# The Canadian Federal Election of 2015

# The Canadian Federal Election of 2015

EDITED BY
JON H. PAMMETT & CHRISTOPHER DORNAN

DUNDURN
TORONTO

Editor: Dominic Farrell
Design: Courtney Horner
Cover Design: Courtney Horner
Printer: Webcom

**Library and Archives Canada Cataloguing in Publication**

The Canadian federal election of 2015 / Jon H. Pammett and Christopher Dornan, editors.

Includes bibliographical references and index.
Issued in print and electronic formats.
ISBN 978-1-4597-3334-3 (paperback).--ISBN 978-1-4597-3335-0 (pdf).--
ISBN 978-1-4597-3336-7 (epub)

1. Canada. Parliament--Elections, 2015. 2. Canada--Politics and government--2015-. 3. Elections--Canada--History--21st century. 4. Voting--Canada. I. Pammett, Jon H., 1944-, editor II. Dornan, Chris, editor

JL193.C3586 2016 324.971'074 C2016-900861-4
C2016-900862-2

1 2 3 4 5 20 19 18 17 16

We acknowledge the support of the **Canada Council for the Arts** and the **Ontario Arts Council** for our publishing program. We also acknowledge the financial support of the **Government of Canada** through the **Canada Book Fund** and **Livres Canada Books**, and the **Government of Ontario** through the **Ontario Book Publishing Tax Credit** and the **Ontario Media Development Corporation**.



Printed and bound in Canada.

**VISIT US AT**

Dundurn.com | @dundurnpress | Facebook.com/dundurnpress | Pinterest.com/dundurnpress

Dundurn
3 Church Street, Suite 500
Toronto, Ontario, Canada
M5E 1M2

# CONTENTS

CHAPTER 1 7
The Long Goodbye: The Contours of the Election
*Christopher Dornan*

CHAPTER 2 23
Stephen Harper and the 2015 Conservative Campaign: Defeated but Not Devastated
*Faron Ellis*

CHAPTER 3 57
Back to the Future: The Resurgent Liberals
*Brooke Jeffrey*

CHAPTER 4 85
From Third to First and Back to Third: The 2015 NDP Campaign
*David McGrane*

CHAPTER 5 117
The Bloc Québécois in a Rainbow-Coloured Quebec
*Éric Bélanger and Richard Nadeau*

CHAPTER 6 141
Opportunities and Obstacles: The Green Party of Canada's 2015 Campaign
*Susan Harada*

CHAPTER 7 163
Roll Back! The Conservatives Rewrite Election Laws, 2006–2015
*Louis Massicotte*

CHAPTER 8 195
Mounting a Local Campaign
*Allan Thompson*

CHAPTER 9 225
Like, Share, Vote: The CTV/Facebook Partnership and the 2015 Election
*Mary Francoli, Josh Greenberg, and Christopher Waddell*

CHAPTER 10 253
A Debate About *The Debates*
*André Turcotte*

CHAPTER 11 275
"Because It's 2015": Gender and the 2015 Federal Election
*Brenda O'Neill and Melanee Thomas*

CHAPTER 12 305
Polling and the 2015 Federal Election
*David Coletto*

CHAPTER 13 327
It's Spring Again! Voting in the 2015 Federal Election
*Harold D. Clarke, Jason Reifler, Thomas J. Scotto, and Marianne C. Stewart*

CHAPTER 14 357
The Fall of the Harper Dynasty
*Jon H. Pammett and Lawrence LeDuc*

APPENDICES
Appendix A: The Results in Summary 381
Appendix B: The Results by Constituency 383

Notes on Contributors 415

# CHAPTER 1

## The Long Goodbye: The Contours of the Election

Christopher Dornan

For a party and a government whose modus operandi had been incrementalism, it all came to a shuddering and definitive end. The project of remaking Canada according to an image of conservatism, step by step, was over. The new government, anathema to everything the previous government stood for, would deliberately run deficits, legalize marijuana, expedite entry to the country of tens of thousands of refugees from war-scarred Islamic nations, and award citizenship to people who hid their faces in public on grounds of religious belief and cultural practice.

The Conservative Party of Canada under Stephen Harper — or, more properly, Stephen Harper's Conservative Party, since he was its founding leader and executive authority — had taken four elections to inch its way to majority government. In 2004, the party lost the general election but brought the Liberals to minority status, the first toehold in the Conservative climb to office. In 2006, the Liberal minority was defeated and replaced with a Conservative minority, and the Liberal leader resigned. In 2008, the Conservatives were returned with a greater number of seats — still not quite enough to command a majority but sufficient to ensure that the Liberal leader resigned. In 2011, the Conservatives at last won the majority they had so assiduously sought. The Liberals were reduced to third-party status, with only thirty-four seats, while the Conservatives won 166. For the third time in a row, the Liberal leader resigned following the election.

Some governments are content to manage the affairs of the nation. Others take power with revolutionary intent. Harper's Conservatives made no secret of their missionary zeal to demolish what they saw as an intrusive, arrogant, condescending, and economically irresponsible state apparatus, entrenched after decades of Liberal rule. But the revolution would be carried out by accretion, via the accumulation of myriad government decisions and policy implementations. Canadian priorities and imperatives would change by increments.

The goal was not to impose a new hegemony on a resistant population, as though an occupying force had seized control. The social engineering the Conservatives had in mind was altogether more ambitious. It was to transform the default thinking of the country, to shift what counted as common sense. The goal was to manufacture consent for the axioms of Conservative rule, the most prominent of which was that the role of government was to empower individual enterprise, not to command-plan how people should live through costly, unwieldy, and obnoxious bureaucratic measures funded by taxes that throttled prosperity.

This, the Conservatives calculated, was the long route to staying in power into the twenty-first century the way the Liberals had all but owned the government of the twentieth. After all, elections are so much easier to win when the electorate already consents, when the majority of voters share the values and perspective of one party, preferring those over the values and perspectives of the other parties. An agreeable electorate is pre-convinced; they do not have to be persuaded at great effort and expense of something they are not inclined to believe. Over almost a decade, the Conservative government did all it could to make its core precepts the launching pad for its perpetual re-election.

And yet it did so with ham fists. It was extremely effective in targeting, bludgeoning, and belittling its political opponents. And it used the instruments of power to promote its structure of values, from renaming a national museum to opening an Office of Religious Freedom, from killing the long-gun registry to doing away with the long-form census. But it conducted itself throughout as though either ignorant or dismissive of the first part of Dale Carnegie's famous maxim: in order to influence people, one must win friends.

All political parties are fiercely partisan — and necessarily so. They all have designs on power and they are all committed to frustrating one another's ambitions. But the Harper Conservatives behaved more like a cult than a traditional party. They did not treat their opponents as honourable adversaries; they saw them as enemies, and they saw enemies everywhere. They made no effort to understand the positions of other parties or interest groups in order to effect negotiations and arrive at accommodations. The Conservatives would no more negotiate with the NDP or the Liberals than they would negotiate with terrorists. And since they perceived the political structures and institutions of the country as creations of their ideological antagonists, rigged against them, they felt no obligation to honour past practices. Oddly, for conservatives, they had little respect for tradition — except when it served their political ends. And for a party in which Christian faith was so important to so many, they were curiously uncharitable toward anyone not a member of their political sect.

It was a government of resentment from the outset, a government as devoted to settling scores as to implementing a policy program. There were times when it seemed as though the Conservatives *had* no policy program beyond vilifying their enemies, that the true mission of the Conservative government and the best safeguard of the interests of the country, as they understood it, was to prevent anyone else from ever forming a government. And because the Conservative grievances attached to anyone outside their ranks, they often extended to sectors of the electorate. The Harperites not only chafed at the other parties and the strictures of Parliament, at the public service, the courts, the media, the scientific community, unions, and universities — all of which they saw as arrayed against them — they too often comported themselves as angry at the very people they represented.

The Conservative government did not pretend to engage in political dialogue. Whether in Question Period, in parliamentary committees, or in rare media appearances, ministers and MPs simply refused to answer questions, instead parroting prepared speaking points and attack lines. Legislation was packaged in enormous omnibus bills while debate in the House was curtailed, so that the laws of the land were enacted without traditional review by the Commons. When one judges Parliament a theatre of intransigent animosity, what profit is there in arguing for one's position? The Conservatives simply dispensed with what they saw as a charade. The naked exercise of power is, one supposes, a form of transparency.

But if a party expends almost no effort to persuade the public of the virtues of its policies, it is next to impossible to effect a political paradigm shift of national values. Hence the grandiose attempt to re-engineer Canadian groupthink to align with Conservative principles was doomed. One cannot win friends by alienating people.

Not only did the Conservatives fail to rewrite basic Canadian values, in all likelihood it was those values that proved their undoing. Canadians differ on whether tax credits offered to families for child care are preferable to a national daycare system, whether punitive jail sentences for criminal offenders are a deserved deterrent or simply vindictive, whether deficit spending on infrastructure is an economic stimulus or an invitation to fiscal recklessness — and they do so heatedly. But in the main, they react badly to power exercised spitefully, to a political arena drained of respectful disagreement, to a politics in which denigration is not just a means but the goal.

The Harper Conservatives were constitutionally, even insistently, inconsiderate of others. Pollsters identified a "desire for change" as the salient feature of the 2015 campaign, but this was really a euphemism. On election night there was nothing remotely incremental about the outcome. It was a repudiation, pure and simple. It took the Conservatives four elections to win a majority. It took one term of majority government for them to lose office and terminate the reign of Stephen Harper. In his victory speech that night, the newly elected Prime Minister Justin Trudeau caught the fundamental mistake — the character flaw — of the defeated government. "Conservatives are not our enemies," he told his supporters and the country, "they are our neighbours."

Given the Conservative failure to effect a sea change in the country's attitudes and perspectives, the party's prospects for re-election in 2015 turned on the arithmetic of how the vote would split between the three major parties — with the Bloc Québécois and the Greens perhaps eating away at Liberal and NDP vote share — and how that vote would translate into seat returns. With some 70 percent of the country opposed to the Conservatives, in retrospect the government's defeat seems inevitable, but at the time the outcome came as a surprise to almost everyone. Going into the election, it seemed perfectly possible that the Conservatives could be returned to power. Even in the last days before the vote, the talk among the punditry was of the role of the governor general should no single party carry sufficient seats to command the confidence of the House. By the eve of the election, it seemed altogether likely the Liberals could win the most seats, but no one was talking openly about a Liberal majority.

## THE 30 PERCENT SOLUTION

Stephen Harper was not just prime minister. He was by any standard an imposing political figure. Uncharismatic, certainly, but firm, assured, calm, guided by and unshakeable in his convictions, and steeled by experience both in the domestic political arena and on the world stage. The most popular kids win election as president of the student council. Stephen Harper was the school principal. After almost a decade in power, he was the embodiment of the strong man: an emotionally cool father figure who knew what was best for his charges and would protect them against their own worst instincts, whether they appreciated it or not.

Perversely, his strategists counted his unpopularity as a political strength. Voters who disliked him did so not because he was corrupt or weak or venal or stupid — he was none of those things. He was, in fact, the opposite of those things. He was disliked for the same reason teenagers invariably dislike the principal — because he was in charge, because he was authoritarian. The Conservatives assumed that in perilous times of extremist threats and economic fragility, authority trumps likeability. What matters is the person one wants making the decisions that matter. Sometimes the best credential for being in charge is actually being in charge.

The Conservatives called the election with all the advantages of a majority government and the unshakeable support of 30 percent of the electorate. On that alone their strategists calculated they could bully their way back into office. Yes, more than two-thirds of the country was set against them, but a federal election is a choice between options, and who were Harper's opponents? An irascible socialist who had won the leadership of a party that was only the Official Opposition on a fluke (the appeal of a charismatic and now dead leader, the collapse of Bloc support, and the fickleness of Quebec voters) and a vacuous, we-generation motivational speaker, who on the strength of his dead father's name had inherited leadership of a diminished party, a rump of what it once was.

All the Conservatives had to do was put a stark choice before the voters, project an aura of unperturbable competence, maintain ultra-disciplined message control, outspend their opponents on advertising and cross-country appearances, and wait for Angry Tom or Just-Not-Ready Justin to self-destruct. In the heat of the campaign, one or both of them would eventually pick the wrong side of a volatile issue or say the wrong thing. If the Conservatives could maintain the split in the opposition, neither the NDP nor the Liberals would be able to marshal the returns to unseat the government outright. If the Liberals eroded support for the NDP, so much the better. If one of the two opposition options collapsed — likely the Liberals — the Conservatives could round on Mulcair's socialists with their full arsenal. Meanwhile, any international incident, the kind of thing that showed a world in jeopardy, surely played to the strengths of the prime minister and the government.

At eleven weeks, the campaign was more than twice as long as most recent campaigns. In a 2007 amendment to the Canada Fair Elections Act, the Conservatives had set a fixed date for voting day. A seventy-eight-day campaign — almost a quarter of a year — was intended to deplete the cash reserves of the opposition parties while giving them plenty of opportunity to cause trouble for themselves. If the two major rival parties undermined each other over the course of the campaign, that was the luck the Conservatives were trying to conjure. Misfortune for their squabbling opponents might grow the Conservatives' share just a little beyond their base, and that was the roadmap to staying in power.

Even if they were returned with only a minority, the Conservatives and Stephen Harper had experience wielding authority under two previous minority governments. They had manhandled Stéphane Dion and Michael Ignatieff in turn; presumably they could do the same to Tom Mulcair and Justin Trudeau.

## EVENT MANAGEMENT

The Conservatives no doubt liked the way things began. Harper conveyed the very image of prime ministerial bearing as he made the visit to Rideau Hall on the morning of August 2 to ask the governor general to dissolve Parliament, and then as he spoke to reporters from behind a podium bearing the Royal Coat of Arms of Canada before heading off on the campaign trail.

Mulcair, meanwhile, opened his campaign standing in front of a Canadian flag at the Canadian Museum of History in Gatineau, with the

Houses of Parliament in the background across the river. Alone at a podium, no members of his party around him, he delivered a statement and declined to entertain questions from reporters. He was presenting himself as the prime minister-in-waiting. By aping the style and manner of Stephen Harper, he had chosen to fight an image war on terrain already claimed by his opponent.

And Trudeau? As Harper and Mulcair were speaking, Trudeau was on an aircraft heading to Vancouver where he was scheduled to march in the city's Pride Parade. He had made a commitment to appear and chose to honour it despite the election call. Among the commentariat, the news media, and Conservative and NDP party operatives, this was seen as a risible blunder, a telltale sign that the Liberal campaign team were amateurs who did not understand how a federal election campaign should be run. Mulcair had cancelled his attendance at the parade in order to stay in Ottawa for the call of the election.

So, on the very first day of the campaign, Harper and Mulcair stood behind lecterns, two solitary older men in suits and ties, rooted in place, clutching for gravitas, both using the architecture of the nation's capital as the inert backdrop to their campaign launches. The images Canadians saw of Trudeau that day showed him in full motion at the other end of the country, as far away as he could get from Harper's corridors of power, central to an event celebrating diverse sexuality when Conservative Party policy was opposed to same-sex marriage. There he was beaming in shirtsleeves on the streets of Vancouver, being enthusiastically embraced by cheering, happy crowds and embracing them in turn. Almost all of these images were captured and uploaded for circulation on social media by people who were at the parade, not by the parliamentary press corps. The parliamentary media were all back in Ottawa. There were no crowds of people in a jubilant mood snapping selfies and streaming them on Periscope at the Harper or Mulcair launch events, because crowds of people had not been invited.

To the bewilderment of the Conservative and NDP electoral machines, what was supposed to be a Trudeau campaign gaffe proved to be a triumph of retail politics.

This sort of freewheeling among the electorate was unthinkable to the Conservatives, who were ever wary of the unscripted moment and on guard against protestors hijacking campaign events in order to ruin things. Harper's appearances were meticulously staged and seriously policed. In addition to the prime minister's RCMP protection detail, the Conservatives hired former members of the Canadian military to provide security. A campaign run on the persona of the prime minister as the country's principal-in-chief demanded events that were disciplined, dignified, and upbeat, like school-spirit rallies — there would be no outbursts from troublemakers at the back of the classroom. Only vetted party faithful were invited and admitted. And while it seemed as though Trudeau had made it a campaign goal to take a selfie with every living Canadian from coast to coast, at first Conservative organizers tried to prevent attendees at Harper's appearances from recording or publicizing the events in any way — including posting photographs on social media.

Reporters were limited to asking five questions a day, one allocated to a member of the local media and the other four to journalists paying to travel with the Harper tour. As Justin Ling of *Vice* pointed out, for the privilege of posing the occasional question to the country's leader during an election campaign, national journalists were required to pay the Conservative Party some $78,000. The prime minister's campaign appearances were so well orchestrated that the only disruption was the booing and heckling directed at the media from party supporters.

By the end, of course, there was nothing dignified about Harper's campaign events, as the party enlisted the disgraced former mayor of Toronto Rob Ford, and resorted to gimmicky game show sound effects to count off the cost to taxpayers of Trudeau's election promises.

## WHAT'S THE NUMBER, JUSTIN?

The first of the leaders' debates, organized by *Maclean's* magazine, came only four days into the campaign. Here, the smart thinking went, was where Trudeau — inexperienced, an intellectual lightweight, prone to dinner-theatre emoting — was most at risk. The question that was supposed to demolish Trudeau, to expose him as nothing more than addle-brained charisma, came from Mulcair, not Harper. Once Trudeau had embarrassed himself nationally — once he had been revealed to be truly not up to the job — that would clear the way for the two grown-ups to get down to the brass knuckle fight Mulcair wanted and Harper was confident he could win: a contest between two strong, unyielding, and uncharismatic personalities; a sharp choice on spending, taxation, and social policy. The climactic battle between Right and Left.

The question Mulcair put to him was intended to leave Trudeau floundering, because the question is a trap. Trudeau had chided Mulcair for his promise to repeal the Clarity Act, which requires a "clear majority" for any vote in favour of Quebec separation to be valid. Mulcair saw his opportunity. What, he demanded to know, was the precise majority Trudeau would require in order to accept a vote in favour of separation? Mulcair goaded Trudeau: "What's his number? What's your number, Mr. Trudeau? ... What's the number, Justin?"

The question is a trap because there is no correct number. But instead of equivocating, Trudeau supplied what Mulcair least expected: an actual figure. "You want a number, Mr. Mulcair? … I'll give you a number. Nine. My number is nine. Nine Supreme Court justices said one vote is not enough to break up this country, and yet that is Mr. Mulcair's position."

We should not read too much into a single truncated moment of election theatrics, but Trudeau's answer was triply effective. First, it was Mulcair, the former lawyer, who ended up looking flustered, caught by his own trap. The Conservatives had invited Canadians to grill Trudeau as though in a job interview, but he had just fielded an especially belligerent question in a way that outsmarted the older guy. Second, it invoked the Supreme Court. It amounted to a declaration of confidence in the position and wisdom of that body — an allusion to Harper's petulant public spat in 2013 with Chief Justice Beverley McLachlin. Third, and most telling, it was *clever*.

Trudeau's detractors, and the Conservative propaganda engine in particular, had portrayed him as just a walking hairdo, a glamour boy. With one word — "Nine" — he showed that there was a brain at work too. He may have possessed a different type of intelligence from Mulcair and Harper — disparaged by some as mere emotional intelligence — but it was a dangerous mind nonetheless, not least because Mulcair and Harper did not understand how it worked and were baffled by its appeal. It was as though Trudeau were broadcasting on a frequency that neither Mulcair nor Harper could pick up.

## TAX AND SPEND

The Conservative platform offered no grand architectural vision for the nation. Conservatives by definition abhor collectivist schemes. Instead, the platform rested on four main planks. The first was ensuring prosperity through the trade deals the government had negotiated: CETA (the Comprehensive European Trade Agreement) with the European Union; and the Trans-Pacific Partnership, concluded and announced late in the campaign. The second was the reduction of the tax burden through income splitting and a series of boutique incentives for everything from home renovation to children's education savings plans. The third consisted of measures intended to keep Canada safe from threats from abroad and terrorists and criminals at home. The fourth was the demonstration of responsible fiscal management through balancing the budget.

Though the Harper government had run six straight annual deficits, by the 2014–15 fiscal year there was a budget surplus of $1.9 billion, which the Conservatives trumpeted as proof of their astute financial stewardship. More than that, they had elevated the promise of a balanced budget to a sacrosanct ethic. They had made it all but unthinkable for a party to propose deficit spending as part of its electoral appeal.

The NDP deplored Conservative policies as favouring corporate interests and the wealthiest Canadians over the disadvantaged and the middle class, and they promised measures that would redress these injustices. But they concluded that it would be political suicide if they did not loudly insist that they, too, were committed to balanced budgets. Otherwise, the Conservatives would fear-monger about an NDP government wrecking the economy by printing money to pay for its socialist agenda. The effect was to suggest that on the question of spending and taxation, the NDP would hold to Conservative principles.

On August 27, the Liberals announced that they would almost double federal infrastructure spending over the next decade, from $65 billion to $125 billion, both as an economic stimulus and to upgrade for the twenty-first century the country's crumbling central nervous system of roads, bridges, and transit systems: the very stuff essential to moving goods and people around. In order to pay for this, a Liberal government would run "modest" deficits of some $10 billion a year before balancing the budget in its fourth year in office.

Both the Conservatives and NDP derided the plan as folly, but the Liberals had political cover. No less a figure than David Dodge, a former governor of the Bank of Canada, had co-written a paper in 2014 for the law firm Bennett Jones that may well have been the inspiration for the Liberal gambit. Dodge argued that in the current environment making a fetish of balancing the budget was myopic and actually worked against the country's economic interests. He advocated taking advantage of historically low interest rates to invest in infrastructure in order to improve productivity. Rather than garroting public spending in order to meet an artificial target in balancing the budget, Dodge argued that the sensible government priority should be to gradually reduce the public debt-to-GDP ratio. This, he said, could be done while still spending on much-needed infrastructure.

In one bold move, the Liberals managed to not only vividly distinguish themselves from the NDP but to outflank them too, positioning themselves to the left of the traditionally leftist New Democrats, whom the Liberals could now paint as Conservative quislings. At the same time, they suggested that the Conservative mantra of balanced budgets was a canard, and that the truly responsible fiscal manager would find more creative solutions to the country's economic doldrums. Attacking what had been established as an economic truism was a risky proposition, but it would prove to be less risky than the NDP's supposed caution in promising to balance the budget.

## CITIZENSHIP

A month into the campaign, in the small hours of September 2, sixteen people fleeing the civil war in Syria piled into an inflatable boat designed to hold eight and pushed off from Bodrum, Turkey, heading for the Greek island of Kos. Five minutes later the dinghy capsized and three members of a single family drowned. One of them was three-year-old Alan Kurdi. Photographs of the child's lifeless body lying face down on the beach gripped the attention of the world. As soon as it was revealed that the Kurdi family had been trying to join relatives in Vancouver, the Syrian refugee crisis became a Canadian election issue. In short order this would become entwined with whether Muslim women should be permitted to wear the niqab during Canadian citizenship ceremonies, whether dual citizens convicted of terrorism or treason should be stripped of their Canadian citizenship, and whether Canadian citizens should be invited to inform on one another to the national police force.

Both Mulcair and Trudeau called for Canada to open its borders to refugees trying to escape the conflicts in the Middle East. While visibly moved by the images of Alan Kurdi's body, Harper remained steadfast. This was not a government to be panicked into precipitous action just because others — the opposition, the media, members of the public — had worked themselves into a state of over-excitement. It was not a government to be buffeted by the chattering classes. Harper framed the matter as a public safety priority, not a humanitarian concern. The NDP and Liberals wanted thousands of additional refugees admitted as soon as possible. Harper decried this as a security risk. He vowed to attack ISIS as the root cause. Bombs were the answer, not entry visas.

To those who viewed what was happening in Syria and southern Europe as a humanitarian crisis, the Conservative response was compassionless, isolationist, and paranoid, in that it saw the hordes of refugees as a mass of potential terrorists. But the public as a whole rewarded the Conservatives with an uptick in the polls.

Then, on September 15, the "niqab issue" seized the campaign. In 2011 the Conservative government had instituted a policy that required Muslim women taking the oath of citizenship to remove their face coverings at the public ceremony, even though the women would have revealed themselves to court officials in private in order to establish their identities. A woman named Zunera Ishaq, a devout Sunni, launched a court challenge and in February 2015 a Federal Court judge struck down the policy. The government appealed. With a month to go in the election campaign, the Federal Court of Appeal upheld the previous court's ruling and the Conservative government announced that it would appeal to the Supreme Court.

The issue reverberated across the country. Harper had made himself clear on the question six months previously when the court first ruled against the government policy. "It is offensive," he said, "that someone would hide their identity at the very moment where they are committing to join the Canadian family." The implication was that people unwilling to abandon specific cultural practices on government edict — practices that just happen to be specific to a particular culture — should not be welcome in the Canadian family, no matter the opinion of the courts.

Trade deals and boutique tax credits aside, here was a stark choice the Conservatives could put to the electorate: what sort of Canada do you want? They were certain the Canadian public was on their side. They certainly knew how voters in Quebec would react. Anyone foolish enough — or principled enough — to defend the niqab would forfeit Quebec.

Tactically, the Conservatives were right. For NDP and Liberal candidates canvassing for votes, defending the right of a woman to take the oath of citizenship in a veil was a doorstep liability. (Allan Thompson in this volume offers a first-hand account of how the niqab issue was received in his rural, southwestern Ontario riding.) It was difficult enough to dispel the misconceptions — to explain patiently that these Muslim women would indeed have already revealed themselves in private, just as they are required to do in banks, airport security lines, and passport control, where everyone must confirm their identity. Explaining the principle at stake was even more challenging. For the Liberals and NDP, anyone about to be confirmed as a Canadian citizen should be free to present themselves at the ceremony just as they present themselves in public in their daily lives. It is not against the law to wear a niqab in Canada, either as a tourist, an international student, a business visitor, a permanent resident, or a citizen. Why should it be prohibited just at the moment that citizenship is being publicly conferred? But this is not a persuasive argument to someone who sees the niqab as an alien cultural practice that should have no place in Canada. In an interview with CBC, Harper suggested the Conservatives would consider preventing any federal public servant from wearing the niqab.

Although both the NDP and the Liberals applauded the court ruling and opposed the government policy, the Conservatives released a French-language advertisement that accused Trudeau of being disconnected from the values and priorities of Québécois but made no mention of Mulcair. It was the NDP, however, that would feel the effects of the controversy most keenly. Quebec had rewarded the NDP with fifty-nine seats in the 2011 election and vaulted them into Stornoway as the Official Opposition. Though the party knew all too well that its position on the issue was playing badly in Quebec, in the first French-language leaders' debate, on September 24, Mulcair took a principled stand. Support for the NDP in Quebec never recovered.

At almost the same time, the government announced that under the provisions of Bill C-24 — the Strengthening Canadian Citizenship Act that had become law in May — it had revoked the citizenship of Zakaria Amara, who was serving a life sentence having pled guilty to planning to bomb downtown Toronto. Both the NDP and the Liberals vowed to repeal the legislation, but again the principle at stake was hard to explain and defend on the doorstep: that Canadian citizens are governed by Canadian laws; that if a citizen breaks these laws, mechanisms are in place to bring them to justice; that citizenship is not something that any government should be allowed to revoke; and that the provisions of this law created two classes of citizens, one with more rights than the other. But Trudeau had found a way to state plainly why he believed C-24 was objectionable and dangerous, and he deployed it on September 28 during the Munk leaders' debate. Borrowing the cadence of Gertrude Stein, he insisted that: "A Canadian is a Canadian is a Canadian."

But perhaps some Canadians, the Conservatives insinuated, were behaving in ways that were not Canadian. In November 2014 the Conservatives had passed the Zero Tolerance for Barbaric Cultural Practices Act. On October 2, in one last overt reference to alien others residing in Canada, Minister of Immigration Chris Alexander called a press conference to promise an RCMP snitch line to which Canadians could report barbaric practices on the part of their neighbours.

Tactically, each of these Conservative measures had its utility. Cumulatively, they were a strategic fiasco. They were an insistent reminder of the divisive, abrasive, and authoritarian personality of the Conservative regime. They may have stoked the party's base, but they galvanized those who desperately wanted rid of the Harperites. In the final days of the campaign, as the NDP's prospects faded, voters committed to ousting the Conservatives gravitated toward the "sunny ways" of the Liberal alternative.

Clearly, for the Conservatives, the long campaign was a mistake. They expected that over the course of gruelling weeks Trudeau would embarrass himself. In fact, the campaign gave him ample opportunity to present himself to the electorate, and the more voters saw of him the more he grew on them. Meanwhile, the Conservative effort to belittle him as a Gen-X slacker with presumptions started to unravel. Retired parents in their sixties and seventies think well of their children coming of age in their late thirties or early forties and want the best for them. Trudeau emerged as the very image of that generation. The "Just Not Ready" ad, which the Conservatives had released in May and kept in heavy rotation, became the 2015 equivalent of the Kim Campbell Progressive Conservatives' attack on Jean Chrétien back in 1993. In an ad that played on Chrétien's partial facial paralysis, the Conservatives had asked: "Is this the face of a prime minister?" It only worked to make Chrétien sympathetic. Similarly, the "Just Not Ready" ad invited voters to size up Justin Trudeau. As they did, more and more began to think he might be the best of the candidates. The ad managed to make him prime ministerial.

And while the Conservative campaign bet heavily on Harper's stature as a father figure, it neglected to strategically consider that Trudeau was also a father — a young, energetic, cheerful father, against whom Harper, by the end, looked like a sour, sullen old man.

The chapters that follow parse the election with scholarly attention, examining each of the party campaigns in turn, the impact of the debates, the role of the pollsters, gender issues in the election, voting behaviour, political coverage in an utterly changed media environment, and the experience of a first-time candidate.

They are a time capsule of analysis.

# CHAPTER 2

## Stephen Harper and the 2015 Conservative Campaign: Defeated but Not Devastated

Faron Ellis

"No regrets" is what Stephen Harper said as he conceded defeat in the 2015 election. Harper was undoubtedly reflecting on his nearly ten years in power and the quarter-century he participated in one of the great transformations in Canadian party politics, at least as much as he was commenting on the previous eleven-week campaign and the election night results. By the measure of seats won and standing in the House of Commons, the 2015 election results were the worst for Harper during his tenure as leader of the united Conservative Party of Canada.[1] Although the party won ninety-nine seats, identical to what it garnered in its first contest as a reunited party in 2004, that total represented a lower proportion of Commons seats (29.3 percent) than it did in 2004 (32.1 percent). Further, in 2004 it held the Liberals to a minority government and soon claimed its own victories in 2006, 2008, and 2011. In each election it increased its share of votes and seats. Until this time.

When viewed through the prism of party competitiveness, Harper did achieve something in 2015. He left the party in a relatively competitive position, especially when compared to 1993, the last time a conservative party completed nearly a decade in power. The base of support that was built on the foundations of the old Reform-Alliance and Progressive Conservative parties held strong throughout Harper's tenure and remained especially strong through a difficult 2015 campaign. In terms of raw numbers, the Conservative Party earned only slightly fewer total votes in 2015 than in 2011, its most successful campaign, and over one and a half million more votes than in its inaugural 2004 contest. Post-election analysis will likely reveal that it lost ground because it failed to mobilize as many new voters as did its competitors during an election that saw turnout increase. It also lost support among recently hard-earned additions to its coalition, particularly among new Canadians. And it was decimated in many of Canada's major metropolitan centres. But the base held. "Rock solid," according to members of the Conservative campaign team.

**Table 2.1: Conservative Party of Canada Election Results (2004–2015)**[2]

| Year | Result | Total votes | Percentage of total votes | Seats | Percentage of seats |
|---|---|---|---|---|---|
| 2015 | Liberal majority | 5,600,496 | 31.9 | 99 | 29.3 |
| 2011 | Conservative majority | 5,835,270 | 39.6 | 166 | 53.9 |
| 2008 | Conservative minority | 5,209,069 | 37.7 | 143 | 46.4 |
| 2006 | Conservative minority | 5,374,071 | 36.3 | 124 | 40.3 |
| 2004 | Liberal minority | 4,019,498 | 29.6 | 99 | 32.1 |

Source: Elections Canada

The Conservative Party entered the 2015 campaign confident that its base was solidly behind it, but aware that it would face a "time for change" ballot question that clearly favoured its competitors. With upward of two-thirds of the electorate telling pollsters they wanted a change, and with the Harper Conservatives' style, tone, and temperament in government reinforcing their opponents' narrative, campaign strategists knew the magnitude of the hill they had to climb. Add the natural fatigue voters tend to develop for any leader after ten years in power, the accumulated baggage of several relatively small but symbolically significant scandals, and a growing list of organized anti-Harper special interest groups, and the task of re-election seemed monumental.

Monumental but not unachievable. After all, much had been accomplished over the party's years in power. The Conservatives had rebalanced the government books, brought Canada's debt-to-GDP level down to what they inherited in 2006, and they could claim other enviable economic policy successes associated with their free trade agenda, tax reductions, and an overall stemming of the growth in government. The party's outreach strategy had recruited voters from formerly unsupportive segments of the electorate, both regionally and demographically, and the party continued to be a fundraising behemoth. Harper's leadership poll numbers were typically strong and all evidence indicated that the base continued to remain loyal, at between 25 to 30 percent of voters throughout the majority government period between 2011 and 2015.[3] The Conservatives believed they could limit the impact of the "time for change" narrative by promoting another, one that played to their strengths: leadership, security, and the economy. These themes would be presented in the context of Harper's experience and would be juxtaposed against Liberal leader Justin Trudeau's lack thereof in an effort at framing their preferred ballot question: Who is most capable of keeping the economy strong and Canadians safe? Answer: Stephen Harper, even if you don't like him and his *style* very much.

Conservatives were certain that the young Liberal leader would falter at some point during the exceptionally long campaign. When that occurred, they believed, adding another 5 to 7 percent of the electorate to the stable Conservative base seemed achievable, if they could execute an effective campaign. That level of success would also be conditional on the NDP maintaining its support, particularly in Ontario, something that would allow the Conservatives to eke out marginal wins based on advantageous vote splits. All of this seemed feasible, and so at the outset of the campaign a strong minority win was considered a distinct possibility. If absolutely everything broke right, a majority was not unthinkable. However, Conservatives knew that even a modest minority victory would see them surrender power; whether that occurred in days or months would be determined only by how strong or weak that minority was.

What resulted, however, was an unfocused, at times disorganized, campaign effort. The Conservatives offered a platform that promised moderate, conservative governance and only a small selection of targeted policies as incentives to vote for them. They offered no galvanizing signature policy element similar to the 2006 GST-cut promise, or a powerfully motivating agenda such as the 2011 mantra of keeping the Bloc Québécois from controlling an unorthodox coalition of power-grabbing carpetbaggers. Their 2015 campaign narrative was unfocused, more similar to their unsuccessful 2004 effort than to any of their victorious campaigns. Their much vaunted organizational superiority failed to materialize, in as much as the Liberals were at least as prepared to target, track, and deliver their vote as were Conservatives. The Conservatives definitely had more money to spend than did their opponents, but they were unprepared when the Liberals staked out what Conservative strategists believed to be untenable policy positions, Trudeau failed to stumble, and the NDP refused to co-operate by maintaining its vote share. When the "change" vote galvanized around the Liberals late in the contest, the Conservative campaign tried to preserve as many of the long-term gains the party had achieved over the previous decade, and live to fight another day.

## THE CAMPAIGN TEAM

### The Leader

Much has been written about Stephen Harper, his mindset, and his purported purposes for pursuing power.[4] His legacy will ultimately be analyzed within the two broad categories of his contribution to conservatism and the Conservative Party on the one hand, and his contribution as prime minster on the other. Although we will leave analysis of those legacies to others, a number of consistent themes emanate from the existing literature, are corroborated by his behaviour, and are relevant for understanding how he and the Conservatives approached the 2015 campaign.

It is useful to recall not only the past dozen years during which Harper united Canadian conservatism and led it to government but also his participation in the movement that divided Canadian conservatives in the first place. Much of what he experienced then conditioned his strategic outlook and his understanding of what needed to be done to bring about, as he put it in his address to the 2002 Canadian Alliance convention, "a permanent political institution" based on conservative principles capable of competing for power in the twenty-first century.

Harper witnessed first-hand the chaos that was Reform's inaugural experience in Parliament and knew instinctively that if conservatives were going to succeed they would need to demonstrate a great deal more discipline and political maturity.[5] Particularly problematic for Reform-Alliance were the party's populist impulses, the expressions of which were antithetical to the kind of centralized message discipline deemed necessary for a successful political party. It was decided that these would have to be jettisoned,[6] as would the harder edges of Reform's social conservatism. Social conservatives would be welcome in the envisioned coalition, but clear lines across which they would not be allowed to drag the party would be established and enforced. This initially focused on the issue of abortion choice, but later included gay rights, among other issues that were noticeably absent from the 2015 campaign.[7]

Harper succeeded by establishing a centralized regime of strict message discipline.[8] He learned from mistakes, such as those that occurred during the 2004 election campaign when accusations of a social-conservative hidden agenda dogged the Conservative campaign and limited its electoral appeal.[9]

Message discipline, imposed from the centre, continued to be a feature of Harper's tenure as prime minister. Sharply partisan and at times unnecessarily antagonistic, the tone could be justified during his two minority terms by the need to be perpetually election-ready.[10] But the style and tone did not change once the party secured a majority in 2011. Indeed, the aggressive partisanship only intensified, to the point where even erstwhile friends were accusing them of contempt of Parliament, if not of democracy itself. Despite garnering strong reviews when he did move off the "garrison mentality" messaging,[11] he repeatedly refused to change his style and resisted attempts to remake his image. Several feeble attempts at branding him as a sweater-wearing, piano-playing cat lover failed primarily because he was much more comfortable with the authenticity of being who he was: a suburban middle-class policy wonk who just wanted to make the country a little bit better by making its federal government a little bit smaller.[12] Notoriously introverted, he rarely indulged outsiders' queries about just what made him tick. His response to Peter Mansbridge's prodding during the obligatory leader's interview for the CBC's *The National* was instructive. After admitting that he probably had a few personal regrets over the course of his political career, he abruptly declared: "But I'm not going to bare my soul here." Nor anywhere else on the 2015 campaign trail.

If Harper was reluctant to embellish his virtues, critiquing his opponents' vices, real or perceived, was an activity at which he and the Conservatives excelled. No rival within the government or society would be spared the sharp, deeply partisan, and at times seemingly gratuitous venom spewed by Conservatives when challenged on their vision or on their means of achieving ends. On the international stage, Harper's steely resolve and forceful approach, such as when he famously told Vladimir Putin that he would shake the Russian president's hand only long enough to tell him to get out of Ukraine, served him well and was typically met with public approval. Even his excessively partisan approach to Parliament could be understood as an expected, albeit unfortunate, condition of participation in that arena. But when the same approach was used in dealing with the national media, the public service, provincial governments, the courts, environmentalists, academics, artists, and any other group that could be tangentially associated with the interests of "urban elites," the public grew increasingly estranged from the tone and practices of Harper and the governments he led.

## Candidates

For the first time in four campaigns, the Conservatives proceeded with a more or less full round of candidate nominations. Party executive director Dustin Van Vugt managed the day-to-day aspects of a process that saw few incumbents receive formal protection from challengers, as had typically been the case during the minority government situations between 2004 and 2011. Still, of the 159 sitting Conservative MPs at dissolution, 32 decided to retire and 116 were acclaimed as Conservative candidates. Only three incumbents lost contested nomination battles, most notably controversial Calgary MP Rob Anders and Minister of State Lynne Yelich. Anders's service dated back to the Reform days (1997), when he succeeded Harper as MP for Calgary West. Yelich was first elected as an Alliance MP in 2000. Their losses contributed to the exodus of many experienced MPs. Among those were eight sitting Alberta incumbents including twenty-two-year veterans Diane Ablonczy and Leon Benoit, and fifteen-year stalwart

James Rajotte, Saskatchewan's Garry Breitkreuz (1993) and Maurice Vellacott (1997), and British Columbia's Dick Harris (1993). Retirements from other regions included a number of the few remaining former Progressive Conservative MPs such as Ontario's Gary Schellenberger and Nova Scotian Gerald Keddy. By the time nominations closed, the Conservatives had 211 non-incumbent candidates, of whom only sixty-seven had to win contested nominations.

Although a significant number of backbench and junior minister retirements had been anticipated, the number was not expected to be abnormally high when compared to other parties that had been in power for nearly a decade. What was unanticipated was the exodus of senior Cabinet ministers the Conservatives were counting on to win seats in strategic ridings but who made late decisions to not seek re-election. Harper had clearly communicated to his Cabinet that he expected those not planning to seek re-election to make their intentions clear well in advance of the 2015 campaign. Prior to his untimely passing, Finance Minister Jim Flaherty adhered to Harper's wishes, as did Government Whip Gordon O'Connor. Others, including former PC leader Peter MacKay, British Columbia's James Moore, Ontario's John Baird, Quebec's Christian Paradis, and Manitoba's Shelly Glover made their decisions in the spring of 2015, leaving the Conservatives with a significantly depleted front bench. In the minds of Conservative strategists, the exodus all but eliminated the option of complementing their planned leader-focused campaign with a "Team Harper" subtext.

## The National Campaign Team and Organization

After five elections, turnover in national campaign staff is inevitable, and the Conservatives typically viewed elections as an opportunity to both benefit from the wisdom of experienced campaigners as well as renew the team with the fresh ideas and approaches that accompany newcomers. At least until 2015.

Long-serving operatives whose talents were noticeably absent in 2015 included the late senator Doug Finley who campaigned on conservative teams going back to the Reform days. Finley held specific responsibility for candidate recruitment and vetting in 2006 and 2008, an arm of the operation that came under scrutiny for its lack of rigour in 2015. Also gone was Patrick Muttart, known as the creative mind behind past campaigns and chief architect of the Conservatives' political marketing approach, another aspect of the 2015 campaign that was criticized for not being able to grow support beyond the loyal base.[13] Also missing in 2015 was a strong, stable, and capable central figure who could be counted upon to calmly pilot the ship through the unpredictable choppy waters that all campaigns encounter. This was a role capably filled by Ian Brodie in earlier campaigns and by Nigel Wright in 2011. Wright would have an impact in 2015, but not as a member of the campaign team.

The 2015 team was much more insular than in the past. Harper had repeatedly demonstrated that he only trusted those closest to him and in particular those who were currently on the payroll. Hence, when Harper appointed former Prime Minister's Office (PMO) Chief of Staff Guy Giorno as campaign chair, and told campaign director Jenni Byrne to assemble the same team that served them well in 2011, the team consisted primarily of former PMO and party operatives. The results led to a number of predicable patterns of behaviour summarized by the colloquialism, "When in doubt, go with what got us here."

Conservative strategists would attempt to strictly control the message as per their PMO roles. When that was not possible, they would reflexively shelter Harper to the point of trapping him in a prison of their own making. Despite some dissenting opinions within the senior ranks of the Conservative team, access to Harper was severely restricted in an attempt at keeping him from moving off script, on his own or as a result of him enduring unlimited media questioning. They viciously attacked all competing messages, and never considered retreat. Even more importantly, the final lines of authority within the chain of command all led back to personnel associated with the PMO rather than the "outsiders" who had held final authority in the successful 2011 campaign and who tended to offer fresher perspectives and bolder, albeit riskier strategies. Hence, innovative was not a descriptor that could be used to characterize the Conservative's 2015 campaign effort.

This reliance on insiders could be seen in the other figures who rounded out the team's senior ranks. Among them was Harper PMO Chief of Staff Ray Novak, a veteran who had served in each of his offices from 2002 onward. Novak travelled with Harper on the leader's tour until his presence became a distraction during the criminal trial of Senator Mike Duffy, which fortuitously was also the same time the war room needed some direction. He and Byrne, who had also been travelling with Harper on tour, returned to Ottawa in late August and remained there for the duration of the campaign. Their return to the war room marked a turning point in the Conservative campaign — it not only exemplified the old adage that "you can't properly run a campaign from the tour," it also revealed an already increasingly problematic question regarding the organizational structure: Which one of the three principals, Giorno, Byrne, or Novak, if any of them, was ultimately in charge? This question was never answered and remained a point of open debate to the end. Described by campaign insiders as a three-headed monster, the leadership structure, with its absence of an ultimate authority, was an operational deficiency that created confusion, inefficiencies, and communication errors at critical junctures.

Aside from Harper, the most visible member of the team was campaign spokesperson Kory Teneycke, another former PMO operative, who was tasked with front-line communication. Other key personnel included long-time Harper adviser Ken Boessenkool who, in taking leave from his consulting practice to help with the campaign, was the closest thing to an outsider within the top ranks of the operation, having served in Harper's Opposition Leader's Office but not in the PMO. Another veteran of past Reform-Alliance-Conservative leader's tours, Ian Todd, would manage the tour. Dennis Matthews, former ad manager in the PMO, led the advertising initiative, while PMO staffer Sean Speer crafted the platform. Former PMO policy adviser Matt Wolf managed the rapid response team. Rachel Curran worked with Boessenkool on scripting and Lynette Corbett supported communications. Research and polling was supervised by PMO director of market research, Brooke Pigott. Data collection and focus group testing were contracted out to Andrew Enns of NRG Research Group, but, like advertising, research was primarily an in-house operation.

An example of the limited use of outside talent became evident mid-campaign, when the media thought it newsworthy to make a multi-day story out of learning the Conservatives had received strategic advice from Australian campaign guru Lynton Crosby. Although interpreted at the time as a sign of a significant strategic change of direction by a floundering campaign, in reality Crosby had been providing limited strategic advice for years and was only tangentially involved in the 2015 campaign, reviewing polling data and providing a mid-campaign strategic report. In it, he advised the party to campaign solely on the economy, not on the "culture war" issues many in the media accused Harper of instigating.

After winning only a slim minority victory in 2006, the Conservatives established a "permanent" war room, which they maintained throughout their two minority governments. Dubbed "the fear factory," the seventeen-thousand-square-foot command centre contained among other amenities a state-of-the-art broadcast studio, designed to give the Conservatives the capacity to bypass the national media and their perceived anti-Conservative biases. After staffing the facility on a more or less permanent basis until 2011, the war room was mothballed once the Conservatives obtained a majority. Campaign veterans who had become used to attending semi-annual strategy sessions during the minority years noted that they were not summoned to Ottawa for any serious discussions for the first three years of the majority government, until preparations for 2015 began in earnest in February of that year. Several cited the lack of a permanent war room as a contributing factor in their relative lack of preparedness for the 2015 campaign. For 2015, the Conservatives leased war-room space in the downtown Ottawa building that already housed the party's national headquarters. Modest in comparison, it was nevertheless fully equipped to meet the needs of the approximately eighty staff who would occupy it during the campaign.

Harper's tour was the first to take to the air, using a Flair Air 737 during much of August and then a larger Air Canada Airbus 319. Though the plane had room for journalists, there was no attempt made during the campaign at mending fences with the national media, which the Conservatives had long viewed with contempt and treated accordingly.[14] Rather, the media continued to be limited to the familiar routine of being allowed to ask only five questions at Conservative campaign events. Conservatives again attempted to bypass the national media and reach voters either directly through their mass television ad buys and innovative radio ads, or through appeals to regional media, with particular emphasis on ethnic media, and through a series of web pages and social media tools. The tour spent most of its time in the metropolitan areas of central Canada, Ontario in particular, and in British Columbia. It held only about a half-dozen events in the Atlantic provinces, one in each of the Yukon and Northwest Territories, and less than a dozen in total on the Prairies. The tour spent more time in Quebec than in the Atlantic and Prairie provinces combined. It held more events in British Columbia than in all three Prairie provinces combined. It organized over fifty events in Ontario, with twenty of those in the Greater Toronto Area. Approximately forty staff accompanied Harper on tour. As usual, his wife Laureen joined him, but unlike in previous campaigns his two children Ben and Rachel joined the tour for much of August.

## FINANCING THE CONSERVATIVE CAMPAIGN

The Conservatives' strength in fundraising has been well documented, with the party typically raising as much annual revenue as both its major national competitors combined. Party and election finance reforms brought in by the Chrétien government in 2004 benefitted the Conservatives, as did the further reforms to contribution limits brought in by Harper in 2007. With the end of per-vote, government-financed allowances in 2015, all parties had to strengthen their individual donor appeals, and the Conservatives again demonstrated that they could out-fundraise their competitors. (More detail on party financing laws may be found in Chapter 7.) As the data in Table 2.2 demonstrate, the Conservatives raised larger amounts between election years during the period of allowance phase-out than they raised in the periods between previous elections.

Table 2.2: Conservative Party Revenue, 2004–2014
(in thousands of dollars)

| | 2004* | 2005 | 2006 | 2007 | 2008 | 2009 | 2010 | 2011 | 2012 | 2013 | 2014 |
|---|---|---|---|---|---|---|---|---|---|---|---|
| Contributions | 10,910 | 17,847 | 18,641 | 16,984 | 21,179 | 17,702 | 17,420 | 22,738 | 17,258 | 18,101 | 20,113 |
| Number of contributors | 68 | 107 | 109 | 107 | 112 | 101 | 95 | 110.3 | 87.3 | 80.1 | 91.7 |
| Mean dollar value per contributor | 160 | 107 | 171 | 158 | 189 | 175 | 183 | 206 | 198 | 226 | 219 |
| Transfers (from candidates, associations, leadership contestants) | 39 | 225 | 287 | 92 | 152 | 65 | 20 | 130 | 170 | 4,211 | 2,757 |
| Total contributions and transfers | 10,950 | 18,073 | 18,928 | 17,076 | 21,331 | 17,767 | 17,437 | 22,868 | 17,428 | 22,312 | 22,870 |
| | | | | | | | | | | | |
| Allowances | 7,914 | 7,331 | 9,388 | 10,218 | 10,439 | 10,351 | 10,431 | 11,212 | 9,670 | 6,695 | 3,719 |
| | | | | | | | | | | | |
| Total contributions and allowances | 18,863 | 25,404 | 28,317 | 27,294 | 31,770 | 28,118 | 27,868 | 34,080 | 27,098 | 29,007 | 26,598 |

* December 7, 2003, through December 31, 2004

Despite the higher costs associated with generating more revenue from individual contributions, by the end of 2014 the Conservatives had accumulated over $14 million in its Conservative Fund.[15] They raised another $24 million in the first nine months of 2015, including $10 million from July to the end of September. They were awarded a final allowance payment of nearly three-quarters of a million dollars in the spring of 2015 and were confident they would spend most of their $54 million limit by the time the campaign ended. Bridge financing was easily obtained, given the party's proven fundraising track record and the expectation that half of their 2015 spending total would be rebated once the votes were tallied. These amounts were not unusual given the party negotiated a $15 million loan to finance its 2008 campaign and $10.2 million in 2011.[16] Conservative constituency associations were also flush with funds, reporting over $22 million in total net assets at the end of 2014. With over three hundred of its candidates eligible for the 60 percent refund on expenses, most Conservative constituency associations will be financially well-positioned moving forward.

## BRANDING, PLATFORM, AND COMMUNICATIONS

That Harper and the Conservative Party had been actively brand-conscious from their earliest days is also well documented. Integrating branding with their disciplined message control strategies and relentless demonizing of their opponents allowed them to successfully develop their market-oriented campaign techniques[17] and manufacture minimum winning coalitions from 2006 onward. The 2015 campaign plan was to proceed in a similar fashion, with the variations necessary given the different criteria involved with defending a decade-long record in government. They adopted a "three paths to victory" strategy that included emphasizing Harper's leadership, security issues at home and abroad, and the economy, which they believed would ultimately lead to their preferred ballot question: Who is most capable of protecting Canadians and their livelihoods? The platform highlighted the government's economic achievements while cautioning about the risks of choosing either of the main competitors. It would contain a series of micro-targeted initiatives but no galvanizing signature policy proposal. Attempts to negatively define their competitors would be accomplished through their advertising program, which mirrored successful previous campaigns, although it was much less hard-hitting than were the 2008 and 2011 campaigns. Conservatives understood that the best political advertising builds upon ideas already held by target audiences. Accordingly, they understood that too harsh a critique of their main target, Liberal leader Trudeau, ran counter to the general public perceptions of him as genuinely likeable and would therefore likely prove ineffective. Further, a campaign that was too sharp-edged would likely engender a significant backlash by reinforcing the Conservatives' negatives among a public that understood their tactics and viewed them as overly aggressive, at times abrasive, and often unnecessarily divisive.

The Conservative record in government dictated much of the platform, both because they were sincerely proud of their economic accomplishments and because neither the public nor their opponents were going to let them run away from their record. Upon receiving their majority in 2011, they immediately completed unfinished business from their minority years by repealing the national long-gun registry, stripping the Canadian Wheat Board of its grain marketing monopoly, passing omnibus crime legislation, and preparing the 2012 budget, its first of four designed to wrestle the $36 billion deficit back into balance in time for the 2015 election. The 2009–10 stimulus spending the Conservatives had been coerced into implementing would continue to be wound down, corporate taxes would continue to drift lower, and program savings would be found in all departments. Small, boutique-style tax credits or targeted spending measures would be included in each successive budget, but achieving balance was paramount, meaning little fiscal capacity remained for any new initiatives. Not that Conservatives were interested in creating any large federal social program initiatives — just the opposite. So determined were they to hamstring their opponents that when "balance" was reached in 2015, they decided to spend all the remaining surplus fiscal capacity by fulfilling the 2011 commitments and enhancing child support payments to Canadian parents, thereby ensuring that if their competitors wanted to introduce any new major initiatives they would have to either cancel popular Conservative programs or run deficits. These were options the Conservatives were confident their opponents would not dare to consider, or at least find very difficult to justify.

Conservative strategists understood that their fiscal decisions left them in the same position as their opponents, hence their lack of a signature major initiative in their platform. But they were confident that Canadians had reached a consensus on fiscal matters that clearly favoured their approach over any of the unpalatable options their opponents might propose.[18] They would offer thin gruel primarily because they did not anticipate the Liberals' planned-deficit strategy. Accordingly, they had no meaningful response when the Liberals' planned-deficit gambit gained traction mid-campaign.[19]

Conservatives also failed to anticipate, or properly calculate, the cumulative impact of the large number of groups and individuals they had alienated during four years of relative austerity. As they saw it, every savings initiative was met with sensationalized media coverage accompanied by spokespersons for the aggrieved. Conservative strategists understood that the likes of public sector unions, environmentalists, and cultural elites were never going to be part of any Conservative coalition, so offending those voters had no net negative impact on their base support. But when budget restraints impacted normally sympathetic voters, veterans for example, and the government's response to their objections differed little from the dismissive, often contemptuous responses they provided their parliamentary opponents and other known foes, the Conservatives appeared to be not only restricting their growth potential but also chipping away at their base support. They also appear to have underestimated how much motivation their aggressive tone and style provided opponents and the cumulative impact this would have on the swing voters they needed to add to their base in order to succeed. It is one thing to discount individual voters who are never going to cast a ballot in your favour. It is quite another to provide them with four years of increasingly intense motivation to organize anti-Harper campaigns dedicated to convincing others to also not vote Conservative.

## Platform

Prime Minister Stephen Harper began unveiling the Conservative platform on the first day of the campaign and continued with near-daily policy announcements until releasing the full platform document in week nine of the eleven-week campaign. Long gone were the days of the Reform *Blue*

*Book*, where parties would reveal their entire platform at the beginning of the campaign. Not that the Conservatives had many secrets. The platform relied heavily on their record in government and offered little new aside from a few boutique policy measures. The Conservatives delayed releasing their complete platform until late in the campaign in part to allow the Trans-Pacific Partnership (TPP) trade agreement to be included. More importantly, they continued fine-tuning their pitch up to that point, and by the time the formal platform document was released the Conservatives had narrowed their focus to one defining issue: the economy. They knew the risks of banking everything on the very subtle economic argument they were making but believed it was their only hope in the late stages of a campaign where victory appeared to be slipping away. They asked voters to give the Conservatives credit for the relatively good shape of the Canadian economy and not risk turning the government over to its irresponsible opponents at a time of global economic instability. A "knife-edge" argument, as Conservative strategists described it. Or, as Harper did in his introductory letter to the platform: "In this election, Canadians have a clear choice: a choice that carries the greatest of consequences for our economy, for our jobs, and for our families. Amid a global economy that is once again weak and in turmoil, Canada's economy remains stronger than most — but it's fragile, and needs protection from instability elsewhere in the world."

The economic emphasis was accentuated by the fact that although an image of Harper appeared on the platform document cover, his name did not. In fact, aside from his introductory letter, Harper's name did not appear in the document again until page sixty-eight and appeared only ten times in the entire 159 pages.[20] Nor did the words "leadership" or "security" appear on the cover. The document carried the formal title *Protect Our Economy: Our Conservative Plan to Protect the Economy*. If that was too subtle, the cover image had Harper surrounded by campaign signs — three in the background with the formal tag line, and one prominent foreground sign declaring: ECONOMY #1 PRIORITY.

The platform document was professionally produced. A text-heavy document, it contained only fifty-six images, all but two of which included Harper. No Cabinet minister or candidate was featured. Just Harper, meeting with veterans, with families, with seniors, with Ukrainians, with Wayne Gretzky, et cetera.

The content was organized using six broad themes, with order of appearance indicating importance. It began with seven pages extolling the virtues of balanced budgets, low taxes, and the Conservatives' record on both, underpinning strategists' lingering hopes Canadians would reconsider their flirtation with the Liberals' planned-deficits proposals. The section concluded, as did each of the six major sections, with a list of "AT RISK" items, distinguished from the rest of the blue-highlighted document by their red text and a large red X. Each of these was designed to bolster the comparative components of the campaign strategy. A fourteen-point section outlining the Conservatives' plans for a "stronger economy" followed, as did a seven-point section listing their plans for "hard-working families and seniors."

Not until the halfway point of the document did an eight-point section detailing their plans for a "more secure Canada" appear, followed by an even briefer five-point plan for "safe streets," and a concluding fourteen-point plan for "strong communities."

The final four pages contained a costing of the platform, meant to truly underscore the differences between what the Conservatives were offering compared to their rivals. It included small surplus budgets in each year of the plan, achieved primarily by keeping expenditures modest. Of the sixty-four items, the vast majority totalled in the single or, at most, double-digit millions of dollars. Only the reincarnated home renovation tax credit exceeded $1 billion, and then only in the final year of the plan. New platform commitments would be kept to less than $8 billion in total over four years, totalling only $0.54 billion in the first year, rising to $2.7 billion in the fourth. Thin gruel indeed.

## Advertising and Communications

Formal campaign preparedness began under Dimitri Soudas during his brief tenure as Conservative Party executive director. Conceptualized to ensure that Harper reconnected with voters, the goal of the party's communications efforts would be to drive home the narrative of Harper's strong, stable leadership juxtaposed against the poor judgment of Justin Trudeau.[21] The plan was detailed in its goals, included a much stronger online and social media presence than in past campaigns, and attempted to create a "Conservative Digital [N]ation." Campaign staffer Dennis Matthews, who had apprenticed under Muttart, assembled the in-house marketing team; it produced campaign ad material using the in-house staff along with outside writers, contracted camera crews, and other production staff hired on a freelance basis. Matthews continued a campaign that had been conceived prior to Trudeau assuming the Liberal leadership and had been unfolding since the day he ascended to that position. In 2013, immediately following the Liberal leadership convention and before Trudeau had time to make his first speech as leader in the House of Commons, the Conservatives released two ads on YouTube, versions of which would quickly air on TV and radio. They also launched an anti-Trudeau web page.

The ads revealed the first phases of a strategy that would be followed through to the end of the 2015 campaign, albeit with significant tweaks along the way. The first ad openly mocked Trudeau, using unflattering video footage and background carnival music to drive home the message that he was "in over his head." The second ad directly juxtaposed Trudeau's experience with Harper's by mocking Trudeau's previous occupations and comparing those to Harper's record of achievement.

By the spring of 2014, the Conservatives began running another series of ads — three shorter ones in this round. They included a sharper attack on Trudeau by using his public statements and policy proposals. More hard-hitting, these ads attacked Trudeau's "sociological approach" to terrorism, his position on legalizing marijuana, and his comment that "the budget will balance itself." The Conservatives ran these ads in heavy rotation on prime-time TV shows, newscasts, and sports broadcasts. But unlike with the previous ad campaign, they were not immediately posted to YouTube or available on the party's web pages. At the time, Conservative strategists were using their web pages to test even more hard-hitting ads. These used negative headlines about Trudeau, including one controversial ad that incorporated ISIL (Islamic State of Iraq and the Levant) video into its message about Trudeau's perceived lack of commitment to fighting terrorism.

By the spring of 2015, the Conservatives were ready to launch their full advertising assault. The earlier ad campaigns appeared to be working, inasmuch as pollsters were registering a decline in Liberal support and confidence in Trudeau as a future prime minister. Although Tom Mulcair had the NDP leading in most public opinion polls, the Conservatives correctly believed that Trudeau was still their main competitor, and with this in mind prepared to launch their most important ad campaign. When asked about the risk of driving up NDP support even further by continuing to focus on Trudeau, Conservative campaign spokesman Teneycke dismissed that notion with the prescient observation: "I don't think you can ever kill the Liberal Party in Canadian politics."

Two ads were again produced. One featured Trudeau's résumé undergoing scrutiny by a workplace hiring committee, a format borrowed from the Manitoba provincial NDP, who used it against the Progressive Conservatives in their 2011 campaign. After reviewing his "credentials" on a number of issues, it concluded with the tag line, "Justin Trudeau, just not ready." Mild in comparison to the previous barrage, and certainly much less caustic than those unleashed on former Liberal leaders Stéphane Dion in 2008 or Michael Ignatieff in 2011, the ads were judged by media analysts to be very effective.

In a telling moment in the ad, occurring before the "just not ready" tagline appeared, a panellist states that she is "not saying no forever, but not now." Conservative research over the previous two years indicated that no matter how hard they tried to denigrate Trudeau, Canadians either liked him or at minimum wanted to like him. They did have concerns over his perceived lack of maturity and lack of experience, but they didn't find him offensive and tended to believe that denigrating him too harshly bordered on bullying. Hence, a malicious onslaught would only reinforce negative perceptions of the Conservatives and so would prove counterproductive. Many voters also believed that he would indeed be prime minister someday and most seemed comfortable with the idea. This left the Conservatives to reason they had only one option: try to ensure that day would not occur in 2015.

The companion ad featured Harper calmly, competently working at his desk late into the evening, dealing with the many complex economic and security issues faced by a prime minister. It closed with a reference to the Conservatives' preferred ballot question about leadership: "Stephen Harper: Proven Leadership." In an unintended foreshadowing of the election night results, the final frames feature Harper leaving the prime minister's office and shutting off the lights as he exits.

By mid-campaign, as Harper's approval numbers began to tank, Conservatives changed tactics by releasing their "Stephen Harper isn't perfect" ad. Although criticized for acknowledging a deficiency, it clearly signalled the strategic shift in their approach to the leadership question. The ad featured a series of Canadians talking about the economy and their fears about what might happen if a non-Conservative government was elected. Conservatives would employ this strategy of playing up their opponents' perceived negatives rather than continuing to extol Harper's virtues through to the end of the campaign.

By Thanksgiving, their ads were accusing Trudeau of being "economically clueless" and declaring that his policies would mean "hard-working Canadians" risked losing everything as a result of accepting his reckless strategy of incurring $10 billion deficits and a "$1,000 tax hike on the typical worker." Another ad provided a direct comparison between the two leaders, telling Canadians that they had a "big decision" to make and offered up a checklist comparing Harper to "Justin."

The Conservatives' final national advertising gambit urged voters to not accept their opponents' "time for change" narrative. In a complete reversal of tactics, it had Harper declaring that "this election isn't about me." It hit the airwaves in heavy rotation during the Toronto Blue Jays' playoff series broadcasts and was immediately interpreted as an open acknowledgement that for the first time in his tenure, Harper had become a liability to his party.

A final set of regional television ads aired primarily in Ontario on the last weekend of the campaign. They continued to focus on Trudeau's fiscal plans while attempting to solidify the connection between him and Ontario premier Kathleen Wynne that the Conservatives had been trying to exploit since she began actively campaigning against them on the first day of the contest. The animosity between Harper and Wynne had been long-standing, very public, and bitter. Understanding that Wynne had many supporters, the Conservatives calculated that most of those were concentrated in urban Toronto ridings, which they had long since given up on winning. They further calculated that considerable opposition to her fiscal policies existed in the suburbs, where Conservatives had won by narrow margins in 2011 and where they were now trying to save seats. The ad recognized the limited impact Conservatives were having denigrating Trudeau and moved to tarnish the Liberal brand more generally by associating it with "the same Liberals who crippled Ontario under a mountain of debt, taxes, and wasteful spending."

As in past campaigns, the Conservatives did not rely solely on television ads. Harper had good radio appeal, and they made creative use of that medium. Each day during the final weeks of the campaign, the Conservatives broadcast across a wide variety of radio formats an ad featuring Harper speaking directly to listeners. Conservatives have always appreciated the potential of commercial radio and made heavy use of its relative affordability and messaging flexibility, which allowed them to easily tailor different messages to different markets. They have also tended to like "talk" format because it skews toward older, more conservative voters — something that allowed Harper to create a sense of intimacy with listeners.

The national Conservative campaign also placed ads in local newspapers late in the campaign and distributed flyers. Some targeted Chinese- and Punjabi-speaking voters by claiming that because Trudeau did not share their socially conservative values he would bring drugs and brothels to their communities. These ads constituted an extension of their ongoing strategy of giving unprecedented access to local and ethnic media organizations in attempting to be included in more of their news content, a strategy they successfully executed in the 2011 election.[22]

The national campaign also purchased the front pages of most Postmedia and Sun newspapers on the final weekend before the vote. In place of the newspapers' headlines, a giant yellow Conservative ad appeared. Not by accident, the yellow ads looked remarkably similar to Elections Canada branding and warned Canadians that voting anything other than Conservative "will cost you." Explanations followed the headline, but the visual impact was paramount and was reinforced by a ballot-style checkbox marking a "Conservative" vote.

The Conservatives also deployed a full array of social media promotions. Most included some of the best party-produced graphics of the campaign, allowing the Conservative rapid response team to do at least as good a job as the other parties at effectively utilizing social media.

Hence, although the Conservatives' advertising and branding strategy resources were heavily skewed toward television, they attempted to leave no advertising stone unturned, making use of all mediums within the limits of the available resources.

## CAMPAIGN DYNAMICS

When the Harper government included fixed election dates in its 2007 electoral law reforms, the stated intention was to limit a sitting majority government's ability to enhance its re-election chances by controlling the timing of the next vote. The law was flexible enough, however, to allow minority governments to seek an earlier renewal by way of prime ministerial discretion, as Harper exercised in 2008, or in cases where it lost a formal confidence vote as in 2011. It did not prescribe a fixed length for the campaign, and revisions contained in their 2014 Fair Elections Act amendments included provisions for proportionally increasing campaign expense limits in situations where campaigns ran longer than the now customary five weeks, as had happened with the nearly eight-week 2006 campaign. By the summer of 2015, Conservative strategists were already incorporating a much longer than usual campaign into their plans, and on the August long weekend Harper made it official by visiting the governor general and asking for dissolution to officially begin a campaign that he claimed had already started. Harper's rationalization had some legitimacy, given the leaders were preparing for the first of several leaders debates that would be held later that same week. Behind the scenes, however, Conservatives believed that the exceptionally long campaign would serve their strategic interest in three critical respects.

Initially, Conservatives have never been shy about dipping into their war chest to finance pre-writ advertising, always secure in the knowledge that enough money remained, or could be raised, to allow them to spend the maximum during the writ period. They were equally confident that their competitors could not afford similar pre-writ extravagances. In 2015, however, they faced new entrants into the pre-writ market, the vast majority of which were anti-Conservative third-party organizations ready to promote one simple message: *Vote for anybody but Harper and his Conservatives.* Indeed, Engage Canada's anti-Harper ads had already aired in June, accusing the Conservatives of increasing income inequality and cutting health-care spending. Conservative strategists took the threat seriously given that they attributed Wynne's 2014 Ontario election victory to the boost she received from anti-Conservative interest group advertising. Conservative strategists estimated that anti-Harper third-party spending by organizations such as Unifor, Leadnow, and Engage Canada could top $20 million prior to a more conventional, early-September election call when the legal restrictions on third-party spending would reduce those amounts to a negligible total. When combined with the anticipated fallout from testimony at the Mike Duffy Senate expense trial, Conservatives believed they risked starting a post-Labour Day campaign as much as 10 percentage points behind in the polls, a deficit from which they knew they could not recover. Eliminating interest group spending for an additional six weeks would force the anti-Harper forces to marshal their efforts in other ways.

An eleven-week campaign would also provide Trudeau more opportunities to make mistakes. The Conservatives reasoned that Trudeau's words and actions, amplified by the more intense media scrutiny expected during the formal campaign period, would expose enough of his own weaknesses to sufficiently backstop their mild attack ads, making their case while insulating them from a backlash. The long campaign period would also benefit the Conservatives in that they were the only party capable of spending anywhere close to the $54 million national party campaign expense limits. The benefits would be compounded if the Conservatives could hold back large proportions of those funds for late-campaign advertising blitzes.

The Conservatives were hoping to launch the campaign by announcing agreement on the Trans-Pacific Partnership trade agreement, the centrepiece to the trade plank in their economic platform. But when negotiators failed to finalize the deal before the recessing of Parliament at the end of July, the decision was made to proceed with the campaign and use the TPP as best they could once the deal was finalized. When that occurred with only two weeks remaining in the campaign, it failed to materially impact the campaign dynamics. On its own, the TPP may or may not have significantly moved votes had there been more time to debate its merits, but it did symbolize the lack of any signature policy item in the Conservatives' 2015 campaign.

From the start, the 2015 campaign resembled their failed 2004 effort more than their successful 2006 endeavour. After careful analysis of what went wrong in 2004, Conservatives fixed many of the problems by moving away from their obsession with details, which the electorate perceived as little more than campaign white noise. By 2006, they simplified their message down to five priorities with one signature proposal: the 2 percent GST cut. Why Conservative strategists chose to execute a 2015 campaign strategy that quickly appeared unfocused and lacking any ability to define its own narrative will be debated for some time to come. The results, however, became clear early and dogged the Conservatives, who ultimately had no simple and compelling narrative to counter exogenous campaign developments.

The entire pre-Labour Day campaign period illustrated this dynamic. Harper spent the first two weeks of August dutifully and meticulously executing the strategy of juxtaposing his leadership against the alternatives, reminding Canadians about the government's role in supporting the relatively healthy but still fragile and threatened economy and in ensuring Canadians' security at home and abroad. Minor policy announcements, a near daily occurrence, included tax breaks for apprentice training, reinstating the home renovation tax credit, banning travel to terrorist-controlled zones, and taking in an additional ten thousand refugees over the next four years. Along the way, he attempted to pick fights with provincial governments, past and present. Most, such as Alberta's NDP premier Rachel Notley, refused to engage. Ontario's Wynne, on the other hand, was only too eager to oblige.

Harper's tour events typically ran on schedule and as planned, at least until the tight security and message-control techniques supplanted the planned daily message as the main news item emerging from the tour. Conservatives had developed campaign-event participant screening techniques over the years as an element of their message control strategies. Tight security served to keep their events free from the very vocal type of protesters their polarizing style of politics attracted. But early in the campaign it became known they were also requiring participants to sign a disclaimer forbidding distribution of pictures and accounts of the events. While that practice was abandoned soon after it became public, the careful screening and the strategy of entertaining only five media questions continued.

Both became visibly problematic during the second week of the campaign, when the media used all of its questions to ask Harper to reconcile the seemingly contradictory testimonies of former second-in-command

Nigel Wright and former legal adviser Benjamin Perrin emerging from the Duffy trial. Sticking to the "do no further damage" strategy, at each event Harper would run out the clock by repeating his mantra that only two people were involved, Duffy and Wright. Both were held accountable, had been or were in the process of being disciplined, and he had nothing further to add. This rendered news coverage of the tour diametrically opposed to the Conservatives' preferred narrative at the same time it reinforced their opponents' ballot question.

Coverage of Harper's events typically began with stories about the trial itself, including evidence suggesting other members of the inner circle, primarily Chief of Staff Novak, were involved, or at a minimum had knowledge of Wright's $90,000 personal cheque to Duffy. These were followed by stories outlining Harper's responses, or lack thereof, and only occasionally by a story about his main talking point of the day.

When repeating Harper's unchanging position became less newsworthy, Conservative event participants provided the media with another unflattering angle to cover. When the predictability of Harper's media encounters became too much for many of the assembled partisans, some began openly jeering reporters. Harper did little to intervene, nor did event organizers when sparring matches between attendees and the media erupted. The malaise peaked when one outraged partisan's expletive-laced attack on a reporter received several days' of blanket national media coverage. Further complications arose out of the Conservative tour organizers' insistence on providing only minimal prior notice of events to both the media and local Conservative campaigns. The short notice regarding when and where campaign events were to occur helped keep protesters away. However, it also made it much more difficult for media to cover events and complicated matters for local campaign organizers, who were hard-pressed to fill rooms. As the campaign continued, visible evidence of less-than-capacity crowds at Conservative events presented bad optics and more advance time was incorporated. Event attendance increased, as did the number of protesters.

An accumulation of self-inflicted distractions also hampered the Conservative campaign. Daily messaging was often overshadowed by the effects of sloppy or careless planning, such as when Scouts Canada took exception to the Conservatives using uniformed Scouts to promote their conservation promises, or when the Terry Fox family took exception to the annual Marathon of Hope charity event being linked to the Conservative campaign. Voices from the past continued to haunt them, such as when suspended Senator Patrick Brazeau penned a 1,600-word tirade accusing Harper of being a "control freak" and urging Canadians to vote the Conservatives out. Sloppy social media promotions were critiqued for using generic photographs of places and items different from what was being promoted. And although all parties had to deal with troublesome candidates, when it was revealed that a Conservative candidate had been caught on film by the CBC urinating in a cup while on a service call in a customer's kitchen, prior to his being vetted and approved as a candidate, the overall media narrative presented the Conservative campaign as disorganized and adrift, if not floundering altogether. Much of the coverage included critiques from "anonymous" but nevertheless "senior" Conservative insiders who described the 2015 campaign in terms more reflective of the 2000 Alliance campaign[23] than any Harper had led.

Nevertheless, throughout it all the Conservatives remained competitive in what pollsters were reporting was shaping up to be a close three-way race. Although their problems in the Atlantic provinces were evident early, they were gaining ground in Ontario and at times led nationally, an eminently satisfactory position according to Conservative strategists, who knew how much worse it could have been heading into the Labour Day weekend.

When the Syrian refugee crisis exploded on the campaign trail, however, Harper's response revealed a number of weaknesses that were bubbling beneath the surface. In a genuinely sympathetic initial response, Harper called the images of three-year-old Alan Kurdi's lifeless body lying face down on a beach "heartbreaking." But he refused to alter his plans, insisting that fighting ISIL terrorism was a key component of any responsible strategy. Citing security concerns and the enormity of the situation, he would not alter the planned acceptance of ten thousand additional refugees, although he announced later that he would shorten the time frame to one year from four. Conservative strategists maintained that Harper read the public mood better than any of the other leaders, and they had the national poll numbers to support that contention. After an initial dip downward, the Conservatives' response appeared to give the party a boost. Indeed, toward the end of September the Conservatives were leading in poll aggregations with several individual polls indicating they had opened up a substantial lead over the second-place Liberals and the plummeting NDP. But all of this masked a deeper problem, of which the war room was fully aware: Harper's leadership numbers were declining rapidly and had been doing so for some time. Further, he was losing credibility on economic leadership, formerly his greatest strength. Reports from Canadians' doorsteps by candidates clearly indicated that even Conservative supporters were becoming increasingly hostile toward their leader, and for the first time in his tenure his leadership was a net negative for the party. It was at this time they began to shift their message track to de-emphasize his leadership, first admitting he was "not perfect," and then claiming that the election was not about him after all.

Another defining issue for the Conservative campaign emerged when a Federal Court ruled that contrary to government policy, Muslim women could indeed take the Canadian citizenship oath while wearing a face-covering niqab.[24] Again, Conservatives appeared to be fully onside with public opinion, at least with respect to the specific requirements at citizenship ceremonies. Attributing their bump in the polls to their measured refugee stance, their proposal to deport dual citizens convicted of terrorism while stripping them of their Canadian citizenship, and their determination to fight the courts over the niqab, they decided to double down on what are loosely referred to as "culture war" issues. On a day Harper was off the campaign trail preparing for a leaders debate, the Conservative war room organized an event at which Cabinet ministers Chris Alexander and Kellie Leitch announced the Conservatives would create a new "barbaric cultural practices" hotline. Harper went further when he declared that a re-elected Conservative government would follow Quebec's lead in dealing with sensitive accommodation issues, leaving many to speculate that the Conservatives might proclaim a ban on the niqab in the public service and for those seeking services from the federal government. Conservative strategists maintain that Harper had merely been unclear when he first broached the subject, intending only to state that he would deal with the difficult issue sensitively, as had the Quebec government. But his failure to clarify matters in the ensuing days only reinforced the impression that Conservatives were prepared to use what high-profile detractors like Calgary mayor Naheed Nenshi called "dog-whistle" politics to win at any cost. Many Canadians, including soft Conservative supporters, recoiled. This was an unadulterated low point for a prime minister who had repeatedly extolled the virtues of pluralism and for a party that had resisted temptation to use ethnicity and immigration as negative wedge issues to divide the electorate.[25] Not only had Harper worked hard to eradicate those lingering anti-immigrant Reform elements from his Conservatives, his government directed policy in exactly the opposite direction, seeking to bring more new Canadians into their coalition rather than pit them against "old stock" voters. At least until now.

As the Conservatives continued to attempt to finesse the issue, opportunity opened for their opponents to capitalize. Candidates were reporting a backlash from constituents at the same time they were receiving contradictory communications from the war room. Campaign chair Giorno began urging a return to economic messaging, while campaign director Byrne advocated even greater emphasis on cultural values. All the while, Trudeau was gaining momentum and the Conservatives had provided him with a quintessentially Liberal issue to rally further support. His simple and direct "a Canadian is a Canadian is a Canadian" retort stood in stark contrast to the Conservatives' complex and mixed messaging. The issue helped further deflate Mulcair's NDP who had already began a steady slide in the polls prior to the niqab issue (see Chapter 3 for further analysis of the NDP campaign). Trudeau's handling of the issue solidified another fact Conservatives were now forced to acknowledge. If Trudeau had not imploded yet, they certainly could not count on that happening at all in the 2015 campaign. In the final week, they would adjust as best they could to accommodate for that mistaken strategic assumption.

---

Although the Conservatives targeted Trudeau as their primary threat from the beginning, they repeatedly underestimated his capabilities while making errors in their strategies for dealing with him. Evidence came early in the campaign when prior to the first leaders debate, campaign spokesperson Teneycke deliberately lowered expectations for Trudeau by claiming that "if he comes on stage with his pants on, he will probably exceed expectations." Not only did Trudeau attend fully clothed, he exceeded expectations. He continued to improve his performance in the succeeding four debates while Harper, although not performing poorly, delivered only solid or stable performances. Another example occurred during the Munk debate on Canada's foreign policy when the audience openly chuckled after Trudeau was asked how he would deal with Putin. War-room scripter Boessenkool tweeted that the incident was a defining moment that signified Trudeau's imminent demise. Yet Trudeau left that debate with most pundits scoring him as the outright winner (see Chapter 10).

Conservatives also failed to anticipate the Liberals' strategic decisions to challenge two of the Conservatives' narratives head-on. Despite Trudeau providing plenty of advance notice that he would confront the "just not ready" narrative when he was asked about it at the *Maclean's* debate, the Conservative campaign was dumbstruck when the Liberals addressed the charge directly in their own advertising. Further, rather than considering the possibility that the strategy might succeed, they believed the tactic was the beginning of the implosion they were anticipating and therefore developed no immediate counter-strategy. They also failed to anticipate the Liberals' planned-deficit strategy. Once revealed, they again misinterpreted it to be a mistake on their competitor's part. They were wrong on both accounts. By the time they realized as much, they had become so heavily invested in their own economic narrative that reversing course would likely have been counterproductive, even if they had an alternative narrative in waiting, which they did not.

So the Conservatives entered the final week of the campaign knowing that they would not win enough seats to survive as a government even if they managed to eke out a minority victory. The more likely result would see the Liberals win the election; the best the Conservatives could hope for was to keep them to a minority, quickly replace Harper as leader, and take on Trudeau again sometime in 2016 or 2017.

It was at this point the Conservative campaign deployed what appeared to be its most bemusing campaign tactics. At each tour event they created a mock game show atmosphere with Harper playing host to a "regular tax-paying Canadian" who would count out fake dollars until they totalled what Conservatives estimated were the costs to the average Canadian family of the Liberals' campaign promises. Most observers panned the theatrics as amateurish gimmickry and openly wondered how Harper would allow himself to participate in such an undignified end to his political career. While Harper had been initially cautious about the plan, he was not beyond using stunts. Earlier in the campaign the Conservatives had used a giant safe to illustrate their "tax lock" legislation promise. In previous campaigns, Harper had used fake dollars while lampooning the Liberal sponsorship scandal. So he agreed to try the game show stunt for a day; when his reservations were confirmed by media criticism, he was ready to discontinue it. But Conservative strategists pointed out that in spite of the ridicule, they had gotten their single most important economic message through. Not only was this a rare occurrence for them in 2015, they argued that the stunt could provide them, for the first time ever, the opportunity to finish a campaign by punching through their primary message. So on it went.

The Conservatives also endured much criticism for including Toronto political power brokers Doug and Rob Ford in their late-campaign rallies in Harper's childhood hometown of Etobicoke. Although a seemingly incomprehensible manoeuvre to outside observers, there was some method to their apparent madness. Conservatives knew Rob Ford was definitely a distraction and liability. But his inclusion was a concession to his brother, Doug, whom the Conservatives still considered an asset. Not only was Doug Ford skilled at taking on Ontario premier Wynne with more credibility than the Conservatives could muster, he was in possession of a 191,000-name list of identified supporters to which the Conservatives desperately wanted access. Their research indicated that half of the Ford brothers' supporters had voted Liberal in the last provincial election. Hence, while it appeared as though the Conservatives were scrambling to preserve their core base of support, they did not see it that way. They believed that many suburban Toronto voters would listen to Doug Ford even if they were no longer listening to the Conservatives and that he could sway substantial numbers of votes toward them at the last minute. Not that they were under any illusions about winning big in the 905 region around Toronto. But knowing their base was solid, they believed Ford could improve their fortunes enough to limit the damage and help them survive in a few additional ridings. Be that as it may, Harper and his team knew that the overall election outcome had been determined prior to any of the final-week campaign shenanigans, and on the final flights of the 2015 leader's tour they prepared for the transfer of power and Harper's resignation as leader.

## CONCLUSION

There are very few positives that can be gleaned from the 2015 Conservative election results. Certainly organizers were relieved that the party was not completely decimated. They took solace in knowing that their defeat was not as substantial for them as the NDP's was for it. The new ninety-nine-member Conservative caucus would form the Official Opposition, albeit absent considerable talent given that eight former Cabinet ministers lost their re-election bids. They made gains in Quebec, winning twelve seats in the Quebec City area, their most under Harper. Their twenty-nine Alberta victories were also their most ever. But they lost five Alberta contests, surrendering two in Calgary and three in Edmonton. In every other province the Conservatives lost seats on declining vote shares.

Conservatives were shut out in the Atlantic provinces after capturing twelve seats there in 2011, winning at least one in each province. The Newfoundland and Labrador results were not unexpected, the party having faced difficulties there since 2008 when then-premier Danny Williams first launched his "Anybody But Conservative" campaign after a bitter fallout with Harper over equalization payments. In Nova Scotia, the Conservatives had hoped to retain at least a couple of the four seats they won in 2011 but knew that was unlikely, hence the lack of leader's tour events in that province. Their New Brunswick results were undoubtedly the most disappointing in the region. After steadily increasing their seat count and proportion of vote in each successive election since 2004, the Conservatives were shut out in the province. Considering the fact that they had campaigned hard there, it was an especially bitter pill to swallow. Further, not only was the Atlantic Conservative caucus obliterated, their proportion of the vote was severely depleted in each province, to their lowest share of the total vote during Harper's tenure as leader.

As bad as the Atlantic results were, in terms of seat losses the Ontario numbers were worse. The Conservatives lost forty seats in a province where redistribution provided them with fifteen more opportunities for victories, dropping to only thirty-three from the seventy-three they won in 2011. Their 35 percent share of the Ontario vote was their worst showing since 2004, as was their 2015 seat total. They were completely shut out of Toronto, and won only three seats in the rest of the Greater

Toronto Area. They won most of the seats outside of Ontario's metropolitan areas, but were shut out of the urban centres and lost all ten of the province's northwestern seats.

The Conservatives' western Canadian results look good in comparison. In fact, having won fifty-four of their ninety-nine seats in the West, their forty-second parliamentary caucus will again be dominated by western MPs. But the Conservatives lost seats and vote shares in three of the four provinces. Their British Columbia caucus was more than halved, from twenty-one to only ten based on a 15 percent decline in their vote share. They lost every Vancouver seat, were shut out on Vancouver Island, and won only three of twenty-three seats in the entire Greater Vancouver Area. Their Manitoba caucus was similarly reduced, dropping from eleven to only five based on a similar decline in vote share. They lost all nine ridings in Winnipeg and the surrounding area. Overall, 2015 represented their worst results in these provinces since the party's merger. Although their Saskatchewan losses were modest in comparison, ten victories was their worst under Harper and was based on their lowest vote share since 2004. Immediately following the election, the Conservatives announced that Stephen Harper had resigned as leader. The new caucus elected Edmonton-area MP Rona Ambrose as interim leader and the party began structuring a process to choose a permanent leader. Thus ended a remarkable period in Canadian politics that saw Harper first divide, then reunite and lead conservatives to a decade in power before losing the 2015 election to a party many had predicted they would replace as Canada's natural governing party.

Conservatives have four years to rebuild prior to the next federal election. Acting as Official Opposition, their ninety-nine-member caucus will provide them with ample opportunity to remain relevant to Canadian voters on a day-to-day basis while presenting themselves as a credible alternative to the Liberals. The Conservative Party remains organizationally strong and well-financed. The leadership selection process that awards one hundred points to each riding association will require national efforts by most serious contenders and present opportunities to rebuild in regions of relative weakness, particularly Atlantic Canada, Quebec, and Canada's metropolitan areas. Re-establishing trust with ethnic voters based on a renewed commitment to pluralism will also be key. Most importantly, the Conservatives have the opportunity to define for themselves a core set of classical-liberal, pluralist, fiscally conservative principles that will allow them to build a new minimum winning coalition. Keeping social conservatives and rural votes onside while attempting to accommodate an increasingly libertarian mainstream political culture will be challenging, but not impossible. The Harper era of Canadian conservatism clearly demonstrated the potential for success, as well as the limitations of attempting to instigate an enduring change in partisan alignments by a party devoid of a defining core identity.

## NOTES

1. This essay reflects in part interviews with a number of people associated with Conservative campaigns since 2004. Although most had no problem with being identified, I have again committed to anonymity for all and sincerely thank them for their time, insights, and help in making this a more accurate and complete analysis.
2. Elections Canada, www.elections.ca.
3. See ThreeHundredEight.com for aggregate polling numbers through this period.
4. See Tom Flanagan, *Harper's Team: Behind the Scenes in the Conservative Rise to Power*, 2nd ed. (Montreal and Kingston: McGill-Queen's University Press, 2009). For more recent offerings see John Ibbitson, *Stephen Harper* (Toronto: McClelland & Stewart [Signal], 2015); and Ken Boessenkool and Sean Spear, "Ordered Liberty: How Harper's Philosophy Transformed Canada for the Better," *Policy Options*, December 1, 2015, http://policyoptions.irpp.org/2015/12/01/harper/.
5. Faron Ellis and Keith Archer, "Reform at the Crossroads: The 1997 Election," in *The Canadian General Election of 1997*, ed. Alan Frizzell and Jon Pammett (Toronto: Dundurn, 1997), 111–34; and Faron Ellis, "The More Things Change …: The Alliance Campaign," in *The Canadian General Election of 2000*, ed. Jon H. Pammett and Christopher Dornan (Toronto: Dundurn, 2001), 59–89.
6. Faron Ellis, *The Limits of Participation: Members and Leaders in Canada's Reform Party* (Calgary: University of Calgary Press, 2005).
7. Faron Ellis, "Twenty-First Century Conservatives Can Continue to Succeed," in *Crosscurrents: Contemporary Political Issues*, 8th ed., ed. Mark Charlton and Paul Barker (Toronto: Nelson, 2015), 17–36.
8. See Lawrence Martin, *Harperland: The Politics of Control* (Toronto: Penguin Canada, 2011).
9. Faron Ellis and Peter Woolstencroft, "New Conservatives, Old Realities: The 2004 Election Campaign," in *The Canadian General Election of 2004*, ed. Jon H. Pammett and Christopher Dornan (Toronto: Dundurn, 2004), 66–105.

10. Tom Flanagan, *Winning Power: Canadian Campaigning in the 21st Century* (Montreal and Kingston: McGill-Queen's University Press, 2014), 125–42.
11. Tom Flanagan, "Something Blue: The Harper Conservatives as Garrison Party," in *Conservatism in Canada*, ed. James Farney and David Rayside (Toronto: University of Toronto Press, 2013), 79–94.
12. See Paul Wells, *The Longer I'm Prime Minister: Stephen Harper and Canada, 2006–* (Toronto: Random House Canada, 2013).
13. Faron Ellis and Peter Woolstencroft, "A Change of Government, Not a Change of Country: The Conservatives and the 2006 Federal Election," in *The Canadian Federal Election of 2006*, ed. Jon H. Pammett and Christopher Dornan (Toronto: Dundurn, 2006), 58–92.
14. See Jennifer Ditchburn, "Journalistic Pathfinding: How the Parliamentary Press Gallery Adapted to News Management Under the Conservative Government of Stephen Harper" (master's thesis, Carleton University, 2014).
15. Conservative Party of Canada, Financial Statements, December 31, 2014.
16. Elections Canada, www.election.ca.
17. See Susan Delacourt, *Shopping for Votes: How Politicians Choose Us and We Choose Them* (Madeira Park, BC: Douglas & McIntyre, 2013).
18. See Darrell J. Bricker and John Ibbitson, *The Big Shift: The Seismic Change in Canadian Politics, Business, and Culture and What It Means for Our Future* (Toronto: HarperCollins, 2013).
19. See Ken Boessenkool and Sean Speer, "How the Deficit Gambit Stunned Conservatives into Silence," *Maclean's*, October 30, 2015, www.macleans.ca/economy/how-the-deficit-gambit-stunned-conservatives-into-silence/.
20. Alternatively, the word *Conservative* appears nearly four hundred times. See *Protect Our Economy*, Conservative 2015 campaign platform.
21. See Tonda MacCharles, "Conservatives Lay Out Re-Election Strategy in Secret Document," *Toronto Star*, February 10, 2014, www.thestar.com/news/canada/2014/02/10/conservatives_lay_out_reelection_strategy_in_secret_document.html.
22. See April Lindgren, "Toronto-Area Ethnic Newspapers and Canada's 2011 Federal Election: An Investigation of Content, Focus and Partisanship," *Canadian Journal of Political Science* 47, no. 4 (December 2014): 667–96.
23. Ellis, "The More Things Change. . . ."
24. The Supreme Court of Canada had previously ruled in 2012 that women could testify in court while wearing the niqab.
25. For analysis of the Harper Conservatives' "ethnic outreach" program and its impact on government policy see, Inder Marwah, Triadafilos (Phil) Triadafilopoulos, and Stephen White, "Immigration, Citizenship, and Canada's New Conservative Party," in *Conservatism in Canada*, ed. James Farney and David Rayside (Toronto: University of Toronto Press, 2013), 95–119.

# CHAPTER 3

## Back to the Future: The Resurgent Liberals

Brooke Jeffrey

When Prime Minister Stephen Harper dropped the election writ on August 2, 2015, the Liberal Party found itself in third place in the polls, well behind the first-place NDP and even the second-place Conservatives. This was particularly ominous for the party since the Liberals earlier had risen from the ashes of their humiliating 2011 election defeat and seemed to be on the comeback trail. In fact, they had occupied first place in the polls for much of 2014 and early 2015. But their decline since the spring of 2015 had been steady and significant. For several months it had been apparent that the Conservatives were reduced to their core support of roughly 30 percent, suggesting to most observers that the upcoming election would be a contest between the NDP and the Liberals for the nearly 65 percent of the Canadian electorate who were intent on replacing the Harper government at all costs. To the Liberals' dismay, in the early days of the campaign that contest seemed to have been won by the NDP. Yet by early September, the Liberals' recovery was clearly under way and by October 2 the tables had been turned. The party soared to first place in the polls and never looked back. On October 19 the resurgent Liberals obtained a comfortable majority of 184 seats, while the Conservatives were reduced to the status of Official Opposition with ninety-nine seats and the NDP fell back to its more traditional role of third party with forty-four seats. Within days, Justin Trudeau became the twenty-third prime minister of Canada.

## THE CONTEXT OF THE LIBERALS' VICTORY

The Liberals' come-from-behind victory was of unprecedented scope in Canadian electoral history. For the party to have even been in contention after its 2011 electoral disaster was a remarkable feat. Many observers had written the Liberals off as past their prime, heading for political oblivion or a merger with the NDP. To not only survive but come from third place at the beginning of the campaign to triumph over a better-financed and governing Conservative Party, which had used every conceivable tactic to ensure its advantage, as well as an NDP Opposition leader with far more experience and gravitas, was nothing short of astonishing.

How did this remarkable turn of events come to pass? As this chapter outlines, the Liberals conducted what could only be described as a campaign for the ages, one which in many respects was also unprecedented. In addition, they took full advantage of numerous tactical blunders by their opponents. But first, the Liberal Party of Canada did what it has so often done in the past: rebuild, reorganize, and rejuvenate its brand. Had it not done so with painstaking care over the four-year period leading up to the 2015 election, not even a perfect campaign could have achieved the astonishing result. To fully appreciate the magnitude of the Liberals' accomplishment, it is important to recognize the situation the party faced after its crushing defeat in 2011. Its unprecedented third-place finish, with only 19 percent of the popular vote, left it with just thirty-four seats in the House of Commons and a major challenge if it was ever to regain its former status.

The party's vaunted electoral machine lay in ruins. Its base in Quebec had been destroyed. Its traditional support in Atlantic Canada and Ontario had been reduced to a pathetically small urban rump. Western Canada, which had been a source of declining Liberal support for decades, was now an arid wasteland for it. The situation appeared so grave that political commentator Peter Newman declared the party was finished. "They have no power base. Every party must have a power base," he argued, concluding it would be impossible for the Liberals to rebuild on all fronts at once.[1]

In addition, the party was close to bankruptcy, having failed utterly in its half-hearted attempts to emulate the superior direct-mail fundraising machine of the Conservatives, and staggering under the financial burden of so many general elections and leadership conventions in such a short period of time. Indeed, it was now facing the necessity of seeking a fourth party leader in less than eight years, Michael Ignatieff having resigned immediately after the 2011 election. And, with Stephen Harper's deliberate moves to eliminate public subsidies for political parties, it was difficult to see how the party could ever raise sufficient funds to mount a credible campaign in the future.

Perhaps most important of all, during the 2011 campaign the party had yet again failed to articulate either a meaningful alternative to the Conservatives' narrative of small government, or its own positive vision for the country. Nor had the party been willing to defy the Conservative fiscal mantra of lowering taxes and balancing budgets. The Liberals' inability to address any of these issues in three consecutive elections had led many to conclude that liberalism itself, and not just the party, was on the verge of disappearing from the political scene in Canada. Author Peter Newman's dire prediction of the "death of liberal Canada,"[2] for example, was reinforced by pollster Darrell Bricker and columnist John Ibbitson's claims that the appeal of the centre-left had disappeared entirely and, as a result, "the Conservative Party will be to the twenty-first century what the Liberal Party was to the twentieth, the perpetually dominant party, the natural governing party."[3] While others were less convinced of the Liberals' ultimate demise, many believed the 2015 election would be the last chance for the Liberal Party of Canada to recover its major party status. As the chapter on the Liberals in the previous edition of this series concluded, "The Liberal Party should not be counted out on the basis of this election, but nor should its recovery and eventual return to power be taken for granted. Much will depend on the willingness of the Liberal membership to come together and contribute to the party's rebuilding, and on the party's ability to return to basics and define essential liberal values in the context of the twenty-first century."[4]

## THE DELAYED LEADERSHIP RACE

With enthusiasm and precision, the Liberals did exactly that — returned to basics. Unlike after their 2006 and 2008 defeats, this time the party executive recognized the importance of avoiding shortcuts. Rather than pursue a costly and divisive leadership race in the immediate aftermath of the election, it was decided that the contest to choose Michael Ignatieff's successor would not begin until January 2013, a decision that undoubtedly was made easier by Stephen Harper's governmental majority and fixed election date legislation, since the next federal election was not scheduled until October 2015. In the meantime, former Liberal leadership candidate and MP Bob Rae was appointed interim leader of the party. He filled this position with competence and attracted considerable public recognition for the party. Indeed, Rae's influence in the House of Commons was such that the Conservatives soon launched several attack ads against him, apparently concerned that he might become the next permanent leader of the party.

The leadership race itself unfolded in relative obscurity, with a large field of nine candidates, comprised of virtual unknowns as well as a smattering of backbench MPs and former Cabinet ministers, including Marc Garneau and Martin Cauchon. The wild card was rookie MP Justin Trudeau, son of the former prime minister, who had earlier ruled himself out as a candidate and only entered the race after Bob Rae announced that he would not run for the leadership.

Perhaps the most striking feature of the various leadership "debates" over the course of early 2013 was the high degree of civility among the candidates and the lack of any significant differences of opinion on policy matters. However, as the race progressed it became increasingly clear that Trudeau was the likely winner. He received endorsements from most of the caucus and prominent members of the non-parliamentary wing of the party, as well as a number of key players in Dalton McGuinty's Liberal government in Ontario. Trudeau's popularity with the general public also increased over time, and his campaign raised record amounts of money. (In fact, his revenue exceeded requirements and his campaign turned over a substantial balance to the party at the end of the leadership race.) Recognizing the inevitable, three of the candidates actually withdrew from the race in the early stages. With Trudeau's overwhelming first-ballot victory in April 2013, it soon became evident that a new era in the party's history was about to begin.

Certainly this was clear to Harper and his advisers. Within *minutes* of Trudeau's victory, the airwaves were filled with Conservative attack ads claiming that the Liberals' new leader was "just not ready," a campaign that repeated the Conservatives' earlier efforts with Dion and Ignatieff to define the party's leaders for voters before they could do so themselves. However Trudeau's response — that he would ignore such negative advertising in favour of the high road — appeared to have more traction with the public than did a similar response from his predecessors.[5] One reason for this difference was the party's superior financial resources, which allowed the Liberals to counter the Conservative ads with their own. Humorously mocking those negative ads with ones showing Trudeau in a positive light as a teacher and highlighting his background, the Liberal ads proved both popular and effective.

One puzzle is why the Conservatives continued with the "just not ready" ads. Even Harper's former mentor, University of Calgary political scientist Tom Flanagan, warned that the Conservative ads were "just not working" and advised the Conservatives that they should try a different approach.

His views were echoed by former Progressive Conservative prime minister Brian Mulroney. In what would prove to be a prescient interview, Mulroney argued that Trudeau's biggest advantage after nearly eight years of the Harper government was "he's not Harper. My point to the Conservatives is to be very careful how you treat this fellow. Because you're not dealing with a Stéphane Dion. You're not dealing with a Michael Ignatieff here. You're dealing with a different generation, a different product of that life."[6]

Trudeau's candidacy had, in fact, been predicated on several assumptions and conditions that would prove significant in the lead-up to the next election. The first was that there would be no merger with the NDP, an option that several senior Liberals and New Democrats, including Jean Chrétien and Ed Broadbent, had mused about publicly on a number of occasions between the 2008 and 2011 elections.[7] The second was that the party must at all costs avoid negative campaigns, and instead fight a positive battle against the Harper Conservatives based on Liberal values. The third was that the party must end the divisive internecine war that had contributed to its recent electoral defeats.[8] Fourth, and most significant in the short term, the party must move quickly and decisively to rebuild its organization long before the next federal election. As Trudeau and his advisers knew only too well, the legendary Big Red Machine was, in fact, a broken-down wreck.

Trudeau and his closest advisers, including former Queen's Park staffers Gerald Butts (Dalton McGuinty) and Katie Telford (Gerard Kennedy), and Cyrus Reporter (a former aide to Chrétien-era minister Allan Rock), all of whom had also been architects of his leadership victory, moved quickly to begin the party's major rebuilding exercise. Also aiding Trudeau in this rebuilding process would be two long-time friends who occupied key positions in the party hierarchy. Stephen Bronfman assumed the duties of revenue officer by appointment of the new leader, while another long-time family friend, Anna Gainey, was elected party president at the Liberals' January 2014 convention, thereby ensuring the close co-operation between parliamentary and volunteer wings of the party, something that had often been lacking in the recent past.

## THE REBUILDING PROCESS

### The Fundraising Challenge

Among the Liberals' first priorities was fundraising. Not only had the party been slow to master the new technique of direct mail but it had only recently acquired a national membership list (called Liberalist). This would form the core group of potential donors. Compared with the Conservatives, the party's efforts were substantially behind, both in terms of total revenue raised and also in terms of the total number of donors. With the implementation in 2004 of Jean Chrétien's legislation eliminating corporate and union donations to political parties, this had proved a crucial problem for the Liberals as well as for the NDP, and a decade later the Liberals were still trailing the Conservatives badly. In the last quarter of 2011, for example, the party had raised $2.8 million compared with $4.1 million for the Conservatives.

Although Trudeau's popularity undoubtedly helped, it was the Liberals' determined focus on updated mailing lists and relentless email solicitations from their rapidly expanding membership that ultimately paid off. By fall 2013, Elections Canada reported the party had already surpassed the Conservatives in the total number of donors, reaching thirty thousand compared with twenty-one thousand. By the end of 2014, aided by the party's new bagman Stephen Bronfman and fundraising expert Christina Topp (a former colleague of Butts at the World Wildlife Fund), the Liberals' total revenue had increased 40 percent over the previous year and, at $15.8 million, was nearly double the amount raised by the NDP, despite its Official Opposition advantage.

Still the Conservatives continued to outpace the Liberals in terms of amount of money raised. In the first quarter of 2015, with the election looming, Stephen Harper's party dominated the fundraising contest with reported revenue of $6.3 million, or more than the Liberals ($3.8 million) and NDP ($2.3 million) combined. Moreover, the gradual elimination of public subsidies for political parties impacted both the Liberals and the NDP far more than the Conservatives. Nevertheless, it was clear by early 2015 that the Liberal Party would have more than enough funds to conduct a credible electoral campaign. With Harper's subsequent decision to launch the formal election period earlier than expected, the Conservatives' superior finances might well have been expected to have an impact on the eventual results. Instead, as outlined below, it was the Liberals' greatly improved finances that played a part in their eventual victory over the NDP.

## Modernizing the Party Apparatus

The party's reorganization was led by Katie Telford (who had run Trudeau's leadership campaign and was promptly named national campaign co-chair), along with Gerald Butts (now Trudeau's chief of staff), and Jeremy Broadhurst (the national director of the party and a former chief of staff to interim leader Bob Rae). Telford, whose background with Gerard Kennedy as well as with Trudeau had involved logistics and organization, once declared that "I love numbers, they never lie." Together with Butts, who had earlier worked for pollster Michael Marzolini at his Pollara polling firm, they moved quickly to introduce several new concepts and technologies to the party's national operation. All of these innovations were designed to bring the party "out of the dark ages," according to one senior Liberal, who described the party as having fallen "light years" behind the Conservatives in virtually all aspects of campaign preparation over the previous decade.

All of these innovations also involved recruiting individuals who were experts in various aspects of the new technologies of election campaigns. Significantly, many of them had little or no previous formal connection to the Liberal Party despite their liberal leanings. However, most of them were known to the leader or his key advisers in some way from previous activities, and accepted these new positions on the strength of these past relationships, despite the daunting challenge the party faced and the potentially limited opportunities for career advancement it offered, a scenario remarkably similar to the party's last major rebuilding exercise after the decisive 1984 defeat.

Among the team's innovations was an in-house pollster. The Liberals, like other parties, had long employed an independent polling firm to conduct opinion polls for them — most recently Pollara — but the substantial cost had generally meant that these efforts were limited, especially outside of election periods. In difficult times they were almost non-existent. (During the 1988 election, for example, the party was so financially strapped that it was forced to simply add a few questions to a pre-existing commercial poll; similar compromises had taken place in 2008 and 2011.)

The recruitment of former Alberta Liberal blogger and Pollara employee Dan Arnold as an in-house pollster in March 2014 was therefore a significant development and one that would have important consequences for the campaign. From his early work with focus groups and his close collaboration with other elements of the campaign team to ensure the party's messaging was consistent with public opinion, he proceeded to develop a seat projection model that proved remarkably accurate (predicting 177 seats, it came within ten seats of the actual result). Arnold was described by other members of the team as an invaluable asset, and "integral in translating the data and applying it strategically to all aspects of the campaign."[9]

Closely related to this new approach in polling was the party's determination to get up to speed on the use of "Big Data," a technique long utilized by the Conservatives, and one on which the NDP was already working hard. The basic concept involves marrying voters' lists and/or lists of known supporters with extensive demographic data in order to microtarget the party's message to individual voters or groups, and also to ensure the party's campaign volunteers have the information to improve their performance at getting out the vote. To this end, the Liberals recruited a former Ph.D. candidate in microbiology and expert in statistics and computer modelling, Sean Wiltshire, to be their first director of analytics.

Together, Arnold and Wiltshire provided essential information to the campaign team and advice to individual Liberal candidates through the Team Trudeau Candidate College held months before the election was called. As Jeremy Broadhurst noted, the Big Data approach "can help you make better decisions about how to deploy volunteers and where to be targeting those door knockers and phone callers in a way that maximizes your chances of identifying the vote and getting the vote pulled on election day." At the same time, however, Broadhurst also acknowledged that "you can collect all the data you want but do you have people on the ground who are trained up or know how to use it?"[10]

The need for training led logically to the creation of another new post at the Liberals' national headquarters, a director of volunteer mobilization, a position filled by another newcomer, Hilary Leftick, who had most recently worked as the coordinator of POP Montreal, a major music festival. From an earlier era of local wine and cheese parties to identify supporters and the impromptu organization of canvassing teams in ridings once the writ was dropped, the party under Leftick quickly moved to a sophisticated, nationwide volunteer organization that would soon be the envy of its political opponents. Starting in October 2014, a full year before the next scheduled election, the party organized "Days of Action" for supporters, which eventually saw every riding in the country canvassed by volunteers on weekends. By the day the writ was dropped, the Liberals had some eighty thousand volunteers on the ground. At the same time, banks of trained volunteers were calling supporters across the country for months before the election began. One source estimated that this coordinated at-the-door and telephone canvassing had resulted in 3.8 million contacts with voters, some 1.1 million of whom had declared they would vote Liberal.[11]

Finally, the party's modernization involved a greatly updated web presence and email communications with the membership, including extensive use of social media, a task taken on by Sarah Cowan (daughter of former Liberal Senate leader James Cowan), and Tom Pitfield (son of former senator Michael Pitfield), who assumed the title of director of digital strategy.

## Candidate Selection: Building a Strong Liberal Team

As the above sections on the rebuilding process have demonstrated, one consequence of the Trudeau team's determination to drag the party into the twenty-first century was generational change. The host of new players recruited as experts and behind-the-scenes strategists were a strikingly similar cohort of forty-something professionals with young children — much like Trudeau himself — a situation frequently referred to in media coverage of the key organizers. The assembling of such a new team had the added advantage of allowing Trudeau to avoid becoming embroiled — or being *seen* to be involved — in a continuation of the debilitating internecine warfare between the Chrétien and Martin forces.

This scenario also played out in the search for strong candidates to carry the Liberal banner in the 2015 election. Unlike his two predecessors, Trudeau had little difficulty attracting good new candidates, who, thus, had not been involved in the party's earlier battles. At the same time, the significance of developing a strong team of candidates was obvious to the Liberal campaign organizers, who realized that Trudeau's lack of experience would be a key argument made against him by both the Conservatives and the NDP. Many of the candidates the party recruited were young entrepreneurs and professionals with families, a striking visual example of the potential changing of the guard within the Liberals' parliamentary ranks.

In the end, the Liberals were successful in recruiting an impressive group of candidates in all regions of the country and they did so in record time. When the writ was dropped unexpectedly early, on August 2, the Liberals had more candidates already nominated (294) than either the Conservatives (291) or the NDP (253). As a result, they were able to use them to their advantage in media events and advertising ("Team Trudeau" is ready) long before the official campaign began.

Trudeau announced in September 2013 and December 2014 that he had created two advisory panels to assist him in key policy areas where he was judged to be weak, namely economic policy and defence and foreign policy. For the former, he appointed well-known economic journalist and author Chrystia Freeland (the newly selected Liberal candidate in the Toronto riding of University-Rosedale) as the co-chair of his economic advisory panel, which also included prominent Toronto financial adviser Bill Morneau, the party's candidate in Toronto Centre. Similarly, retired lieutenant-general Andrew Leslie (the aspiring Liberal candidate in Orléans) was appointed co-chair of Trudeau's advisory committee on foreign policy and defence, another of whose members was retired Royal Canadian Air Force pilot Major Steve Fuhr (Kelowna-Lake Country), a vocal critic of the Harper government's proposed F-35 purchase. (Significantly, all of these candidates went on to win their ridings.)

The party was also successful in recruiting a diverse range of candidates, something that Trudeau emphasized strongly. An unprecedented eighteen Liberal candidates were of Aboriginal descent, while another forty-eight were visible minorities or self-described "first-generation" Canadians. In addition, the party was quick to note the large number of prominent francophones running as Liberal candidates in Quebec, despite the widespread media view that the NDP was firmly entrenched there. Although the party did not meet an aspirational goal of gender parity, slightly more than one third of the Liberal candidates were women, greatly assisting Trudeau's stated commitment to appoint women to 50 percent of Cabinet positions if his party were to win.

Interestingly, the party additionally classified its candidates by background and experience, presumably in an effort to distinguish itself from the Conservatives in some cases, and to counter Conservative accusations of weakness in others. For example, fully 111 Liberal candidates were described as business people or entrepreneurs, while another twenty-three were identified as either veterans or police officers. One figure that clearly distinguished the Liberals from the Conservatives, and incidentally highlighted Trudeau's own experience, related to the number of professors and teachers, a category claimed by seventy-two candidates. Finally, no doubt to counter the argument that the party was dominated by inexperienced candidates (fewer than forty were incumbent MPs) and hence could not field a Cabinet knowledgeable about the workings of Parliament, the Liberal website pointedly noted that one-third of its candidates (112) had previously been elected at some level in Canada and several candidates were former Liberal MPs who had lost their seats during the Harper years. As well as showcasing the quality of the candidates who would be running on the party's slate, the stress placed on the experience of the strong

Liberal team highlighted Trudeau's bench strength for Cabinet selection, something they hoped would be a contrast with the NDP.

It was in the area of candidate selection that some difficulties arose for Trudeau and his team — difficulties that were largely of their own making. The first problem arose out of the party's decision in June 2014 to require all Liberal candidates to vote pro-choice on the issue of abortion, following the party's official position, regardless of their personal beliefs. This directive caused a certain degree of angst among potential candidates in various ridings, something that was not unexpected; however, when the question of the applicability of this directive to existing MPs arose, the issue became one that caused the Liberals more serious difficulty. Trudeau first appeared to suggest that sitting MPs would be "grandfathered," a position publicly declared by known anti-abortion MPs Lawrence MacAulay and John McKay. It was only when the NDP seized upon the issue and mocked Trudeau's "two-tier" pro-choice policy that he was forced to clarify his position, declaring that sitting MPs would be permitted to run again but would be bound by the same rules as new candidates.

This issue paled in comparison with the one created by Trudeau's early declaration that all nomination contests would be open. This commitment, intended to demonstrate a break with the past and the many problems caused by leadership interference at the riding level, effectively precluded him from appointing candidates to increase gender balance or diversity, a provision that had been added to the Liberal constitution for that specific purpose. It also prevented him from appointing the so-called "star" candidates whom his team was busy recruiting. Not surprisingly, this commitment — intended to avoid political conflicts — actually served to engender several of its own.

A sign of things to come emerged in February 2014, when Christine Innes, the wife of former Liberal MP Tony Ianno, was barred from running as a candidate for the nomination in the riding of Trinity-Spadina, allegedly due to improper behaviour on the part of her campaign team. Innes promptly launched a $1.5 million lawsuit against Trudeau and the Liberals' Ontario campaign chair, David MacNaughton.

Even more damaging and controversial were the lengthy (and less credible) efforts of the campaign leadership to ensure that Andrew Leslie became the nominated candidate in Orléans, a riding that he did not live in and to which he had no connections, and in which the local favourite, lawyer David Bertschi, had deep roots, impressive credentials of his own, and a lengthy history in the party. The eventual disqualification of Bertschi by Katie Telford and Dan Gagnier in their roles as campaign co-chairs, after he had been "green-lighted" by the party's official screening committee, proved extremely unpopular with long-standing local Liberals, and might well have caused the party to fail to regain the former Liberal stronghold from the Conservative incumbent had it not been for the national trend.

Adding insult to injury, in late August the Liberals inexplicably announced that disgraced Conservative MP Eve Adams would be allowed to run for the Liberal nomination in the riding of Eglington-Lawrence, a move that infuriated Liberals there and elsewhere. Adams, whose earlier exploits in shopping for a winnable Conservative riding had been well publicized, had been forbidden from running for that party in any riding after several accusations of improper influence and bullying had surfaced. The situation escalated when popular provincial Liberal MPP Michael Colle, whose riding overlapped with the federal one, vowed to put forward a candidate of his own to ensure that Adams would win the nomination "over my dead body." Colle, a legendary organizer and veteran campaigner, made good on his promise as his choice of Marco Mendicino, a lawyer and well-known Liberal in the riding, defeated Adams handily. (Mendicino went on to defeat Finance Minister Joe Oliver in the federal election.) Long after the nomination battle was over, photos of Justin Trudeau sitting beside Eve Adams at the press conference announcing her acceptance by the Liberals continued to surface, and contributed to a cynical view among some Liberal rank-and-file about the leader's commitment to open nominations, as well as some voters' ongoing concerns about his political judgment.

Finally, as became apparent throughout the course of the actual election campaign, the Liberal vetting process for candidates was not immune to the problems caused by individuals' past participation on social media. Luckily for the Liberals, however, it was also true that their political opponents were encountering similar and often more significant problems in this area, leading many observers to suggest that this whole new problem of social media would need to be seriously addressed before the next federal election.

## Policy Development

The Trudeau team was intent on ensuring that the party was not seen to be devoid of policy positions before the election, even though they were also committed to "keeping their powder dry" regarding the actual platform until the writ was dropped. They therefore used the party's regularly scheduled 2014 policy convention, held in Montreal, to highlight issues they wished to have identified with the party, such as fairness for the middle class, and democratic reform. They also invited a number of well-known experts in these fields to participate in the process, by presenting keynote addresses or speaking to breakout groups. Perhaps the most revealing of these was the introductory session in which Chrystia Freeland interviewed former U.S. Treasury Secretary Lawrence Summers, who at the time was serving as president of Harvard University. Both Freeland and Summers were known to be concerned with income disparity, and their discussion — foreshadowing the eventual platform — focused on the question of how to create stable economic growth "that benefits everyone."

The convention was essentially the last formal setting in which policy development took place. With hardly a perfunctory nod to party resolutions, the campaign team set about developing the election platform *in camera*, much as Jean Chrétien had done. The consultations with the party membership continued instead through the party's now highly developed web correspondence, where the primary concern was to ensure members felt included in the discussion, and the policy team obtained valuable input on perceptions of priorities and policy preferences.

Heading the team's platform development process was Mike McNair, a former policy adviser to Stéphane Dion and Michael Ignatieff who had also served as director of the Liberal Research Bureau. McNair served as the coordinator of the various policy committees that had been established by the leader, which involved candidates, caucus members, and outside experts. McNair was described by numerous colleagues as the "real architect" of the platform that was eventually released midway through the election campaign.

In the meantime, however, Trudeau's pre-writ policy pronouncements were designed to reflect, once again, generational change as well as a positive Liberal vision. As a result, although they were few and far between, they succeeded in attracting considerable attention from the general public as well as from other parties. Among these declarations were the aforementioned commitment to a pro-choice position, the proposal to decriminalize marijuana (announced, significantly, in British Columbia), and the decision to remove Liberal senators from the Liberal caucus.

At the same time, platform development continued apace. The broad outlines of the Liberal emphasis on middle-class families had been delivered repeatedly by Trudeau over the course of 2014 and early 2015. In May 2015, for example, Trudeau announced the party's "fairness" package proposal, which included a more generous (but also means-tested) child-care benefit than the one offered by the Conservatives, and a tax break for the middle class. To compensate, the Liberals would cancel the Conservatives' plan to introduce what most experts considered to be an extremely unfair provision for income-splitting for families (a separate proposal from the already existing income-splitting measure for seniors that the Liberals would not touch), and increased taxation of the top 1 percent of income earners, with a 33 percent tax bracket for those earning more than $200,000 per year. This position, considered radical and risky by some advisers in light of earlier Liberal platforms that feared either to raise taxes or run deficits, was nevertheless positively received. In June, Trudeau followed up with an announcement of the Liberals' thirty-two-point plan to address the democratic deficit by ensuring more open and transparent government, and revealed the party's Real Change logo at the same time.

These announcements, however, met with limited success in terms of increasing polling numbers, and it was increasingly clear to the campaign team, as the summer of 2015 continued to deliver bad news in this regard, that the only way to significantly improve their prospects would be to include in the platform a dramatic measure that would clearly demonstrate they were indeed the party that offered the greatest change from the governing Conservatives. As we shall see, it was a decision that changed the course of the campaign.

## THE DRAMATIC LIBERAL CAMPAIGN

Virtually everyone other than the Conservatives had long since agreed that the 2015 election would be about change and who could best bring that change about. For the Liberals, in third place at the start of the campaign, the plan to demonstrate that they were the best choice to do so appeared to be in great difficulty before the writ was even dropped. Both their ad firm (Bensimon Byrne) and other advisers, such as former Martin operative David Herle, argued that the NDP had already won the battle to be seen as the party of change, and that the Liberals would have to adopt another strategy. The slogan already chosen for the Liberal campaign, *Real Change*, is "not going to work," John Bensimon wrote in an email to Butts that was later distributed to all staff. Both he and Herle also strongly urged Trudeau's inner team to adopt a negative advertising campaign.

Butts and Telford disagreed. In his response to the Bensimon email, Butts wrote, "We will win this on hope and hard work."[12] As a result, the team stayed committed to the plan they had worked on for the past two years, a plan that involved promoting the party as the agent of change, and the leader as the best person to accomplish it. With Trudeau's low standing in the polls at the start of the campaign, this was clearly an act of faith, but one that paid off handsomely in the end.

### The Crucial Role of the Leader

Given the Conservatives' relentless attacks on Justin Trudeau after he assumed the leadership of the party, it is hardly surprising that his performance, both before and during the election campaign, was of crucial importance in the Liberal victory. Although he enjoyed a fairly lengthy honeymoon with the general public in 2013 and 2014, the number of minor gaffes and missteps began to accumulate. Taken together, his various miscues appeared to support the Conservative message that Trudeau was "just not ready" to be prime minister, and the Liberals' polling numbers began to fall as a consequence. As a result of such perceived gaffes as his reference to hockey when discussing Russian incursions in the Ukraine, his expressed admiration for the repressive Chinese government, and his quip about the Conservatives and CF-18 fighter jets in reference to Iraq, the Liberal leader began to cause considerable unease among Liberal supporters and strategists as well as the general public.

Trudeau's decision to support the Conservatives' anti-terrorism bill, C-51, in the early spring of 2015 seemed to cement these concerns. As the Liberals' numbers declined precipitously, it was the NDP, who had opposed the bill unequivocally, that began to surge in the polls. Worse still, in addition to the apparent movement of large swaths of previously undecided voters to the NDP camp, there were signs that Liberals were deserting the party as well. Many rejected Trudeau's description of his position as "nuanced" and were furious about what instead appeared to them to be a rejection of the party's commitment to human rights and the Charter of Rights and Freedoms. As one Liberal insider said, "We lost volunteers over it.... Candidates were hearing about it at the doorstep." Some disgruntled party members even withdrew their financial support.[13]

As a result of Trudeau's uneven performance, when the writ was dropped on August 2, one of the biggest concerns among Liberals was whether the leader would be able to acquit himself well in the various leaders' debates, facing off with two much more experienced and knowledgeable opponents. Their fears were echoed by public opinion polls showing Canadians in general did not have high expectations of Trudeau. As former Liberal strategist Rob Silver commented, "It was very easy to imagine a scenario where, coming out of the (first) *Maclean's* debate, the narrative from the media and the chatterers was: There were two potential prime ministers on stage tonight and we're really sorry, Mr. Trudeau, you weren't one of them." Yet it was in these debates that Trudeau not only survived but shone, and in the process redefined his image with the electorate. His performance, like so much of the Liberal campaign, was based on several years of hard work and preparation. Recognizing that the debates could well prove to be a deciding element, Trudeau's inner circle had prepared him with mock debate sessions for over a year.

Trudeau worked assiduously to overcome the perception that he was a policy lightweight. From a somewhat shaky start in the first *Maclean's* debate, on August 6, Trudeau ended the evening strongly, having demonstrated an unapologetically aggressive approach toward the other two leaders and a solid knowledge of the issues. Perhaps most important was his ability to use every opportunity to communicate the party platform, including the proposed income tax fairness and open government initiatives. At the same time, his closing remarks were a deliberate calculation on the part of the inner team that he must address the issue of his readiness to govern head-on. "In order to know if someone is ready for this job, ask them what they want to do with this job, and why they want it in the first place," he told viewers, a message that he repeated throughout the campaign.

One Liberal candidate, Adam Vaughan, commented afterward, "I think what Canadians saw was a guy … who is not like the ads have been saying. He *is* ready. And that changes the conversation on every doorstep."[14]

Trudeau turned in another strong performance in the *Globe and Mail*'s debate on the economy on September 17, with several polls suggesting the Liberal leader had equalled or bested Stephen Harper, while Tom Mulcair trailed badly.

In the two French-language debates, Trudeau managed to score points as well. Held in Quebec, where the NDP appeared to be holding on to its Orange Wave for much of the campaign, the Liberal leader adroitly extricated himself from the niqab debate by pointing at Harper and declaring that "getting rid of this man" was the most important issue in the campaign, and pointing out to the Conservative leader: "You have more men in your caucus who oppose abortion than [there are] women in Quebec who wear the niqab."*(translation)*

But it was in the final English-language debate, a debate held at the Munk School of Global Affairs in Toronto that focused on foreign policy issues, where Trudeau outdid himself. Given that foreign policy was expected to be the most challenging subject area for him, his soaring performance left his opponents behind. As one media commentator concluded, "Even if you disagreed vehemently with his positions, you couldn't deny he delivered them with conviction. Throughout the night, he clearly articulated Liberal policies, defended them with passion, threw in some good zingers (Harper's northern strategy was "all dogs, no sled"), and, most importantly, never tripped up."[15] And when NDP leader Tom Mulcair criticized his father's handling of the October crisis, apparently in reference to Liberal support for Bill C-51, Trudeau delivered a stirring defence of his father's legacy, including the Charter of Rights, that elicited cheers from the audience and several days' worth of positive coverage in the media.

In addition to the debates, Trudeau was winning other battles on the ground. As the campaign progressed, the positive images of Trudeau happily interacting with Canadians of all ages and backgrounds continued to mount. In the end, it became obvious to everyone that he was a natural campaigner, a politician who genuinely enjoyed meeting people and, even more significantly, listening to their views, something neither Harper or Mulcair could realistically claim. His strength on the hustings provided much-needed momentum for the party and ensured that it had a fighting chance despite its slow start.

As public opinion polls demonstrated, the Liberal leader's image and popularity continued to mount steadily throughout the campaign. The party then took advantage of his unexpectedly strong contribution by scheduling several more large public events. Perhaps the most notable was the massive Liberal rally held in Brampton, Ontario, on October 4. One of the largest political rallies in decades, and reminiscent of a legendary rally held in Toronto in 1968 for Pierre Trudeau, the Brampton rally saw more than five thousand Liberals and members of the general public respond enthusiastically to Trudeau's campaign speech. The event was widely reported and media clips continued to circulate for days, once again feeding the growing momentum the party was enjoying. And, as the following section demonstrates, the Liberals' ad campaign was also quick to take advantage of this momentum.

## The Innovative Ad Campaign

Advertising campaigns are often considered to be an important element of a party's successful election campaign, but the one launched by the Liberal Party in the 2015 election stands out as one of critical importance to its success in convincing Canadians that their leader was ready and that the Liberals were the party of real change. Despite earlier misgivings about the direction the campaign team was determined to pursue, the firm of Bensimon Byrne developed an ad campaign that succeeded brilliantly in promoting the campaign themes. It broke the mould in many respects and was later directly credited by Butts and Telford for much of their success. This was particularly noteworthy since the firm was a prominent commercial ad agency and was not primarily known for political work, although it had handled the campaigns of Dalton McGuinty and Kathleen Wynne.

To begin with, as mentioned above, the firm tackled the Conservatives' claim that Trudeau was not ready to govern, despite conventional wisdom that argues one should never make reference to an opponent's ad message. Not only did the so-called "ready" ads break this cardinal rule, they also defied the earlier recommendation of David Herle and others to "go negative," focusing instead on a positive Liberal message. The first of the "ready" TV ads had Trudeau stating that what he was "not ready for" were job losses and an economic recession, before outlining his own economic promises. Broadcast first in the summer, the ad was used again shortly before the writ was dropped in August.

A second TV ad showed Trudeau walking up a down escalator, indicating once again that he was "not ready," but this time he was not ready to put up with Canadians having to struggle to get ahead because of the Conservatives' lack of a solid economic plan. That ad was shown widely and was even more successful than the previous one according to the Liberals' internal polling. By election day, it had reportedly attracted three million views online. Later in the campaign the firm used footage from the massive Liberal rally in Brampton, showing Trudeau speaking to the partisan crowd and looking prime ministerial. The ad, shown over the Thanksgiving weekend, was designed to showcase the momentum the Liberals had developed at that point, and concluded with a fade-out of the rally image to a one-word text: *Ready*.

A final TV spot, one that proved highly effective, aired very late in the campaign. It featured Hazel McCallion, the legendary former mayor of Mississauga. This was an effort to cement Liberal support in the Toronto and surrounding "905" region, and among seniors, by having McCallion denounce last-minute efforts by the Conservatives to cast doubt on the Liberals' plans for the seniors' income-splitting measure and other platform planks. McCallion's spot concluded with the statement that the Tories were fear-mongering and asked, "Do I look scared, Stephen?" A long-time supporter of Trudeau, McCallion had had numerous run-ins with the Harper Conservatives over the years and was more than willing to tackle them head-on.

Finally, it should be noted that the financial reserves of the party also allowed them to make good use of print media advertising, another area where previous Liberal campaigns had faltered. Perhaps the most significant was a hugely costly full-page ad that appeared in the *Globe and Mail* and newspapers across Canada on Saturday, October 10, the Thanksgiving weekend, and also the weekend of advance polls. The eye-catching ad contained testimonials from five well-known individuals with no connection to the Liberal Party, praising the Liberals' economic platform and particularly their plans to invest in infrastructure and the Canada Child Benefit. They included former governor of the Bank of Canada David Dodge; Larry Summers, the director of U.S. president Barack Obama's National Economic Council; Ken Battle and Sherri Torjman of the highly regarded Caledon Institute of Social Policy; John Tory, the Conservative mayor of Toronto; and Hazel McCallion. And, as with the later TV advertisements, the ad concluded with the modified Liberal slogan: *Real Change Now*.

## The Platform as Closer: Progressive but Credible

Although the broad direction of the Liberal platform in a range of policy areas had been publicly available on the party's website for some time — under the rubrics of "Invest Now in Our Future," "Help the Middle Class," and "Open, Honest Government" — it was only with the launching of the campaign that details of specific measures began to be outlined. Justin Trudeau used various campaign events as launch pads for these.

It soon became evident that the platform was well-developed and comprehensive. In addition to commitments to eliminate a variety of measures implemented by the Harper Conservatives, it offered a centre-left package of Liberal initiatives that were well-received by various experts and NGOs. This was significant for the party since, among its priority commitments, was a pledge to return to "evidence-based decision-making" and the use of scientific knowledge and expertise. The Liberals' appreciation of, and commitment to, a merit-based and professional public service was also reiterated on numerous occasions. This culminated in a dramatic open letter to public servants from Justin Trudeau on September 25, which helped to cement the party's support in the National Capital Region.

One significant departure from earlier Liberal platforms was the lack of a companion costing document until fairly late in the campaign, on

September 25. Since the 1988 election, in which John Turner had been assailed relentlessly with demands for the costs associated with the Liberal platform, no political party had dared to publish a platform without such a document. However the Liberals simply stated that their costing would be available once most of their platform planks were announced and fleshed out. Interestingly, no widespread political storm ensued despite criticism from the NDP and Conservatives, who had already released their fiscal plans.

In the end, this decision proved to be among the most crucial of the whole campaign. While Trudeau's strong early debate performances, the innovative Liberal ads, and early platform plank announcements had all contributed to a situation in which the end of the first month of the campaign saw an entrenched three-way race — no small accomplishment for the Liberals given their last-place start — it was proving impossible for any party to take the lead. Indeed, some analysts were beginning to consider the possibility of a Conservative minority if the Liberals and NDP continued to receive relatively equal voter support.

According to some advisers, the Liberal team had already taken a risk by raising taxes, even though the tax increase affected only the wealthiest Canadians, and even though at the same time they were providing a tax break for middle-class Canadians. But this measure had not been sufficient to distinguish the Liberals from the NDP, who were proposing to raise corporate taxes as a means of financing some of their commitments. A lengthy debate ensued among the members of Trudeau's inner team as to what measure should be announced to attempt to break the logjam. In the end, following a discussion led by Butts, the decision was taken to announce that the Liberals would run three small deficits of roughly $10 billion dollars each, balancing the budget only in the fourth year of a Liberal term, in order to finance a multi-billion dollar infrastructure plan to stimulate the economy and create jobs. This decision was made somewhat easier by the decision of the NDP to commit to balanced budgets throughout their potential first mandate, a cautionary approach that left them promising many social programs that would only be implemented in the distant future.

When Trudeau announced the plan on August 27, both the Conservatives and the NDP predictably criticized it severely, but he continued to hype the proposal on every possible occasion, including during the leaders' debates. Citing numerous experts who argued that small deficits were irrelevant and also that low interest rates made this the ideal time for such a badly needed investment in deteriorating infrastructure (a proposal that incidentally appealed to municipal politicians across the country), Trudeau soon saw the party's numbers rise in the polls. The Liberal team concluded that the decision was indeed the one that allowed them to break away and lay claim to the title of party of real change. Subsequently, the September 21 announcement in Orléans, Ontario, that the party would cancel the Conservatives' costly F-35 fighter jet purchase produced a similar surge in the polls, as did the open letter to the public service a few days later on September 25.

Interestingly, all of these announcements appeared to catch both the Conservatives and the NDP off guard, and their subsequent attacks on the Liberals and on their deficit plans, in particular, likely backfired by reinforcing voters' awareness of the Liberal plan. Other actions of the Liberals' two major opponents also proved useful to the Liberal campaign in unexpected ways as well, as the following section outlines.

## THE POSITIVE IMPACT OF OPPOSITION ERRORS ON LIBERAL FORTUNES

Without question, the Liberal campaign, despite its competence, benefitted substantially from a number of tactical errors by the Conservatives. To begin with, as the above analysis has demonstrated, Stephen Harper's decision to conduct an extraordinarily long eleven-week campaign proved to be a serious mistake. It allowed Justin Trudeau to redefine himself to Canadians as someone who was ready to govern, and it allowed Canadians time to decide that the Liberals, not the first-place NDP of August, were the best situated to defeat the Harper Conservatives. Nor did the Liberals run out of money, as Harper's advisers had apparently hoped. In addition, the length of the campaign meant that there was a good chance that any minor miscues by Trudeau were likely to be easily forgotten by the electorate.

The Conservatives committed another tactical error that was sufficiently grave to not only be remembered but play a significant role in altering the course of the campaign. When photos appeared in Canada and around the world of the body of a young boy who had drowned in a failed attempt to flee

Syria with his family, Conservative immigration minister Chris Alexander's insensitive and politically tone-deaf response provided the Liberals with an unexpected opening, which Trudeau was quick to seize. His commitment to bring twenty-five thousand refugees to Canada by the end of the year appeared decisive, offering national leadership in an apparent vacuum. The incident and the fallout from it provided countless opportunities for Trudeau to underline Liberal values in his speeches and debates.

The Conservatives' tactic of emphasizing the niqab issue in the late stages of the campaign also backfired dramatically. The move was most popular in Quebec, and they had expected to benefit from it there. But NDP leader Tom Mulcair's categorical opposition caused the already declining NDP fortunes to plummet precipitously, thereby reinforcing the Liberals as the party of choice to beat the Conservatives. Although Trudeau also opposed the Conservative move, he had provided a more nuanced and comprehensive explanation of his position and, more importantly, had highlighted the liberal values of tolerance and compassion driving his reponse, values to which Canadians, and Quebecers, responded strongly. Moreover, the Conservatives' divisive niqab ploy had the unintended consequence of reviving the fortunes of the Bloc Québécois, all the while delivering minimal benefits to the Conservatives themselves. In the end, the Liberals received significant support from francophone voters in Quebec and more than half of the seats in that province for the first time since Pierre Trudeau's 1980 election, and much of the credit, according to pollsters, came from the last-minute decision by many Quebecers that the Trudeau Liberals were best positioned to defeat the Harper Conservatives.

Lastly, the desperation demonstrated by the Conservatives' final campaign rallies in the Toronto suburbs, which were attended by the notorious Ford brothers, generated so much negative coverage that it managed to overshadow the one real misstep of the Liberal campaign, namely the revelation that national campaign co-chair Dan Gagnier had been providing advice to the oil industry about how to lobby a future (presumably Liberal) government.

As for the NDP, several of their early decisions left the Trudeau team mystified but delighted. Tom Mulcair's last-minute decision to pull out of the national broadcast consortium's scheduled debate, having earlier agreed to participate despite Stephen Harper's absence, arguably deprived him of an early opportunity to outshine Justin Trudeau, his less-experienced opponent and principal adversary, on the national stage. Mulcair's subsequent subdued performances in the five debates that were held — where he was apparently determined to appear prime ministerial and avoid confrontation — were equally perplexing. Even more significant was the failure of the NDP platform to distinguish the party as the instrument of change. Their decision to promise balanced budgets throughout a four-year mandate, which curtailed much of their program (in the same way that Michael Ignatieff had been limited in 2011 by his decision to neither raise taxes nor run a deficit), left many observers concluding that the NDP had fallen victim to their own polling data and assumed that an overabundance of caution was required if they were to maintain their position as the presumed front runner.

## THE ONTARIO FACTOR: A MIXED BLESSING?

Although Ontario Liberal premier Kathleen Wynne could hardly be described as an opponent, some Liberals in the early days of the campaign began to think of her efforts as a type of friendly fire. The actions of Wynne's government, especially on the issue of sex education in Ontario schools, had had an unfortunate but noticeable and negative impact on the Liberals' fortunes before the campaign even began. Her unprecedented intervention during the federal campaign — motivated by her resentment of the innumerable policy decisions of the Harper government, which she felt had disadvantaged her province and/or her government purposely — was seen by some Liberal strategists as a mixed blessing, particularly given her low overall approval ratings (31 percent) in the province, which was a key battleground if the Liberals were to make significant progress. As one Liberal insider stated, "There wasn't much strategy in Wynne's sorties to help Trudeau.... To be perfectly honest, she just wanted to get out there against Stephen Harper herself."[16]

On the other hand, it became clear that Wynne's direct support for Trudeau was beneficial in the early stages of the campaign when the party had not yet found its footing or improved its third-place standing. In addition, pollsters noted that "nearly a million Ontarians had voted for Wynne's provincial Liberals in 2014 but had not voted for the federal Liberals in 2011."[17] This, the Liberals knew, was a crucial challenge, as the number of Liberals who had stayed home or shifted their vote in 2011 was substantial, and could spell the difference between victory or defeat in many Ontario ridings. In the end, as the results came in on election night, it was evident that Ontario would indeed return to the Liberal fold and Justin Trudeau would owe at least some of his success to his provincial counterpart.

As outlined above, many of Trudeau's key advisers had come from Wynne's inner circle and that of her predecessor, Dalton McGuinty, a reality that appeared to guarantee her access to the new prime minister as well as influence. As Trudeau fleshed out the composition of his new Prime Minister's Office in the weeks and months following the election, this disproportionate influence of Ontario advisers — and the apparent lack of comparable input to his inner circle from other regions of the country, particularly Quebec — did begin to surface as a source of comment and concern in the media. However, Trudeau's appointment of a strong, regionally representative Cabinet, and stated plans to meet with all of the premiers on a range of issues early in his tenure, seemed to have diminished the concern over what some critics had referred to as the "Ontario factor."

## VICTORY EXPLAINED: THE LIBERAL RESURGENCE

On October 19 the Liberal Party of Canada returned from the wilderness to form a majority government with 184 seats and nearly 40 percent of the popular vote. Moreover, the party elected members in every region of the country, including the francophone regions of Quebec, and so could now be considered as a national political party once more.

A major victory in and of itself, the win constituted a stunning turnaround for a party that had been left for dead barely four years earlier. What can explain such a dramatic reversal of fortunes? As this chapter has demonstrated, the party won both the air and the ground wars. It also reimagined its electoral machine, adopting twenty-first century techniques that now make it the envy of the other parties. There can be no doubt that the lengthy rebuilding process under Trudeau from the moment he assumed the leadership of the party in April 2013 was a crucial factor in the Liberal victory.

Nor should Trudeau's own role, and that of the various supporting actors, be downplayed. To some extent, his family name and appearance, as Brian Mulroney predicted, must be recognized as having enabled his campaign to be taken seriously in the early days, but his own natural ability on the hustings, his "sunny ways," as well as his growing confidence and competence, must also be recognized as having made a valuable contribution.

Still, an argument can be made that underlying much of the explanation for the Liberal victory is the return to Liberal values that Trudeau and his team articulated, not only through their platform but also in the leader's countless speeches and debate performances. While issues such as the Syrian refugee crisis and the Conservative plan to introduce income-splitting provisions that would benefit primarily the wealthy may have provided the opportunity, it was Trudeau who seized upon them to communicate, often with passion, his commitment to ideals such as fairness, equality of opportunity, and respect for diversity. This argument about the importance of Liberal values was strongly supported by the findings of an EKOS/Canada 2020 poll released a month after the election. According to EKOS president Frank Graves, "the election shifted from being an election about the economy to a historic election about values."[18]

It was also the Trudeau team that finally broke the mystical barrier of the Conservative fiscal mantra of balanced budgets and low taxes, asserting that both deficits and increased taxes could be useful tools to allow governments to provide valuable programs and services to citizens, and Graves's poll indicated that this, too, was an important factor. "It was pretty clear," he said, "that the values vision that Trudeau and the Liberals were offering up, backed up by an accounting framework that says we actually are going to find the money to do this, is what won the election for them."[19]

Of course, a new Liberal government, with a new leader and a large number of new caucus members, and faced with immediate and serious policy challenges, will now test the ability of the Trudeau Liberals to handle the reins of power. As one Liberal insider remarked, "It may be that winning the election was the easy part." As a result, it is too early to tell whether the Liberals are in the process of re-establishing a "dynasty,"[20] or whether the electorate's determination to remove the Harper Conservatives at all costs will have benefitted the Liberals this time to an extent that will not be possible in future when they face the electorate after four years in power.

## NOTES

1. Peter Newman, *When the Gods Changed: The Death of Liberal Canada* (Toronto: Random House, 2012).
2. Ibid.
3. Darrell Bricker and John Ibbitson, *The Big Shift: The Seismic Change in Canadian Politics, Business and Culture, and What It Means for Our Future* (Toronto: Harper Collins, 2013).
4. Brooke Jeffrey, "The Disappearing Liberals: Caught in the Crossfire," in *The Canadian Federal Election of 2011*, ed. John H. Pammett and Christopher Dornan (Toronto: Dundurn Press, 2011), 73–74.
5. See Michael Ignatieff's pointed comments about this in his memoir, *Fire and Ashes: Success and Failure in Canadian Politics* (Toronto: Random House, 2013), 123.
6. Mark Kennedy, "Brian Mulroney Cautions Tories to Tread Carefully with Trudeau," *Ottawa Citizen,* September 4, 2014.
7. See, for example, former prime minister Jean Chrétien's interview with Evan Solomon on *Power and Politics* on CBC Radio, June 11, 2011, www.cbc.ca.
8. For a comprehensive discussion of the issue, see Brooke Jeffrey, *Divided Loyalties: The Liberal Party of Canada 1984–2006* (Toronto: University of Toronto Press, 2010).
9. Rachel Aiello, "Some Boys Want to Be Prime Minister, I Wanted to Grow Up to Be Allan Gregg," *Hill Times*, November 2, 2015, www.hilltimes.com/feature/hill-life-people/2015/11/02/some-boys-want-to-grow-up-to-be-prime-minister-i-wanted-to-grow-up-to-be/44006.
10. Glen McGregor, "The Big Data Election: Political Parties Building Detailed Voter Records," *Ottawa Citizen*, October 20, 2014, http://ottawacitizen.com/news/national/the-big-data-election-political-parties-building-detailed-voter-records.
11. Paul Wells, "The Winner Takes It All," *Maclean's*, Special Edition, November 2, 2015: 39.
12. Quoted in Althia Raj, "Justin Trudeau's Liberals: 'We Had a Plan and We Stuck to It,' and They Won," *Huffington Post*, October 25, 2015, www.huffingtonpost.ca/2015/10/25/justin-trudeau_n_8382304.html.
13. Quoted in Richard Warnica, "The Liberal Resurrection," *National Post*, October 24, 2015.
14. Quoted in Althia Raj, "Justin Trudeau's *Maclean's* Debate Performance Reassures Liberals," *Huffington Post*, August 7, 2015, www.huffingtonpost.ca/2015/08/07/macleans-debate-justin-trudeau-federal-election_n_7957916.html.
15. Tasha Kheiriddin, "The Munk Debate: Mulcair Slumps, Trudeau Soars, Harper Coasts," *i*Politics, September 29, 2015, http://ipolitics.ca/2015/09/29/the-munk-debate-mulcair-slumps-trudeau-soars-harper-coasts/.
16. Quoted in Paul Wells, "The Making of a Prime Minister: Inside Trudeau's Epic Victory," *Maclean's*, Special Edition, November 2, 2015: 24.
17. Ibid.
18. Quoted in Mark Kennedy, "Liberal Values Won Election, Says Poll," *Ottawa Citizen*, November 19, 2015, A12.
19. Ibid.
20. For more detail, see Leduc, Pammett, et al., *Dynasties and Interludes: Past and Present in Canadian Electoral Politics,* 2nd ed. (Toronto: Dundurn, 2016).

# CHAPTER 4

## From Third to First and Back to Third: The 2015 NDP Campaign[1]

David McGrane

Throughout 2014, the NDP remained in third place in public opinion polls as Canadians seemed enamoured of Justin Trudeau, the Liberals' new leader, and the Conservatives' base remained fiercely loyal. The roller coaster that followed is the subject of this chapter. The NDP gradually climbed from third place to first place in the polls during the first six months of 2015. When the federal election campaign began in the first week of August, NDP strategists found themselves in the unprecedented position of directing the campaign of the most popular party. The events that followed brought the party back down to earth again.

The 2015 campaign was the first in Canadian history in which the NDP entered as Official Opposition and the first in which the party started with a solid base of seats in Quebec. The party was better financed than at any time in the past, and it had a relatively modernized campaign machinery, which it had improved over the decade prior to the campaign. The NDP's election team was seasoned and experienced, as many of them had been involved in the NDP's historic breakthrough in the 2011 election under the leadership of Jack Layton. Public domain polling as well as internal polling indicated that if the election were held when the writ was dropped there was a strong likelihood that the NDP would win a minority government (see Chapter 12). In its entire electoral history, the CCF-NDP had never entered a federal campaign with media and pundits declaring it as the "front-runner." The dream of finally forming a federal government appeared entirely plausible after decades of election-night disappointments.

In response to its lead in the polls at the outset of the campaign, the NDP initially adopted a strategy that did not directly attack the Liberals; instead, it worked to present itself as the only credible and safe government-in-waiting to replace the Conservatives. It consistently attempted to set up the narrative of a two-way NDP/Conservative race. While this strategy appeared to be working at the mid-point of the campaign, it was overcome by subsequent events. Controversy around its position on banning the niqab at citizenship ceremonies and questions about how the party could pay for its spending commitments given its commitment to a balanced budget dogged the party. By the end of the campaign, the central claims of the NDP that it was the only party that could beat the Conservatives and that it represented "safe" change as opposed to that promised by the "risky" Liberals started to ring hollow. The NDP's support went into a slow and steady decline as the Liberals gradually supplanted it as the primary alternative to the Harper Conservatives. Instead of resulting in the NDP's dream coming true, the 2015 federal election was a bitter disappointment for the party as it lost over half of its seats and saw the Liberals form a majority government. The party had been returned to its traditional third-place position in federal politics.

## GOING FROM THIRD TO FIRST: JANUARY 2015 TO AUGUST 2015

At the end of 2014, the NDP was mired in third place with around 20 percent of the projected popular vote. The Liberals had opened a lead in the polls since Justin Trudeau had become leader, garnering support ranging from 32 percent to 39 percent while the Conservatives were consistently polling around 30 percent. Despite the fact that the party was the Official Opposition in the House of Commons, the NDP's internal polling was confirming what public polls were saying: Trudeau's extended honeymoon was showing no signs of ending and the Conservatives were remaining very competitive.[2] NDP leader Tom Mulcair reacted in January of 2015 by making major changes to the party's senior staff. In particular, he brought in Alain Gaul, who had worked for him during Mulcair's time as minister of the environment in the Quebec government of Jean Charest, as his chief of staff, and Brad Lavigne, who had been the national campaign director for the NDP's successful 2011 campaign. These changes were in addition to the hiring of Anne McGrath as national director at party headquarters in April 2014. McGrath had been Jack Layton's chief of staff from 2008 to 2011.

The senior campaign team's first goal was to return the party's national support to around 25–26 percent and improve Mulcair's levels of popularity before summer set in. With a projected fall election, the strategists assumed there would be a quiet summer, with little movement in voting intentions, as Canadians were busy vacationing. The party could then head into a campaign starting sometime after Labour Day with a more popular leader and support closer to the levels of the Conservatives and the Liberals.

Since becoming NDP leader in 2012, Mulcair had become renowned for holding the Conservative government accountable in the House of Commons. His aggressive style in Question Period on issues surrounding corruption in the Senate had earned him the moniker "Prosecutor in Chief." A less flattering meme was "Angry Tom," which often came up in mainstream media and referred to Mulcair's supposed temper and alleged inability to get along with his colleagues. Internal research illustrated that while Mulcair was well liked by voters who knew him, there was still a lack of name recognition. However, the more voters heard about Mulcair and his personal story, the more that they liked him. It was believed by party strategists that there was an opportunity to increase the NDP's support if Mulcair could become better known.

The NDP had made the unorthodox decision to announce two of its major policies for the campaign, a national plan for $15 per day child-care spaces and a $15 per hour federal minimum wage, in the fall of 2014. These policy announcements were made very early to allow thorough scrutiny by the media prior to the campaign and to get the media talking about something else other than Trudeau's rise in the polls. Aware of the controversy that arose during the June 2014 Ontario provincial election when the media picked up on a letter from some disgruntled NDP members stating that NDP leader Andrea Horwath had drifted to the right of Kathleen Wynne's Liberals,[3] the federal NDP had crafted these two policies to firmly cement the party as "progressive" in comparison to the Trudeau Liberals and to draw attention to the fact that the Liberals had made few policy announcements.

Building on the success of these two pre-election policy rollouts in the fall of 2014, strategists decided to get Mulcair out of the House of Commons in the first part of 2015. They sent him on a leader's tour around Canada to raise his profile in regional media in places where the party's support had weakened and needed to be rebuilt, as well as to seats held by the Conservatives that the NDP would need to win to form government. Instead of responding to invitations, the party started to create events around the country to showcase their leader. The party also increased the frequency with which the leader appeared on national television programs like CTV's *Power Play*.

The themes of Mulcair's speeches during this tour and his national media appearances began to shift away from Conservative corruption to talking about kick-starting Canada's economy and protecting the middle class. Mulcair looked increasingly prime ministerial as he gave major speeches outlining NDP policies, such as cuts to taxes on small businesses, infrastructure plans, and an agenda for Toronto, to groups like the Federation of Canadian Municipalities and the Economic Club of Canada. Mulcair also began to refer to his own middle-class upbringing as one of nine children and the fact that he was a father and a grandfather. He stressed his experience as a Cabinet minister in the Quebec provincial government of Jean Charest and he pointed out that he had stood by his principles when he resigned from Cabinet over the privatization of a provincial park. The party let it be known that he was working on an autobiography that would explore his personal experiences and political journey. Mulcair's brand was becoming more clearly established: an experienced leader who personified the "middle-class values" of honesty, hard work, standing up for what you believe in, and the importance of family.

The sharpening of Mulcair's brand was reinforced by the NDP caucus' decision to oppose the Harper government's Bill C-51, anti-terrorism legislation produced as a response to the 2014 armed attack on the House of Commons by Michael Zehaf-Bibeau. The NDP claimed that Bill C-51 would endanger civil rights. When the legislation was first introduced, in early 2015, polls showed the bill to be overwhelmingly popular with Canadians, so Mulcair was seen to be taking a risk opposing it. The Liberals were certainly more circumspect in their response to the bill. Indeed, Trudeau and the party supported the bill, with the caveat that they would introduce amendments once in power. Mulcair's gamble appeared to pay off, though, as Canadians' support for Bill C-51 dropped steadily as more information about it became known. Party strategists felt that Mulcair's opposition to Bill C-51 displayed his conviction, something that compared well to Trudeau's penchant for political expediency.

The federal NDP received an unexpected boost from the Alberta NDP's surprise election win. A media narrative had emerged that the NDP had been on a losing streak in federal by-elections, provincial elections, and even mayoral races in Toronto and Winnipeg since the party's success in the 2011 federal election. The Alberta NDP's win turned that narrative on its head and illustrated the party could win in the most unexpected of places. Party strategists felt that the Alberta election shifted the momentum away from the Liberals and to the federal NDP. In late May 2015, the party began a $2 million pre-election television advertising campaign, with ads entitled, "*Un pays qui vous ressemble*" and "Bring Change to Ottawa." The commercials, which were virtually the same in French and English, featured Mulcair touting his commitment to middle-class values and his focus on restarting Canada's economic growth.

Overall, the NDP staff felt that the developments of the first six months of 2015 were very fortuitous. Polling indicated the NDP had gradually become more competitive during the winter. Then, following the Alberta provincial election, internal polling showed the NDP shooting past the Conservatives and Liberals into first place with approximately 35 percent of the national vote. A Forum poll taken on August 2, the day that the writ was dropped, was especially heartening for the party. The poll placed the NDP's support at 39 percent, found Mulcair was the most preferred prime minister, and projected that the NDP would be only ten seats short of a majority government if the election were held that day.[4] This situation was much better than what the strategists had hoped for back in January.

In addition to rebuilding the NDP's national support, the second goal of the party's senior staff in early 2015 was to finalize the party's campaign machinery so that it was completely "election ready." The federal NDP had adopted a model of "perpetual election preparation" following the 2011 federal election.[5] They had put elaborate structures in place to train volunteers, create a national voter contact database — called Populus — vet and recruit candidates, mobilize local electoral district associations, research voter opinion, reach out to stakeholders, and centrally fundraise. Given the organization that had already taken place, the work that was necessary in the months from January to August 2015 was more a matter of putting the finishing touches on what had been planned as opposed to starting from the ground up. Indeed, the party had set an internal goal of being election-ready by the beginning of April in the event of an early election call.

Given the scale of the election campaign that it was planning, the party created a budget that called for the spending of $24 million by the party headquarters, the full legal limit for a five-week campaign. Whereas in the 1990s and early 2000s NDP party headquarters resembled a fledging NGO, party headquarters in the lead-up to the 2015 federal election looked more like the head office of a Fortune 500 company. The party's headquarters on Laurier Street in Ottawa, which had housed roughly forty permanent employees during 2014, swelled to 250 employees in nine departments: fundraising, war room, tour, administration, digital, products/research, policy/platform, organization, and targeted ridings. Each department had its own director, reporting to Anne McGrath, the national campaign director. The party had made the decision to bring as many functions of the campaign as possible in-house. As such, the party was prepared to run its own call centre, design all of its printed materials, administer its own online presence, do all of its own fundraising, and perform its own research and data analytics. Extensive consultations on the platform with stakeholder groups, federal caucus members, and party members had been completed and the drafting and costing of the final document had begun. Many candidates had been nominated in key ridings and party staff in Ottawa were closing in on completion of a slate of well-qualified and disciplined candidates. As it would turn out, the NDP's campaign would see some "bozo eruptions" by its candidates over controversial social media comments but it would be no worse than the other parties.[6] More importantly, the number of NDP women candidates and NDP candidates from other equity-seeking groups was promising to be impressive (see Chapter 11). An eight-day "Ontario Tour for Change" was organized in early July as a practice run for an actual leader's tour during an election. The tour even included mock debate preparation to practise how Mulcair and his team would react to a debate in the middle of an election campaign.

At this time, organizers were hired for every province to report to Ottawa and be responsible for ensuring that local campaigns were functioning well and were on track to meet their targets. Some provinces had more than one organizer to focus on special regions such as Vancouver Island and Toronto. Quebec was a special case. The party hired roughly one hundred staff to dedicate to its Quebec operations during the election. The party set up a head office for the Quebec NDP campaign in Montreal as well as five regional offices throughout Quebec. Party strategists were cognizant of the fact that many of the Quebec NDP MPs who had been elected four years earlier had actually never run local campaigns and the campaign team understood that the party's infrastructure in Quebec was underdeveloped. The regional offices were created to help deal with these issues; they would be able to provide direct support to local campaigns and provide immediate and in-person organizational assistance to campaigns that were struggling. It should be noted that, like NDP's regional offices elsewhere in Canada, the Montreal office and the party's regional offices in Quebec had only "ground-game" responsibilities, like organizing voter contact. "Air-game" responsibilities, like television and online advertising, as well as relations with media, were run out of party headquarters in Ottawa.

Whereas in the past the NDP had relied on local volunteers and the labour movement in its election preparation, the elaborate organization that been created in the lead-up to the 2015 election was made possible by the gradual professionalization of the party that had been going on over the last decade.[7] A volunteer-based election planning committee (EPC) of party members had met periodically during 2014 and 2015, but it played the role of approving plans presented to it as opposed to creating or implementing those plans. Union representatives had been part of the EPC and a representative of the Canadian Labour Congress (CLC) was invited to sit in on the NDP's morning meetings during the campaign. However, similar to 2011, the labour movement was making plans quite separately of the NDP to run its own campaign, aimed at its members all over Canada and designed to inform them on such issues such as jobs, pensions, health care, and child care. It wanted to give its members the knowledge they needed to vote without specifying which party they should support. The CLC also targeted eighty-eight ridings in English Canada (double the number targeted in 2011), where it ran campaigns parallel to those run by the party, designed to help elect a new NDP candidate or defend an NDP incumbent. In these targeted ridings, union staff would organize their members to volunteer for the NDP, communicate directly with local unionists to outline the reasons that they should vote NDP, and set up meet-and-greet sessions between union members and NDP candidates. However, some individual unions that were unaffiliated to the NDP did give strategic aid to Liberal candidates in ridings where they felt that the Liberal had a chance to unseat a Conservative.

In the past, the Fédération des travailleurs et travailleuses du Québec (FTQ) had supported the Bloc Québécois. In 2015, the FTQ announced that it would target its efforts on a handful of seats held by Conservatives and support the party with the best chance of defeating the Conservative in that riding. In practical terms, this meant that the FTQ would be supporting the efforts of a number of NDP candidates in and around Quebec City.

Despite changes to election laws in 2004 that prohibited direct union support in the form of financial donations or seconding of union staff, the NDP had been able to adapt to and overcome this challenge to assemble the most sophisticated, well-organized, and well-financed campaign machine it its history. While there was some scrambling to get all of the last-minute details into place before the summer, NDP strategists felt confident that they had the organization in place to carry out the ground game and air game necessary to compete with the other two major parties. While the party's stated goal was to form a government (either minority or majority), it was actually targeting 170 seats, which would have been just enough to form a majority government.

## MAINTAINING FIRST PLACE: AUGUST 2 TO LABOUR DAY 2015

NDP strategists admitted to being caught off guard when the writ was dropped at the beginning of August. After Tom Mulcair's late July tour of Ontario, some senior personnel had even scheduled vacations for August, believing that a brief hiatus was possible before the election was called in September. The party already had an entire five-week campaign planned out and prepared to be implemented, something that had been in place since March due to persistent rumors that the prime minister might call a spring election. However, there were no plans for a campaign stretching from August to October. In such an extended campaign, the legal limit for central spending would be double what had been instituted in 2011. Also, the NDP would need more content to fill up an eleven-week campaign and had to plan several extra weeks of the leader's tour.

However, these organizational challenges were not seen as insurmountable. Strategists decided to send Mulcair on a full-fledged leader's tour, although a decision was made not to initially use a chartered airplane. As was originally planned, Mulcair would start using his official campaign plane after Labour Day. Strategists also decided not to run any television commercials in August. They felt that Canadians would be paying only superficial attention to the campaign in August and they wanted to save their money for the final weeks when voters were confirming their decisions and the NDP could be facing a barrage of attack ads from its competitors.

The initial strategy devised by the NDP for August could be best described as its government-in-waiting strategy, though the party never actually used the term, because it did not want to sound arrogant. Interestingly, the NDP's strategy was relatively similar in both Quebec and English Canada. Strategists felt that, like English Canadians, Quebecers were looking for a credible and well-prepared agent of change to replace Harper. All across Canada, the NDP decided to frame the election around the ballot box question of "Which party is ready to bring change to Ottawa?"

The NDP's government-in-waiting strategy consisted of five elements, which became apparent throughout the first month of the campaign and can be seen in Table 4.1 (see following page). The table utilizes the same research design as found in the chapter on the NDP campaign in *The Canadian Federal Election of 2011*.[8] The analysis was performed through the inductive coding of all of the news releases issued by the federal NDP during the campaign using computer-assisted qualitative data analysis software (CAQDAS) called NVivo 10 that calculates "percentage coverage" and which is based on the number of characters coded into a particular theme.[9]

## Table 4.1: Percentage Coverage of Themes in 2015 Federal NDP Press Releases

| Weeks 1 and 2 (August 2–August 16) | Weeks 3, 4, and 5 (August 17 to September 6) | Week 6 and 7 (September 7–September 20) | Week 8 and 9 (September 21–October 4) | Week 10 and 11 (October 5–October 19) |
|---|---|---|---|---|
| NDP team: 30% | NDP team: 33% | Attack Trudeau: 28% | Attack Trudeau: 33% | Attack Trudeau: 46% |
| CPC corruption: 17% | Attack Harper: 31% | Health care: 21% | Mulcair's leadership: 33% | TPP: 38% |
| Mulcair's leadership: 14% | Economy/Protecting middle class: 17% | NDP team: 14% | Attack Harper: 19% | Attack Harper: 28% |
| Attack Harper: 14% | Attack Trudeau: 14% | Mulcair's leadership: 13% | NDP team: 20% | NDP team: 26% |
| Time for a change: 13% | Time for a change: 13% | Infrastructure: 12% | Environment: 20% | Health care: 20% |
| Economy/Protecting middle class: 13% | Foreign affairs: 11% | Attack Harper: 8% | Foreign affairs: 6% | Mulcair's leadership: 15% |
| Senate: 12% | Mulcair's leadership: 8% | Manufacturing: 7% | TPP: 6% | Auto sector: 8% |
| Agriculture: 7% | Fiscal responsibility: 8% | Economy/Protecting middle class: 8% | Northern Canada: 6% | Environment: 7% |
| Fiscal responsibility: 4% | Tourism: 6% | Women's issues: 6% | Youth issues: 6% | Time for a change: 6% |
| Small business taxes: 4% | Attack Kenney: 6% | Foreign affairs: 4% | CPC corruption: 5% | Strategic voting: 4% |
| Environment: 3% | Retirement security: 4% | Immigration: 4% | Immigration: 4% | Arts and culture: 4% |
| Child care: 1% | Sports: 4% | Aboriginal issues: 3% | Post-secondary education: 3% | Protect the CBC: 4% |
| Consumer protection: 1% | CPC corruption: 4% | Fiscal responsibility: 3% | Elections Act: 3% | Bill C-51: 4% |
| Official languages: 1% | Frontline police: 4% | Child care: 3% | Seniors: 3% | Housing: 4% |
| Bill C-51: 1% | Wildfires and floods: 4% | Higher corporate taxes: 3% | Health care: 3% | LGBT issues: 4% |
| Federal minimum wage: 0.5% | Ring of Fire: 3% | CPC corruption: 3% | Disabilities issues: 3% | Foreign affairs: 4% |
| Women's issues: 0.5% | Aboriginals 3% | Environment: 2% | Respect for science: 3% | Poverty: 4% |
| | Women's issues: 3% | Housing: 2% | Veterans: 3% | Internet freedom: 3% |
| | Seniors poverty: 3% | Retirement security: 2% | Forestry: 3% | Aboriginal affairs: 3% |
| | Manufacturing: 3% | Youth issues: 2% | Employment insurance: 3% | Support from Quebec academic community: 3% |
| | Child care: 3% | Time for a change: 1% | CBC: 2% | Child care: 0.5% |
| | Attack Goodale: 3% | Labour Day: 1% | Economy/Protecting middle class: 2% | Democratic reform: 0.5% |
| | Bill C-51: 1% | Federal minimum wage: 0.5% | Child care: 2% | |
| | Small business taxes: 2% | Higher taxes for wealthy: 0.5% | Time for a change: 2% | |
| | Veterans: 0.5% | | Manufacturing: 2% | |
| | Federal minimum wage: 0.5% | | Aboriginal affairs: 2% | |
| | Environment: 0.5% | | Auto sector: 1% | |
| | | | Dairy supply management: 1% | |

The first element of the NDP's government-in-waiting strategy involved Mulcair. Undoubtedly, a government in waiting needs a prime minister in waiting. As such, building off the party's activities in the first six months of 2015, the NDP's campaign was quite leader-centric in August. As can be seen in Table 4.1, touting Mulcair's leadership qualities and experience was an important theme of the party's news releases. The party's research indicated that voters who were hesitating between the Liberals and the NDP saw Mulcair as a serious politician who was reassuring and capable, in contrast to Trudeau, whom they feared was "just not ready," as the Conservative attacks ads had repeated since he had became Liberal leader. Trudeau was "risky" change and Mulcair was "safe" change. Thus, the summary of Mulcair's brand was a simple one: experienced leadership. He was the leader with Cabinet experience who was ready to bring change to Ottawa and repair the damage that Harper had done. He was the type of leader who could manage a $2 trillion economy and be trusted to handle international crises at 3:00 in the morning as you and your children slept. Mulcair's brand was reinforced by the release of his autobiography on August 8, 2015, entitled *Strength of Conviction/Le courage de ses convictions*. The release of the book generated a number of positive media stories detailing Mulcair's upbringing in a large family, his courtship with his wife, his days as a Cabinet minister in the Charest provincial government, his courage to leave his Cabinet minister job and join a party that was historically very unpopular in Quebec, and his life as a father and grandfather.

Second, a government in waiting needs a Cabinet in waiting. In order to establish that the party had an accomplished group of candidates suitable for such a role, the NDP organized a "B tour" to supplement Mulcair's leader's tour, in which the national media was invited to cover news conferences by prominent NDP candidates or sitting NDP MPs. The B tour served several purposes. It boosted the profile of NDP candidates in their local media markets and it filled holes in the leader's schedule when he was travelling or preparing for debates.

Since it can be considered "un-prime ministerial" to engage in biting partisanship, the NDP's other candidates used the B-tour events to attack the other parties. For instance, NDP MP Charlie Angus held an event outside of the Ottawa courthouse where the Mike Duffy trial was taking place to help keep Duffy and the other Conservatives associated with the Senate scandal in the media spotlight.

Of course, since the party was in first place in the polls, the NDP and its staff were also facing questions from the media. In particular, the press was eager to learn what an eventual NDP Cabinet would look like. The B tour highlighted the talent of NDP candidates and reassured voters that Mulcair would have several strong performers to chose from when assembling a Cabinet. One of special note, Andrew Thomson, the NDP candidate in Eglinton-Lawrence, was a former NDP minister of finance in Saskatchewan who since had been working in the private sector in Toronto. Thomson became a spokesperson for the party on fiscal and economic matters. He and other prominent NDP candidates were the figures the party hoped would convince the public of the strength of the NDP team, and as Table 4.1 illustrates, the theme of "NDP team" is actually the most prominent element found in NDP press releases prior to Labour Day.

The third focus of the NDP's government-in-waiting strategy was to intensely criticize the Conservatives and refrain from directly attacking the Liberals. The thinking behind this strategy was to create a two-way NDP/Conservative race, in which the NDP was the sole credible alternative to the Conservative government and Mulcair was the only safe choice to replace Harper as prime minister. The establishment of a two-way, NDP/Conservative race narrative was intended to allow for the setting up of strategic voting appeals at the end of the campaign, assuming the Liberals would fade away gradually and the NDP could benefit from a bandwagon effect at the end of the campaign. It was felt by campaign strategists that attacks by the NDP on the Liberals and Trudeau would only give the Liberal Party's campaign credibility and undermine the two-way NDP/Conservative race narrative.

Further, the Conservatives held the seats in English Canada that the NDP needed to win government. By attacking the Conservatives, the NDP was signalling to progressive voters that it was the party that could beat Conservative incumbents and repair the damage that the Harper government had done. And so, during the summer, the NDP leader's tour spent a large amount of time in ridings held by the Conservatives. When in those ridings, Mulcair's critiques of the Conservatives centred on corruption, the need to abolish the Senate, Canada's weak economic performance, and the simple message that it was "time for a change." Indeed, in Table 4.1, these themes appear as important parts of the NDP's news releases during the summer.

Conversely, NDP news releases barely mentioned Trudeau or the Liberals during the first two weeks of the campaign. In fact, party strategists reported that NDP donors and activists as well as Liberal/NDP switchers in focus groups reacted negatively to NDP attacks on the Liberals; they felt that NDP criticism of Trudeau only helped Harper. Attacks against Trudeau and the Liberals in NDP news releases did not start in earnest until the very end of August and the first week of September, when it became clear that the Liberals were not fading away.

A fourth part of the NDP's government-in-waiting strategy was to consolidate its regional stronghold while focusing on other areas of the country during the campaign. The NDP was solidly in first place in Quebec in its internal polling at the beginning of August and Mulcair was far better liked and more trusted than Harper, Trudeau, or Gilles Duceppe, the leader of the Bloc Québécois. It appeared to be a relatively safe bet that Quebec could be relied upon as the party's regional stronghold and that a block of seats from the province would be the anchor to the NDP's first-ever federal government. In the first couple of weeks, strategists moved to secure their support in Quebec by having Mulcair visit the province and talk about Quebec-specific issues, like ensuring the bilingualism of Supreme Court judges, protecting the beluga whale nursery at Cacouna, and saving the Maritime Search and Rescue centre in Quebec City. In weeks three to five of the campaign, Mulcair visited Quebec three times but did not make new policy announcements at those stops.[10] The leader's tour concentrated more on taking Mulcair to the battleground provinces of Ontario and British Columbia where the party was hoping to take seats away from the Conservatives.

Finally, in order to appear like a government in waiting, the NDP sought to mitigate negative stereotypes of its brand, such as being prone to overspending and being "bad for the economy." As we can see in Table 4.1, during the first month of the campaign, the clear policy emphasis was on economic issues: protecting the middle class, increasing employment, reducing small business taxes, consumer protection, agriculture, the Ring of Fire mining development in northern Ontario, and tourism. Mulcair also tried to present the NDP as a well-rounded party by talking about issues that were not typically associated with the NDP, like veterans affairs, emergency preparedness, sports, and hiring more police officers. When it came to social policy, the NDP emphasized that its ambitious child-care plan would be gradually phased in and limited its significant new social spending promises to increasing the Guaranteed Income Supplement to seniors and restoring funding to shelters for abused women. There was also an emphasis on fiscal responsibility, with the proposal of a law guaranteeing budget transparency and a promise to run a balanced budget in the NDP's first term of office. The NDP repeated this pledge after the Liberals announced their plan to run deficits in order to increase infrastructure spending.

The election campaign prior to Labour Day showed mixed results for the NDP. In order to ensure that Mulcair appeared prime ministerial and in an attempt to manage his time, the NDP had decided that he would only participate in debates that included Harper. As a result, the party was sucked into "debating about the debates" as opposed to talking about its vision for the country. In particular, a controversy about Mulcair's participation in a debate on women's issues was a distraction. Party strategists were disappointed with the fact that despite the results of some polls that showed the NDP and the Conservatives in first and second place with the Liberals in third, the media did not seem to be buying into the narrative of a two-way NDP/Conservative race. The Liberals continued to get significant media attention as a contender to form government, something that only intensified as their polling numbers crept upward at the end of August and the beginning of September.

While the NDP avoided directly attacking the Liberals, the Liberal war room did not reciprocate. The Liberal campaign claimed that Mulcair was saying contradictory statements in English and French, that Trudeau was more feminist than Mulcair because he agreed to the debate on women's issues, that the NDP's federal minimum wage plan would actually help out only a minuscule number of workers, and that the NDP's child-care plan would never be fully implemented because it depending on the NDP winning two majority governments in a row. Old video footage was unearthed in which Mulcair appeared to say flattering things about Margaret Thatcher and that he had been in favour of bulk water exports when he was the minister of environment in the Charest government. Liberal premiers from Ontario and New Brunswick also publicly expressed doubts about Mulcair and NDP policies. The media picked up on several of these Liberal attacks.

By the end of August, the NDP had started to directly attack Trudeau on what they claimed was a $10 billion hole in his fiscal framework. This, they said, would lead to reckless deficits and cuts to important public services in the future. However, these initial NDP attacks did not really bring down Trudeau's popularity, and NDP strategists felt that the Liberals' promises were not receiving the same high level of media scrutiny as the NDP's plans. Due to the NDP's front-runner status, the media had become fixated on the most minute details of the party's spending initiatives and how they were to be financed. Strategists indicated that reporters were also very interested in the question of whether provincial governments would buy into the NDP's plans and if the party's plans might have difficulty being realized as a result of provincial resistance. Questions surrounding how the NDP intended to pay for its campaign promises increased once the party dedicated itself to balanced budgets and the Liberals stated that they were going to run deficits. The NDP was forced to defend itself against the counter-intuitive claim that it was positioned to the right of the Liberals.

While strategists had expected this level of scrutiny and had the resources in place to deal with it, they felt that they were spending large amounts of time explaining and defending their plans as opposed to setting the agenda. Overall, there was a feeling that the NDP's organization was large and professional but not very nimble.

Nonetheless, as Labour Day came, party officials felt good about how their campaign had handled the curveballs that had been thrown their way and felt that the party was in relatively good shape. Despite some criticism about his supposed "fake smile," worn to combat the "Angry Tom" stereotype, Mulcair had performed well in the first debate. The Duffy trial had reinforced the NDP's message on Conservative corruption and news that Canada had entered into a recession proved that the NDP's criticism of Harper's economic record was correct. Harper's somewhat muted response to the photo of a three-year-old Syrian refugee who washed up dead on a shore in Greece put the Conservatives on the defensive over their refugee policy. The media had appeared to accept that the NDP had enough qualified candidates to form a competent federal Cabinet and the narrative around Mulcair's experience and leadership qualities had taken hold. Strategists felt that they had succeeded in convincing Canadians that the NDP was a credible governing alternative to the Conservatives. Internal polling illustrated that Mulcair was popular; there was little fear of an NDP majority; a sizable chunk of voters thought that an NDP win was likely; and there was a high level of comfort with the notion of an NDP/Liberal coalition or an NDP minority government supported by the Liberals. The party's organization on the ground in Quebec and other provinces was working well and its call centre and national database were providing high-quality data in real time.

For these reasons, strategists saw little reason to reverse their government-in-waiting strategy, which appeared to be working as planned. However, an emerging problem was that the Liberals could say many of the same things about their campaign. News about a weak economy, the Duffy trial, Syrian refugees, and an imploding Conservative campaign could be just as beneficial to the Liberals as to the NDP. Trudeau was also drawing large crowds and the narrative about him being "just not ready" was gradually subsiding. The Liberals' risky policy announcement about running deficits to pay for infrastructure had not created the downward pressure on their support that some had predicted. Having out-fundraised the NDP in 2013 and 2014,[11] the Liberals were also well funded for the second half of the campaign despite their aggressive television advertising campaign throughout August.

## FALLING BACK INTO THIRD PLACE: LABOUR DAY TO ELECTION DAY

The NDP's television ads in September were nearly identical in both Quebec and English Canada and they closely corresponded to the NDP's government-in-waiting strategy described above. The focus continued to be on attacking the Conservatives over corruption and their poor economic record while touting the experienced leadership of Mulcair and his middle-class-family background. The party still felt that it could create a two-way NDP/Conservative race and represent Mulcair as a credible agent of change as opposed to Trudeau who was inherently risky. The slogan on Muclair's podium was changed to read, simply, "Experience, Leadership," and those attending Mulcair's rallies were given hand-held signs that read "Defeat Harper." Using CAQDAS software once again, the NDP English and French commercials released in September are analyzed on the next page.

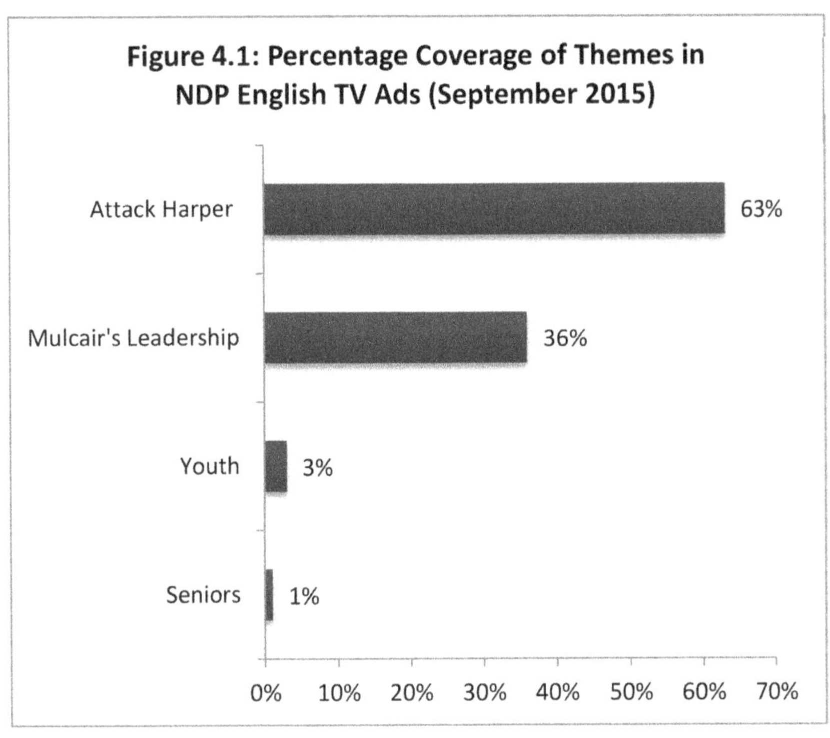
Figure 4.1: Percentage Coverage of Themes in NDP English TV Ads (September 2015)
Attack Harper
63%
Mulcair's Leadership
36%
Youth
3%
Seniors
1%
0%
10%
20%
30%
40%
50%
60%
70%

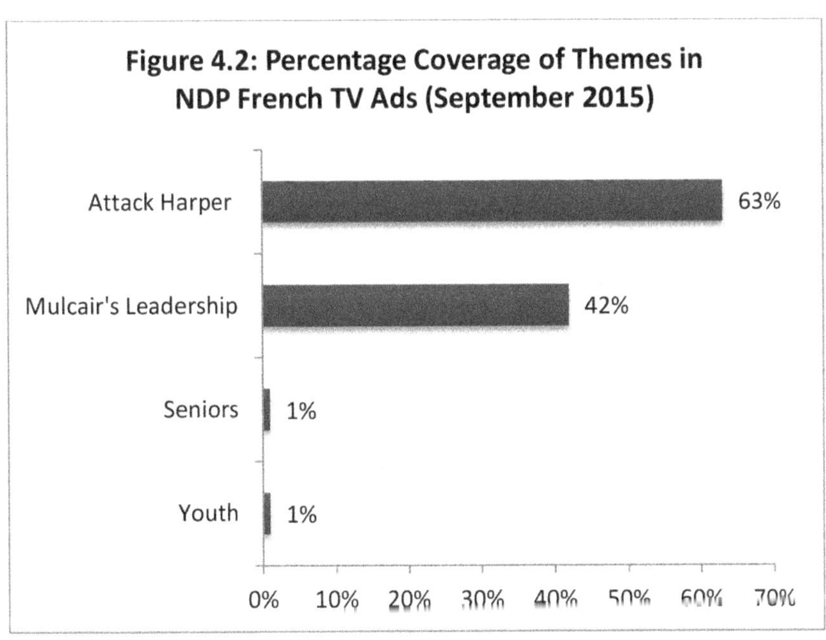
Figure 4.2: Percentage Coverage of Themes in NDP French TV Ads (September 2015)
Attack Harper
63%
Mulcair's Leadership
42%
Seniors
1%
Youth
1%
0%
10%
20%
30%
40%
50%
60%
70%

If we refer back to Table 4.1, we can see that the NDP's team of candidates and attacking Harper remained important themes in Weeks 6 and 7 of the campaign. Economic issues like manufacturing, protecting the middle class, and infrastructure also remained important, and fiscal responsibility was still mentioned.

In response to incessant questions from the media on how the NDP intended to pay for its spending promises, party strategists decided to release the costing document for their platform earlier than planned. The day before the *Globe and Mail* debate on the economy, the NDP released its fiscal plan that proposed to pay for its "long-term investments to help families get ahead" by closing tax loopholes for CEOs and "increasing the tax rate paid by profitable corporations from 15 percent to 17 percent, which [the NDP document noted] is lower than the average it was under Stephen Harper and leaves Canada's rate below the G7 average."[12] The costing document also pledged to balance the budget over all four years of an NDP government's mandate. The party promised that a more detailed platform based on this fiscal framework would be released later in the campaign.

However, two themes emerged in the NDP's press releases from weeks 6 and 7 that indicate the beginning of a subtle shift of strategy for the party had taken place. First, the NDP decided to make several announcements on health care in the middle of September, the boldest being to work with the provinces to create a universal prescription drug program at the cost of $2.6 billion over four years. According to strategists, these ambitious health-care announcements had been planned and third-party valuators had been secured well ahead of the beginning of the campaign. The idea behind presenting the party's health platform in early September was to cement the NDP as a progressive alternative to the Liberals, who had no plan on how to repair the damage done by the Conservatives to Canada's health-care system. The emphasis on the "NDP issue" of health care dovetailed with the ramping up of direct attacks on Trudeau. Table 4.1 illustrates that attacking Trudeau became the top theme within NDP news releases in weeks 6 and 7.

September 16 was an important day in the NDP's campaign due to two events. First, the release of the NDP's costing document set off another round of scrutiny of the party's policies, with the media focusing on how unforeseen circumstances in the future, like the dropping price of oil, might affect spending plans given the party's balanced budget commitment.[13] The Liberal war room was only too happy to repeat these criticisms.[14] NDP strategists strongly believed that, while the Liberals could get away with proposing deficits, the NDP could not. Given the negative stereotypes about the NDP, proposing deficit spending would have led to damaging charges that an NDP government would engage in "out of control spending," leading Canada toward economic ruin. Further, the NDP had been running on balanced budgets since 2006; to change gears in 2015 would have been considered a flip-flop. The decision was made to vigorously defend the party's position on fiscal responsibility by arguing that new spending would be financed through new revenues coming from a higher corporate tax rate, pointing out that the federal government had posted a $1.9 billion surplus in the 2014–2015 fiscal year so going into deficit to pay for social programs was unnecessary. Canadians were reminded that Saskatchewan CCF premier Tommy Douglas had introduced Medicare while running seventeen consecutive balanced budgets.

Second, the release of the NDP's costing platform coincided with an announcement in Trois-Rivières by Denis Lebel, Harper's Quebec lieutenant, stating that a Conservative government would appeal the previous day's Federal Court of Appeal ruling allowing women to take their citizenship oaths while wearing the niqab and reinstate the ban on the practice within one hundred days of being re-elected.[15] NDP strategists pointed to the niqab ruling as a major setback for their campaign in Quebec. In March 2015, the NDP had opposed the Conservative-decreed ban on the niqab at citizenship ceremonies, and strategists considered this a position of principle for the party and the leader. The Bloc Québécois and the Conservatives quickly began to use an Ipsos poll from March 2015 that found that 91 percent of Quebecers supported banning the wearing of the niqab at citizenship ceremonies to claim that the NDP was offside with Quebecers' values.[16] Harper and Duceppe also pointed out that the National Assembly of Quebec had unanimously adopted a motion denouncing the wearing of a niqab during citizenship ceremonies. The issue came to dominate francophone media in Quebec over the last two weeks of September.

The party's internal polling showed the NDP's support in Quebec dropping 17 percent over the course of three days and some NDP candidates even stopped going door to door to avoid the backlash.

Despite the fact that the issue had been a controversial one for the NDP earlier in the year and that operatives had known about its potential to hurt them, a coherent and precise reaction from the NDP was not immediately forthcoming. The debate among party strategists was not about whether the NDP should change its position, but rather how to best explain the party's opposition to banning the niqab at citizenship ceremonies to Quebecers and the rest of Canada. Strategists struggled to find the correct language in a timely manner. Mulcair began with the legalistic argument that he would respect the court's decision and that courts are needed to protect the freedom of religion.[17] He also pointed out that women wearing the niqab would be obliged to uncover their faces for identification purposes prior to the ceremony. At the same time, the media picked up on comments in favour of the ban by the NDP's candidate in Mégantic-L'Érable to claim that there was disagreement in the party over Mulcair's position. The party then shifted gears, with Mulcair arguing that the ban of the niqab at citizenship ceremonies should not be a vote-determining issue and that Canadians should see it as a "a weapon of mass distraction" used by Harper to avoid talking about his poor record on the economy and health care.[18] At the same time, he began to express a greater empathy with Quebecers on the issue that showed he understood how seeing a woman wearing a niqab could create uneasiness.[19] Again, strategists felt they were explaining their position as opposed to setting the agenda. In hindsight, Mulcair's oscillations over the issue may have even kept the issue alive as it gave the media multiple occasions to report something new concerning the NDP and the niqab.

While the issue eventually subsided on its own by the beginning of October, strategists felt that the episode hurt Mulcair's brand in Quebec. Quebecers had believed that the NDP and Mulcair really understood their concerns but the niqab controversy appeared to show otherwise. The Bloc Québécois campaign was given new life. It came out with a commercial attacking the NDP's position that showed niqabs flowing out of a pipeline, a reference to both the niqab controversy and the NDP's qualified support for the Energy East pipeline, which was unpopular among environmentalists in Quebec. The niqab debate also gave the Conservatives a chance to solidify their support around the Quebec City area as they pushed the issue further by proposing the idea of a barbaric cultural practices tip line.

By late September, NDP strategists realized that a perfect storm had fallen upon their campaign and the way that they had strategically positioned their party was now awkward. The NDP had been put on the defensive over how it would pay for its spending programs, given its balanced-budget commitment, and its principled position on the niqab debate led to questions over the solidity of its Quebec regional stronghold, where the niqab debate had helped the Conservatives regain their footing, as they were able to change the channel away from corruption and the Mike Duffy trial. Moreover, the Liberal campaign continued to surge as doubts about Trudeau's readiness to be prime minister waned. Mulcair had done well in the four debates in September but so had Trudeau, Harper, and Duceppe (see Chapter 10). The narrative of a two-way NDP/Conservative race that the party had hoped would be well entrenched as the campaign entered its final weeks was now doubted by both media and the general public. Worse yet, a new narrative began to emerge: that the NDP was losing momentum and its support was in decline.

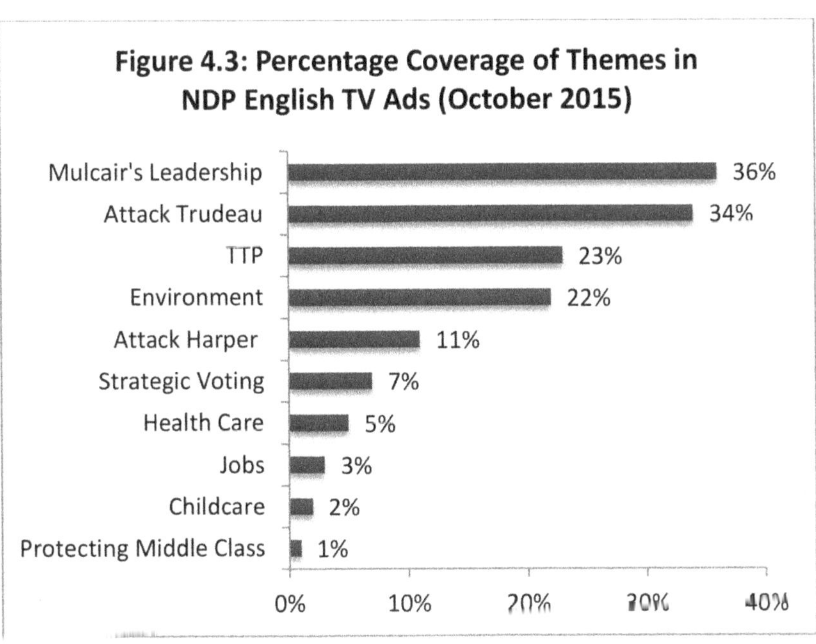

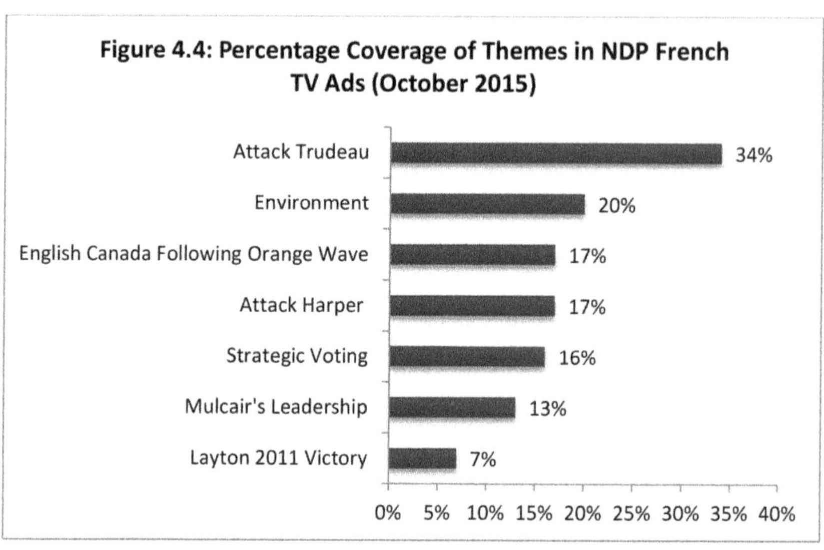


NDP strategists were faced with a tough decision. Should they abandon their government-in-waiting strategy and adopt an entirely new strategy? Or, should they just stay the course? They ended up doing a bit of both, maintaining certain parts of the old plan while adopting new tactics. A content analysis of the NDP's television commercials from October reflects this dual approach.

This analysis of NDP commercials from October reveals that the government-in-waiting strategy was still in effect. One of the NDP's final commercials of the campaign featured Mulcair wearing a suit and tie, sitting on the edge of a desk in what appeared to be a law office filled with books, as he spoke straight into the camera about his plan to help Canadian families. At the end of the commercial, the phrase "Tom Mulcair: Experienced, Principled, Ready for Change" flashed on the screen. The party's commercials still attacked the Conservatives and attempted to reinforce the narrative of a two-way NDP/Conservative race by pointing out that, based on the seat count in the House of Commons at the time of its dissolution, the NDP needed to win only thirty-five additional seats to stop Harper compared to the one hundred additional seats that the Liberals would need. At Mulcair's rallies, the crowds were issued octagonal "Stop Harper" signs and those with NDP lawn signs were given the option to add a smaller "Stop Harper" sign above their local candidate's name. The commercials in Quebec included images of Rachel Notley and Jack Layton while Mulcair told Quebecers that the rest of Canada was getting ready to follow the Orange Wave that Quebec had started in 2011 in order to get rid of Harper.

Yet, there were also some evident changes in the NDP's tactics. Quebec was no longer considered a regional stronghold. Mulcair visited the province more and stressed Quebec issues, such as protecting supply management for the dairy industry and reversing the cuts made to Radio-Canada. More strikingly, as we can see in the analysis of the NDP's news releases from the final weeks of the campaign in Table 4.1 and its October television commercials, the NDP stepped up its direct attacks on Trudeau and the Liberals. Overall, NDP strategists believed that it was important to highlight the differences between their party and the Liberals on ethics, Bill C-51, the Trans-Pacific Partnership, and climate change. Radio ads were launched in English Canada that criticized Trudeau for charging charities $20,000 in speaking fees while he was an MP and voting in favour of "Stephen Harper's spy bill." The NDP repeatedly attacked Trudeau for keeping his position on the TPP secret and not openly opposing a deal that would cost Canadian jobs. Further, the NDP contrasted its hard targets on greenhouse gas emissions with the vague plan by Trudeau to work with the provinces to reduce climate change. In the last week of the campaign, after a member of Trudeau's campaign team had to resign for advising an oil company on how to fast-track a pipeline through a new Liberal government, the NDP released hard-hitting television commercials in French and English that invoked the sponsorship scandal from the Chrétien years.

Another change in tactics appeared to be a shift away from inoculating the NDP's brand against negative stereotypes. As opposed to focusing on economic issues and fiscal responsibility, the NDP's commercials and news releases gave an increasingly prominent role to health care and the environment. The NDP had come out tentatively in favour of the trade agreement with the European Union while waiting to see the final text, and in early August 2015, Mulcair stated that the NDP was "enthusiastically in favour" of the TPP but had some concerns about supply management.[20] In October 2015, it was announced that a TPP deal had been reached, though the final text would not be released until after the election. Nonetheless, the NDP came out very strongly against what it characterized as a secretive deal negotiated by Harper that could weaken environmental laws, raise the price of prescription drugs, hurt the auto sector, undermine supply management in the dairy industry, and increase the surveillance of Canadians as they surfed the Internet. NDP strategists were evidently not worried about any damage to their brand inflicted by opposing a trade deal that was supported by most of Canada's business community.

The NDP's final platform was released on October 9, 2015, just ten days before the election. There were few surprises since nearly all of the policies in the platform had already been announced and the fiscal framework had been released. Still, it was interesting that strategists chose the audacious title of "Building the Country of Our Dreams," a title that contrasted significantly with the more pedestrian labels used by Jack Layton for the platforms he helped to promote.[21]

Indeed, in certain areas, the NDP's platform in 2015 was more ambitious and left-wing than the party's 2011 platform. The 2015 platform promised one million child-care spaces over eight years at $15 dollars a day compared to the 2011 promise of one hundred thousand spaces over four years with no mention of regulating the cost of those spaces. Whereas the 2011 platform contained a vague pledge to lower prescription drug costs when finances permitted, the 2015 platform boldly claimed that an NDP government would work toward universal public drug coverage for all Canadians, something that would lower prescription drug costs by 30 percent. The 2011 NDP platform had been silent on labour policy, free trade agreements, and illicit drugs. The 2015 NDP platform committed to the decriminalization of marijuana and ensuring that trade agreements improved social, environmental, and labour standards in partner countries. Interestingly, the 2015 NDP platform pledged not only to repeal several pieces of labour legislation passed by the Harper government but also to introduce anti-scab legislation. In short, party strategists were going into election day with what was the NDP's most left-wing platform in a decade, couched in a language more utopian than Layton had ever used.[22] Indeed, the federal

NDP 2015 campaign was largely free from criticism of Mulcair's centrism from the left wing of the NDP.[23]

In contrast to the optimistic tone of the title of the party's platform, however, the NDP entered the final week of the election with little momentum. Its ground game appeared to be functioning well. As it turned out, though, the way that the party had strategically positioned itself was now starting to hurt. Much of the NDP's overall strategy since August had been built upon the claims that a) Mulcair was the experienced and safe choice to replace Harper as prime minister, compared to Trudeau who was a political neophyte and risky; and b) the NDP was the party best positioned to beat the Conservatives. In the final weeks of the campaign, the Conservatives' attacks on Trudeau being just not ready and the NDP's attacks on Trudeau's ethical failings and policy positions on climate change, Bill C-51, and the TPP were not resonating. Perhaps, voters had decided that they had seen enough of Trudeau over the marathon campaign to conclude that such attacks were overstated.

NDP strategists had also noticed a troubling feedback loop in their internal polling that was being reported in public-domain polling as well. The drop in NDP support in Quebec over the niqab controversy had created a dip in the NDP's national numbers, which seemed to send a signal to the anybody-but-Harper voters in the rest of Canada, particularly Ontario, that the NDP was not the party that was best positioned to defeat the Conservatives. The NDP's national numbers dropped further as English-Canadian voters shifted to the Liberals. Then, when voters in Quebec saw the NDP's national numbers dropping further, they were themselves less likely to support Mulcair's party. Both mentions of the NDP and positive coverage of the NDP in Canadian newspapers declined in October.[24] NDP strategists had planned for strategic voting arguments down the stretch to hurt the Liberals and help the NDP. In fact, the opposite appeared to be occurring as anybody-but-Harper voters were coming to the conclusion that the Liberals were the party best positioned to topple the Conservative government and that Trudeau was not so risky after all.

## RESULTS: A SHORT-TERM VIEW AND A LONG-TERM VIEW

Table 4.2 compares the average popular vote and seat total of the CCF in 1935 to 1958 and the NDP in 1962 to 2008 to the NDP's performance in 2011 and 2015. It allows us to take both a long-term perspective on the 2015 election results as well as a short-term perspective.

**Table 4.2: CCF-NDP Electoral Results in 1935–1958, 1962–2008, 2011, and 2015**

| Province | CCF Average Vote (1935–1958) | NDP Average Vote (1962–2008) | 2011 NDP Vote | 2015 NDP Vote | CCF Average Seat Total (1935–1958) | NDP Average Seat Total (1962–2008) | 2011 NDP Seat Total | 2015 NDP Seat Total |
|---|---|---|---|---|---|---|---|---|
| NL | 0.2% | 12.3% | 32.6% | 21.0% | 0.0 | 0.1 | 2 | 0 |
| PEI | 1.7% | 7.0% | 15.4% | 16.0% | 0.0 | 0.0 | 0 | 0 |
| NS | 8.1% | 16.9% | 30.3% | 16.4% | 0.7 | 1.1 | 3 | 0 |
| NB | 3.0% | 12.0% | 29.8% | 18.3% | 0.0 | 0.4 | 1 | 0 |
| QC | 1.5% | 6.9% | 42.9% | 25.4% | 0.0 | 0.1 | 59 | 16 |
| ON | 10.7% | 17.5% | 25.6% | 16.6% | 1.1 | 7.3 | 22 | 8 |
| MB | 23.3% | 24.0% | 25.8% | 13.8% | 2.7 | 3.3 | 2 | 2 |
| SK | 34.7% | 30.0% | 32.3% | 25.1% | 7.4 | 3.2 | 0 | 3 |
| AB | 10.2% | 9.7% | 16.8% | 11.6% | 0.0 | 0.1 | 1 | 1 |
| BC | 28.0% | 28.1% | 32.5% | 25.9% | 4.1 | 7.9 | 12 | 14 |
| Territories | 22.3% | 25.2% | 27.8% | 25.3% | 0.0 | 0.6 | 1 | 0 |
| National | 11.1% | 15.9% | 30.6% | 19.7% | 16.0 | 24.1 | 103 | 44 |

First, the short-term perspective. When compared to the NDP's historic breakthrough in the 2011 federal election, the party's performance in the 2015 was disastrous. One of the most striking features of the Table 4.2 is that, with the exception of Prince Edward Island, the NDP's popular vote decreased noticeably in all Canadian provinces between 2011 and 2015. The largest decreases in the party's support came in the eastern part of the country (Quebec, Nova Scotia, Newfoundland and Labrador, New Brunswick) as well as Manitoba.

The NDP suffered less significant decreases in popular vote in the three western provinces and Ontario. In terms of seats, the party's losses came mostly from Quebec and to a lesser extent Ontario. The only positive news for the NDP on election night in 2015 was its performance in Saskatchewan and British Columbia. Despite the NDP's popular vote going down in both of those provinces, the party made modest seat gains.

Due to the redrawing of boundaries and the addition of new seats in the House of Commons, it is difficult to precisely determine which party directly benefitted from the reduction in the NDP's popular vote compared to 2011. However, by examining the first-place and second-place finishes of the NDP, it appears that Liberals were the primary beneficiaries of the NDP's decline. In the forty-four seats that the NDP won, the second-place finishers were the Liberals in twenty-nine seats, the Conservatives in eleven seats, the Bloc Québécois in three seats, and the Greens in one seat. In the eighty-four seats where the NDP placed second, the winner was the Liberals in sixty-four seats, the Conservatives in eighteen seats, and the Bloc Québécois in two seats. Many high-profile NDP incumbents who were running for re-election in 2015 ended up being beaten by Liberals. While the Liberals did take seats away from the Conservatives, it is undeniable that much of the Liberals' majority victory came through winning seats in areas of Canada that voted for the NDP in 2011.

However, if one takes a long-term perspective, a different picture emerges. On a national level, the NDP's forty-four seats in the 2015 election represent approximately double the CCF-NDP average seat count in the time period from 1935 to 2008. Similarly, the 19.7 percent of the popular vote that the party received in 2015 is noticeably higher than the 11 percent averaged by the CCF during its existence and the 15.9 percent averaged by the NDP from 1962 to 2008. Whereas the CCF-NDP was almost non-existent in Quebec throughout most of its history, the party retained sixteen seats in the province in 2015. Indeed, the NDP took over a quarter of the vote in Quebec in 2015, whereas the NDP averaged 6.9 percent from 1962 to 2008. In Atlantic Canada, the NDP's 2015 popular vote was markedly higher than that typically received from 1962 to 2008. In Ontario, the NDP's 2015 popular vote and seat count was similar to the way the party performed in that province prior to 2011. The NDP's seat total on the Prairies in 2015 is relatively similar to the party's performance on the Prairies in its historic 2011 victory and similar to the CCF-NDP's electoral history in that region prior to that election. Finally, as noted above, the British Columbia 2015 results are encouraging for the party as it won two additional seats compared to 2011 and its 2015 seat total is almost double the NDP's historical total.

Overall, the 2015 election has returned the federal NDP to its traditional position as the "third party" in a two-and-a-half party system. If we take a historical perspective, we can see that the NDP has come back to the level of the electoral performance that it enjoyed during the 1980s, which had been the party's most electorally successful time period prior to the stunning 2011 breakthrough. The most notable difference between the current era and the 1980s is that the NDP is now electorally competitive in Quebec.

## CONCLUSION: ORGANIZATIONAL STRENGTH AND STRATEGIC WEAKNESS

Despite the disappointing results, the NDP has several organizational strengths coming out of the 2015 campaign and it appears to be united. The party has been thoroughly professionalized and its ground game performed well throughout the campaign. The party has garnered considerable experience in using sophisticated techniques of digital campaigning, volunteer mobilization, fundraising, micro-targeting, and voter contact. The NDP's new database system is up and running and it will be continually improved, as NDP provincial parties will likely use it in various upcoming provincial elections. The NDP had a stellar third quarter of fundraising in 2015, beating out the Liberals and coming just behind the Conservatives.[25] While the party estimates that it spent approximately $30 million in the 2015 election, due to the longer campaign, it expects to retire its debt soon and it has four years to rebuild its finances before the next federal election.

Thomas Mulcair has established a national profile as a strong, serious, and bilingual leader with a compelling personal story. Despite the party's disappointing election results, Mulcair's continued leadership of the party was not internally questioned in the immediate aftermath of the election. It appears that most party members and caucus members were relatively comfortable with the 2015 platform and are not looking for a change in ideological direction.

While the NDP and the labour movement have become much more independent of each over the last two decades, both are now comfortable in their new relationship and the party will likely continue to have the strong support of unions in the form of parallel campaigns on the ground and advertising campaigns that indirectly support the NDP. Indeed, in 2015, the NDP won in thirty-six out of the eighty-eight ridings in English Canada in which the labour movement ran parallel campaigns.

Finally, over the past four years, the NDP's infrastructure and electoral district associations have been built up within Quebec. In 2015, the NDP still retained a base of seats in Quebec along with 25 percent of the popular vote. Undoubtedly, the NDP is better organized in Quebec, more bilingual, and more attuned to Quebec issues than in any previous time in its history. While there are questions remaining about the exact relationship between the labour movement and the NDP in Quebec, the FTQ support did help elect at least one NDP candidate, Karine Trudel, in Jonquière.

For the most part, the regrets expressed by NDP strategists coming out of the 2015 campaign centred around strategic errors as opposed to weaknesses or problems in organization. The party's challenges came in its air game not in its ground game. Perhaps the future challenges for the NDP may be less about organization and more about how to manoeuvre through the tough strategic context that it now faces. Canadian federal politics appears to have returned to a two-and-a-half-party system similar to that which prevailed for most the second half of the twentieth century. In this context, the Liberals and the Conservatives could come to dominate media attention, with the NDP having to fight to be heard. Justin Trudeau is a young and popular leader who has a large reservoir of goodwill on which he can draw after a decade of the Harper Conservatives' rule. Indeed, he seems to be trying to develop a strong emotional connection with Canadian voters based on his personal image and what he calls his new, positive vision of politics. Nonetheless, recent Canadian elections have shown that parties can rebuild quickly after defeats, as the federal Liberals did after their disappointing results in the 2011 federal election. Given the NDP's organizational strengths developed over the last decade, there is little reason for the party to give up hope. Strategies come and go as political dynamics change. On the other hand, solid political organizations, like the one that the NDP has constructed, can take years to build.

## NOTES

1. The information contained in several sections of this chapter was obtained by telephone interviews with NDP officials conducted between November 2, 2015, and December 1, 2015. An agreement was made with those interviewed to publish their names but not to attribute any exact quotations or information to a particular person. The following NDP party officials graciously agreed to be interviewed: Anne McGrath (national campaign director), Karine Fortin (deputy national director), Brad Lavigne (senior campaign adviser), Rebecca Blaikie (campaign director for Quebec), Lucy Watson (national campaign co-ordinator), George Soule (director of media), David Hare (director of operations), Steve Moran (director of debate preparation), Karl Bélanger (deputy lead on leader's tour), Emily Watkins (director of stakeholder relations), Danny Mallett (director of political action for the Canadian Labour Congress), Raoul Gébert (regional director for Mauricie/Lanaudière/Centre du Québec), and Thomas Linner (war room researcher).
2. See Éric Grenier, "Trudeau's Liberals Led in 2014, but What Does 2015 Hold?" CBC News, December 30, 2014, www.cbc.ca/m/touch/news/story/1.2877711.
3. "Andrea Horwath Campaign Leaves Prominent NDP Supporters 'Deeply Distressed,'" CBC News, May 23, 2014, www.cbc.ca/news/canada/toronto/ontario-votes-2014/andrea-horwath-campaign-leaves-prominent-ndp-supporters-deeply-distressed-1.2652766.
4. Forum Research, "NDP Leads in First Post-Writ Poll," August 3, 2015, http://poll.forumresearch.com/post/334/new-democrats-headed-for-solid-minority/.
5. David McGrane, "Election Preparation in the Federal NDP: The Next Campaign Starts the Day After the Last One Ends," in *Permanent Campaigning in Canada*, ed. Alex Marland, Thierry Giasson, and Anna Esselment (Vancouver: UBC Press, forthcoming).
6. Mike Strobel, "Campaign Bonanza of Bozo Eruptions," *Toronto Sun*, September 27, 2015, www.torontosun.com/2015/09/27/campaign-bonanza-of-bozo-eruptions.
7. Lynda Erickson and David Laycock, "Modernization, Incremental Progress, and the Challenge of Relevance: The NDP's 2008 Campaign," in *The Canadian Federal Election of 2008*, ed. Jon Pammett and Christopher Dornan (Toronto: Dundurn, 2009), 98–135; and David Laycock and Lynda Erickson, "Modernizing the Party," in *Re-*

*viving Social Democracy: The Near Death and Surprising Rise of the Federal NDP*, ed. David Laycock and Lynda Erickson (Vancouver: UBC Press, 2015), 84–108.
8. David McGrane, "Political Marketing and the NDP's Historic Breakthrough," in *The Canadian Federal Election of 2011*, ed. Jon Pammett and Christopher Doran (Toronto: Dundurn, 2011), 77–110.
9. QSR International, *NVivo 9 Basics* (Doncaster, Australia: QSR International, 2010), 54.
10. Mulcair stopped at a corn roast in St-Jerome on August 22 where he talked about how the NDP's campaign would be positive. He stopped in Montreal on August 28 where he stated that a New Democratic government would not finance a stadium for the eventual return of the Expos. He stopped on September 3 in Brossard to speak about a policy that he had unveiled earlier in the day in Toronto concerning increasing the GIS for seniors.
11. Mark Burgess, "The Permanent Campaign Meets the 78-Day Campaign, and Falls Apart," in *Canadian Election Analysis 2015: Communication, Strategy, and Democracy*, ed. Alex Marland and Thierry Giasson (Vancouver: UBC Press, 2015), 19.
12. NDP New Release, "Long-Term Investments to Help Families Get Ahead," September 16, 2015.
13. One example was Althia Raj, "Kevin Page: NDP's 'Thin' Fiscal Plan Puts Mulcair on Spot," *Huffington Post*, September 18, 2015, www.huffingtonpost.ca/2015/09/18/kevin-page-ndp-fiscal-mulcair_n_8161864.html.
14. Liberal Party of Canada, "More Economists Blast Flawed NDP Costing," September 21, 2015, www.liberal.ca/more-economists-blast-flawed-ndp-costing/.
15. Stephanie Marin, "Niqab aux cérémonies de citoyenneté: Ottawa ira en Cour supreme," *La Presse*, September 16, 2015,www.lapresse.ca/actualites/justice-et-affaires-criminelles/actualites-judiciaires/201509/16/01-4901016-niqab-aux-ceremonies-de-citoyennete-ottawa-ira-en-cour-supreme.php.
16. Annabelle Blais, "Le Bloc juge «grotesque» d'être comparé au Front national," *La Presse*, September 19, 2015,www.lapresse.ca/actualites/elections-federales/201509/19/01-4902055-le-bloc-juge-grotesque-detre-compare-au-front-national.php.
17. Marie Vastel, "Le niqab devient une arme électorale," *Le Devoir*, September 19, 2015, www.ledevoir.com/politique/canada/450528/le-niqab-devient-une-arme-electorale.
18. Andy Blatchford, "Mulcair Digs in on Niqab Stance, Despite the Fact It Could Cost the NDP Votes in Quebec," *National Post*, September 25, 2015, http://news.nationalpost.com/news/canada/mulcair-digs-in-on-niqab-stance-despite-the-fact-it-could-cost-the-ndp-votes-in-quebec.
19. Pierre-André Normadin, "Niqab: Mulcair accuse ses adversaires d'aller trop loin," September 24, 2015, *La Presse*, www.lapresse.ca/actualites/elections-federales/201509/24/01-4903434-niqab-mulcair-accuse-ses-adversaires-daller-trop-loin.php.
20. CBC, "Tom Mulcair Says Stephen Harper Is 'Weak and Vulnerable' on TPP Talks," August 4, 2015,www.cbc.ca/news/politics/canada-election-2015-tom-mulcair-says-stephen-harper-is-weak-and-vulnerable-on-tpp-talks-1.3178689.

21. Layton's platforms had been titled "New Energy, a Positive Choice" (2004), "Getting Results for People" (2006), "A Prime Minister on Your Family's Side, for a Change" (2008), and "Giving Your Family a Break: Practical First Steps" (2011).
22. Further analysis comparing the 2015 NDP platforms to past platforms of the party can be found in David McGrane, "Ideological Moderation and Professionalization: The NDP Under Jack Layton and Tom Mulcair," in *Canadian Parties in Transition: Recent Evolution and New Paths for Research,* 4th ed., ed. Alain-G. Gagnon and A. Brian Tanguay (Toronto: University of Toronto Press, n.p.).
23. A mix of NDP supporters and left-wing non-NDPers, led by Naomi Klein, did put out a document entitled "The Leap Manifesto" in the middle of September 2015. It called for the complete decarbonization of Canada's economy by 2050, a guaranteed basic income, a national child-care program, and higher taxes on corporations and the wealthy. However, it did not specifically criticize the NDP in any way, nor did it even mention Mulcair and the party. It was aimed more at the electorate as a whole and all Canadian politicians. See www.leapmanifesto.org.
24. Denver McNeney, "Letting the Press Decide? Party Coverage, Media Tone, and Issue Salience in the 2015 Canadian Federal Election Newsprint," in *Canadian Election Analysis 2015: Communication, Strategy, and Democracy*, ed. Alex Marland and Thierry Giasson (Vancouver: UBC Press, 2015), 74–75.
25. From July 1 to September 30, 2015, the NDP raised $9 million, compared to $7.3 million for the Liberals and $10 million for the Conservatives: Canadian Press, "Election 2015 Fundraising Results: Liberals Raised Less Money Than Tories, NDP," October 30, 2015, www.huffingtonpost.ca/2015/10/30/liberals-first-at-ballot-box-but-third-in-fundraising-sweepstakes_n_8434614.html.

# CHAPTER 5

## The Bloc Québécois in a Rainbow-Coloured Quebec

Éric Bélanger and Richard Nadeau

Never before has the Province of Quebec elected ten members of Parliament or more from each of four different political parties in a Canadian federal election. Usually, federal party competition in Quebec is limited to two parties, sometimes three, with one of them clearly dominating the others in terms of seats gained in the province. The Liberal Party of Canada was long the dominating force in Quebec (up until 1980); it was followed in succession by the Progressive Conservative Party (in 1984 and 1988), the Bloc Québécois (between 1993 and 2008), and the New Democratic Party (2011). While in some ways the Liberals can be viewed as having reclaimed their dominant position in the 2015 federal election, three other parties also gained significant representation in Quebec in that same contest. Thus, the province currently offers an exceptional diversity in terms of its party preferences, forming a rainbow made up of four political colours — with red being more prominent than the other three.

From a Quebec viewpoint, how did each of these four parties stand before the start of the 2015 campaign?

The Bloc Québécois came out of the 2011 election almost extinguished. For the first time since its creation, it had lost its official party status in the House of Commons, a development that ushered the sovereigntist party into an entirely new era of its existence. Its Ottawa personnel shrank from the usual sixty to eighty people, including its MPs and a research team of ten persons, down to only seven: four MPs,[1] one part-time researcher, one parliamentary assistant, and one press officer.[2] The Bloc also faced difficulty in getting its message and its positions heard by the media and the public, a situation that the party hadn't experienced since the days between 1990 and its 1993 electoral surge.[3] The party was also leaderless following the resignation of Gilles Duceppe, who had actually lost his seat in the watershed 2011 election.[4] As a result, the four years following would prove to be tough times for the Bloc, something exemplified by the succession of no less than three party leaders over that period.

The first BQ leadership race in that period took place in late 2011. Former Bloc MP Daniel Paillé ended up winning the leadership over two other candidates, sitting MPs Maria Mourani and Jean-François Fortin, with 61 percent of the second-round vote. Around fourteen thousand BQ members — representing a little over a third of the total number of registered party members — took part in the mail-in vote.[5]

Although someone with a lot of experience in politics, Paillé was not well known among the public. Having no seat in Parliament, he turned this situation into an opportunity, spending most of 2012 touring Quebec's regions to meet with Bloc members and voters and start a long rebuilding phase. However, Paillé's tenure came to an abrupt end in December 2013 when health issues forced him to resign.

Another leadership race was held that culminated in the June 2014 selection of Mario Beaulieu over sitting MP André Bellavance. Beaulieu, a radical sovereignty supporter and former French-language activist, proved to be a divisive figure within the BQ ranks. His arrival was followed by the resignations of several high-profile members and staff — including Bellavance and Fortin — and by abysmal numbers in popular polls.[6] Barely a year later and only a couple of months before the start of the federal election campaign, it was announced that Mario Beaulieu was stepping aside from the Bloc leadership and that Gilles Duceppe was coming out of retirement to take the party's reins again in the hopes that the Bloc would remain competitive in the upcoming election.

The BQ's clear competitor entering the 2015 election was the New Democratic Party. The NDP had formed the Official Opposition in 2011 thanks to the Quebec "Orange Wave." Indeed, all of the Bloc's lost seats in 2011 went to the NDP, the result of a shift in Quebecers' party preferences that was attributable to fatigue with the BQ, the ideological proximity between these two parties, and the appeal of then–NDP leader Jack Layton.[7] Soon after the election and Layton's untimely death, Quebec MP Thomas Mulcair became the new leader of the party.

In order to help strengthen the NDP's newly found support base in the province, Mulcair and his parliamentary troops acted quickly to represent and defend issues close to Quebecers' interests. For example, many of the NDP's proposed bills and various policy positions during the first two years of the forty-first Parliament directly involved the protection of the French language in various spheres. These included attempts to require the understanding of French as a criterion in the selection of Supreme Court justices, opposition to the appointment of Michael Ferguson (a unilingual anglophone) as auditor general, a proposal to subject all Quebec-based federal offices to a select number of French language norms, and another, to make bilingualism mandatory for senior public officer positions. The NDP also opposed the Conservatives' budget cuts to the Canadian Broadcasting Corporation (CBC) and its French-language counterpart.

Despite the party's attempts to show itself as a strong advocate for Quebec, there was one issue involving the province that turned out to be a hot potato for the NDP during this period. Possibly in an attempt to paint the NDP into a corner on the question of the recognition of a secessionist vote in Quebec, the Bloc Québécois tabled a bill in fall 2012 (C-457) proposing to repeal the Clarity Act. The debate around this bill thus forced the NDP to take a position on the Clarity Act, or rather to remind everyone of its position as it was stated in the party's 2005 Sherbrooke Declaration.[8] The NDP's reply was to table its own bill (C-470), which restated that position: the NDP would recognize as valid a simple majority vote (50 percent plus one) in favour of secession. The New Democrats' move led the other parties to criticize them: the Liberals vehemently opposed the bill and the Conservatives accused the NDP of being a separatist's nest, while the Bloc underlined that the NDP's position maintained the requirement for a "clear" referendum question — something that, according to the BQ, went against the interests of the Quebec nation and did not respect the autonomy of the Quebec National Assembly.[9] The debate over these two bills actually led one Quebec NDP MP, Claude Patry, to leave his party and join the ranks of the Bloc Québécois. It can be said that the BQ's strategy succeeded in that the NDP's image pertaining to Quebec-centric issues was shaken by this debate, both within and outside Quebec (but for different reasons).

Just as the BQ and the NDP hoped to bolster their support in the province, the Conservative Party of Canada also hoped to make gains in Quebec in 2015. To this end, it is worth noting that four of the five Conservative MPs elected in Quebec in 2011 ended up being appointed to the Harper Cabinet. Most prominent among them were Christian Paradis (first as minister of industry, then as minister of international development and for La Francophonie), and Denis Lebel (as minister of transport, infrastructure, communities and, later, intergovernmental affairs), who was also named as Stephen Harper's Quebec adviser.

During the forty-first Parliament, the Conservative government made regular announcements of investments in the province, and particularly in the Quebec City area, where the Conservative Party's voting base was seen as being stronger. For instance, announcements were made (usually by Denis Lebel and/or Stephen Harper himself) regarding the preservation of Quebec City's Maritime Search and Rescue centre, the construction of the city's covered ice rink, the restoration of the city's historical fortifications and of the Quebec Bridge, and the revitalization of the city of Lévis. However, relationships were more tense between the Conservative government and Montreal's administration, with a notable public dispute erupting over the question of whether to include a toll system on the new Champlain Bridge.[10] During the year that preceded the election campaign, another Conservative government position that stirred controversy in the province was its strong support of TransCanada's Energy East pipeline project, which would transport oil from Alberta to New Brunswick, passing through Quebec's territory.

As for the Liberal Party of Canada, it is clear that the arrival of Justin Trudeau at its head in 2013 helped put the party back on Quebecers' radar screen after several years during which there was a relative lack of interest toward it. For the first time since the spring of 2009, the Liberals were polling first in Quebec federal vote intentions during the months that followed Trudeau's selection as party leader, with numbers hovering around 35 percent — a figure practically identical to the final vote that the party would receive in the province in October 2015.

Right from the start of his tenure as leader, Trudeau frequently addressed himself to Quebecers in his speeches, and he quickly acted to establish good relations with Liberal premier Philippe Couillard after his provincial election win in 2014. During most of the period between the 2011 and 2015 elections, the Liberals also advocated a number of positions on Quebec-centric issues that were very much in line with the NDP's positions, including a focus on the protection of bilingualism and the CBC. One NDP MP from Quebec, Lise St-Denis, decided to join the Liberal Party in January 2012, something that was interpreted as a further sign that the NDP's Quebec base remained fragile despite its 2011 success.

---

The political context in Quebec is a particularly important thing to consider when trying to understand the campaign dynamics and the outcome of the 2015 federal election in that province. Two elements are particularly noteworthy.[11] The first is the return to power of the Liberal Party of Quebec in April 2014 after a brief (nineteen months) interlude of the sovereigntist Parti Québécois (PQ) in government. The PQ had been elected as a minority government in 2012 in the wake of massive protests against the ruling Liberals (a period commonly known as the "Maple Spring"). However, the outcome of the following provincial election confirmed the slow decline of the PQ and its constitutional option; its 25 percent of support in 2014 was the lowest vote share registered by that party since 1973. This result possibly signalled a growing lack of interest in the national question among Quebecers.

The second element is the debate that surrounded the PQ government's "Charter of Quebec Values," proposed in 2013. The most controversial provision in this piece of legislation was the ban on the wearing of religious symbols by all public employees. Many actors within (and outside) Quebec society considered that provision to be unconstitutional, as it was interpreted as an attack on the right to express one's religious beliefs. The charter was never adopted, due to the PQ losing power the following spring; but as will become clear below, the Conservative Party did not shy away from bringing the issue of religious accommodation into the 2015 electoral campaign.

## THE 2015 FEDERAL ELECTION CAMPAIGN IN QUEBEC

The party that had the most to gain in Quebec in the 2015 election was the Bloc Québécois. The BQ began literally fighting for its life: as one of Gilles Duceppe's advisers candidly admitted to *Le Devoir* in the middle of the campaign, "the Bloc was almost dead" at the time Duceppe took over the leadership from Beaulieu at the beginning of the summer.[12]

To face the challenge, Duceppe brought back with him his old team of advisers. The party's return to its former ways was evident from the start of the campaign with the unveiling of the first of two Bloc slogans: "*Qui prend pays prend parti,*" a clever inversion of an old and well-known French-Canadian saying ("You adopt the country of your spouse"). The slogan clearly implied that those Quebecers who were in favour of making Quebec a country should adopt the Bloc, or should remain faithful to it rather than support a federalist party. It was the only slogan used by the party during August, indicating that the BQ's strategy in the first stage of this campaign was to (re)connect with its sovereignist base, or at least to reassure the latter of the party's commitment toward sovereignty.[13]

The rest of the Bloc's campaign would mainly be run on the more general question of the defence of Quebec's interests, starting with the release in the first week of September of the party's second slogan: "*On a tout à gagner*" ("We have everything to gain"). We can note that this strategy was the reverse of the Bloc's 2011 one, when the party ended the campaign with a message centred on sovereignty in an attempt to stop the bleeding of supporters moving over to the NDP.[14] The long 2015 campaign (it lasted over two months) may have benefitted the BQ in that it allowed the party to discuss the sovereignty issue early in the campaign before putting it aside for the remaining stretch. It was important for the party to keep the focus of its later campaign much more on the issue of Quebec's interests since doing so allowed the Bloc to question the NDP's record on that front.

As Figure 5.1 illustrates, at the beginning of September the BQ was still about 28 percentage points behind Thomas Mulcair's party in Quebec voting intentions. Not much had moved in public opinion during August and the *Bloquistes* really needed the NDP to start losing support soon if they were to make any substantial gains by October 19. As the figure also makes clear, the rest of the campaign in Quebec evolved in two stages: a steep decline in NDP vote intentions during September, from which all of the three other main parties benefitted; and a slight gain by the Liberals during October. Thus, the campaign in Quebec very much mirrored that in the rest of the country, with the only difference being that the NDP's decline was more dramatic in Quebec because that province was the 2011 home base of the New Democrats.

**Figure 5.1: Vote Intentions in Quebec Over the 2015 Campaign**

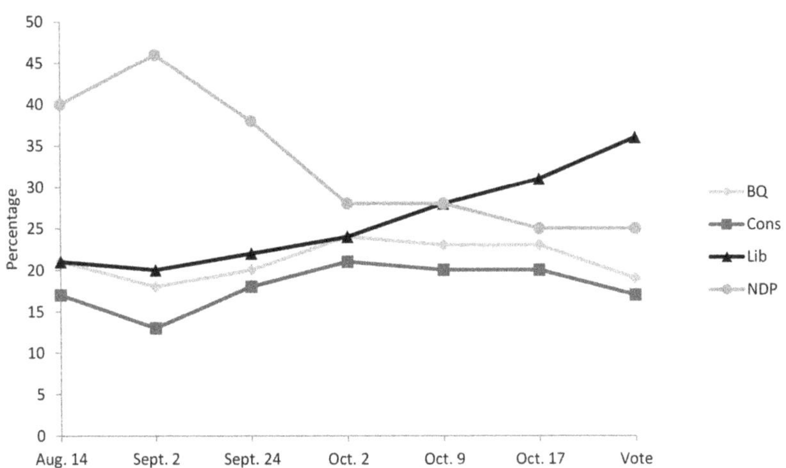


The Bloc wished to make the case that Mulcair and the NDP had not been competent promoters and defenders of Quebec issues and interests in Ottawa and were not in sync with the values of Quebecers. Among other things, two issues served as key pieces of evidence in favour of this interpretation. In August and in the first half of September, Gilles Duceppe took every opportunity he could to criticize the NDP's position on the Energy East pipeline project. Mulcair's view on this project was that it should be embraced for the revenues and the economic development that it would bring to the province, but also that the project should proceed only if it met stricter environmental standards.[15] This was doublespeak, according to Duceppe, and showed that Thomas Mulcair wanted to remain ambivalent so that he could say one thing to Quebecers and another to the rest of Canadians.[16] Duceppe's accusations, fuelled by the ambiguous response from Mulcair, aimed at instilling doubt in the minds of Quebecers about the correspondence between the province's majority opinion on environmental issues (and especially the exploitation of oil resources) and the NDP's position.

The second issue that the Bloc used to further undermine the credibility of the NDP in terms of defending Quebec views in Ottawa was offered to the BQ on a silver platter: it was the Conservative government's decision to challenge the court ruling against the niqab ban at citizenship ceremonies. The Bloc was clearly in favour of the ban proposed by the Conservatives — recall that the 2013 debate over the PQ's Charter of Quebec Values had shown significant support among nationalist Quebecers for the general idea of a ban on religious veils. The Liberals were staunchly against it, which was the expected position coming from a party that had pushed multiculturalism and individual rights for many decades. The New Democrats basically adopted the same position as the Liberal Party on this issue. On September 18, the Bloc decided to highlight the NDP's position on the niqab in a television ad that also recalled Mulcair's stand on Energy East: over an orange background, a pipeline appears. From this, a drop of oil emerges, which transforms itself into a black niqab. While these images are appearing on screen a female voice states, "This is a drop too much; I return to the Bloc."[17]

Following the airing of this ad, Thomas Mulcair spent the next two weeks defending his party's positions on both of these issues. Meanwhile, he was being attacked from all sides, accused again of saying different things in French and English to dupe voters.[18] These two issues notably came up during the first French-language leaders' debate[19] (September 24) as well as in the private network TVA's debate (October 2). It was only on October 4, during his appearance on the Quebec talk show *Tout le monde en parle*, that Mulcair finally clarified his party's stances.[20] He claimed to be personally uncomfortable with the niqab but said that he trusted, and that all Canadians ought to trust, the court's decision on this issue. As for the Energy East pipeline, he took a rather strong stand against it because he argued that it was currently impossible to guarantee the pipeline's safety for the environment due to the Harper government's deregulation in this domain. But these clarifications proved to be too little too late. The damage to Mulcair and his party's credibility was done.[21] Quebec support for the NDP stood at only 28 percent at the beginning of October, barely ahead of the other parties (see Figure 5.1).

With so many Orange Wave voters in Quebec leaving the NDP in the wake of the party's September troubles, the New Democrats had not much chance left of gaining power come October 19. This evolution in Quebec public opinion likely sent a signal to Canadians outside Quebec that the party to back in order to get rid of the Conservative government was the Liberal Party, not the NDP. And once Quebecers saw the Liberals taking flight in the rest of the country, those in Quebec who were seeking the same goal likely started to jump on board the Liberal bandwagon. The Bloc Québécois' strategy thus seems to have had a domino effect: it succeeded in shaking the support base of the NDP in Quebec, which then contributed to a surge in Liberal vote intentions both within and outside of the province.

Of course, the Liberal Party's generally faultless campaign, as well as the relatively good performance of Justin Trudeau in the French-language debates, also helped the Liberals to gain traction in Quebec. The minor faults made, such as Trudeau's funny slip during the second French debate, when he called Duceppe "*mon amour*" (my love), seemed to work in favour of the Liberals, since they showed how relaxed and confident he was. Also important were Trudeau's commitments to reinvest in the CBC and the Canada Council for the Arts,[22] and to reopen the dialogue with the provincial governments, which was a demand made by Quebec premier Couillard to the federal party leaders at the beginning of the campaign.[23] The fact that the NDP's and the Conservatives' attempts at drawing a link between the Dan Gagnier lobbying affair and the sponsorship scandal era[24] — as well as Stephen Harper's efforts at showing with bills and cash register sounds how a Trudeau government would waste taxpayers' money[25] — failed to break the Liberal surge in Quebec illustrates the extent to which many Quebecers had already made up their mind by the last days of the campaign.

To sum up, the dynamics of the federal campaign in Quebec were driven in good part by the Bloc Québécois, but paradoxically the sovereignist party did not really benefit from this situation. The Conservative Party also contributed to the demise of the NDP in Quebec with the introduction of the niqab issue in the campaign; however, Harper's troops gained nothing from it in the end because many Quebecers wanted a change in government. Indeed, as Figure 5.1 shows, the Conservatives remained in fourth place in Quebec throughout this eleven-week-long campaign. That same motivation (i.e., throwing the incumbent out) also helps explain why the Bloc was not viewed as an attractive option either.

The Conservatives' message in the province was focused on convincing Quebecers that their values were "conservative" values (with an emphasis on security and fiscal responsibility)[26] and that their party was the only one that pledged not to intrude on the province's jurisdictions if elected.[27] It seems clear in retrospect that this message did not really take hold. The same can be said of the NDP's promise to balance the federal budget: it clashed with Quebec's progressive constituency, who had just spent the past year protesting against the Couillard government's cost-cutting efforts and who were "suffering from an overdose of government-imposed austerity."[28] It is telling that the NDP's vote intentions in Quebec started to dip the moment Mulcair announced (at the end of August) that he would balance the budget in his first year in office.

## THE 2015 QUEBEC RESULTS IN PERSPECTIVE

Many commentators have used the term "red wave" to describe the performance of the Liberal Party in Quebec during the most recent federal election. However, does this expression accurately reflect reality? Does it account for the party's breakthrough in Quebec and put it into perspective? Do the levels of support received by the other political parties signal some kind of break with previous elections in Quebec? We will discuss these issues using federal election results in Quebec from 1984 to 2015.

## A "Red Wave"?

Is a "red wave" the most appropriate way to refer to the Liberal Party's performance in Quebec on October 19, 2015? It is clear that the progress made by the federal Liberals in Quebec is spectacular, especially when compared to the previous election in 2011. As shown in Table 5.1, the Liberal Party only won 14 percent of Quebec votes and elected seven MPs in that province in 2011. Thus, we can say that support for the Liberal Party of Canada in Quebec jumped over 20 percent under Justin Trudeau and the party increased its number of seats in the province from seven to forty. That being said, this increase is similar in magnitude to how the Liberals performed across all of Canada since the election of 2011: the Liberal vote rose by over 20 percent between these two elections (from 19 percent to 39.5 percent) and the number of elected MPs jumped (from thirty-four to 184 MPs). The Liberal sweep in the Atlantic provinces and the party's sharp increase in Ontario (26 percent to 45 percent; eleven to eighty MPs) put the so-called "Quebec Red Wave" into perspective.

Perhaps the most interesting point of comparison is not geographical, but rather temporal. Table 5.1 shows the results for the Liberal Party of Canada in Quebec since 1984. This starting point is important because these elections followed not only Pierre Elliot Trudeau's departure from politics but also the repatriation of the Constitution in 1982. Several observations emerge from this table. The first is that the Liberal vote in Quebec certainly declined more in the early 1980s than in previous decades, but was far from collapsing. During the six elections that took place between 1984 and 2004, average support for the Liberal Party stood at 35.5 percent, which is very similar to what the party received in 2015 (35.7 percent). Moreover, there were two elections during this period (1997 and 2000) where support for the Liberal Party was higher than the levels seen in 2015, and three others where it was similar to 2015 (in 1984, 1993, and 2004). The last and perhaps most striking observation is that the performance of the Liberal Party in 2015 pales considerably when compared to how the party fared under Jean Chrétien in 2000, when it won no less than 44 percent of the vote in Quebec.

## Table 5.1: Vote Percentages and Number of Seats for Federal Political Parties in Quebec, 1984–2015

| | Liberal | | | Conservative | | | Bloc Québécois | | | NDP | | |
|---|---|---|---|---|---|---|---|---|---|---|---|---|
| Year | Vote % | # Seats | # Seats (PR)* | Vote % | # Seats | #Seats (PR)* | Vote % | # Seats | # Seats (PR)* | Vote % | # Seats | # Seats (PR)* |
| 1984 | 35 | 17 | 28 | 50 | 58 | 40 | - | - | - | 9 | 0 | 7 |
| 1988 | 30 | 12 | 23 | 53 | 63 | 41 | - | - | - | 14 | 0 | 11 |
| 1993 | 33 | 19 | 26 | 14 | 1 | 12 | 49 | 54 | 38 | 2 | 0 | 0 |
| 1997 | 37 | 26 | 29 | 22 | 5 | 17 | 38 | 44 | 29 | 2 | 0 | 0 |
| 2000 | 44 | 36 | 34 | 13** | 0 | 10 | 40 | 38 | 31 | 2 | 0 | 0 |
| 2004 | 34 | 21 | 26 | 9 | 0 | 7 | 49 | 54 | 38 | 5*** | 0 | 4 |
| 2006 | 21 | 13 | 16 | 25 | 10 | 20 | 42 | 51 | 33 | 8 | 0 | 6 |
| 2008 | 24 | 14 | 19 | 22 | 10 | 17 | 38 | 49 | 30 | 12 | 1 | 9 |
| 2011 | 14 | 7 | 11 | 17 | 5 | 13 | 24 | 4 | 18 | 43 | 59 | 33 |
| 2015 | 36 | 40 | 28 | 17 | 12 | 13 | 19 | 10 | 15 | 25 | 16 | 19 |

* To facilitate the comparison of seats won as a function of vote share, the number of Quebec seats for the 2015 election was held constant at 75.

** The votes received by the Canadian Alliance and the Progressive Conservative Party were combined for the 2000 election.

*** Seats under proportional representation were only given to parties having won at least 4 percent of the Quebec vote in a given election.

The data in Table 5.1 also show that support for the Liberal Party declined substantially after 2004 in the wake of the sponsorship scandal. Support for the Liberals was down to 21 percent in 2006, barely increased in 2008 (24 percent), then fell to 14 percent in 2011. The growth in vote share for the party in 2015 seems to mark a return to normalcy, going back to levels of support similar to that of the period from 1984 to 2004. In other words, the rise of the Liberal Party in 2015 seems to have allowed it to offset the damage from the sponsorship scandal, but not return to levels of support similar to what the party enjoyed in Quebec before the repatriation of the Constitution.[29]

How can we explain why so much has been made of this Liberal breakthrough in 2015? We can find an explanation in the distribution of votes between parties and how the first-past-the-post electoral system amplifies these tendencies. For example, during the 1984 and 1988 elections, the Liberals won almost 33 percent of Quebec votes on average, but were up against the Mulroney Conservatives, who received 50 percent of the Quebec votes in 1984 and 53 percent in 1988. From 1993–2004, the Liberal Party maintained and even increased its support, but had to contend with the Bloc Québécois, which won 44 percent of the Quebec vote on average during this period. The case of the 2000 election is striking. The Liberal Party won 44 percent of the votes and outperformed the Bloc, which received 40 percent, but the Liberals managed to elect two fewer members than the BQ (thirty-six versus thirty-eight) due to Liberal support being concentrated in the Montreal West Island and Outaouais constituencies in particular. BQ dominance would continue in 2006 and 2008, prior to the Orange Wave election in 2011. Thus, the 2015 election breaks with all previous elections over the past thirty years, because the Liberal Party benefitted from the demise of its opponents. Between 1984 and 2011, the Liberal Party's main opponent never won less than 38 percent of the province's votes. In 2015, however, its most serious rival, the NDP, only received 25 percent of the Quebec vote.

In 2015, the fracturing of the vote among the opponents of the Liberals, along with the vagaries of the first-past-the-post electoral system, helped to allow the Liberals to regain a significant number of seats in Quebec, a fact that helped to popularize the interpretation of the Liberals coasting to a spectacular victory in Quebec. The third column in Table 5.1, however, puts things into perspective. It shows the distribution of seats in Quebec between 1984 and 2015 under a hypothetical proportional electoral system. These figures show that on average the Liberal Party would have won twenty-eight seats out of seventy-five between 1984 and 2004, with a peak of thirty-three seats in 2000. The Liberals also would have averaged fifteen seats between 2006 and 2011. However, the number of seats that the Liberals would have won under proportional representation in the 2015 election (twenty-eight) is similar to what the party would have averaged between 1984 and 2004 under John Turner, Jean Chrétien, and Paul Martin. This detail clearly illustrates the need to put the Red Wave in Quebec into historical perspective.

## Stability of the Conservative Vote

During the most recent election, the Conservative Party won 17 percent of the Quebec vote and elected twelve MPs in the province. Interestingly, the Conservatives received roughly the same percentage of votes during the 2011 election, but only managed to elect five MPs, mainly due to the NDP's strong performance. Several observers have noted the exceptional nature of the results for the Conservative Party in Quebec in 2015. Its ability to maintain similar levels of support and elect a greater number of MPs, given a political context in which support for the party declined by more than 7 percentage points across Canada (39.5 percent in 2011 to 32 percent in 2015) and its parliamentary caucus numbers melted from 166 to 99 MPs. In fact, Quebec was the only province where the Conservative Party did better in 2015 than in 2011, both in terms of popular support (16.7 percent versus 16.5 percent) and number of MPs elected (twelve versus five).

How does the 2015 performance of the Conservatives in Quebec stack up against its results over the past thirty years? Once again, the results in Table 5.1 are informative. They show that, excluding the exceptional 1984 and 1988 elections, the Conservatives' vote share averaged around 17 percent of the Quebec vote between 1993 and 2011. Thus, the party's performance in 2015 was very much a story of attracting the "normal vote" that the Conservatives ordinarily win in Quebec, at least since 1993. In fact, this stability of the Conservative vote is something that has been maintained over an even longer period of time. With the exception of the 1958 election, when the Conservative Party won 50 percent of the Quebec votes, Conservative support averaged 18 percent in the province between 1963 and 1980, practically identical to the average for the 1993–2015 period.

Table 5.1 also shows that the electoral system and the performance of competitor parties help explain the fluctuations in Quebec Conservative representation in the Canadian House of Commons. While the 1984 and 1988 elections, in which the Progressive Conservative Party elected fifty-eight and sixty-three MPs respectively, stand out — the Quebecer Brian Mulroney led the Progressive Conservative Party in those elections — we see that, more recently, the number of Quebec Conservative MPs varied between zero (2000 and 2004) and twelve (in 2015). It is noteworthy that this record crop of Quebec Conservative MPs in the post-Mulroney period happened in an election where support for the Conservatives in the province was less than it had been in 2008 (22 percent), 1997 (22 percent), and especially in 2006, when Harper's "open federalism" had won over 25 percent of Quebecers.[30] The latter result can be explained by the fact that the growth of the Conservatives in 2006 coincided with a good performance of the BQ (42 percent of the Quebec vote and fifty-one MPs), which resulted in limiting Quebec's Conservative representation to ten MPs.

A re-reading of the Conservative Party's performance in Quebec assuming proportional representation is instructive. The Conservatives would have elected a majority of Quebec MPs in the elections of 1984 and 1988 (forty and forty-one MPs, respectively), and averaged about fourteen MPs thereafter. Under this assumption, the best results for the Conservative Party would have been in 2006 with twenty MPs, and not in 2015, which would have been a rather average election for the Conservatives in Quebec in terms of parliamentary representation. Beyond the fluctuations resulting from the electoral system, the stability of the Conservative vote in Quebec is clear.

## Bloc Québécois Vote in Decline

At first glance, the Bloc Québécois' performance in 2015 may seem paradoxical. The party won 19 percent of the Quebec vote, which is actually the lowest level of support for a sovereignist party in Quebec since the founding of the Parti Québécois in 1968. However, by taking advantage of vote splitting and tapping into concentrations of support in some areas, the Bloc succeeded in electing ten MPs. This contrasts with the 2011 election, where the party only elected four MPs despite winning 23 percent of the vote in Quebec. That being said, the data in Table 5.1 clearly show that the 2015 election is a continuation of a downward trend already apparent in the 2011 outcome. Between 1993 and 2008, support for the Bloc Québécois averaged 43 percent, which ensured that party an average representation of forty-eight MPs in the House of Commons. However, mean support for the BQ in 2011 and 2015 was 21 percent and its average representation was seven MPs (see Table 5.1).

The contrast between the performance of the Bloc in the 1993–2008 elections and those of 2011 and 2015 could not be greater. Admittedly, support for the BQ fluctuated during the first period, peaking when circumstances were favourable to the party (in 1993 with Lucien Bouchard as party leader and in 2004 during the sponsorship scandal) and plummeting during more difficult campaigns (such as in 1997 and 2008). That being said, support for the Bloc Québécois was never lower than 38 percent during this period. The fall in support to 23 percent in 2011 and 19 percent in 2015 signals a significant realignment of Quebecers' voting preferences at the federal level.

The data in Table 5.1 illustrate this decline and how the 2015 election emphasizes this trend. Assuming proportional representation in the House of Commons, the Bloc Québécois would have had an average of thirty-three MPs (out of seventy-five) during the 1993–2008 period. This number would have dropped to eighteen in 2011 and then to fifteen in 2015. The trend is clear and it seems hard to imagine that it can be reversed in the foreseeable future.

## Surge and Decline of the NDP

The case of the NDP is unique. Before the Orange Wave in 2011, support for the party in Quebec had always been limited. For example, between 1962 and 1980, the NDP averaged 7 percent of the vote in the province. Interestingly, this also corresponds to the party's average vote percentages from 1984 to 2008. In this context, it is not surprising that parliamentary representation of the NDP in Quebec was marginal before 2011. Victories by Phil Edmonston in 1990 in a by-election in Chambly and Thomas Mulcair in another by-election in Outremont in 2007 (and again in the 2008 federal election) are the exceptions in a history of repeated failures for NDP candidates in Quebec.

However, it is also interesting to note that support for the NDP in Quebec has nonetheless tended to vary over time. A first success was seen in 1965, when the NDP won 12 percent of the vote in the province. The party peaked at 14 percent of the popular vote in 1988 before collapsing to 2 percent in the 1993, 1997, and 2000 federal elections. Such variations in support can be explained by the influence of such factors as having strong personalities representing the NDP in Quebec (Robert Cliche in the 1960s, John Paul Harney in the 1980s, Thomas Mulcair from 2007 on), a lack of enthusiasm for the Liberal and Conservative parties (as in 1965 and 2008), and a stalling sovereigntist movement (as in the 1980s). That being said, the NDP surge in 2011, both in terms of support (from 12 percent to 43 percent) and seats (from one to fifty-nine), remains surprising, not only because of its magnitude[31] but also because of its unforeseen nature. Of course, an electoral system with proportional representation would have made the 2011 results seem somewhat less exceptional. As shown in Table 5.1, although a PR system would have given the NDP at times symbolic parliamentary representation (as in 2000), at other times such a system would have resulted in the party having a more significant presence in the House of Commons (as in 1988 and 2008). Having said that, it must be admitted that the almost total absence of parliamentary representation for the NDP in Quebec before 2011 almost certainly hindered the party's ability to become more popular in the province, which makes the fifty-nine seats won under the leadership of Jack Layton in 2011 even more spectacular.

The NDP's performance in Quebec in the current election, however, seems paradoxical. On the one hand, there was a significant drop in support for the party (43 percent to 25 percent) and its parliamentary representation fell (from fifty-nine to sixteen members) between 2011 and 2015. But it was also the party's second-best showing in Quebec during a federal election. This fact makes it difficult to speculate about the future performance of the NDP in the province. Some may look at the fact that the NDP is the second largest party in Quebec in terms of popular support and parliamentary representation and read that as a sign of the party's resilience and proof that the party can count on a fairly solid base in the province. Others may see a parallel between support for the Conservative Party in Quebec between 1958 and 1962 and what the future might have in store for the NDP. The Conservatives won 50 percent of the popular vote in Quebec in 1958 before falling back to 30 percent and then settling into an average of 17 percent over the next two decades.

## CONCLUSION: BETWEEN CONTINUITY AND CHANGE

The 2015 Canadian federal election in Quebec is being characterized as an election dominated by change. Many interpretations of the election focus on the gains made by the Liberal Party. On first glance, it would seem that Quebec was swept away by a Red Wave that replaced the 2011 Orange Wave, somehow marking the return of the Liberal Party in Quebec after decades of electoral drought.

In some ways, this characterization does indeed reflect reality. The 2015 election is the first since 1980 in which the Liberal Party finished as the largest party, both in terms of vote share and number of MPs. Compared to its closest competitor, the NDP, the Liberals won 36 percent of the Quebec vote (versus the NDP's 25 percent) and elected forty MPs (versus the NDP's 16). However, putting this election into perspective, we see that the vote share received by the Liberals in Quebec was actually far from spectacular. In fact, it was almost exactly the same as the average vote share that the Liberal Party won in Quebec between 1984 and 2011 (35.5 percent), and well below the 44 percent that the Liberals won in 2000 under the leadership of Jean Chrétien. The complete "rehabilitation" of the

Liberal Party in Quebec is far from over. The 2015 election seems to have allowed the party to erase its previous setbacks that were brought about due to the sponsorship scandal and bring support back to what it was after the repatriation of the Constitution. It remains to be seen over the next few years, however, if the performance of the Trudeau government will allow the Liberal Party to go past this threshold.

The support received by the Conservative Party in 2015 is another manifestation of stability in Quebec electoral behaviour. With some clear exceptions in 1958, 1984, and 1988, the Conservative Party usually receives between 15 percent and 20 percent of the Quebec votes. The 2015 election was no exception to this trend. In fact, not only was the Conservative vote share in Quebec similar to what it won in 2011, but it also corresponds to the average vote share that the party has received in the province between 1993 and 2011. Therefore, it seems that there is a stable, although limited, core of support for the Conservatives in Quebec.[32]

The 2015 election also confirmed the decline of the Bloc Québécois, despite the fact that it increased its representation in Ottawa from four to ten MPs. The party's vote share in the most recent election (19 percent) was even smaller than in 2011 (23 percent), and was the poorest performance for a sovereigntist party in Quebec since the founding of the Parti Québécois in 1968. The sovereignist movement can find some solace in the fact that the BQ's parliamentary caucus increased in number and the party did not completely collapse as was feared prior to the return of Duceppe as leader. However, the number of Bloc MPs is still insufficient to obtain official party status and Gilles Duceppe's resignation (for the second time in a row) deprives the party of an energetic leader and effective debater. What is more, one can note that seven of the ten Bloc MPs were elected with only a third of the constituency vote or less, and their election was mainly attributable to the split between the NDP and the Liberals. Therefore, without a resurgence in sovereignty support or the emergence of a new popular leader — two conditions that currently seem unlikely to be met, at least in the short term — it seems difficult to imagine the Bloc Québécois coming back to prominence in the coming years.[33] Those curious about the future of the Bloc should turn their attention to the upcoming 2018 Quebec provincial election.

A Parti Québécois victory in that election could increase the relevance of the Bloc in Ottawa and put the party in a better position for the 2019 federal election. On the other hand, a Parti Québécois defeat could be fatal for the future of the Bloc Québécois.

Just as in 2011, the NDP's performance in Quebec in 2015 constituted the most unpredictable part of the electoral dynamics in the province. The volatility of the NDP's support was evident not only when comparing the results of the two elections but also when looking at the campaigns themselves. In 2011, the NDP began far behind the BQ, but eventually came from behind to decisively beat them. The opposite happened in 2015. The NDP started the campaign with a seemingly insurmountable lead in Quebec before falling far behind the Liberal Party. This volatility of the NDP vote in Quebec both between and during election campaigns is revealing but makes any prediction about its future difficult. That said, three factors could influence the future success of the NDP in Quebec: The first factor is the future of the Bloc Québécois, which is linked to the outcome of the 2018 Quebec provincial election, as was just mentioned. The Bloc's collapse could allow the NDP to continue benefitting from the support of progressive voters who either voted for the Bloc before or continued to vote for the Bloc. A BQ resurgence would be problematic for the NDP. A second factor is linked to the performance of the Trudeau government. A more complete reconciliation between the Liberal Party of Canada and the Quebec electorate could help erode support for the NDP in Quebec. Finally, the third factor is related to the NDP's national situation and the future of Thomas Mulcair. His departure as party leader would mean that three of the four biggest political parties from the most recent federal election would be led by new leaders by 2019. Due to a greater willingness of voters to base their electoral decision on short-term factors such as the leaders' images and the issues that come up during campaigns, new BQ, Conservative, and (possibly) NDP leaders could be a game-changer for the 2019 federal election.

## NOTES

We thank Gaby González-Sirois and Chris Chhim for their helpful assistance in preparing this chapter.

1. André Bellavance, Jean-François Fortin, Maria Mourani, and Louis Plamondon.
2. Canadian Press, "Maria Mourani garde le cap," *La Presse*, August 29, 2011, A11.
3. Malorie Beauchemin, "Bilan de session du Bloc québécois: 'Ça donne un choc,' dit le doyen du parti," *La Presse*, June 27, 2011, A8.
4. MP Louis Plamondon acted as the Bloc's interim leader until December 2011.
5. Guillaume Bourgault-Côté, "À Paillé de relancer le Bloc," *Le Devoir*, December 12, 2011, A1.
6. Media reports indicate that a BQ internal poll conducted in the spring of 2015 showed only 16 percent support for the party under Beaulieu's leadership, whereas that support nearly doubled once Duceppe was named as the party's possible new leader. See Michel Corbeil, "Retour de Duceppe: Beaulieu a lui-même entrepris les démarches," *Le Soleil*, June 10, 2015, www.lapresse.ca/le-soleil/actualites/politique/201506/09/01-4876726-retour-de-duceppe-beaulieu-a-lui-meme-entrepris-les-demarches.php.
7. See Patrick Fournier, Fred Cutler, Stuart Soroka, Dietlind Stolle, and Éric Bélanger, "Riding the Orange Wave: Leadership, Values, Issues, and the 2011 Canadian Election," *Canadian Journal of Political Science* 46, no. 4 (2013): 863–97; Éric Bélanger and Richard Nadeau, "The Bloc Québécois: Capsized by the Orange Wave," in *The Canadian Federal Election of 2011*, ed. Jon H. Pammett and Christopher Dornan (Toronto: Dundurn, 2011), 111–37.
8. See Policy Committee of the NDP (Quebec Section), *Quebec's Voice and a Choice for a Different Canada: Federalism, Social-Democracy and the Quebec Question*, New Democratic Party orientation document, October 2005.
9. Hugo de Grandpré, "Le NPD veut clarifier la loi sur la clarté," *La Presse*, January 28, 2013, www.lapresse.ca/actualites/politique/politique-canadienne/201301/28/01-4615835-le-npd-veut-clarifier-la-loi-sur-la-clarte.php; Martin Croteau, "Claude Patry quitte le NPD et passe au Bloc québécois," *La Presse*, February 28, 2013, www.lapresse.ca/actualites/politique/politique-canadienne/201302/28/01-4626393-claude-patry-quitte-le-npd-et-passe-au-bloc-quebecois.php.
10. Daniel Leblanc and Les Perreaux, "Ottawa's Plans for a Toll on Champlain Bridge Draw Criticism in Quebec," *Globe and Mail*, May 18, 2014, www.theglobeandmail.com/news/politics/quebeckers-pan-champlain-toll/article18742103/.
11. For more details, see Éric Bélanger and Eva Falk Pedersen, "The 2012 Provincial Election in Quebec," *Canadian Political Science Review* 8, no. 1 (2014): 141–49; Éric Bélanger and Eva Falk Pedersen, "The 2014 Provincial Election in Quebec," *Canadian Political Science Review* 9, no. 2 (2015): 112–20.
12. Guillaume Bourgault-Côté, "L'immense défi de Duceppe," *Le Devoir*, September 8, 2015, www.ledevoir.com/politique/canada/449523/l-immense-defi-de-duceppe.
13. It is worth noting that a sizable number of Bloc candidates in this election were recruited from among the ranks of the provincial Option Nationale party, a

marginal hard-core sovereignist party. See Philippe Teisceira-Lessard, "Option nationale investit le Bloc," *La Presse*, August 5, 2015, www.lapresse.ca/actualites/elections-federales/201508/04/01-4890423-option-nationale-investit-le-bloc.php.

14. Bélanger and Nadeau, "The Bloc Québécois: Capsized by the Orange Wave," 124–26.
15. Martin Ouellet, "Mulcair exprime son préjugé favorable pour Énergie Est," *La Presse Canadienne*, August 12, 2015.
16. Louis-Samuel Perron, "Énergie Est: Duceppe critique la position de Mulcair," *La Presse*, August 13, 2015, www.lapresse.ca/actualites/elections-federales/201508/13/01-4892546-energie-est-duceppe-critique-la-position-de-mulcair.php.
17. This BQ ad can be viewed online at www.youtube.com/watch?v=lVE-N-htzKs.
18. Mulcair's personal credibility was further damaged by press stories, recuperated by the three other party leaders, that reported quotes from his time as a member of the Quebec National Assembly. These old quotes, which showed Mulcair praising Thatcherism in the United Kingdom and being in favour of (or at least not being sufficiently against) the privatization of Mont Orford in Quebec, were interpreted as evidence of a lack of ideological consistency on his part on matters of state intervention and environmentalism. See Joël-Denis Bellavance, "Mulcair hanté par une déclaration sur les politiques économiques de Thatcher," *La Presse*, August 19, 2015, www.lapresse.ca/actualites/elections-federales/201508/19/01-4893719-mulcair-hante-par-une-declaration-sur-les-politiques-economiques-de-thatcher.php; Marie-Michèle Sioui, "Privatisation d'Orford: Mulcair attaqué de toutes parts," *La Presse*, September 20, 2015, www.lapresse.ca/actualites/elections-federales/201509/20/01-4902190-privatisation-dorford-mulcair-attaque-de-toutes-parts.php.
19. Chantal Hébert, "Harper Escapes Bruising as Rivals Take Out Each Other," *Toronto Star*, September 25, 2015, http://startouch.thestar.com/screens/b5055b80-8549-420d-83f6-0d7ec16348ee%7CEhQdcVfd1PAv.html.
20. Marie-Michèle Sioui, "Mulcair 'inconfortable' avec le port du niqab," *La Presse*, October 5, 2015, www.lapresse.ca/actualites/elections-federales/201510/05/01-4906596-mulcair-inconfortable-avec-le-port-du-niqab.php; Marie Vastel, "Mulcair dit qu'il 'étudierait' le projet Énergie Est," *Le Devoir*, October 5, 2015, www.ledevoir.com/politique/canada/451759/tout-le-monde-en-parle-mulcair-dit-qu-il-etudierait-le-projet-energie-est.
21. Chantal Hébert, "The NDP's Quebec Problems Didn't Start with the Niqab," *Toronto Star*, October 1, 2015, http://startouch.thestar.com/screens/bde3ab53-5254-4835-9407-65aa2734b6de%7ChIEf6Ne7szLl.html.
22. Pierre-André Normandin, "Harper a été 'un adversaire de la culture', accuse Trudeau," *La Presse*, September 22, 2015, www.lapresse.ca/actualites/elections-federales/201509/22/01-4902845-harper-a-ete-un-adversaire-de-la-culture-accuse-trudeau.php.
23. Joël-Denis Bellavance, "Trudeau favorable à plusieurs demandes du Québec," *La Presse*, August 22, 2015, www.lapresse.ca/actualites/elections-federales/201508/21/01-4894532-trudeau-favorable-a-plusieurs-demandes-du-quebec.php.
24. Martin Croteau and Pierre-André Normandin, "Harper et Mulcair ravivent le spectre du scandale des commandites," *La Presse*, October 17, 2015, www.lapresse.

ca/actualites/elections-federales/201510/15/01-4910198-harper-et-mulcair-ravivent-le-spectre-du-scandale-des-commandites.php.

25. Isabelle Porter, "Dernier arrêt pour reconquérir Québec," *Le Devoir*, October 5, 2015, www.ledevoir.com/politique/canada/452862/dernier-arret-pour-reconquerir-quebec.
26. Marco Fortier, "Stephen Harper met de l'avant ses 'valeurs québécoises,'" *Le Devoir*, October 16, 2015, www.ledevoir.com/politique/canada/452774/stephen-harper-met-de-l-avant-ses-valeurs-quebecoises.
27. Joël-Denis Bellavance, "Lettre à Couillard: Harper vante son 'fédéralisme d'ouverture,'" *La Presse*, September 19, 2015, www.lapresse.ca/actualites/elections-federales/201509/18/01-4901986-lettre-a-couillard-harper-vante-son-federalisme-douverture.php.
28. Hébert, "The NDP's Quebec Problems Didn't Start with the Niqab."
29. Recall that the Liberal Party performed exceptionally well in Quebec in 1980, winning 68 percent of the vote and electing 74 out of 75 MPs. From 1957 to 1979, average support for the Liberal Party stood at 50 percent in Quebec, with its lowest score being at 39 percent in 1962 due to the breakthrough of the Ralliement des Créditistes under Réal Caouette.
30. See Éric Bélanger and Richard Nadeau, "The Bloc Québécois: A Sour-Tasting Victory," in *The Canadian Federal Election of 2006*, ed. Jon H. Pammett and Christopher Dornan (Toronto: Dundurn, 2006), 122–42; Adela Gotz, "Open Federalism and the 2006 Federal Election in Quebec: Did Quebecers Accept the Olive Branch?" (M.A. thesis, McGill University, 2009).
31. It should be noted that the Conservative surge in Quebec in 1984 was even more spectacular, with a gain of 37 percentage points (from 13 percent to 50 percent) and the election of fifty-eight MPs (compared with just one in 1980). The fall of the party between 1988 and 1993 was commensurate with these gains (decrease of support from 53 percent to 14 percent and reduction of parliamentary representation from sixty-three MPs to a single MP). The rise of the Bloc Québécois is no less spectacular. In 1988, this previously non-existent party received over 49 percent of the Quebec vote and elected fifty-four MPs in 1993. However, in both cases, either public-opinion polls or by-elections (e.g., the 1990 by-election victory of Gilles Duceppe in the riding of Laurier–Sainte-Marie) hinted at these surges.
32. See Andrea Lawlor and Éric Bélanger, "The Blue Electorate in Quebec and Support for the ADQ and the CPC," in *Conservatism in Canada*, ed. James Farney and David Rayside (Toronto: University of Toronto Press, 2013), 293–316.
33. Chantal Hébert, "Election Vote in Quebec Should Cause Renewed Worry in Sovereigntist Ranks," *Toronto Star*, October 30, 2015, www.thestar.com/news/canada/2015/10/30/election-vote-in-quebec-should-cause-renewed-worry-in-sovereigntist-ranks.html; Michel David, "Le lent déclin," *Le Devoir*, October 22, 2015, www.ledevoir.com/politique/quebec/453258/le-lent-declin.

## CHAPTER 6

# Opportunities and Obstacles: The Green Party of Canada's 2015 Campaign

Susan Harada

Not long after the news media projected a Liberal majority on election night, the Green Party's national tour director, Debra Eindiguer, knew the time had come to connect the Greens' Elizabeth May with the Liberals' Justin Trudeau. She arranged a phone call through Trudeau's scheduling assistant. With Liberal celebrations audible in the background, the two leaders had a quick, thirty-second exchange — "Congratulations, congratulations. Looking forward to working with you" — and then the conversation was over, Eindiguer said.[1]

She then followed up with a request for a face-to-face meeting between May and Prime Minister–Designate Trudeau — and that is how it came to be that the Greens' best election news was generated three days after their campaign ended, when May sat down with Trudeau in Ottawa. She used the twenty-five-minute opportunity to, among other things, successfully offer her services to the Liberal-led Canadian delegation heading to the United Nations' climate change conference in Paris (COP21) at the end of November.

The Liberals' inclusion of May on the Canadian COP21 team was a return to the pre-Harper era practice of inviting the opposition.[2] It was also, for the Greens, a signal that their sole member of Parliament might not be sidelined altogether in the forty-second Parliament. Cut back down to "party of one" status in the House, the Greens' best hopes for immediate post-election relevance were pinned to public acknowledgement of May's expertise on the climate change file. As a veteran of climate conferences, May felt that she was likely "the closest thing they have to institutional memory. So by being on the inside, assuming our government wants to do the right thing and get the best possible treaty, my role is to help make that happen by working the networks I have."[3]

On the one hand, inclusion was the chance for May and the Greens to showcase their value as players with global connections who could help Canada make a meaningful contribution while repairing its damaged international environmental reputation. On the other hand, it underscored the political reality that being just one on a long list of high-profile Canadian delegates — from the prime minister to the premiers on down — increased the odds they would be overshadowed. Thus the Greens' COP21 inclusion was, writ smaller, the story of their campaign 2015: unprecedented opportunities competing with significant obstacles.

From the outset of the campaign, a number of elements were aligned in the Greens' favour. The desire for change after ten years of the Harper government, coupled with the long campaign, provided an opening for the Greens to use the long weeks to spread their "doing politics differently" message. They had more resources than ever before — MPs,[4] money — and a claim on the climate file at a time when Canadians were paying attention to environmental issues. There was a flip side to all of this, of course. Their biggest opportunity presented their biggest potential obstacle: a deep desire for change could strategically push aside their party, which had lost popular support in 2011, in favour of a major party with a realistic chance of defeating the Conservatives and forming a government. And even a long writ period was no guarantee their message would get out, a factor that could seriously hamper the Greens at a time when their political rivals were also staking claims on environmental issues. So, these were the competing possibilities the Greens faced as they stared down the eleven weeks to election day: a set of conditions that could either propel them forward in a meaningful way, or make for an electoral journey that would not necessarily be easy, nor end well.

## OPPORTUNITIES LOST

In spite of the opportunities, the election delivered little for the Greens to feel good about as a political party. Their singular achievement was handily retaining May's seat in Saanich-Gulf Islands. She took 54.4 percent of the popular vote, increasing her margin of victory over the second-place Conservatives; it jumped from 10.6 percent in 2011 to an historic 34.9 — the widest margin since the riding's creation in 1988. Her win was no surprise. Since becoming the Greens' first elected MP, she had single-handedly kept herself and her party in mainstream media headlines on a range of issues, racking up numerous honours — best parliamentarian, hardest working MP, best orator — in the process.[5] The party had built a strong local organization when it first set out to get her elected back in 2011, and had kept it going, according to May's co-campaign manager Jocelyn Gifford, in anticipation of the next campaign. "We've been planning for a long time for this," she said, the goal being to "take our strength in Saanich-Gulf Islands and spread it out to other ridings where we can elect Greens."[6]

It was a solid strategy, but the Greens were surprised and dismayed by their inability to turn it into solid results. There is often a gap between the optimistic goals released publicly when a campaign begins and the actual achievements evident once the electoral dust settles, but the Greens' 2015 goals-versus-reality gap was enormous, and telling. At the outset they were aiming for official party status — a minimum of twelve seats — according to Eindiguer. If not that, then at the very least the party hoped to win enough seats to hold the balance of power in what they figured would be a minority Parliament. They were counting on May and the high-profile candidates they had brought on board to deliver seats — especially in British Columbia, but also in parts of Ontario, Quebec, and New Brunswick.[7]

None of this materialized. Not only did the Greens fail to send another MP to Ottawa alongside May, the party's popular vote was sliced in half, from the high-water mark of 6.8 percent (nearly one million votes) set in 2008 down to 3.4 percent (approximately 600,000 votes) — and this in an election that saw voter turnout go up by approximately 7 percent.[8] Only nine of the 336 Green candidates on the ballot logged at least 10 percent of the vote in their individual ridings, the percentage required for a candidate to be reimbursed for campaign expenses: six were in British Columbia, two in Ontario, and one in New Brunswick. This was a slight improvement from the seven in 2011, but well below the forty-one candidates who finished with at least 10 percent in 2008. Only one Green candidate managed a second place finish in 2015. Jo-Ann Roberts, the well-known former CBC Radio host who ran in Victoria, won 32.9 percent of the vote, approximately 10 percent behind the NDP incumbent. Four Green candidates finished a distant third.[9]

By the time election day arrived, May said she knew the Greens' chances were down to two Vancouver Island candidates — Roberts and Paul Manly, a filmmaker and small-business owner in the nearby Nanaimo-Ladysmith riding. Even so, it was "crushing" to watch the results roll in on election night in Victoria with her fellow Greens. According to Eindiguer, people had poured their hearts into running what she believed was the Greens' most professional campaign effort to date. "We had the best staff, the best candidates, more know-how than ever, more money than ever," she said. "I don't know what we could have done differently to elect anyone because we really did do our damnedest. [But] we could not control those variables."

Those variables included hurdles the party has faced in previous elections, and all were tied to its smaller party status: May's exclusion from three of the five leaders' debates; a scaled-back national leader's tour, minus the bells and whistles — the campaign plane, the press corps — that are an integral part of other party leaders' tours; and mainstream media headlines that largely focused on the race between the major parties, not the Greens.

There were also some new impediments. Since 2004, the per-vote subsidy introduced by the Liberal government of the day had provided concrete incentive for Canadians to vote Green; the party's message was that even under the first-past-the-post system no vote was wasted because each one put money directly into its coffers.[10] With the phase-out of the subsidy after the first quarter of 2015, that could no longer be a selling point to attract voters. This was especially problematic during a campaign that saw the Greens caught in the crossfire when strategic voting became a major issue.

There were well-publicized strategic voting initiatives to oust the Harper Conservatives, such as the one spearheaded by the organization Leadnow,[11] along with attendant calls for strategic voting at the expense of the Greens, some of which even came from B.C.-based environmental activists.[12] It contributed to the construction of a narrative that numerous Green candidates encountered right to the end. In Victoria, for example, where based on past voting patterns it was highly unlikely a Green vote would inadvertently elect a Conservative, Roberts ran headlong into the strategic voting push. "People were coming up to us the day of the election saying, 'We love everything you're doing and we believe in your whole platform but we voted for the New Democrats,'" she said. "And they'd say, 'We had to vote strategically, we'll vote for you next time.'"[13]

It was the same story for Claire Martin, the former CBC meteorologist running in North Vancouver: "At the door I was hearing, 'I want to vote for you but I can't, I'm too scared of splitting the vote.'"[14] Mark Brooks in Ottawa West-Nepean discovered the same thing from the voters he encountered: "There is a strong mood out there for change and people are telling me that they would love to vote Green but in this particular election they're going to support the candidate who they think has the best chance of winning."[15]

And those three were by no means the only Green candidates who got that message from voters.

After plunging into the 2015 campaign with such high hopes, and running a tight, professional operation during the writ period, the Greens were once again left grappling with their failure to grow as a national party. They have been on the federal ballot since 1984 — ten general elections over the span of thirty-one years — without making significant inroads, and the issue of their future viability has gained more urgency during their post-election soul-searching, especially given the downward trajectory they have been tracing nationally since 2008.

## THE GREEN SURGE

Following Elizabeth May's historic 2011 win on Vancouver Island, the party set about to rack up more points in the political relevance ledger. It showcased its leader; it began taking electoral steps forward at the regional level in some parts of the country; and it strengthened its fundraising and membership base in the Canadian version of the "Green Surge" that the Green Party of England and Wales experienced in 2014.[16]

Weighing in on issues ranging from Bill C-51 to the Truth and Reconciliation Commission report,[17] May worked both as an MP to try to build a credible profile for herself[18] and as a party leader to try to demonstrate that the Greens were not simply a single-issue environmental party. Her mission was reinforced by a number of Green successes.

In the November 2012 federal by-elections, the Green candidate in Victoria finished a tantalizingly close second, just 1,118 votes behind New Democrat Murray Rankin. Held by the NDP since 2006 and by the Liberals in the eighteen years prior, Victoria had never delivered more than approximately 11 percent of the vote to the Greens since they started running candidates there in 1984. Vaulting to 34.3 percent in that by-election buoyed the party, as did the result of the other 2012 by-election, in Calgary Centre.[19] Although the Greens finished third behind the Conservatives and Liberals there, they more than doubled their percentage of the vote in the process.[20]

And then came some real wins, not just close finishes and popular vote gains. The volatile 2013 provincial election in British Columbia produced some surprising results, including the election of the province's first Green MLA. What began as a close three-way race in Oak Bay-Gordon Head, a riding whose boundaries overlapped part of May's federal district, ended with climate scientist Andrew Weaver overtaking both the long-time Liberal incumbent and the NDP candidate; he increased the Greens' popular vote by more than 30 percent in the process.[21]

A year later, there was another first: voters in the newly created riding of Fredericton South in New Brunswick sent provincial Green Party leader David Coon to the legislature after a campaign that thrust the shale gas industry front and centre as a major issue.[22] And a scant three months before the 2015 federal campaign began, yet another Green made history, this time during the general election in P.E.I., when provincial party leader Peter Bevan-Baker won Kellys Cross-Cumberland with 54.8 percent of the vote, nearly double that of the second-place Liberal incumbent. The P.E.I. Greens had parlayed government accountability issues and riding-level environmental concerns over the realignment of the Trans-Canada Highway into a tightly focused campaign. Only ten years after their designation as an official party, the Greens successfully elected their first MLA.[23]

The provincial wins were punctuated by historic Green victories at the municipal level also. On the heels of May's 2011 breakthrough victory, the federal party's former deputy leader, Adriane Carr, narrowly won a seat on Vancouver's municipal council, running under the local Green Party banner — the first big city councillor in Canada to do so.[24] When she repeated the feat in 2014, she significantly increased her vote share, finishing ahead of her nine fellow council members. She also brought Green Party of Vancouver members with her: two Greens were elected as Park Board commissioners and one was elected as a school trustee.[25]

Along with the party's electoral successes provincially and municipally came growing success in fundraising and a longer list of paid-up party members. Fundraising became particularly important for the Greens after the Conservative government announced it would phase out the per-vote subsidy that had kept the Greens afloat since 2004. After receiving approximately $12.6 million over the decade, the Greens were concerned that the phase-out, combined with their shrunken popular vote in the 2011 election, spelled potential financial disaster. Out of necessity, they sharpened their fundraising efforts, and, like the larger parties, implemented an approach that combined targeted appeals with small but specific goals: a $15 donation to help the Greens combat the Harper government's budget; $5 to hit a looming end-of-year fundraising target; $5 to ensure the Greens' voice wouldn't be drowned out by the other parties' attack ads. The strategy struck a chord. Contributions grew from some $1.7 million in 2012 to $3 million in 2014. In 2014 alone, the number of individual contributors jumped from approximately 9,500 to 24,000. Nearly $3.5 million came in during the first three quarters of 2015; $2 million of that was raised during the writ period.[26]

Just as significant was the growth in paid-up party memberships. After years of being stuck at the twelve-thousand-member mark, even with May ensconced in the House, the party finally cracked through what deputy executive director Craig Cantin called its perpetual glass ceiling.[27] They had twenty thousand signed-up party members by the end of the 2015 campaign. Small change, compared to other parties — the Liberals, for example, claimed three hundred thousand as of December 2014[28] — but still, significant for the Greens.

They sharpened their strategy too, moving from a general "negative opt-out" membership approach to targeted appeals. According to Cantin, those who donated without buying a membership at the same time would be emailed every few months. "We did a Valentine's one, for example, that said, 'You like us. We like you. Let's make it official, become a member,'" he said. "Because they had already given a donation, they could just click this button and they would become a member."

These were the small but telling details of the new approach the party adopted — marks of a growing professionalism that resulted in more successful membership and fundraising campaigns. That, combined with the highest-profile leader they had ever had and visible electoral success at the regional level across the country, fuelled the party's sense of optimism as it headed into the 2015 national campaign.

## THE NATIONAL CAMPAIGN

Only a political party that has struggled for so long to establish a meaningful role for itself would enjoy the symbolic significance of the wallet-sized card on a lanyard that became de rigueur at national headquarters during the campaign. For the first time, the Greens had so many people toiling in their main office that party-issued ID cards — complete with logo, the bearer's photo, and name — were the only way to keep track of them all. They had come a long way from the small basement apartment in Montreal, where former leader Jim Harris's campaign staff often held strategy sessions. Now, a decade later, the lanyard-wearing Green team spilled across two large chunks of office space in downtown Ottawa — the dividing wall torn down to accommodate their info and call centres, along with the digital, fundraising, social media, and communications units. The number of national staff ballooned from the core of fourteen the year prior to 160 by August. An energy that had not been present in 2011 was palpable at party headquarters, even weeks into the exhaustingly long writ period.

According to executive director Emily McMillan, the 2015 campaign showed the difference between working for a party that had never won a seat and working for a party with three previously elected candidates on the ballot. "We've shifted from just wanting to get the issues on the table to realizing how much influence we can actually have if we get some people elected," she said. "We have candidates who are being very serious about their campaigns. They're raising money, they're hiring staff, they're doing a real campaign."[29]

The $4.5 million campaign strategy involved a number of strands: the focusing of resources on specific ridings; the establishment of a professional electoral toolbox and provision of some support for the non-targeted ridings; the use of social media to promote May and to reach as many Canadians as possible; and a full slate of candidates across the country.

The first strand was a larger-scale version of the "Saanich strategy" that had helped elect May in 2011 — select strong candidates, plant them in places with potential for growth, and add the financial and human resources. To that end, they identified fourteen ridings on which to focus. This included eight in British Columbia — five on Vancouver Island (excluding May's riding, which did not need extra support) and three in the Lower Mainland. There were two in Ontario (Thunder Bay-Superior North and Guelph), three in Quebec, and one in New Brunswick (Fredericton). According to McMillan, each of what they called their "focused" ridings received central funding in the order of $100,000, along with campaign directors hired by the national party.

The focused ridings also benefitted the most from the Greens' new electoral system, called "G-Vote," which they developed to replace their older, more limited system. With G-Vote, the Greens hoped to better identify their vote, get that vote out on election day, organize volunteers, and organize sign requests. According to Cantin, the prime mover behind G-Vote, the Greens had just begun to think about using demographic data in 2015, even though other political parties had been using it for some time. "Just the same as when I got in here around 2007 — a lot of people in the party weren't convinced yet on the benefits of knocking on doors," he said. "So it's a learning curve and we're further up the learning curve but we're not right there yet."

Not having reliable voter information banks at the party's disposal automatically put Green campaigns at a disadvantage. In Victoria, Roberts said her campaign was unable to effectively capitalize on the party's growth in the 2012 by-election. "The sign war is a huge part of the campaign and so we wanted to know who had taken signs in 2012 so that we could contact them first to see if they wanted signs in this campaign," she said. But they were hampered by the lack of trustworthy data because G-Vote wasn't fully up and running in time.

Even so, the Greens pressed ahead with deploying their limited range of demographic data. According to Cantin, the labour-intensive nature of working with the data sets available to them meant that they were only able to provide the more detailed information on a consistent basis to the focused ridings. Candidates running elsewhere could access the G-Vote system but only for logistical matters such as organizing volunteers and tracking their electioneering efforts throughout the riding.

The same pecking order was applied to other aspects of campaign support, such as the provision of brochures. Focused ridings could expect to receive them; requests from the others were not automatically accommodated, because much depended on available resources. For the most part, the second strand of the strategy involving national party support for the majority of the local campaigns was "non-monetary" and included such things as brochure and website templates, fundraising advice, talking points, and policy backgrounders. According to McMillan, it was a question of setting strategic priorities for the short term while keeping an eye on the future. "Even though we may not win in other parts of the country, we will want to support those candidates' long-term building."

The third strategic strand involved utilizing digital elements and ensuring social media played a key role in the overall campaign. For the first time, the Greens had a digital director in place, as well as a social media director heading a team that regularly employed Facebook, Twitter, YouTube, Instagram, and live streaming via Periscope to spread the word when there were announcements and events. Their most high-profile use of Twitter came during the leaders' debates. Although May was invited to the English-language debate hosted by *Maclean's* and the French-language debate hosted by the traditional consortium of news organizations, she was locked out of the *Globe and Mail*, Quebecor, and foreign policy Munk debates. Undeterred, she held parallel events. While the *Globe* debate unfolded in Calgary, May played to her live audience in Victoria as well as to her virtual one. She weighed in with answers as if she were standing beside her opponents, speaking directly to the camera and tweeting out nearly two dozen short video clips that were eventually retweeted 11,750 times.[30] She weighed in via Twitter again during the Munk debate,[31] and showed her social media savvy during the one French-language debate she took part in. As the leaders moved into place on the debate set, May shot a sideways glance at the camera and flashed a peace sign. The video of what became known as her "super sassy peace sign" was looped and retweeted, becoming a social media hit.[32]

The Greens' use of all the social media tools at their disposal to create space for May often helped get the attention of the mainstream media, which did not cover the party regularly. It also bolstered her presence during a campaign that once again featured a curtailed national leader's tour. In 2011, with her own future as well as the party's on the line after her two unsuccessful bids for a seat, she only ventured out of her riding twice to campaign for the party in other areas of the country.[33] In 2015, with her seat considered safe,[34] she made nine short forays out of British Columbia, looping through a handful of ridings — mainly the focused ones — in Ontario, Quebec, Nova Scotia, and New Brunswick. The rest of the time she stuck close to home, campaigning for the most part with the candidates running in focused ridings on Vancouver Island and the Lower Mainland.

Putting the B.C.-based Green leader on the road mainly on the West Coast was a smart strategic move to boost candidates in the focused ridings in British Columbia but did little to garner headlines about the Greens in the rest of the country. May thought that if they played it differently — went into Manitoba, Alberta, and Newfoundland and Labrador, for example — her trips would have earned national media; however, given the party's grassroots structure and emphasis on consensus, as leader she could not unilaterally call the shots on the national campaign.[35] In the case of where to dispatch her, the campaign team made a different decision. "I'm not blaming anybody," May said, post-election. "This was my opinion. I might have been wrong. There's no way to know whether it would have made any difference."

Given the number of issues that dominated campaign coverage, such as the plight of Syrian refugees and the niqab controversy, it was difficult for May and the Greens to win attention. She felt that even the release of the party's platform was a tough sell in the mainstream media. Based on the Greens' foundational policy document, *Vision Green*, the platform presented a range of ideas, underscoring the party's message that it was not a single-issue organization. A few planks, such as free post-secondary tuition for domestic students, were new. Some, such as the national pharmacare program, were carried over from the 2011 platform. Other 2011 ideas were amended: the Greens adjusted their proposed carbon tax, for example, from $50/ton of greenhouse gases (GHGs) rising to $60/ton over three years to a different pricing structure of $30/ton over three years.[36]

Finally, the party ran nearly a full slate of candidates across Canada, falling two short of 338. Approximately sixty-five of them — 19.5 percent — were "paper" candidates, including May's daughter Cate Burton, who was listed as the candidate for Berthier-Maskinongé in Quebec. May's campaign co-managers in Saanich-Gulf Islands, Jocelyn Gifford and Marilyn Redivo, were also listed in Quebec ridings. Stacey Leadbetter, the Ontario representative on the party's federal council and also the campaign manager in Whitby, offered to stand as the paper candidate in the nearby Durham riding when she learned the only likely option was to find somebody from British Columbia. She participated in Durham's local debates and built a web presence three days before election day but that was the extent of her campaigning.[37] Rounding out the slate with paper candidates fortified the party's claim — at least on the books — to being a national party deserving of national party treatment, such as a spot in the leaders' debates and more attention in the mainstream media. Here again, May says the full slate was not her position going into the election, but others in the party were committed to running in every riding, "to the extent that people I respect and people on staff that we needed in the election were prepared to quit if I didn't support [it]."

May had also argued that the Green Party should move unilaterally after she was unable to persuade the NDP and Liberals to endorse a "one time only" agreement to defeat the Conservatives. If the Greens, on their own, identified a handful of ridings where not running a Green candidate would benefit the NDP or Liberals, she figured the gesture would resonate with Canadians. In turn, Canadians might then trust her assurances that voting for Greens who were in a position to win — such as Roberts in Victoria — would not inadvertently keep Stephen Harper in office. She was once more in the minority on this. "I wasn't the only one, but it didn't carry the day," she said. "And the argument on the counter side is it's a democracy … if our local members want to have a candidate and we want to make sure Canadians get to express their preference that they want to vote Green, then we have to have candidates in every riding."

The flip side of allowing the grassroots to decide whether they should run a candidate is allowing them to decide whether they should not run one. That is what played out in the B.C. riding of Kelowna-Lake Country, when the Greens' local electoral district association (EDA) made the controversial decision that its candidate would step down and work with the Liberal candidate to defeat the Conservatives.[38] It was a gamble. The riding's combined Green-Liberal vote in the previous two elections was nowhere close to that of the Conservative incumbent, and both times the Greens had finished fourth with no more than 13.7 percent.

According to the Green Party's president, Dave Bagler, the party's federal council voted to allow May to stickhandle Kelowna-Lake Country at her request.[39] After much debate, the Green candidate withdrew and the Greens did not replace him on the ballot. At the same time, Bagler said, the local organization also agreed to not endorse the Liberal, who went on to win the riding with a 7 percent margin. "It was such a struggle to protect the Kelowna-Lake Country decision," May said. "So the most I could do was protect what I regarded as their grassroots decision that they weren't running a candidate. And even that, that was a really big struggle for one seat."

The dissension over whether or how to embrace co-operation with other parties in order to defeat the Harper Conservatives — and how to label such efforts — harkens back to the strategic voting controversy that dogged May during the 2008 campaign. Following news stories that reported that she said she would rather see no Green MPs and a Harper loss than Green MPs in a Harper-led Parliament, May took heat internally and externally. Her words were interpreted as encouragement to vote strategically. The party finally issued a number of statements denying she was endorsing strategic voting at the expense of the Greens, but many felt that the damage had been done, a view that was seen as being confirmed by the results at the ballot box.[40] Questioned later about the sentiment she had expressed in 2008, May stated, "I would still say that. I mean, you have to be a Canadian first."

## THE WEST COAST CAMPAIGN

When Jo-Ann Roberts announced she would be stepping down from her post at the CBC in Victoria, she had no intention of running for office. But it wasn't long before the long-time journalist and popular radio host was approached by both May and the Liberals. After considering both, she opted for the Greens in early 2015. The party's stands on issues around climate change and democratic renewal appealed to her. In short order, she became the party's culture and heritage critic as well as the candidate for Victoria, where she lived, and began her pre-election campaign.

As has been the case in the past, British Columbia was where the Greens consistently polled the highest leading up to the election.[41] Although their national numbers ranged between 2 and 9.6 per cent in early 2015, they began the year at 17 percent in British Columbia in at least one poll[42] and were averaging approximately 13 percent in that province through the spring.[43] As the Greens' deputy national campaign manager, Paul Noble, noted, the party had strong West Coast ties. Originally from British Columbia, Noble left his job as May's legislative assistant in Ottawa to set up the West Coast campaign in August 2014. "The prioritization of environmental issues on the West Coast is higher than anywhere else in the country," he said. "So obviously that plays to our strong suit."[44]

Noble set up shop on the upper floor of a building in downtown Victoria. His first hire was a West Coast campaign coordinator, and he built on that, eventually assembling a regional team of seven people, each responsible for one specialized file, such as West Coast canvassing coordination, West Coast communications, and West Coast volunteer coordination. These regional team leaders trained their counterparts working on the same files for the local campaigns in the focused ridings. Even in the province with the greatest Green electoral success, the party's infrastructure was still at the nascent stage in comparison to its political rivals.

Lining up strong candidates was a priority task spearheaded by May. She worked over a number of years to find high-profile Canadians, "people whose personal reputation was stronger than the Green Party's reputation, basically." Another of her goals was to put strong women in the ridings where the Greens had the best chances. Her sales pitch? Being a Green MP would not mean having to toe the party line: "you are there to work for your constituents; you decide how you're going to vote." Approximately half of the people she approached said yes. In the end, 39 percent of the party's candidates were women, a percentage of female candidates second only to the NDP.[45] Of the Greens' fourteen focused ridings, six had women candidates, and five of those women ran in British Columbia, in ridings with mixed potential for Green growth.

In fact, a close look at all eight of the ridings the Greens focused on in British Columbia provides a snapshot of stellar candidates — journalists, scientists, community activists, business people — who faced uphill battles, especially in a campaign marked by strategic voting initiatives. Five ridings were new, carved out of areas dominated by the NDP and Conservatives in 2011, with Green support at the time averaging about 6 percent. Four years later, by mid-campaign in 2015, polls showed their support had grown — just slightly, but enough that some critics questioned the wisdom of running strong Green candidates in "unwinnable ridings,"[46] given the prospect at that point of a split vote.

In Victoria, where the Greens were the most competitive, they were 5–7 percent behind the NDP when the election was called. Their internal polling showed they had shaved that to 1 percent some ten days out, according to Roberts. With the resignation of the Liberal candidate at the end of September,[47] it was a two-way race locally. But as the dynamics of the larger political campaign unfolded and the Liberals began trending upward nationally, her campaign's mistake, Roberts said, was not being nimble enough to leverage this trend in order to change the strategic voting narrative that had taken hold in Victoria. "What we didn't realize is that not everyone reads the polls the way we read them. Not everybody was going, 'The New Dems are done, the New Dems are done,'" she said. In the meantime, "they [the New Democrats] were [still] handing out flyers … that said a vote for the Greens is a vote for Harper."

Nearby in Nanaimo-Ladysmith, internal polling showed candidate Paul Manly in second place and closing the gap with the NDP, according to campaign manager Ilan Goldenblatt,[48] while external polling showed them in third.[49] Speaking two days before the vote, Goldenblatt said the campaign's momentum was evident through its fundraising success

($105,000 at that point), the number of volunteers (nearly 400), the number of bumper stickers and lawn signs flying out the door (2,250), and the social media hits (94,834 views of Manly's Facebook posts in the week prior). In the Lower Mainland riding of North Vancouver, candidate Claire Martin was not feeling as optimistic. She said she knew going in that her redrawn riding was a long shot, and then toward the end of September their internal polling started to drop off. "There was definitely a Liberal swing," she said. "You could tell it on the streets when you spoke to people. We all felt it."

Martin's riding changed hands, from Conservative to overwhelmingly Liberal, and while she increased the Greens' vote share by 3 percent over 2011, finishing third, the 8.3 percent of the vote she won left her 48 percentage points behind the front-runner. Her results were in line with the other Greens in the focused Lower Mainland ridings: in Burnaby-North Seymour and West Vancouver-Sunshine Coast-Sea to Sky Country, the Greens also finished well behind the first-place Liberals. Nanaimo-Ladysmith played out a little differently, with only 14 percentage points separating the NDP (33.2), Liberals (23.5), Conservatives (23.4) and Greens (19.8). Apart from May's riding, the most significant Green gains came in the newly drawn Vancouver Island ridings. Each of the candidates increased the Greens' popular vote share when compared to corresponding 2011 results, although not nearly enough. Ultimately, all five of the focused ridings on the Island went to the NDP.

## THE ROAD AHEAD

Since the election, May has not slowed down. She has been trying to connect with as many Cabinet ministers as she can to talk about issues she feels are urgent. On the morning I met with her, she was fresh from a forty-five-minute meeting with the new environment and climate change minister, Catherine McKenna, in which they discussed the looming COP21 meeting as well as other Green concerns connected to parks and environmental assessments. Then it was lunch on the run — a cafeteria selection of crackers, cheese, and dip — before this interview, followed by more meetings, including one with a school group from Vancouver Island coming through on a tour of the nation's capital. In other words, life has returned to normal for May as she picks up her constituency and parliamentary duties where she left off before the election was called.

Elsewhere, Green Party members and former candidates are attempting to determine what lies ahead for the Greens in Canada. And this is where their perennial push-pull between political movement versus party, and what direction they should attempt to grow in, comes into play.

Party president Dave Bagler announced his resignation three weeks after the election. "There [were] some campaign decisions that were made that didn't sit [well] with me," he said. "That's not necessarily a bad thing; it's just that I'm likely no longer in sync with the GPC on everything, and certainly not to the extent necessary to be an effective president."

According to federal council representative Stacey Leadbetter, after thirty years, the Greens must do some soul-searching. "It's time for a shakedown," she said. "I know there are some in the party who say it's great — we did really well, we got our policy out here.… I'm like, we lost. We maintained a seat. That to me is not a victory. I'm not overly happy about the outcome of this election."

The fundamental questions now being raised internally circle back to the fact that the Green Party is still a small party with limited resources playing on the national political stage. "You can't pretend you're a big party," said Green vice-president Don Scott. "You have to be more strategic … pick your areas on which you focus."[50]

To that end, Jo-Ann Roberts, for one, wondered whether it would have been wiser to scale right back, perhaps pour all the energy and resources into the five West Coast ridings with the most promise toward the end. "Or should you, for example, not try and run a national campaign and run a B.C. campaign," she said. "Those are bigger questions and ones I hope the party will discuss."

At the back of everyone's mind is the tantalizing "what if" question about electoral reform. What if the Liberal government actually delivers on its promise to change the first-past-the-post system before the next federal election? It would be an unparalleled opportunity for Green growth; at the same time, a new system could also present obstacles. By Fair Vote Canada's basic calculations, the Greens' 3.4 percent of the national vote translates proportionately into eleven seats,[51] but other electoral systems could garner less favourable results for them.

An alternative voting system, which involves voters ranking all the candidates in their riding in order of preference, favours parties that are acceptable as second as well as first choices — and according to late-campaign polls, the Greens were well behind the Liberals and NDP as a second-choice party.[52] Moreover, mapping that polling data onto the 2015 results in the Greens' strongest ridings shows the others would likely still come out on top under the same conditions with the assistance of Green supporters; Greens are divided fairly evenly between those who would rank the Liberals second and those who would choose the NDP.

They would not necessarily fare any better with a system such as Germany's, which only gives parties with more than 5 percent of the vote a proportional share of seats;[53] the Canadian Greens did not meet that threshold in the previous two elections.

Regardless of whether or not Canada's voting system is reformed, the Greens will need to work hard to maintain their claim to being the political party that most effectively champions a holistic approach to environmental stewardship while embracing a philosophy of governmental transparency and accountability. The Liberals have already signalled their intent to be the government of change, one that will move in substantial ways on climate issues and democratic governance. May, who has spent years tilting at the Harper government's policies on those very issues, is undeterred. "I'll be doing the same job I've always done," she said. That job is representing her constituents, holding the government to account, and commending it if it does well. "We're the anti-party party."

That may be. The question is, is it enough to compel Canadians to pay attention to what the Greens have to say, to continue to donate money now that the Harper government has been vanquished, to commit deeply enough to keep investing in party memberships, and to vote for it four years down the road in numbers sufficient to boost its political presence? How the Greens answer it will determine whether they are finally able to plot their own course as a party, or whether they will remain poised on the edge of political relevance, forever subject to external forces beyond their control.

## NOTES

My sincere thanks to all Green Party members and staff, past and present, who took the time to share their experiences and knowledge of the party and its operations with respect to the 2015 federal election.

1. Debra Eindiguer, interview with author, November 5, 2015. Unless otherwise indicated, all quotes from Eindiguer are from this interview.
2. See, for example, Joan Bryden, "'Inclusive' Trudeau Invites Elizabeth May, Other Party Leaders to Paris Climate Change Summit," *National Post*, October 24, 2015, http://news.nationalpost.com/news/canada/inclusive-trudeau-invites-elizabeth-may-other-party-leaders-to-paris-climate-change-summit; and Sonya Bell, "Opposition absence from Durban delegation reflects new majority: Kent," *i*Politics, December 6, 2011. http://ipolitics.ca/2011/12/06/opposition-absence-from-durban-delegation-reflects-new-majority-kent/.
3. Elizabeth May, interview with author, November 16, 2015. Unless otherwise indicated, all quotes from May are from this interview.
4. As well as May, the party's deputy leader, Bruce Hyer, ran again. Hyer was elected as an NDP MP in Thunder Bay-Superior North in 2008 and 2011, and joined the Greens in 2013. See, for example, Susana Mas, "Thunder Bay MP Bruce Hyer Joins Green Party, Doubles Caucus," CBC News, December 13, 2013, www.cbc.ca/news/politics/thunder-bay-mp-bruce-hyer-joins-green-party-doubles-caucus-1.2462983. Another former NDP MP, José Núñez-Melo, ran for the Greens in Quebec. See, for example, "Former NDP MP Jose Nunez-Melo to Run for Greens in Quebec," CBC News, August 16, 2015, www.cbc.ca/news/politics/former-ndp-mp-jose-nunez-melo-to-run-for-greens-in-quebec-1.3192736.
5. Green Party of Canada, "Elizabeth's Story," www.greenparty.ca/en/meet-elizabeth.
6. Jocelyn Gifford, telephone interview with author, October 13, 2015. Unless otherwise indicated, all quotes from Gifford are from this interview.
7. Debra Eindiguer, interview with author, September 2, 2015.
8. In 2011, the Greens won 3.9 percent of the vote (approximately 570,000 votes). While the number of votes they won in 2015 increased due to better voter turnout, their percentage share decreased.
9. All data is from the Elections Canada website: www.elections.ca/home.aspx.
10. Susan Harada, "The 'Others': A Quest for Credibility," in *The Canadian General Election of 2004*, ed. Jon H. Pammett and Christopher Dornan (Toronto: Dundurn, 2004).
11. See the Leadnow campaign entitled "Vote Together" at www.votetogether.ca.
12. See, for example, Justine Hunter, "Environmentalists Turn Away from Greens to Support 'Anybody But Harper' Campaign," *Globe and Mail*, October 15, 2015, www.theglobeandmail.com/news/british-columbia/environmentalists-turn-away-from-greens-to-support-anybody-but-harper-campaign/article26836997/.
13. Jo-Ann Roberts, telephone interview with author, November 13, 2015. Unless otherwise indicated, all quotes from Roberts are from this interview.

14. Claire Martin, telephone interview with author, October 29, 2015. Unless otherwise indicated, all quotes from Martin are from this interview.
15. Roger Smith, "Vote 2015 — Ottawa West-Nepean," *Campaign Politics*, www.cpac.ca/en/digital-archives/?search=Ottawa+West+Nepean.
16. See, for example, John Harris, "The Green Surge: Is This the Party That Will Decide the Election?", *Guardian*, January 21, 2015, www.theguardian.com/politics/2015/jan/21/green-surge-party-that-will-decide-election. It should be noted that the surge did not translate into Green electoral gains in May 2015. See, for example, Peter Walker, "Greens Fail to Add to Single Seat Despite Highest-Ever Share of Vote," *Guardian*, May 8, 2015, www.theguardian.com/politics/2015/may/08/green-party-uk-election-highest-ever-share-vote-caroline-lucas.
17. See, for example, Canadian Press, "Green Party Leader to Present Five Dozen Amendments to Anti-Terrorism Bill," *Maclean's*, March 30, 2015, www.macleans.ca/politics/ottawa/green-party-leader-to-present-five-dozen-amendments-to-anti-terrorism-bill/; and "For the record: Political leaders on residential schools," *Maclean's*, June 2, 2015, www.macleans.ca/politics/for-the-record-political-leaders-on-residential-schools/.
18. Susan Harada, "House Rules: Can the Green Party's Elizabeth May Rescue Democracy in Canada?", *The Walrus*, May 2012.
19. There were fifteen federal by-elections between 2012 and 2014. Of those, the Greens did well in two, won an average 3.5 percent of the vote in eleven, and did not run candidates in two. As noted by Feigert and Norris, by-election successes in Canada have historically been built on "transient support" in a system characterized by "stable dealignment" that can benefit minor parties. Frank B. Feigert and Pippa Norris, "Do By-Elections Constitute Referenda? A Four-Country Comparison," *Legislative Studies Quarterly* 15, no. 2 (May 1990): 183–200.
20. All data is from the Elections Canada website. See www.elections.ca/content.aspx?section=ele&document=index&dir=pas/2012b/59035&lang=e and www.elections.ca/content.aspx?section=ele&document=index&dir=pas/2012b/48006&lang=e.
21. See, for example, "B.C.'s Greens Win First Provincial Seat," CBC News, April 7, 2015, www.cbc.ca/news/canada/british-columbia/b-c-s-greens-win-first-provincial-seat-1.1322651.
22. See, for example, Jane Taber, "How the New Brunswick Green Leader Made His 'Historic' Win," *Globe and Mail*, September 23 2014, www.theglobeandmail.com/news/politics/how-the-new-brunswick-green-leader-made-his-historic-win/article20738635/; and Daniel McHardie, "New Brunswick Election: Party Leaders Focus on Jobs, Shale Gas in Debate," CBC News, September 22, 2014, www.cbc.ca/news/canada/new-brunswick/new-brunswick-election-party-leaders-focus-on-jobs-shale-gas-in-debate-1.2761028.
23. See, for example, "Green Party Leader Peter Bevan-Baker Makes P.E.I. Political History," CBC News, May 5, 2015, www.cbc.ca/news/elections/prince-edward-island-votes/green-party-leader-peter-bevan-baker-makes-p-e-i-political-history-1.3060491.
24. Former Green Party national deputy leader David Chernushenko was elected to Ottawa City Council in 2010 but did not run under the Green Party banner. Similarly, former Green Party national president John Streicker was elected to Whitehorse City Council in 2012 but not under the Green banner.

25. See Carr results at "Official Results of the 2014 Civic Election," City of Vancouver, http://vancouver.ca/election/results.aspx;. and Wendy Stueck and Pauline Holdsworth, "Green Party of Vancouver Grows in Power Despite One Win on Council," *Globe and Mail*, November 17, 2014.
26. Information provided by the Green Party of Canada.
27. Craig Cantin, interview with author, September 17, 2015. Unless otherwise indicated, all quotes and information from Cantin are from this interview.
28. Adrian Wyld, "Liberal Party Says Membership Numbers Have Skyrocketed Under Trudeau," CTV News, December 10 2014, www.ctvnews.ca/politics/liberal-party-says-membership-numbers-have-skyrocketed-under-trudeau-1.2142400.
29. Emily McMillan, interview with author, September 22, 2015. Unless otherwise indicated, all quotes and information from McMillan are from this interview.
30. Cindy E. Harnett, "Not Invited to Debate, May Unleashes Volley of Tweets from Victoria," *Times Colonist*, September 17, 2015, www.timescolonist.com/news/local/not-invited-to-debate-may-unleashes-volley-of-tweets-from-victoria-1.2062489; and "See Elizabeth May's Tweets and Videos from Thursday Night's Debate," *Times Colonist*, September 17, 2015, www.timescolonist.com/see-elizabeth-may-s-tweets-and-videos-from-thursday-night-s-debate-1.2062513.
31. "Elizabeth May, Again Excluded, Tweets Her Way into Munk Debate Conversation," CBC News, September 29, 2015, www.cbc.ca/news/politics/canada-election-2015-munk-debate-green-party-elizabeth-may-tweets-1.3248026.
32. Craig Silverman, "People Can't Stop Watching This Vine of Elizabeth May Dropping a Peace Sign," BuzzFeed News, September 25 2015, www.buzzfeed.com/craigsilverman/sassy-elizabeth-may-won-the-debate#.inp5wmwzB.
33. Susan Harada, "Party of One: Elizabeth May's Campaign Breakthrough," in *The Canadian Federal Election of 2011*, ed. Jon H. Pammett and Christopher Dornan (Toronto: Dundurn, 2011), 139–66.
34. See, for example, Dogwood Initiative, http://votebc.dogwoodinitiative.org/saanichgulf_islands; and VoteTogether, https://www.votetogether.ca/riding/59027/saanichgulf-islands/.
35. The national campaign manager leads the overall effort, and reports to the Greens' federal council, which, among other things, sets the budget. As leader, May is a member of council.
36. See, for example, Seth Klein, "Some Strengths and Weaknesses in the Green Party Platform," Canadian Centre for Policy Alternatives, September 18, 2015, http://behindthenumbers.ca/2015/09/18/some-strengths-and-weaknesses-in-the-green-party-platform/; Kathleen Harris, "Green Party Platform Promises to Expand Rail, Eliminate Tuition," CBC News, September 9, 2015, www.cbc.ca/news/politics/canada-election-2015-green-party-platform-1.3220976; and Sunny Dhillon, "Green Party Pushes for Sustainable Jobs, Climate Plan in Platform," *Globe and Mail*, September 9, 2015, www.theglobeandmail.com/news/politics/green-party-unveils-platform-pledging-infrastructure-cash-housing-and-no-deficit/article26279348/.
37. Stacey Leadbetter, telephone interview with author, November 16, 2015. Unless otherwise indicated, all quotes and information from Leadbetter are from this interview.
38. See the July 16, July 17, and July 20, 2015, posts on the *Kelowna-Lake Country* Facebook site at www.facebook.com/KelownaGreenPartyCanada?fref=nt.

39. Dave Bagler, telephone interview with author, November 17, 2015. Unless otherwise indicated, all quotes and information from Bagler are from this interview. He announced his resignation to council on November 8, effective November 22, 2015.
40. Susan Harada, "The Promise of May: The Green Party of Canada's Campaign 2008," in *The Canadian Federal Election of 2008*, ed. Jon H. Pammett and Christopher Dornan (Toronto: Dundurn, 2009), 162–93.
41. See, for example, Éric Grenier, "February 2015 Federal Polling Averages," ThreeHundredEight.com, March 9, 2015, www.threehundredeight.com/2015/03/february-2015-federal-polling-averages.html.
42. "Landscape Frozen as We Enter Election Year," EKOS Politics, www.ekospolitics.com/index.php/2015/01/landscape-frozen-as-we-enter-election-year/.
43. See, for example, Éric Grenier, "March 2015 Federal Polling Averages," ThreeHundredEight.com, April 17, 2015, www.threehundredeight.com/search?updated-max=2015-04-21T10:15:00-04:00&max-results=6&reverse-paginate=true&start=6&by-date=false; and Éric Grenier, "April 2015 Federal Polling Averages," ThreeHundredEight.com, May 11, 2015, www.threehundredeight.com/search?updated-max=2015-05-13T10:00:00-04:00&max-results=6&start=66&by-date=false.
44. Paul Noble, telephone interview with author, September 16, 2015. Unless otherwise indicated, all quotes and information from Noble are from this interview.
45. Joan Bryden, "Canada Election 2015: Number of Female Candidates Goes Up Since 2011," *Huffington Post*, September 30, 2015, www.huffingtonpost.ca/2015/09/30/almost-1-800-candidates-from-23-parties-on-ballot-only-one-third-are-women_n_8224034.html.
46. Murray Dobbin, "Come Clean, Ms. Green," Murray Dobbin's blog, September 23, 2015, http://murraydobbin.ca/2015/09/23/come-clean-ms-green/.
47. "Liberal Candidate Cheryl Thomas Resigns over Facebook Comments," CBC News, September 30, 2015, www.cbc.ca/news/canada/british-columbia/cheryl-thomas-liberal-candidate-resigns-1.3251338.
48. Ilan Goldenblatt, telephone interview with author, October 17, 2015.
49. See "Riding-Level Polls Show Many Mid-Island Voters Still Undecided," Dogwood Initiative,https://dogwoodinitiative.org/media-centre/media-releases/island-polling-oct-7-2015.
50. Don Scott, telephone interview with author, November 18, 2015.
51. "Trudeau Must Fix the Voting System: Fair Vote Canada," Fair Vote Canada, http://campaign2015.fairvote.ca/trudeau-must-fix-the-voting-system-fair-vote-canada/.
52. "Liberals Lead by Six Points Nationally in Nanos Tracking," Nanos Research, October 15, 2015, www.nanosresearch.com/library/polls/20151015%20Ballot%20TrackingE.pdf; and "End of an Era: For a Second Time, a Trudeau Is Headed to 24 Sussex as Liberals Poised to Win Election," Ipsos North America, www.ipsos-na.com/news-polls/pressrelease.aspx?id=7031.
53. "Election of Members and the Allocation of Seats," *Deutscher Bundestag*, www.bundestag.de/htdocs_e/bundestag/elections/arithmetic/arithmetic/199936.

# CHAPTER 7

## Roll Back! The Conservatives Rewrite Election Laws, 2006–2015

Louis Massicotte

This chapter summarizes the reforms brought in from 2006 to 2015 to Canadian electoral legislation as well as the debates they ignited, and follows earlier contributions to this book series.[1] Election law reform is usually a quiet field in the big picture of Canadian politics, but during the Harper era, it became at times a major issue. The clashes that took place can better be understood as conflicts between the views of the Conservative government and what could be called the "conventional wisdom" that had prevailed since the 1960s among political parties, academics, and election officials with regard to election legislation.

The conventional wisdom held that the decline of electoral turnout was a major problem and that voting should be facilitated instead of made more cumbersome, as there was no evidence of cheating. The Conservatives were convinced that fraud at the polls was rampant, and that the protection of the integrity of the voting process necessitated tighter checks on voter identification and place of residence, even if this possibly had the effect of keeping some voters out of the polling stations.

According to the conventional wisdom, the chief corrupting influence on the voting process was big money, and it was believed that a level playing field should be established and preserved. Contributions to political parties should be regulated, donations from some sources should be prohibited, and state subsidies of parties were welcome. It was also believed that spending by third parties should be prohibited, or at least limited. The Conservatives believed that third-party spending was fine, that both corporate and labour union contributions, and the direct subsidies to parties that replaced them in 2003, were wrong, and that the notion of a level playing field amounted to a limit on free speech. On the other hand, they did not object to fiscal incentives for political contributions or reimbursements of election expenses, though they did agree with the idea of contribution limits.

The conventional wisdom also held that fair elections necessitated a powerful and independent referee that should do more than supply election materials. Elections Canada should not only prosecute those who broke the law, however powerful they might be, but actively encourage higher turnout, intervene in court cases, and mobilize academic knowledge in order to improve the election laws. The Conservatives were initially skeptical of all this and became increasingly defiant of what they saw as Elections Canada's activism, particularly since they became the target of high-profile lawsuits launched by the institution.

Both sides were suspicious of each other's motives. Supporters of the conventional wisdom increasingly saw the Conservatives as serial election cheaters who blamed the referee for repressing too zealously their acts of political turpitude, had a U.S. Republican-style agenda for hampering the vote for their opponents, and wanted to financially choke their rivals in order to replace the Liberals as Canada's natural governing party. They saw the Conservatives as wanting to roll back the trends that had prevailed from the 1970s to the early 2000s, and revamp election laws for their own partisan advantage. The Conservatives saw the conventional wisdom as the agenda of the Ottawa establishment and its academic lackeys, who were trying to preserve the centre-left consensus that had prevailed since the Trudeau years. Like all true revolutionaries, they felt no qualms about confronting the conventional wisdom head-on and imposing their own views if they were in a position to do it.

Some measures taken by the Conservatives during their first term, like elections at fixed dates or empowering Elections Canada to appoint returning officers, squared well with earlier trends. The break appeared to come in late 2008, with the provocative announcement that state subsidies would be phased out unilaterally. Changes to the redistribution rules, if beneficial for Conservatives, went in the direction of greater fairness. Yet the Fair Elections Act (Bill C-23), arguably the most controversial election law measure in Ottawa since the Wartime Elections Act of 1917, will likely dominate any assessment of election reform under Harper because of the breadth of the innovations it brought and the degree of hostility it generated.

## ELECTIONS AT (NOT SO) FIXED DATES

The power to dissolve Parliament and to call new elections has been a valued weapon in the arsenal of the executive since the origins of the British Parliament. This prerogative originally allowed the Crown to get rid of a restive legislature in the hope that voters would return a more pliable one. Following the introduction of responsible government, it became an accepted constitutional convention that this power would be used at the request of the Cabinet, and more exactly of the prime minister. In practice, this meant that elections were scheduled by the party in power at dates that would help to ensure its re-election, or postpone its defeat. Through astute decisions regarding the timing of the federal elections in 1997 and 2000, Jean Chrétien contributed to his own re-election. Not surprisingly, his opponents saw this ability to schedule election dates conferred an unfair advantage on the "ins" — an opinion that found an echo in the public at large.[2] The Conservative election platform for 2006 promised to "introduce legislation modelled on the B.C. and Ontario laws requiring fixed election dates every four years, except when a government loses the confidence of the House (in which case an election would be held immediately, and the subsequent election would follow four years later)."

The government moved quickly on this issue and, on May 30, 2006, Bill C-16 was tabled in the House of Commons. By then, three provinces had adopted legislation to the same effect.[3] The bill refrained from amending the requirement in the Constitution Act, 1867, that elections were to be held every five years. Rather, it inserted a clause in the Canada Elections Act providing that each general election must be held on the third Monday of October in the fourth calendar year following polling day for the last general election. However, this was made subject to the proviso that "nothing in this section affects the powers of the Governor General, including the power to dissolve Parliament at the Governor General's discretion." Subsequent events would emphasize how important this loophole was. Bill C-16 became law in April 2007. The extent of the party consensus underlying the measure is illustrated by the fact that in the House of Commons no recorded division was requested either at second or third reading.

The unanimity mentioned above may have had to do with the fact that in the minority situation then prevailing, Bill C-16 actually gave the opposition parties, if they agreed among themselves, the opportunity to determine the date of the next election, for nobody denied that should the government be defeated in the House before the end of the parliamentary term, it would be entitled to call an election. What was not realized by everyone, however, was that the wording of the measure effectively contradicted the government platform's implicit promise that a snap election would be held *only if the government had been defeated in the House*. As was the case before, the governor general's power to dissolve Parliament could *always* be exercised, and this power was to be used at the request of the prime minister. This became obvious on September 7, 2008, when Prime Minister Harper successfully requested an early election, stating that the existing Parliament had become "dysfunctional." The governor general accepted this request and the opposition parties did not seriously question this decision, which was made during the summer recess.[4]

The 2011 election did not take place at the expected date either, this time because the government was defeated on a no-confidence vote and obtained a dissolution. In 2015, the election was held according to schedule. The wisdom of having elections at fixed dates was then questioned because they allowed the wealthiest parties to escape the spending ceilings provided by the Elections Act by airing political advertising a few months before the election was called.

## THE FEDERAL ACCOUNTABILITY ACT, 2006

The 2006 election was held in the shadow of the sponsorship scandal, which discredited the ruling Liberals and contributed mightily to the Conservative victory. A sweeping package of ethical measures figured at the very beginning of the Conservative legislative agenda. It included a reform of the financing of political parties; a ban on secret donations to political candidates; the toughening of the Lobbyists Registration Act; a reform of government appointments; the cleaning up of government polling, advertising, and procurement of government contracts; real protection for whistle-blowers; the creation of a parliamentary budgeting authority; and the strengthening of the powers of the auditor general and the ethics commissioner. As well, it strengthened access to information legislation, auditing and accountability in departments, and created a Director of Public Prosecutions office.

The first piece of legislation introduced by the new government was the Federal Accountability Act, which dealt with most of the issues outlined above. This act contained measures that touched on a number of areas, but this chapter will focus on changes to political finance rules.

One of the principal changes made related to the Election Expenses Act. In 2003, before he left politics, Prime Minister Chrétien had forced the adoption of a major change to the basics of the system established in the 1974 Election Expenses Act by altering the rules on contributions.[5] Corporations and labour union contributions to the central organizations of political parties were banned, though they were still allowed for constituency associations, candidates, or nomination contestants, subject to a $1,000 combined ceiling. Individuals were still allowed to contribute, but their donations were capped at $10,000 per year to any combination of party, constituency associations, candidates, or nomination contestants. As both changes were expected to reduce sharply the flow of money to parties, a per-vote subsidy to parties was established as a compensating measure, and became a very important source of revenue for parties.

Despite its well-known opposition to government subsidies to parties, the new Conservative government initially went in the same direction as the 2003 reform, by a) eliminating the loophole left in 2003 that allowed for some contributions by unions and corporations, and banning completely corporations and labour unions from contributing; and b) reducing further — from $10,000 to $1,000 — the amount that could be contributed by individuals.[6] Considering the minority context and the presence of an opposition-dominated Senate, the Federal Accountability Act had a relatively smooth passage in an otherwise rather acrimonious Parliament.[7]

## THE ABOLITION OF PARTY SUBSIDIES

The situation changed completely in late November 2008. Barely six weeks after having been returned with an increased number of seats, but still in a minority position, Harper inadvertently committed a major faux pas, as the Financial Update of the minister of finance provided, among other provocative measures, for the outright abolition of party subsidies. The opposition parties, being far more dependent than the ruling party on such subsidies for financial survival,[8] were outraged. Their anger led to an attempt to topple the incumbent government and to replace it with a Liberal-NDP coalition relying on Bloc Québécois support. The attempt failed, but keeping the subsidies intact ranked high on the list of concessions that the government had to make in order to survive.[9]

Once the Conservatives won a majority in 2011, they were in a position to fulfill their explicit election promise of abolishing party subsidies, which they did as soon as possible. In June 2011, the budget speech announced the government's decision to gradually phase out allowances to political parties. The $2.04-per-year vote allowance was reduced by $0.51 increments starting April 1, 2012, with complete elimination due by April 1, 2015. It was claimed that this measure would generate savings of about $30 million for the government.[10] It has been computed that, from 2004 to 2015, the total subsidy amounted to $266 million: $98.1 million for the Conservatives, $74.9 million for the Liberals, $54.6 million for the NDP, $25.7 million for the Bloc Québécois, and $12.6 million for the Greens.[11]

## IDENTIFICATION REQUIREMENTS FOR VOTERS

The Conservative platform of 2006 did not promise any specific action regarding the identification of voters at polling stations. The government measure that dealt with this issue, Bill C-31, introduced in October 2006 and adopted in June 2007,[12] stemmed from recommendations made by the Canadian House of Commons Standing Committee on Procedure and House Affairs in June 2006.[13] Its purpose was to improve the integrity of the electoral process by reducing the opportunity for electoral fraud or error.

Until then, election officers had no right to demand identification documents from voters at polling stations. Indeed, from 1970 to 1993 they had been explicitly *prohibited* from requesting that electors produce a birth certificate or naturalization papers. Starting in 1993, they were empowered, if they had doubts concerning the identity or right to vote of a person, to request that the person show "satisfactory proof of identity." The voter could instead take an oath.

In its 2006 report, the committee had stated the following:

> Many Canadians have expressed concern about the *potential* for fraud and misrepresentation in voting. Members of the Committee share this *concern*. While *we have no means of knowing how widespread this problem is*, the fact that it exists undermines the integrity of the electoral process.... In our society, most important activities require that an individual be able to furnish some form of proper identification, often with a photograph. In the case of voting, we do not believe that it would be unreasonable to impose a similar requirement.[14]

The government responded positively to this report, and in October 2006 introduced a measure enacting its recommendations.[15] Under Bill C-31, electors were required, before voting, to provide polling officials with one piece of government-issued photo identification showing their name, address, and photograph, or two pieces of identification authorized by the chief electoral officer (CEO) showing their name and address, or to take an oath and be vouched for by another elector (with identification). Oath takers had to be informed of the qualifications necessary for voting and of the penalties for violating the law. The third reading of this measure was supported by all parties but the NDP, which had concerns on how it would impact low-income people, people who lived in small, remote communities, and Aboriginal people, many of whom did not have the required identification.[16]

As it turned out, it was soon discovered that other matters should have been given closer scrutiny during the consideration of Bill C-31. In a post-mortem study of by-elections held in Quebec three months later, the chief electoral officer discovered a major problem caused by the new requirement that voters should provide evidence as to their residential address. Over one million Canadians on the electoral register actually did not have a specific residential address and could not fulfill the recently introduced requirement. According to Elections Canada, as many as 80 percent of all electors in Nunavut, and about a quarter of electors in Saskatchewan and Newfoundland, would encounter this problem and could see their right to vote challenged at the next election.[17] Political parties were duly informed of these unintended consequences of the bill.

The government reacted in November 2007 by introducing Bill C-18 as an amendment to the Elections Act.[18] Polling officials were directed to accept as proof of residence a non-residential address (like Rural Road 3) that appeared on the elector's identification, provided that this address matched the elector information on the list of electors. Persons vouching for another elector would also be able to show proof of residence in this manner when the address on the piece of identification would not otherwise permit them to prove that they resided in the polling division. Like C-31, this measure secured the support of all parties but the NDP.[19]

The new voter identification requirements were challenged in 2010 under section 3 of the Charter. The plaintiffs argued that the new voter identification requirements impeded or limited the exercise of the right to vote by those persons who did not have standard documentary proof of their identity and residence available to them. Although it agreed that the identification requirements interfered with the right to vote, the Supreme Court of British Columbia ruled the interference to be a reasonable limit pursuant to section 1 of the Charter. The voter identification provisions of the legislation were considered to be a proportionate response to a concern about voter impersonation and other kinds of electoral fraud. The Court of Appeal for British Columbia later upheld that decision.[20]

## VISUAL IDENTIFICATION OF VOTERS

Another loophole left by C-31, the issue of the visual identification of voters, occasioned a major, if short-lived, clash between the chief electoral officer and MPs from all parties. The new requirements did not explicitly oblige a veiled woman to show her face at the polling station before being allowed to vote. She could refuse to remove her veil when asked but be allowed to vote nevertheless, either by presenting two other pieces of identification without a photo, or by taking an oath and being vouched for by a voter having identification.

This issue had reached prominence during the March 2007 provincial election in Quebec. A decision by the provincial chief electoral officer, based on legal advice, to allow women to vote without showing their faces, ignited an outburst in the media that approached "mass hysteria" levels days before the election,[21] forcing the CEO to use his power to adapt the legislation in order to force women to uncover their faces before voting. The issue was revisited the next fall, this time for federal elections. Eleven days before three by-elections were held in Quebec, MPs sitting on the Standing Committee on Procedure and House Affairs urged the federal chief electoral officer to do the same as his provincial counterpart in Quebec. This Chief Electoral Officer Mayrand refused to do, quoting the Supreme Court's ruling in *Haig v. Canada (Chief Electoral Officer),* and arguing that his power to adapt the legislation was "intended to facilitate the voting process, not to restrict electors' fundamental rights." The most he would do was to ask election officials to invite anyone whose face was concealed to uncover it "in a manner that is respectful of their beliefs," and to oblige voters who declined to do so to take an oath as to their qualification.[22] He was not swayed by the unanimous adoption of a motion urging him to reconsider his decision, nor by statements of party leaders supporting the move.

On October 26, 2007, the government introduced Bill C-6, which required all voters to have their faces uncovered at polling stations in order to enable polling officials to identify them visually. The bill was read a second time in November and referred to committee, but did not proceed further. The Liberal and NDP spokesmen then stated that the bill addressed a problem that did not exist and raised Charter concerns. The consensus of all parties in the committee seemingly evaporated once the by-elections had been held. This issue, it should be noted, was different from the one that surfaced during the 2015 campaign, namely whether a woman should be allowed to wear a niqab while being sworn in as a Canadian citizen.

## THE LONG AND DIFFICULT SEARCH FOR A NEW REDISTRIBUTION FORMULA

That the Harper government intended to alter the formula for redistributing seats in the House of Commons among provinces did not come as a surprise to anyone, as the Conservative platform in 2006 promised to "restore representation by population for Ontario, British Columbia, and Alberta in the House of Commons while protecting the seat counts of smaller provinces."[23] The Conservatives had expressed their dissatisfaction with the existing formula in 2003. They had a strong case for doing so.

The redistribution rules are found in section 51 of the Constitution Act, 1867. However, since 1949, these rules can be altered at will by Parliament, subject to a privilege granted in 1915, known as the senatorial rule, which provides that "a province shall always be entitled to a number of members in the House of Commons not less than the number of senators representing such province." This rule in turn cannot be removed unless all provinces agree.

The existing formula had been devised in 1985 under the Mulroney government with the purpose of preventing substantial increases in the size of the House over time. As the representation of the slow-growth provinces was frozen by the combined application of the senatorial floor rule and of the grandfather clause, which guaranteed that no province would lose seats, this goal was realized at the expense of the faster-growing provinces of Ontario, British Columbia, and Alberta, which did not get as many new seats as their population growth warranted. For example, in 2001, they ended up with about 56 percent of seats while having 61 percent of the population. Such built-in disadvantages were expected to grow over time. Any ruling party with a strong contingent of western MPs would have challenged such an arrangement.[24]

Quebec, a large but slow-growth province, became for some the focus of discontent, as under the existing rules, it was expected to have more seats than Alberta and British Columbia combined (seventy-five to sixty-eight) while having a smaller population (7.9 to 8 million in 2011).[25] Most of the distortions, however, came from the operation of the senatorial floor rule, which froze the representation of the Atlantic provinces at thirty-two, giving them 10 percent of the seats with less than 7 percent of the population.

The Conservatives, assuming quite reasonably that the senatorial clause would be impossible to remove, believed that the only way to get a fairer distribution was to increase the total size of the House, despite an earlier statement from Stephen Harper, then a Reform party MP, suggesting that 273 seats would be appropriate.[26]

The complexity of the issue, as well as the Conservatives' lack of a majority in the Commons until 2011, explain why the government came up with no less than three different formulas within five years. The first one (Bill C-56), disclosed in May 2007, would have resulted in a House of 342 and increased representation for Alberta and British Columbia. However, while the latter were both expected to have one MP for 105,000 inhabitants, Ontario would have one per 115,000. The Ontario legislature understandably protested against a scheme seemingly premised on the assumption that representation by population was good for some provinces but not for others. The outcome of the 2008 election shattered the political assumptions underlying the proposal: the Conservatives made no gains in Quebec, but won eleven seats more in Ontario. The removal of the clause that had offended Ontario was announced a few weeks later.

A second formal proposal was made in April 2010 (Bill C-12), and provided for a House of 338 seats. This time, there was no reason to placate Quebec, which would have become the only slow-growth province to be under-represented in the Commons. Quebec's National Assembly in turn protested,[27] while the Bloc Québécois insisted that Quebec should be entitled to 25 percent of the seats in perpetuity because it had been recognized as a nation. Moreover, projections for future censuses suggested that by 2031, the three faster-growing provinces would remain sharply under-represented.[28]

The 2011 election, in which Harper's Conservatives gained a majority, set the stage for the conclusion of this saga, as the government was now in a position to impose its will. In October 2011, Bill C-20, the Fair Representation Act, was tabled, and became law by December of the same year (SC 2011, c. 26). Quebec's objections were met with a provision that its representation would be proportional to its population, fulfilling the promise made in the Conservative 2011 election platform. On second reading, the bill was opposed by all opposition parties but the sole Green MP, who voted against all subsequent stages. Allocation of time orders shortened the second and third reading as well as the report stage of the bill.

The working of the formula can be summarized as follows: First, the population of each province is divided by an "electoral quotient," set at 111,166 for the 2011 redistribution.[29] Second, the resulting numbers are re-adjusted in order to account for the "senatorial clause" and the "grandfather clause." Then the "representation clause" is applied, which pertains only to provinces whose populations were overrepresented in the House of Commons at the completion of the last redistribution process. If such a province were under-represented based on the calculations above, it would be given extra seats so that its share of House of Commons seats assigned to all ten provinces is proportional to its share of their population. In 2011, this provision applied only to Quebec, which gained three seats more. The process is completed by the addition of three seats, one per territory (see Table 7.1).

For the 2021 readjustment and each subsequent readjustment, the electoral quotient will be increased by the simple average of provincial

**Table 7.1: Allocation of Seats in the House of Commons**

| Province/ Territory | Population estimate | ÷ Electoral quotient | = Initial seat allocation | + Senatorial clause | + Grandfather clause | + Representation rule | = Total seats | Increase 2001-2011 | Average population |
|---|---|---|---|---|---|---|---|---|---|
| British Columbia | 4,573,321 | | 42 | - | - | - | 42 | 6 | 108,889 |
| Alberta | 3,779,353 | | 34 | - | - | - | 34 | 6 | 111,157 |
| Saskatchewan | 1,057,884 | | 10 | - | 4 | - | 14 | none | 75,563 |
| Manitoba | 1,250,574 | | 12 | - | 2 | - | 14 | none | 89,327 |
| Ontario | 13,372,996 | | 121 | - | - | - | 121 | 15 | 110,521 |
| Québec | 7,979,663 | 111,166 | 72 | - | 3 | 3 | 78 | 3 | 102,303 |
| New Brunswick | 755,455 | | 7 | 3 | - | - | 10 | none | 75,546 |
| Nova Scotia | 945,437 | | 9 | 1 | 1 | - | 11 | none | 85,949 |
| Prince Edward Island | 145,855 | | 2 | 2 | - | - | 4 | none | 36,464 |
| Newfoundland and Labrador | 510,578 | | 5 | 1 | 1 | - | 7 | none | 72,94 |
| Yukon | 34,666 | n/a | | | | | 1 | none | 34,666 |
| Northwest Territories | 43,675 | n/a | | | | | 1 | none | 43,675 |
| Nunavut | 33,322 | n/a | | | | | 1 | none | 33,322 |
| Total | 34,482,779 | | | | | | 338 | 30 | 102,020 |

Source: Adapted from Elections Canada, www.elections.ca/content.aspx?section=res&dir=cir/red/allo&document=index&lang=e

population growth rates since the preceding readjustment. No projections were offered by the government.

In addition, for the first time in Canadian redistribution history, provincial populations will be based on Statistics Canada's annual population estimates rather than on census figures, in order to correct for what was described as "net undercoverage in the census" and provide a more accurate representation of total provincial population. However, within each province, seats will continue to be apportioned on the basis of census figures.

The new formula has the effect of increasing the total number of seats so as to better reflect population growth in Ontario, British Columbia, and Alberta, while maintaining the *number* (though not the *proportion*) of seats for six slower-growing provinces, and maintaining the proportional representation of Quebec according to population. Still, the three faster-growing provinces remain under-represented (63.2 percent of the population, 58.8 percent of the seats), which leaves wide open the possibility that the formula may be revisited in the future.

## THE REDISTRIBUTION OF 2013

Once the new redistribution rules were adopted, the redistribution process went on smoothly, and in conformity with the timetable established by the Electoral Boundaries Readjustment Act.[30] In December 2011, the chief electoral officer published a statement outlining the number of seats each province would be entitled to on the basis of its population figures. Ten boundary commissions, one for each province, were appointed in February 2012. The dates for publishing a proposal, holding public meetings, and tabling a final report varied from province to province. For Ontario and Quebec, proposals were made public during the summer of 2012, public hearings thereon took place during the next fall, and the reports were tabled in February 2013.[31] A total of 126 objections pertaining to seven provinces were filed with the House of Commons Standing Committee on Procedure and House Affairs and submitted to the commissions, which made a final decision thereon by the summer of 2013. The representation order enacting the new constituency boundaries was published on October 5, 2013, with the proviso that it would come into force only if the next election were called on or after May 1, 2014. These boundaries were used at the 2015 election.

Only forty-four of the existing 308 ridings survived unaltered, including the four Prince Edward Island seats, for which the redistribution commission had recommended the status quo. Only three districts (out of 338) had populations exceeding the 25 percent maximum deviation allowed by the act. They were Labrador in Newfoundland and Labrador, Kenora in Ontario, and Avignon-La Mitis-Matane-Matapédia in Quebec. Excluding these three "exceptional circumstances districts," only twenty ridings (in 2003: seventeen) had populations exceeding the applicable provincial quota by more than 15 percent. The populations of the 338 new districts ranged from 26,728 to 132,443, while under the 2011 population figures, the previous 308 ranged from 26,728 to a whopping 228,997. In June 2014, Parliament adopted a statute that altered the names of thirty-one districts, mostly adding parts of the district to the name, which allowed "Leeds-Grenville-Thousand Islands and Rideau Lakes" and "Beauport-Côte de Beaupré-Île d'Orléans–Charlevoix" to beat "West Vancouver-Sunshine Coast-Sea to Sky Country" by a whisker.

The political impact of the new boundary changes was important. A transposition of the votes cast at the 2011 election into the boundaries of the new districts was published by Elections Canada.[32] While in theory all parties stood to get some of the thirty additional seats, the Bloc Québécois and the Greens actually kept their existing numbers under the new boundaries (four and one respectively), the New Democrats got 109 instead of 103, and the Liberals thirty-six instead of thirty-four. The undoubted winners were the Conservatives, with 188 seats instead of 166 — a net gain of twenty-two.[33]

This did not come as a surprise, and did not result in accusations of gerrymandering. Twenty-seven additional seats went to Ontario, British Columbia, and Alberta. The Conservatives had won 71 percent of all seats in these three provinces in 2011, and the average Conservative riding there had 88,881 electors, against 78,122 and 82,335 for ridings won respectively by the NDP and the Liberals. Throughout the country, all but four of the nineteen districts with more than 100,000 electors had gone to the Conservatives. The latter were bound to win from the redistribution.[34]

During the 2015 campaign, much was made among experts about the fact that their seat projections seemingly revealed the existence of a bias in favour of the Conservatives, as the latter tended to win notionally more seats than the other parties when all three were tied. In the end, however, the Liberals were more than able to overcome this bias, even winning a majority with only 39.5 percent of the vote and a 7.6 percent lead over the Conservatives.

## ENFORCEMENT OF THE ELECTIONS ACT

Complaints relating to the application of the Elections Act are directed to the commissioner of Canada Elections, who is empowered to determine whether there is a basis for the allegation and, if so, to conduct an investigation. If the commissioner believes that an offence under the act has been committed, he may refer the matter to the director of public prosecutions, who decides whether to initiate a prosecution.

Few Canadians remember it, but election law litigation was once a major competition sport in this country. During the last decades of the nineteenth century, as many as one-quarter of sitting MPs saw their election challenged in court. Here and elsewhere, the waning of election law as a lucrative area of legal practice in the twentieth century was viewed as an indication that election cheating had almost disappeared. Yet, during the period covered by this chapter, one election came very close to being voided, and there were at least two major breaches to the Elections Act, both involving the ruling party, which damaged the reputation of Canadian electioneering and shattered the relationship between Elections Canada and Conservative MPs: the "in–and-out" dispute and the "robocalls" scandal.

### In-and-Out[35]

The Elections Act provided for distinct limits on national party and local candidates election expenses. A party could reach the national limit and be prevented from spending more on its national campaign, while in many constituencies the projected expenses of its candidates might still fall short of the local limit by huge amounts. If local candidates were required to pay for expenses that, in view of their nature, should be paid for by the national campaign, the law would be formally complied with, as neither the national nor the local spending limit would be breached. However, this would mean that the national campaign was actually evading the national spending limit by transferring some of its expenses to local candidates through communicating vessels.

Such was the case with some election expenses claimed by the Conservative Party in the 2006 election. While reviewing the returns of expenses submitted by some local Conservative candidates for the 2006 election, Elections Canada officials spotted substantial amounts that were supposedly spent on national TV advertising and inquired about them. It was found that the Conservative national campaign had transferred a total of $1.2 million to at least sixty-seven local candidates, who immediately sent the money back to the party's head office to pay for television and radio advertisements. The ads were duly attributed to the local campaigns, though these ads were actually identical to those aired by the national campaign.

The chief electoral officer took the view that these ads were not legitimate constituency expenses and so were not eligible for a 60 percent reimbursement. He therefore refused to pay a total of $780,000 to the local candidates who had participated in what he alleged was a breach of the act. The Conservative Party decided to sue the chief electoral officer in court over this decision. Meanwhile, opposition parties attacked the government in the House and in the Standing Committee on Procedure and House Affairs, which summoned campaign directors as witnesses. The dispute was inflamed in April 2008 when Elections Canada and the RCMP, in order to get documents, raided the headquarters of the Conservative Party in Ottawa in full view of the media, which had presumably been tipped off about the event. Resentment against Elections Canada grew within the Conservative administration.

In January 2010, the Federal Court ruled in favour of the Conservatives, saying that the suspicions entertained by the chief electoral officer did not support his decisions or constitute reasonable grounds to suspend indefinitely the reimbursement of the challenged expenses.[36] However, in February 2011, this ruling was unanimously reversed by a three-judge panel of the Federal Court of Appeal, which found that the decision was reasonable.[37]

In February 2011, three days before the decision of the Federal Court of Appeal in the *Callaghan* case on the issue of the CEO rejecting expense claims, a second case was opened when four senior Conservative Party campaign officials, two of whom had been thereafter appointed to the Senate, were charged by Elections Canada with overspending more than $1 million in the 2006 election.[38]

Both cases found their epilogue a few months later. On November 10, 2011, under a deal accepted by an Ontario judge, the charges against the four Conservative officials were dropped, in favour of guilty pleas by the organizations for which they made the decisions. The Conservative Party and the Conservative Fund pleaded guilty to the charges of having overspent and having filed election records that did not set out all expenses, and were fined the statutory maximum of $52,000. The more serious charges of having done so *willfully* were withdrawn.[39] In March 2012, the Conservative Party capitulated in the *Callaghan* case by dropping the appeal the Supreme Court had accepted to hear, and agreed to repay $230,198 for its role in the scheme.[40]

## Robocalls

In May 2011, on election day, at around 10 a.m., thousands of voters in the electoral district of Guelph, Ontario, received the following phone call:

> This is an automated message from Elections Canada. Due to a projected increase in voter turnout, your poll location has been changed. Your new voting location is at the Old Quebec Street Mall, at 55 Wyndham Street North. Once again, your new poll location is at the Old Quebec Street Mall, at 55 Wyndham Street North. If you have any questions, please call our hotline at 1-800-443-4456. We apologize for any inconvenience this may cause.

Anyone closely familiar with the standards of election management in Canada would have smelled a rat, as such very last-minute changes to polling locations would have exposed Elections Canada to serious charges of mismanagement, or worse. Yet, between 150 and 200 unsuspecting voters went to the indicated location, only to realize they had been lied to. There had been no change in their polling location, and the message did not originate from Elections Canada.[41] Following complaints from outraged voters, Elections Canada undertook an in-depth investigation, the results of which found their way to the media in February 2012, igniting a scandal that lingered throughout the Conservatives' third term as a government. Two issues were raised: First, who was responsible for the calls? Second, did such calls have an impact on the outcome of the election? Both issues found their way to the courts.

The inquiry on the source of automated calls focused on the Conservative campaign in Guelph and led to the *Sona* case.[42] On August 14, 2014, the communications director for the Conservative campaign in Guelph, twenty-six-year-old Michael Sona, was found guilty of the offence of preventing or endeavouring to prevent an elector from voting. Sona, the court said,

> was an active participant in an ill-conceived scheme initiating in the offices of the local Conservative candidate in the Guelph riding during the May 2011 federal election. This scheme was initiated, designed, and ultimately activated with the goal to prevent or endeavour to prevent targeted non-Conservative supporters from voting.... The plan involved the sending of some 7,000 automated telephone calls to targeted telephone numbers on the day of the election May 2, 2011, indicating that the polling stations for those individuals had been changed to another location.... The automated telephone calls had been sent through the services of an Alberta company, RackNine. Those services were provided to a fictitious individual named Pierre Poutine at a cost of approximately $160. The payment for those services came from prepaid credit cards and contact with RackNine initially was by way of a "pay as you go" phone. Both the phone and the credit cards were paid for by cash and the account with RackNine was set up under the fictitious name of Pierre Poutine in order

> to attempt to ensure that the creator or creators of this plan could not be traced.... Mr. Sona has been found to be a major and active participant in this plan.[43]

The judge concluded that "the conduct of Mr. Sona on the days leading up to the May 2, 2011, federal election was egregious and had considerable impact not only on this particular community, but also on our democratic process."[44] In November 2014, Sona was sentenced to imprisonment for nine months to be followed by a twelve-month probation period. It has been said that this was the first incarceration for an offence against the Elections Act.[45] Sona appealed the sentence, as, for opposite reasons, did the Crown. Sona was released on bail meanwhile.[46] The case was still pending at the time of writing.

The emotion created by the robocalls revelations ran high, with demonstrations taking place in no less than twenty-seven Canadian cities. Many asked whether the elections in those ridings the Conservatives won by close margins should be annulled due to electoral fraud. Soon after the robocall scheme was revealed, legal proceedings were launched by the Council of Canadians before the Federal Court of Canada, challenging the election of six Conservative MPs.[47] Justice Mosley's ruling was made in May 2013.[48] While refusing to void the six elections, the judge stated that, on the basis of the evidence, misleading calls were made to electors in ridings across the country, not only in the six ridings at stake, and that the purpose of those calls was to suppress the votes of electors who had indicated their voting preference in response to earlier voter identification calls. While refusing to say that the Conservative Party or its candidates were directly involved in the campaign to mislead voters, he added:

> I am satisfied, however, that the most likely source of the information used to make the misleading calls was the CIMS [Constituency Information Management System] database maintained and controlled by the CPC [Conservative Party of Canada], accessed for that purpose by a person or persons currently unknown to this Court. There is no evidence to indicate that the use of the CIMS database in this manner was approved or

> condoned by the CPC. Rather the evidence points to elaborate efforts to conceal the identity of those accessing the database and arranging for the calls to be made.[49]

The issue at stake was whether these fraudulent acts had a major impact on the credibility of the vote. The judge concluded that "the evidence in this proceeding does not support the conclusion that the voter suppression efforts had a major impact on the credibility of the vote."[50] The possibility that robocalls would become a kind of Canadian Watergate was quashed in April 2014, when the commissioner of Canada Elections concluded that there was insufficient evidence to believe that an offence was committed.[51]

### Challenges Against Sitting MPs

Disputes over spending or contributions broke the careers of Conservative MPs Dean Del Mastro and Peter Penashue. Half a dozen official agents of Conservative and Liberal candidates were prosecuted for offences against the election expenses provisions of the act.[52] All were found guilty. The election of a Conservative in Etobicoke Centre was first voided in May 2012, but revalidated by the Supreme Court of Canada five months later.[53]

### Five-Year Limit on Expatriate Voting

The restriction on the right of Canadians who had lived outside the country for more than five years to vote was struck down as unconstitutional by an Ontario judge in May 2014.[54] The government announced it would appeal the decision, but lost when it tried to have the decision suspended before the appeal was decided.[55] The government reacted by introducing legislation that would have scrapped the register of Canadian electors abroad and obliged Canadians living outside the country to register again once the election had been called.[56] Ultimately, this proved unnecessary, as the Ontario Court of Appeal, in July 2015, overturned the earlier decision.[57] At the time of writing, the Supreme Court of Canada still had to decide whether it would grant leave to appeal that decision.

## BILL C-23, THE FAIR ELECTIONS ACT

This was by far the most controversial measure adopted by the Conservatives in the area of election law. A useful way to deal with this measure is to distinguish the process that led to its adoption from its substance.

### The Process

Anyone remotely familiar with the history of Canadian electoral legislation knows that for a long time the rules governing the electoral process were seen as just another area where the government of the day could impose its will on opposition parties. Yet, by the late 1930s, Canadians had devised a different approach that relied on the interaction of technical expertise, represented by the chief electoral officer, and all-party parliamentary committees, with the government relying on both to come up with a measure that secured wide support. In contrast with the fierce parliamentary battles that surrounded Macdonald's Franchise Act of 1885 or the Wartime Elections Act of 1917, the evolution of modern Canadian electoral law has followed a more consensual pattern.

That pattern can be summarized as follows: The post-election statutory report of the chief electoral officer offered suggestions for improvement that were administrative in nature. The report, together with private members' bills dealing with election law issues and suggestions from the public, was referred to a committee of the House of Commons. The committee heard evidence from the chief electoral officer and from other witnesses. Its report, which reflected compromises among the various political parties, was acted upon thereafter through a government bill that enacted the committee's conclusions and was passed without any fanfare. Should parties strongly disagree among themselves, no action was taken, or the issue could be referred to a Royal Commission, as occurred in 1989. There have been departures from this approach. Examples are Chrétien's introduction in 1996 of the electoral register and later of party subsidies. In the latter case, what the majority of the day imposed was undone by the majority of another day.

Bill C-23 was a deliberate, though not entirely unprecedented, departure from the standard approach. Both Elections Canada and opposition members were completely left out of the preparation of the measure, which was announced out of the blue by the government.

The bill represented the culmination of a long-simmering feud between the ruling party and Elections Canada.[58] The roots of the dispute can be traced to the court battle on third-party spending in 2000. Stephen Harper, then chairman of the National Citizens Coalition, led the assault against the new provisions of the Elections Act that limited third-party spending, while Chief Electoral Officer Jean-Pierre Kingsley was involved in the defence of the legislation as it stood. Further, in 2001, Harper wrote a letter in support of an activist who posted election results on his website in violation of the prohibition against this contained in the Elections Act. The letter included insulting references to Elections Canada staff and personal attacks against the chief electoral officer himself.

Harper took office as prime minister in January 2006. In February 2007, Jean-Pierre Kingsley left his position to become president and CEO of the Washington-based International Foundation for Electoral Systems (IFES). Superintendent of Bankruptcy Marc Mayrand, a lawyer by training, was nominated by Harper as chief electoral officer, endorsed by the House Committee on Procedure and House Affairs, and formally appointed on February 21, 2007, through a unanimous resolution of the House of Commons.

Relations quickly soured between the ruling party and Elections Canada. This was largely due to the in-and-out and robocalls inquiries, which were seen by the Conservatives as a vendetta against their party. As an observer noted, "every election since Stephen Harper became prime minister has been associated with some Conservative battle with Elections Canada, some scandal over broken rules."[59]

A Bloc Québécois motion expressing "full and complete confidence in Elections Canada and the Commissioner of Canada Elections" was carried 152 to 117 in the House on April 29, 2008, with all Conservatives standing for the nays.[60] Such an open display of defiance from the ruling party was completely unprecedented in the history of the institution. Worse was to come.

The 252-page Bill C-23 was introduced on February 4, 2014. Its public consideration occasioned numerous firsts. Both the chief electoral officer and the commissioner of Canada Elections publicly objected to many changes brought in by the measure. About 180 academics signed an open letter attacking some of its features, and up to 460 signed a second letter demanding that the bill be withdrawn.[61] A blue-ribbon group of nineteen foreign election experts also published an open letter expressing their concern "that Canada's international reputation as one of the world's guardians of democracy and human rights is threatened by passage of the proposed Fair Elections Act."[62]

All major newspapers in the country came out against the bill in their editorial pages, some of them repeatedly.[63] Former auditor general Sheila Fraser, who had played a major role in exposing the sponsorship scandal to the light, called the bill "an attack on our democracy." The minister saw the need to answer criticism in the media.[64] In the end, a Conservative-dominated Senate committee pre-studied the bill and came up on April 15 with a proposal for amendments, and the government backtracked on some controversial provisions ten days later. The bill was passed by the House on May 13, with all opposition parties voting against.

### The Substance[65]

The amendments enacted by C-23 were aimed at involving the political parties in the regulatory work of Elections Canada, and diminishing its power over them. Under the new act, the CEO is required to issue to the various political entities non-binding guidelines and interpretation notes on the application of the legislation, and can provide binding written opinions on the application of the act only at the request of registered political parties.

The legislation created an Advisory Committee of Political Parties, to be consulted before the issuance of any guideline or interpretation note.[66] The CEO is also required to issue an opinion on an activity or practice that the party or its registered associations, candidates, nomination contestants, or leadership contestants propose to engage in. The Advisory Committee is to be consulted in preparing an opinion. An opinion is only binding with respect to the activity or practice of the party (or its registered associations, candidates, nomination contestants, or leadership contestants) in question. Otherwise, for other purposes, the opinion is not binding on the CEO and the commissioner, although it has precedential value for them until a contrary interpretation is issued by means of a guideline, an interpretation note, or an opinion. Before the CEO issues any guideline, interpretation note, or opinion, however, it must be posted for thirty days on the CEO's website. Where the CEO is responding to an application from a political party, he or she must pre-publish his or her response.

The legislation limits the power of the chief electoral officer to adapt the Canada Elections Act "for the sole purpose of enabling electors to exercise their right to vote or enabling the counting of votes."

The power of the CEO to communicate with electors is limited to certain specific aspects of the electoral processes. The provision that hitherto allowed the CEO to try to offer help to persons or groups who were most likely to experience difficulties in exercising their democratic rights was deleted. The act now states that the CEO may still implement public education initiatives and information programs to make the electoral process better known to students at the primary and secondary levels, and must ensure that any communications with electors are accessible to persons with disabilities.

The power of the CEO to carry out studies on alternative voting processes has been made subject to prior approval of the committees of the Senate and of the House of Commons that normally consider electoral matters. With respect to the implementation of alternative *electronic* voting methods, prior approval of the Senate and the House of Commons is required before the process may be used for an official vote.

Future chief electoral officers will have ten-year tenures and cannot be reappointed, while the former incumbents, including the present one, could stay in office until retirement. The CEO has been made subject to the requirement in the Conflict of Interest Act for public office holders to avoid conflicts of interest, recuse themselves in the event of a conflict, and not act in a manner that takes improper advantage of their office after their term of office.

One of the most controversial innovations of Bill C-23 is the severance of the connection between the chief electoral officer and the official responsible for investigations of alleged violations of the act, known as the commissioner of Canada Elections. The chief electoral officer lost to the director of public prosecutions the power to appoint the commissioner, and has been specifically excluded from consultation whenever the director appoints a new commissioner for a non-renewable term of seven years. The chief electoral officer and Elections Canada staff have been put on the same footing as candidates and party staff, and excluded from filling this office. The chief electoral officer has also lost the power to direct the commissioner to make an inquiry if he believes that an offence has been committed. The Department of Public Works has also insisted that the commissioner's office be moved away from Elections Canada's offices, against the opposition of the commissioner himself.[67]

Other provisions of Bill C-23 are likely to have a more direct impact on Canadians. The view, widespread among Conservatives if unsupported by evidence, that fraud at the polls was rampant, led to a tightening of the rules governing the identification of voters. First, voter information cards cannot be authorized by the chief electoral officer as a type of identification for an elector. Second, the old practice of vouching, whereby a person could vote if another qualified elector vouched for him or her, which had been preserved under the 2007 amendments, was banned and has been replaced by an attestation. Electors who have established their *identity* (but not their residence) through two authorized identification pieces may establish their *residence* by taking a prescribed oath in writing.[68] It remains to be seen whether these requirements have the effect of deterring some voters.[69]

Bill C-23 also included far less controversial innovations. For example, a fourth advance polling day was added, so that advance polling is now available on the Friday, Saturday, Sunday, and Monday, the tenth to seventh days before polling day.[70] This was appropriate, as the percentage of voters voting in advance has jumped from 5.4 percent in 1997 to 10 percent in 2008 and 14 percent in 2011.[71]

Bill C-23 also removed the ban on the public transmission of election results before all the polls in the country closed. There had been a long-running battle by a British Columbia resident against this ban, a battle supported by both the CBC and Harper (when he was president of the NCC). This battle had finally been judicially concluded in 2007 when the Supreme Court of Canada upheld the ban by the smallest possible majority.[72] Another attempt in 2011 also failed.[73] However, as had been expected for a long time, Harper used Bill C-23 to repeal the ban, one which it must be admitted many others found unrealistic in the age of the Internet.

With respect to election expenses and political contributions, Bill C-23 increased the limit on political contributions from $1,200 to $1,500, and mandated a further increase of $25 per year in the future. The maximum amount that a regular candidate and a leadership contestant could contribute to their own campaign, without the amount being subject to the $1,500 ceiling on contributions, was increased to $5,000 and $25,000 respectively. The use of loans to evade donation limit laws was banned. Reimbursements of election expenses to candidates who overspend will be reduced, pursuant to a sliding scale that penalizes these candidates. The $150,000 limit on election expenses incurred by third parties will cover the pre-election period, not just the campaign period itself. The ceiling on election expenses for parties and candidates was marginally increased, but the government had to drop a controversial provision that would have allowed them not to include the commercial value of services provided to a political party to solicit contributions.

Critics found so many causes for outrage in C-23 that most overlooked a clause that had the effect of allowing the prime minister to increase unilaterally and markedly the maximum amount of election expenses.[74] Since their introduction in 1974, the limits on the amounts that could be spent by parties and candidates were set with no regard to the duration of the election campaign. If the campaign lasted twice the standard thirty-seven days, parties and candidates would be allowed to spend, on a daily basis, only one-half of what they would otherwise have spent. Under C-23, however, if an election campaign lasted longer than the standard thirty-seven days, the election expenses limit would be increased accordingly by adding to it the product of 1/37 of the election expenses limit and the number of campaign days in excess of thirty-seven.[75]

Few foresaw that this paved the way for a well-heeled government party, by doubling the length of the election campaign, to increase the spending limit by the same proportion, allowing it to outspend its poorer rivals without breaching the law. On July 29, 2015, it was revealed that the prime minister intended to do just that, which was confirmed a few days later when the longest election campaign in Canadian history — seventy-eight days — was called.

## CONCLUSION

The Harper government is now history. Justin Trudeau's new government is unlikely to endorse its legacy without amendment. In a ministerial mandate letter, the prime minister instructed the new minister of democratic institutions to "bring forward proposals to introduce amendments to the Canada Elections Act to make the commissioner of Canada Elections more independent from government. In addition, repeal the elements of the Fair

Elections Act which make it harder for Canadians to vote and easier for election law breakers to evade punishment." Further, the new minister was invited to bring forward a proposal to establish a special parliamentary committee to consult on electoral reform, "including preferential ballots, proportional representation, mandatory voting, and online voting," and to provide options to create an independent commissioner to organize future leaders' electoral campaign debates. Also ordered was a review of the spending limits imposed on political parties and third parties during elections and a proposal for imposing "reasonable limits" on spending between elections.[76]

The most far-reaching commitment made by the new government was, of course, to ensure that the 2015 election will be the last one conducted under first-past-the-post. "Ranked ballots" (i.e., presumably, Australian-style alternative voting) and proportional representation are envisaged as alternatives to the first-past-the-post system. However, MPs will clearly be in control of the process, and their misgivings will have plenty of opportunities to be heard. Legislation will be brought forward within eighteen months. The Conservatives contend that any change to the electoral system must be submitted to a referendum.

## NOTES

1. Louis Massicotte, "Electoral Reform in the Charter Era," in *The Canadian General Election of 1997*, ed. Alan Frizzell and Jon H. Pammett (Toronto: Dundurn, 1997), 167–91; and "Electoral Legislation Since 1997: Parliament Regains the Initiative," in *The Canadian Federal Election of 2006*, ed. Jon H. Pammett and Christopher Dornan (Toronto: Dundurn, 2006), 196–219.
2. See Bryan Schwartz and Andrew Buck, "Fixed Elections Dates," *Underneath the Golden Boy* 5 (2008): 5, n. 26.
3. At the time of writing, all provinces but Nova Scotia and all the territories but the Yukon provided for elections at fixed dates.
4. The decision to call an early election in 2008, without the government having been defeated in the House, was challenged, on constitutional grounds, by the non-governmental organization Democracy Watch before the Trial Division of the Federal Court of Canada, which, in September 2009, denied the application. See *Conacher v. Canada (Prime Minister)*, [2010] 3 F.C.R. 411. In May 2010, the Federal Court of Appeal upheld that decision [2011] 4 F.C.R. 22. See Doug Stoltz, "Fixed Dates Elections, Parliamentary Dissolutions, and the Court," *Canadian Parliamentary Review* 33, no. 1 (2010): 15–20, available at www.revparl.

ca/33/1/33n1_10e_Stoltz.pdf; Guy Tremblay, "The 2008 Election and the Law on Fixed Election Dates," *Canadian Parliamentary Review* 31, no. 4 (2008): 24–25, available at www.revparl.ca/31/4/31n4_08e_Tremblay.pdf; and Adam Dodek, "Fixing Our Fixed Election Date Legislation," *Canadian Parliamentary Review* 32, no. 1 (2009): 18–20, available at www.revparl.ca/32/1/32n1_09e_Dodek.pdf. For a critical comment on the decisions of the courts, see Andrew Heard, "*Conacher* Missed the Mark on Constitutional Conventions and Fixed Elections Dates," *Canadian Forum Constitutionnel* 19, no. 1 (2010): 129–40, available at https://ejournals.library.ualberta.ca/index.php/constitutional_forum/article/viewFile/17260/13861.

5. For a summary of developments in the 2000s, see Pauline Beange, "Canadian Campaign Finance Reform Since 2000: Path Dependent or Dynamic?", paper presented at the annual general meeting of the Canadian Political Science Association, Ottawa, Ontario, May 2009, available at www.cpsa-acsp.ca/papers-2009/Beange.pdf.
6. The contribution limit was to be adjusted for inflation, so it was $1,100 from 2008 to 2011, and $1,200 from 2012 to 2014. Bill C-23 increased the limit to $1,500 effective January 1, 2015. This part of the measure was not controversial.
7. The various stages of the passage of the bill by both House and Senate are summarized in a document prepared by the Library of Parliament: "Bill C-2: The Federal Accountability Act," LS-52E, December 2006, available online at www.parl.gc.ca/Content/LOP/LegislativeSummaries/39/1/c2-e.pdf, accessed on July 15, 2015.
8. According to 2007 figures that were circulated at that time, the public subsidy represented 86 percent of total revenue for the Bloc Québécois, 63 percent for the Liberals, and 57 percent for the NDP. The Conservatives got the largest chunk of the subsidy, but this was the source of only 37 percent of their revenue.
9. There is little evidence regarding how the public felt about party subsidies, but an Ipsos poll conducted in December 2008 found 61 percent opposed them and 36 percent supported them: http://westernstandard.blogs.com/shotgun/2008/12/poll-canadians.html.
10. See www.budget.gc.ca/2011/plan/chap5-eng.html and s. 445 of the Canada Elections Act. The provision phasing out party subsidies can be found in the 644-page omnibus bill Keeping Canada's Economy and Jobs Growing Act, SC 2011 c. 24 s. 181.
11. See www.mlpc.ca/RU2015/RU15079.HTM.
12. SC 2007 c. 21.
13. Standing Committee of the House on Procedure and House Affairs, *Thirteenth Report: Improving the Integrity of the Electoral Process. Recommendations for Legislative Change*. This report, which had the support of almost all parties, is available online at www.parl.gc.ca/HousePublications/Publication.aspx?DocId=2287023&Language=E&Mode=1&Parl=39&Ses=1.
14. Ibid., 25. Emphasis added.
15. *Government Response to the Thirteenth Report of the Standing Committee on Procedure and House Affairs. Improving the Integrity of the Election Process*, 2006, available at www.parl.gc.ca/HousePublications/Publication.aspx?DocId=2418739&Language=E&ode=1&Parl=39&Ses=1.
16. See remarks by Libby Davies, MP, *Hansard*, November 8, 2006, www.parl.gc.ca/HousePublications/Publication.aspx?Pub=Hansard&Doc=79&Parl=39&Ses=1&Language=E&Mode=1.

17. See remarks by Mario Laframboise, MP, citing Elections Canada figures, *Hansard*, December13,2007,www.parl.gc.ca/HousePublications/Publication.aspx?Pub=Hansard &Doc=37&Parl=39&Ses=2&Language=E&Mode=1#OOB-2272040.
18. SC 2007 c. 37.
19. The objections of the NDP were not directed against Bill C-18 per se, but rather against the original Bill C-31. The bill was passed in committee without amendment and there were no recorded divisions at the major stages of its parliamentary consideration.
20. *Henry v. Canada (Attorney General (AG))*, 2010 BCSC 610; 2014 BCCA 30.
21. These are Chief Electoral Officer Blanchet's very words. See Senate Standing Committee on Legal and Constitutional Affairs, May 16, 2007, www.parl.gc.ca/Content/SEN/Committee/391/lega/44645-e.htm?comm_id=11&Language=F&Parl=39&Ses=1. Many also felt that the concerns raised by the media, about women being allowed to vote wearing burkas or niqabs, had been overblown. For a similar reaction, see Commission de consultation sur les pratiques d'accommodement reliées aux différences culturelles (Bouchard-Taylor Commission), *Rapport. Fonder l'avenir. Le temps de la conciliation* (Québec, 2008), 73–74.
22. Standing Committee on Procedure and House Affairs, September 13, 2007, available at www.parl.gc.ca/HousePublications/Publication.aspx?DocId=3070382&Mode=1 &Parl=39&Ses=1&Language=E.
23. Conservative Party of Canada, *Stand Up for Canada, Federal Election Platform, 2006*, 44. See www.cbc.ca/canadavotes2006/leadersparties/pdf/conservative_platform20060113.pdf.
24. See Andrew Sancton, "The Principle of Representation by Population in Canadian Politics," paper prepared for the Mowat Centre for Policy Innovation, March 2010, available at http://mowatcentre.ca/wp-content/uploads/publications/2_the_principle_of_representation.pdf, accessed on November 8, 2015.
25. Ironically, under the formula that was finally enacted, this oddity remains, as Alberta and British Columbia have been granted an aggregate seventy-six seats against Quebec's seventy-eight.
26. See Louis Massicotte, "'What Place for Quebec? A Study of Federal Electoral Redistribution," a study prepared for L'Idée Fédérale,' *Réseau Québécois de discussion sur le fédéralisme* (2009), 19, n, 39.
27. Resolution passed on April 22, 2010, www.saic.gouv.qc.ca/affaires-intergouvernementales/positions-historiques/motions/2010-04-22-chambre-communes.pdf.
28. In the absence of projections for future censuses in government documents, this point was made by Louis Massicotte, "'Rep. by Pop.'? Le projet de loi C-12 sur la redistribution," *Policy Options Politiques* (May 2010): 57–60, available at http://policyoptions.irpp.org/wp-content/uploads/sites/2/assets/po/the-fault-lines-of-federalism/massicotte.pdf.
29. According to the government, this figure reflected the average riding population prior to the last seat readjustment in 2001, increased by the simple average of provincial population growth rates. See www.democraticreform.gc.ca/eng/content/fair-representation-act-moves-every-province-towards-rep-pop.
30. The timetable was slightly altered by the 2011 act, so as to speed up the process.
31. For an interprovincial comparative analysis of the proposed boundaries, see Michael Pal and Melissa Molson, "Moving Toward Voter Equality. Mowat Center Report

on the Proposed Federal Electoral Boundaries for Ontario" (November 2012), 4, available at http://mowatcentre.ca/wp-content/uploads/publications/55_moving_toward_voter_equality.pdf.

32. See www.elections.ca/content.aspx?section=res&dir=cir/trans2013&document=index&lang=e.
33. Elections Canada was not instructed to transpose the results of the 2008 election into the new boundaries, but Poll Maps did, with the following outcomes. The Conservatives would have won 164 seats instead of 143, the Liberals eighty-six instead of seventy-seven, the Bloc Québécois fifty-one instead of forty-nine, the NDP thirty-five instead of thirty-seven, while two independent MPs would have been returned in each case. No majority would have been won by any party, but the Conservatives would have been much closer to winning one than they actually were. See http://fed2013.pollmaps.ca/.
34. This author's computations, based on the electoral enrollment in each electoral district in 2011.
35. For a summary of the dispute, see http://voices-voix.ca/en/facts/profile/elections-canada.
36. *Callaghan v. Canada (Chief Electoral Officer)*, [2011] 2 FCR 3, available at http://reports.fja.gc.ca/eng/2011/2010fc43.pdf. The decision offers a reliable factual summary of the Conservative "scheme" (as the court called it) that led to this case.
37. *Canada (Chief Electoral Officer) v. Callaghan*, [2011] FCA 74, available at http://decisions.fca-caf.gc.ca/fca-caf/decisions/en/item/37078/index.do.
38. Steven Chase, "Tory Senators Facing Charges from Elections Canada over Election Spending," *Globe and Mail*, February 24, 2011.
39. Laura Payton, "Conservative Party Fined for Breaking Election Laws," CBC News, November 10, 2011.
40. Postmedia News, "Conservatives Drop Appeal of 'In and Out' Ruling," *National Post*, March 6, 2012.
41. In the end, the Liberals won the riding by six thousand votes, an increase over their 2008 score, which itself ran against the trend in the province.
42. *R. v. Sona*, 2014 ONCJ 606 (Hearn), available at www.ontariocourts.ca/search-canlii/scj/scj-en.htm.
43. Ibid.
44. Ibid.
45. Laura Payton, "Dean Del Mastro's Bid to Reopen Trial Is Dismissed," CBC News, February 18, 2015, available online at www.cbc.ca/news/politics/dean-del-mastro-s-bid-to-reopen-trial-is-dismissed-1.2961536, accessed on July 8, 2015.
46. *R. v. Sona*, 2014 ONCA 859 (LaForme), available online at http://canlii.ca/t/gfgd1.
47. The ridings represented by these MPs were Winnipeg South Centre, Saskatoon-Rosetown-Biggar, Elmwood-Transcona, Nipissing-Timiskaming, Vancouver Island North, and Yukon. All had been won by the Conservatives by close margins, ranging from 18 to 1,827 votes.
48. *McEwing v. Canada (AG)*, [2013] 4 FCR 63, available at http://reports.fja.gc.ca/fra/2013/2013cf525.pdf.
49. Ibid., 148.
50. Ibid., 151.

51. Commissioner of Canada Elections, *Summary Investigation Report on Robocalls: An Investigation into Complaints of Nuisance Telephone Calls and of Telephone Calls Providing Incorrect Poll Location Information in Electoral Districts Other Than Guelph During the 41st General Election of May 2011*, April 2014, available online at www.cef-cce.gc.ca/rep/rep2/roboinv_e.pdf, accessed on July 8, 2015.
52. Bruce Cheadle, "Elections Canada Fights Lengthy Battles over Campaign Expense Reporting," June 7, 2013, available online at www.660news.com/2013/06/07/agent-for-former-conservative-mp-wajid-khan-pleads-guilty-under-elections-act/, accessed on July 9, 2015; Canadian Press, "Jacques Chouinard plaide coupable à des infractions à la loi électorale," *La Presse*, January 24, 2014.
53. *Opitz v. Wrzesnewskyj*, [2012] 3 SCR 76, available online at https://scc-csc.lexum.com/scc-csc/scc-csc/fr/12635/1/document.do, accessed on July 25, 2015.
54. *Frank et al. v. AG Canada*, 2014 ONSC 207, available online at http://canlii.ca/t/g6r5z, accessed on July 15, 2015.
55. *Frank v. Canada (AG)*, 2014 ONCA 485, available online at www.ontariocourts.on.ca/decisions/2014/2014ONCA0485.pdf , accessed on July 15, 2015.
56. Bill C-50, Citizen Voting Act. The bill was given second reading and sent to committee, but had not been adopted when Parliament was adjourned in June 2015. It lapsed when Parliament was dissolved.
57. *Frank v. Canada (AG)*, 2015 ONCA 536, a split decision (two to one, Justice Laskin dissenting), available online at www.ontariocourts.ca/decisions/2015/2015ONCA0536.htm, accessed on July 20, 2015. Actor Donald Sutherland made an impassioned plea for expatriate voting. See "I'm Canadian — and I Should Have a Right to Vote," *Globe and Mail*, July 28, 2015.
58. For an illuminating background summary, see Kate Heartfield, "The Harper Conservatives and Elections Canada," *Ottawa Citizen*, February 3, 2014, http://ottawacitizen.com/opinion/the-harper-conservatives-and-elections-canada, accessed on July 11, 2015.
59. Heartfield, op. cit.
60. See the *Debates of the House of Commons*, April 29, 2008, 5200–229 and 5242–258.
61. "An Open Letter to Prime Minister Stephen Harper and to the Parliament of Canada," March 11, 2014, available online at http://democracy-arts.sites.olt.ubc.ca/files/2014/03/OpenLetter_BillC23_March11_2014.pdf; and Melissa Williams et al., "An Open Letter on the Fair Elections Act," *Globe and Mail*, April 23, 2014, available online at www.theglobeandmail.com/globe-debate/an-open-letter-from-academics-on-bill-c-23/article18114166/?page=all, both accessed on July 31, 2015. One of the very few academics who supported the measure was exposed as a former defeated Conservative candidate.
62. "We believe that this Act would prove [to] be deeply damaging to the electoral integrity within Canada," *Globe and Mail*, March 19, 2014.
63. "Don't Undermine Elections Canada," *National Post*, March 11, 2014; "Federal Elections Bill Needs Major Changes," *Montreal Gazette*, March 11, 2014; "Slow It Down, Mr. Poilievre," *Globe and Mail*, March 10–14, 2014; "The Fair Elections Act: Kill This Bill," *Globe and Mail*, March 23, 2014, and "A Less Bad Fair Elections Act Is Not Good Enough." *Globe and Mail*, April 15, 2014; André Pratte, "Des raisons de se méfier," *La Presse*, March 15, 2014.

64. Pierre Poilievre, "Why the Fair Elections Act Is, In Fact, Fair," *Globe and Mail*, March 24, 2014.
65. For a detailed summary of the provisions of the bill and the amendments brought thereto, see Michel Bédard, "Legislative Summary, Bill C-23, an Act to Amend the Canada Elections Act and Other Acts and to Make Consequential Amendments to Other Acts" (Library of Parliament: Publication No. 41-2-C-23-E, revised September 11, 2014), www.parl.gc.ca/About/Parliament/LegislativeSummaries/bills_ls.asp?source=library_prb&ls=C23&Parl=41&Ses=2&Language=E&Mode=1, accessed on July 13, 2015.
66. The Advisory Committee is comprised of the CEO (as chair) and two representatives of each registered political party. It is expected to meet at least once a year. The purpose of this committee is to provide the CEO with advice and recommendations relating to elections and political financing. Its advice and recommendations are non-binding on the CEO.
67. Joan Bryden and Bruce Cheadle, "Chief Investigator Yves Côté Pushed Back on Move from Elections Canada," *Huffington Post*, July 15, 2015. The commissioner had publicly questioned the wisdom of severing his office from Elections Canada, but was maintained in office.
68. For details, see ss. 143 SQ of the act, as amended.
69. The Council of Canadians and the Canadian Federation of Students challenged the new identity requirements in court and tried to prevent their application in the 2015 election. On July 17, 2015, a judge of the Ontario Superior Court of Justice refused to do the latter: *Council of Canadians v. Canada (AG)*, 2015 ONSC 4601, available online at www.ontariocourts.ca/en/2015ONSC4601.htm, accessed on July 20, 2015.
70. This measure had been lingering since 2007, with four government bills providing for expanded voting opportunities dying on the order paper in succession: C-55 in May 2007; C-16, November 2007; C-40, June 2009; and C-18, April 2010.
71. Elections Canada, *The Electoral System of Canada*, 2nd. ed. (Ottawa: Elections Canada, 2007), 31; *Report of the Chief Electoral Officer on the 41st General Election of May 2, 2011*, 34, www.elections.ca/content.aspx?section=res&dir=rep/off/sta_2011&document=index&lang=e. In 2015, a record 20.7 percent of the votes were cast at advance polls, a clear indication that this was a timely innovation.
72. *R. v. Bryan*, [2007] 1 SCR 527. Earlier, Bryan had lost in trial, won in the B.C. Supreme Court, and lost again in the Court of Appeal of British Columbia.
73. *CDN Broadcasting Corp. v. Canada (AG)*, 2011 ONSC 2281 (Ontario Superior Court of Justice), available online at www.canlii.org/en/on/onsc/doc/2011/2011onsc2281/2011onsc2281.html, accessed on July 31, 2015.
74. For a premonitory piece, see Alice Funke, "Here Is How the Prime Minister Could Erase Our Election-Day Choice," *Maclean's*, June 3, 2015.
75. Canada Elections Act, paras. 430(2) and 477.49(2).
76. Prime Minister's Office, "Minister of Democratic Institutions Mandate Letter," November 2015, available at http://pm.gc.ca/eng/minister-democratic-institutions-mandate-letter, accessed on November 13, 2015. The full Liberal agenda on parliamentary reform, a thirty-two-page document entitled *Real Change: A Fair and Open Government* had been unveiled in June 2015: see www.liberal.ca/files/2015/06/a-fair-and-open-government.pdf.

## CHAPTER 8

# Mounting a Local Campaign

Allan Thompson

Spoiler alert: I didn't win the election.

---

As the federal Liberal candidate in the southwestern Ontario riding of Huron-Bruce, I came a relatively close second on October 19. Keep in mind that Huron-Bruce is considered a Tory bastion. In 2011, the Conservative incumbent won with 29,255 votes (55 percent of the popular vote), demolishing the Liberal candidate, who finished a dismal third, with 8,784, far behind the NDP, in second with 13,493. The 2011 calamity was the Liberal Party's worst ever showing in Huron-Bruce.

In 2015, my campaign team and I managed to put the Liberals back in contention, finishing second with 23,129 votes to 26,174 for incumbent Ben Lobb and pushing the NDP back into third at 7,544, followed by the Greens with 1,398.

This chapter is devoted to the story of a local campaign and must be told in the first person, since I was a candidate. The fact that the election date was set years in advance allowed for years of planning. Short of giving away confidences, I want to share as much as I can about that process because, in my experience, we rarely, if ever, look closely at what goes into mounting a local campaign.

As a political reporter with the *Toronto Star*, I had spent nearly a decade on Parliament Hill and covered three major campaigns — the 1995 Quebec referendum as well as the 1997 and the 2000 federal election campaigns. But for all that, I had virtually no concept — none — of what is involved in organizing a run for office at the riding level. As a reporter,

I spent most of my time with leaders and Cabinet ministers, and during elections, I covered the party leader tours by riding the planes and buses with the rest of the press corps. Yes, those stops with the leaders would invariably bring us into contact with ordinary candidates running for the position of member of Parliament. But to be honest, those local candidates most often seemed like props for the national campaign as we slavishly focused our attention on the horse race among the leaders.

What a revelation it has been to build a campaign at the local level from the ground up. I was most struck by three things: the degree of volunteer effort by hundreds who joined in the democratic process, the profound and exhilarating interaction with ordinary people on their doorsteps or out in the community, and the bone-crunching pace of a modern election campaign. To fully understand the process it is important to look at the stages in the campaign — the nomination contest, the pre-writ period, and the formal election that begins with the dropping of the writ. Along the way, I will touch on some cross-cutting themes: building a campaign organization, interaction with voters, the role of the media, and how the campaign strategy in a rural riding intersects with the national story.

---

In my case, from beginning to end this election campaign lasted 881 days — two years, four months, and twenty-eight days. That's the time from my first formal point of contact with the Liberal Party organization in Huron-Bruce through to the day of the election. For the final eighteen months I was campaigning almost full-time.

Before we plunge into the campaign itself, however, a glance at the riding of Huron-Bruce and then a brief biography.

The boundaries of the riding known since 1976 as Huron-Bruce have shifted over the years. The riding is nestled along the shores of Lake Huron and comprises all of Huron County and the southern part of Bruce County. It is one of the most rural ridings in the country with no major urban centres, no train stations, and no airports beyond municipal landing strips. Everyone in Huron-Bruce lives on a farm, on a country road, or in a small town. The Huron County part — Ontario's agricultural heartland — has long been considered a Tory stronghold. Over the years, bits and pieces of Bruce County, which lies to the north and was traditionally more Liberal, were added to the riding.

From the 1950s to the 1993 election of Jean Chrétien's Liberals, the area was held by a series of long-serving Progressive Conservative MPs. In the 1993 Chrétien sweep, Huron-Bruce fell to Liberal candidate Paul Steckle, who many regarded as a rather conservative, blue Liberal. He won the riding five times, operating as something of a maverick — opposing his own party on such issues as abortion, gay marriage, and gun control. Steckle held the riding narrowly when Stephen Harper's Conservatives took power in 2006 but didn't run again in 2008, when thirty-one-year-old Ben Lobb, a member of a prominent Huron County family, won for the Conservatives. Lobb was re-elected by a landslide in 2011.

I was born and raised on a farm near the village of Glammis in the Bruce County part of the riding. I went through school there, and while studying journalism at Carleton University, held my first reporting jobs back home at the weekly Kincardine *Independent* and *Teeswater News*. Most of my full-time career in journalism was spent with the *Toronto Star*. I worked at the newsroom in Toronto from 1987 to 1994 and on Parliament Hill from 1994 to 2003 — essentially the Chrétien era. In 2003, I took up a position as a journalism professor at Carleton but continued to freelance for the *Star* and wrote a column on immigration issues for it until 2012.

Although I was focused on my journalism career during most of this period, I did briefly contemplate running for the Liberals in Huron-Bruce in the 1993 election. I went as far as to draft a letter addressed to Chrétien, offering myself up as a candidate, and made preliminary contact with the riding association. But in the end, I backed off and stayed in journalism.

Midway through the Stephen Harper decade, I had a sort of personal epiphany. I could no longer stand on the sidelines and watch what Harper was doing to my country. So I decided that I had to do something, and that something was to seek election and to try to take a seat away from the Tories. I joined a political party for the first time in my life, signing up with the Liberals in time to vote for Justin Trudeau in his successful 2013 bid to become leader.

From the outset, I set my sights on Huron-Bruce. While some advised me the riding was unwinnable, I was determined to run there because of my family roots and my sense that Huron-Bruce needed a stronger voice in Ottawa. I was very conscious of the fact that I had not lived in the riding since my early twenties. But I felt that my rural upbringing and ongoing connection there combined with my work experience gave me a foot in both worlds and would help me to represent the area effectively.

After mulling things over with my wife, in the spring of 2013 I sent an email to a family friend who was also a long-time member of the Huron-Bruce Federal Liberal riding association. In the message I said I was contemplating seeking the Liberal nomination in Huron-Bruce but wanted to know if there was a preferred candidate in the wings. I was told the field seemed open.

And so it began.

## THE NOMINATION CONTEST

On my visits home in the coming months, I began to piece together, one by one, a network of local Liberal supporters who had at one time or another been active with the party at the provincial or federal level. Some of the contacts were obvious, as they were current members of the riding association executive. But dozens of others I contacted weren't listed anywhere. They were just known Liberals and one contact led to the next. At each stop, I introduced myself, outlined why I was thinking of running, and asked for support and more names. Time and again I explained I wasn't yet ready to go public with my campaign but was seeking support for my eventual run. Most said yes — some quite enthusiastically — but others needed more convincing, or were waiting to see who else would emerge as a candidate.

Early in 2014, I had to make decisions about when to go public with my nomination bid and how to formalize my organization. While the election in October of 2015 seemed far away, there was some buzz that Harper might once again ignore the fixed election date and go early. I was scheduled to go on a six-month sabbatical from Carleton as of July 1, so my plan was to launch my nomination bid in July in hopes the nomination meeting would be held in the autumn, leaving me close to a year to establish a presence in the riding, build up my team, and bolster my name recognition.

While no one had declared publicly any intention of seeking the nomination in Huron-Bruce, I could only assume that, like me, others could be at work under the radar. I assumed that some of those who had sought or held the nomination before might want to run again.

My formal campaign organization began to take shape in January and early February of 2014. I connected with former MP Paul Steckle, who said he would be remaining neutral in the nomination contest, but as chair of a candidate recruitment committee, he invited me to come and introduce myself to the group at a private meeting near Seaforth in late February.

Things were in motion now. I had applied to attend the Liberal Party of Canada's Biennial Convention, being held the weekend of February 21–23 in Montreal, as a delegate from Huron-Bruce. My mission in attending the convention — over and above immersing myself in the party now led by Trudeau — was to establish what I had to do next to complete the party's elaborate "green light" vetting process for prospective candidates. It was only as I was heading up the escalator to the convention floor that it dawned on me I would likely bump into former colleagues in the press gallery and would have to explain why I was a delegate at a Liberal convention. When the inevitable happened, I awkwardly declined to comment on why I was attending the convention, but I assume that most figured it out. I knew that my candidacy would not be big news — the place was awash with potential candidates — but any news at all, even a passing reference in a tweet or blog, would essentially launch my campaign in Huron-Bruce. And I wasn't yet ready to launch. Fortunately, none of my former press gallery colleagues mentioned me in their reports.

I was equally fortunate in that I was able to connect with a number of key figures at the convention. And I was thoroughly impressed by my first contact with Trudeau — although I only saw him from a distance. The party slogan, *Hope and Hard Work*, spoke to me in a way that political slogans rarely do.

To formally seek the nomination, I needed the signatures of close to one hundred riding association members in Huron-Bruce. So I began selling $10 memberships and seeking signatures. And, in accordance with Elections Canada guidelines, I also had to open a bank account and appoint a financial agent to handle donations to my nomination campaign.[1] The green light package was like a lengthy job application. It also required a criminal record check, a credit-rating statement, references, and extensive details about my work, personal life, public statements, and online presence. Later, I would go through two lengthy and intrusive telephone interviews with party officials vetting contestants.

In late March, I reached out to the person who would become the cornerstone of both my nomination bid and my eventual election campaign. Rod MacDonald is a career Liberal from Kincardine who worked over the years on numerous provincial Liberal campaigns and also held positions at Queen's Park under the David Peterson administration and later with Premier Dalton McGuinty. By coincidence, Rod is married to a distant cousin of mine, who was born and raised in Glammis. While Rod and I had known of each other for years, we had met only in passing before I arrived at his door in late March to ask him to manage my nomination bid. Rod prefers to remain in the background when it comes to politics, so I will respect his wishes. But suffice it to say that he was instrumental in the organization and campaign effort that I am about to describe. Indeed, that is an understatement. Together, we built a campaign organization that combined the best of 1970s- and 1980s-style grassroots politicking with social media and the modern database technology and campaign structures advocated by the Trudeau Liberals. And we came close to winning.

Apart from Rod and members of my family, I'm not going to name campaign workers and supporters. There are simply too many who played a role and it would be unfair to name some and not others. I also need to respect confidences and privacy. As a result, many won't get the public acknowledgement they so richly deserve. You can find them in my Facebook posts.[2] And they know who they are.

But those types of people are the heart and soul of any campaign. One of the great revelations for me was that volunteers are at the very core of our democracy, people who donate their time, effort, and creativity to the political process at the local level. Every single member of my campaign worked for free, some of them on a full-time basis for months on end. I still find that nothing short of remarkable. The fact that ordinary people can and will get involved in electoral politics in this country is the magic sauce that makes our democracy work.

Throughout the late winter and early spring of 2014, I began weekly conference calls with members of my campaign team. The focus was on recruiting "captains" in virtually every community in the riding to sell party memberships on my behalf to supporters. These recruiters were provided with a campaign kit — in a bright red folder — containing instructions as well as copies of my biography and Liberal Party membership forms. I also began actively fundraising and, under strict Elections Canada guidelines, raised thousands of dollars to support my nomination bid, funds used to cover the cost of printing, establishing web and social media platforms, and for fuel to keep my car going over the thousands of kilometres travelled to campaign in a large, rural riding.

In June, I effectively moved back to Huron-Bruce, setting up shop on the family farm just outside Glammis, where I created a home office and put in a dedicated phone line. My wife and son carried on with their lives in Ottawa, but for all intents and purposes I was now a resident of Huron-Bruce, visiting Ottawa for a few days every month or so. And when they could, Roula and our son, Laith, would join me on the campaign trail.

In late June, with "green light" approval under my belt, I settled on Monday, July 14, as the day to publicly launch my nomination bid. The Monday would be a "soft launch" through the news media and my own social media platforms, with a public launch event on Wednesday, July 16, at my sister's pub in Tiverton, the King's Pearl. My hope was that this dual launch would generate almost a week's worth of valuable earned media coverage and perhaps give pause to some potential competitors. I was right on both counts.

I am, by training, a journalist. So establishing a media presence was crucial to me and an exciting challenge, but it was also a bit of a mind-bender at times, as I found myself on the other side of the microphone. The local media scene consists of fourteen or so weekly newspapers (most owned then by Sun Media — now a division of Postmedia — and a handful by my former employer Torstar), a half dozen radio stations, and several online media outlets. There are no daily newspapers in the riding (the nearest dailies are in Owen Sound, Kitchener, and London) and no TV stations. The CTV affiliate in London has a midwestern Ontario correspondent, based out of Wingham.

In the week prior to my launch, I contacted virtually every single reporter and editor in the riding to ask if they would agree to an embargo if I would conduct interviews in advance of my campaign launch. Most agreed and I proceeded to do interviews on the condition outlets wouldn't publish before midnight on Sunday. At the national level, the *Ottawa Citizen* and the website *i*Politics also agreed to an embargo.

How my candidacy was portrayed by the media and viewed by ordinary voters was central to me as a novice politician with no history as a candidate in Huron-Bruce. I hoped to avoid the "parachute candidate" label. I wanted to highlight the experience I had gained as a political reporter and university professor while living away from the riding, but also make clear I was someone with local roots and a meaningful connection to Huron-Bruce. In all of the promotional material generated for my launch, I described myself as someone who was born and raised on a farm near Glammis, a Bruce County native who went off to university, studied journalism, worked at local weeklies, then made a career at the *Toronto Star* and as a university professor before coming back home to seek office. My campaign launch press release put it this way:

> Fed up with the Harper government, Thompson has come back home to Huron-Bruce to seek the nomination in hopes of helping Justin Trudeau's Liberals take back the riding and form a government in the next election.
>
> "I decided that I could no longer stand on the sidelines while Stephen Harper runs down or dismantles some of the pillars of Canadian democracy," Thompson said. "I'm running because I want to get rid of Stephen Harper. The people of Huron-Bruce and all Canadians deserve better.
>
> "I want to restore integrity and principled leadership to Canadian politics."

At the same time as I was preparing for the news media launch, I was also preparing a substantial social media presence of my own. As a candidate, I created a dedicated "politician page" on Facebook,[3] a new Twitter account,[4] a campaign website,[5] a weekly Monday morning newsletter to be sent to my growing email list,[6] and a candidate blog called Allan2015.com, which would eventually host more than eighty entries. Later, I also opened an account with SoundCloud.com to post audio recordings of interviews and speeches.[7] All of my media platforms went live that Sunday evening and through the night.

On YouTube,[8] I launched a campaign video called "The Huron-Bruce Shuffle."[9] In a spoof of Bob Dylan's "Subterranean Homesick Blues," the video featured me, standing silently in front of the Glammis sign, as my campaign message flipped by on a computer screen I was holding. (Dylan's version used flashcards.) Over my shoulder, a band with musicians on harmonica, guitar, and a Celtic drum played a catchy tune they'd composed in the ditch while we set up the camera and microphones.

Monday morning was nothing less than a media blitz, with coverage of my nomination bid and catchy launch video on virtually every media platform in the riding. I got major play in the *Ottawa Citizen* and mentions in the *Star*, *National Post*, *i*Politics, and Owen Sound *Sun Times*. As I had hoped, the thrust of the coverage was very much in keeping with my messaging.[10]

My campaign launch event at the pub on Wednesday was attended by more than one hundred people — including former MP Paul Steckle and long-time MPP Murray Elston — and generated another round of positive media coverage. Laith operated the video camera and also took still photos. We posted it all to social media. And in a practice that I would keep up throughout the campaign, I recorded my own speech and then issued a press release written in a journalistic style that was not overly partisan, replete with actual quotes as well as snippets from some of my endorsements by Liberal supporters. Several media outlets carried the press release verbatim as a news story.[11]

Now that I was officially a nomination contestant, the campaign kicked into high gear. By combing through community calendar entries, and with advice from campaign supporters, I set up a grinding schedule that took me to every corner of the riding — to fairs, church suppers, and many other community events — a schedule that would only intensify as election day approached. I kept a map in my office, marking off the locations I'd visited in an effort to reach as many communities as possible. At virtually every stop, I would post almost simultaneously to my blog, Twitter, and Facebook — all of which were constantly updated through a highlights scroll on my website that included pictures and video clips. My use of a "selfie stick" that held my iPhone at arm's length to snap photos of me with others on the campaign trail became a running joke.

In my early encounters with voters, a few things surprised me. One was the number who seemed unaware a federal election was in the offing, or who, upon hearing that I was a Liberal Party candidate, immediately began talking about provincial politics, even though the provincial election had only just come and gone a year prior. Confusion over the distinction between the provincial Liberals and Justin Trudeau's federal party would remain an issue until the very end, as would the hostile opposition among many in the rural riding to Ontario premier Kathleen Wynne and to anything and everything attached to the "Liberal" brand.

But there were also many who expressed outrage about the Harper government, shared stories about their struggles to get by, and also talked about their outright disgust with politics and politicians. I dutifully recorded these comments — unvarnished — in my blogs and Facebook posts.

In the end, only one challenger for the nomination came forward, a family doctor from Clinton named Maarten Bokhout, who was the policy chair in the riding association and had contested the nomination unsuccessfully in 2008 and 2011. I took Maarten's candidacy seriously as he was a resident of Huron County — seen by some as an advantage in Huron-Bruce — and was also known to many through his practice and as the acting medical officer of health in Huron. And from the publicly available information on Liberal membership in the riding, we could see that Maarten was actively recruiting supporters.

In September and early October, I held a series of ten wine-and-cheese events across the riding. Hosted in private homes, Legion halls, and other venues, these events served as fundraisers and opportunities to recruit new Liberal Party members to support my nomination bid. At each event I would mix and mingle, then give a short stump speech and answer questions. My messaging was straightforward: that it was time for a change, that Justin Trudeau was providing a positive and optimistic agenda in contrast to Harper's negativity, and that I had the background and experience to be a good local candidate for the Liberals.

The nomination meeting was held Monday, October 20, 2014, at the community centre in Lucknow, a town located on the border between Bruce and Huron counties. We had aimed to sell more than five hundred memberships and also put in place a network of regional chairs across the riding to get out the vote. We decorated the hall with large Allan2015 posters and had small placards with my picture glued to paint sticks as well as some larger signs. I took care to make sure there would be a proper media table at the front of the room and briefly seconded my Twitter and Facebook accounts to a campaign volunteer so that updates could be posted throughout the speeches and the voting. I used all of my media platforms to document the event, posting my speech to YouTube and my blog.[12] While the final tally in nomination contests is not released publicly by the Liberal Party, it was obvious in the room that I had won overwhelming support from among the six hundred or so who cast ballots.

"Welcome to the first day of the 2015 election campaign," I said in my acceptance speech. The election was almost exactly one year away.

## THE PRE-WRIT CAMPAIGN

I'd already been campaigning full-time for almost six months when I won the nomination, so in some respects I just carried on. But there were some marked differences. As a nominated candidate, I was now plugged in to the Liberal Party of Canada's campaign network, which included receiving free advice on how to better brand my Twitter and Facebook profiles and also daily emails from the Liberal communications team with information about policy positions on key issues and some suggested tweets. As a candidate, I also joined a weekly conference call with other candidates, led by party officials in Ottawa.

On the ground, in addition to going to other people's events, I began to stage my own. One I dubbed the HaveYourSayCAFE, which consisted of me dropping in on coffee shops and restaurants where I would place a sign on the table saying: "I want to be your MP in Ottawa. Please tell me what's on your mind." I'd also publicize the appearances on Facebook and Twitter and then, as soon as possible after the events, post a blog or short description on Facebook, documenting what people had to say.[13] At every stop, I also gathered email addresses for my Monday newsletter, which described my campaign events in the third person.

In the evenings, I would hold Pub&Politics events along the same lines as the coffee shops, again advertising ahead of time through social media and then plunking a sign on my table, inviting people to come over and chew my ear.[14]

Some on my campaign team were skeptical of these events, wondering just how many people I was reaching. But we came to realize that not only was I engaging those who stopped to talk, but I was also being noticed by others around and by hundreds or even thousands who followed along on social media.

Speculation was still rife that Harper could call a snap election — perhaps even before Christmas, or possibly in the spring — so my team had to assume an election footing. Shortly after the nomination, I announced the appointment of former MPP Murray Elston and riding association president Virginia Schenk as co-chairs of my campaign. We held an organizational meeting for a campaign committee that would now grow outward from my nomination team to include my fellow contestant, Dr. Bokhout, as well as former MP Paul Steckle, long-time MPP Jack Riddell, and other members of the riding association. The committee — about twenty people — had chairs for key responsibilities, such as fundraising, sign placement, communications, volunteers, data gathering, and so on.

Central to our strategy in the pre-writ period was to continue to build my campaign organization, to bolster my name recognition and reputation across the riding, and to identify Liberal voters and potential supporters. As a nominated candidate, I was now receiving more requests to participate in events, so much of the work of maintaining my calendar was taken over by campaign volunteers. But I continued to personally manage my Facebook and Twitter feeds and my blog and newsletter. Facebook was used for brief descriptions of encounters and Twitter, by definition, was restricted to 140-character messages and links to other platforms. The blogs were essentially columns, written in my voice, describing my encounters with voters, inside details of the campaign, or the events that I attended. They were very journalistic in tone. The Monday morning newsletter, delivered by email at around 7 a.m. to close to one thousand subscribers, featured brief, one-paragraph descriptions of my activities the week prior and also contained hyperlinks to posts on the blog, Facebook, and Twitter, and news about upcoming events.

With the election drawing closer, we had decisions to make about how to best use my time. The Liberal Party was providing backing and training for the creation of an elaborately structured campaign organization focused on building up teams of local volunteers, making contact and having conversations with potential supporters, and then aggressively identifying the vote and preparing for election day. Early on, I was invited, along with some members of my team, to attend "Campaign College" events for briefings and training sessions on the party's election strategy. Although some of what was discussed is confidential, much of the Liberal Party approach is in the public domain and is also described elsewhere in this volume. The focus was on a "snowflake" model that would decentralize organization to the community level, essentially creating cells of volunteers across the riding. It was in some ways reminiscent of the old-style system of establishing poll captains.

The support from above was tremendous and, in retrospect, clearly benefitted the party in many ridings. But as I watched my counterparts in urban ridings begin to aggressively knock on doors a year out from election day, I wondered about the application in a rural setting. My campaign manager and I concluded that in the early stages I could more meaningfully engage with voters by attending community events. We would ramp up the door-knocking closer to the writ. Here is our logic: in the city, where people are less likely to know their neighbours, you meet voters one by one, either on their doorsteps or at public events. But in a riding made up of rural areas and small towns, there is an enormous logistical challenge to getting to every doorstep. At the same time, in such ridings many people do know their neighbours and at public events will often know virtually every person in the room and immediately recognize a stranger. For me as a candidate, this meant there was enormous value in attending events, talking to as many people as possible, identifying support and potential volunteers, but also being seen and creating a buzz. And I would then attempt to amplify that buzz by posting all of my activities to Facebook, Twitter, and, eventually, Instagram, to bolster a well-earned reputation as a hard-working candidate who was getting around the vast riding. I would often joke online or in speeches about my attempts to eat my way across Huron-Bruce.

The differences between a rural and urban campaign may seem obvious. My sprawling rural riding contained fourteen municipalities — major towns — as well as dozens of smaller towns and villages. These towns are not just another version of the often very similar neighbourhoods one finds in an urban setting. They are miles apart, literally and figuratively. That meant that every town had to be visited, as often as possible, and local contacts cultivated. My campaign organization recognized the distance from one end of the riding to the other, with two very distinct regional operations, one for the Huron County municipalities and the other for Bruce County. On a typical day, I would travel several hundred kilometres to visit three or four communities.

In November, I had the first of several high-profile visits when Senator Jim Munson, a friend and former journalist who had been appointed by Chrétien, came to Huron-Bruce to talk about a subject dear to his heart — the needs of families dealing with autism spectrum disorder.[15]

In early December, I travelled to Ottawa for another of the Campaign College events for candidates. In addition to training on media messaging, fundraising, and the basics of campaign organization, these team-building exercises also allowed candidates from across the country to meet each other in Ottawa and to spend some time with Trudeau — time that included photo shoots with the leader. We were also allowed to attend the final Liberal caucus meeting of the fall session and the Liberal Christmas party, a kick for those of us new to all of this.

Winter brought additional challenges for me, as I was committed to return to teaching a full course load at Carleton for the winter term after my sabbatical. Like most other candidates, I had to hold down a job while seeking office. The difference for me was that my job at Carleton was a seven-hour drive from where I was living in Huron-Bruce. With my classes and office hours clustered on Wednesdays and Thursdays, and my other work, which included committee tasks and grading assignments and exams, able to be accomplished by phone or online, I was able to come up with a weekly schedule for the winter months that usually saw me leave Glammis late Tuesday and return to the riding by midday on Friday to take up a full Friday-Tuesday schedule of campaign events.

I travelled mostly by car and with some good fortune managed to keep up this pace without once being storm-stayed. In the riding, a famous snowbelt, I had numerous encounters with blocked roads, meticulously avoiding roadways that were officially closed, but in retrospect sometimes taking risks by driving — legally — through whiteouts and snowsqualls on secondary roads. In one blog, I described driving on a back road in snow so thick that the only way to navigate was to look up at the tops of the hydro poles.[16]

Former prime minister Paul Martin spent a day with me on the campaign trail, on February 25. Bedevilled by winter weather, we dodged closed roads to get Martin from whistle stops in Port Elgin, Glammis, Tiverton, and Kincardine to our main event, a major speech at the Legion hall in Goderich. The largest population centre in the riding, Goderich was a crucial battleground for me and an important place to showcase my connection to Martin, whom I had come to know on Parliament Hill and through his support for some of my Africa-related work at Carleton. Martin was nothing short of remarkable, extolling my virtues in media scrums and his address and also delivering a barnburner speech at the expense of the Harper government. The event generated front-page coverage.[17]

Martin's intervention was followed up by a visit in mid-May by retired general Roméo Dallaire, a personal friend whom I came to know as a reporter with the *Star* and because of my reportage on the Rwanda genocide, Dallaire's personal struggles with post-traumatic stress disorder (PTSD), and his work on behalf of war-affected children and child soldiers. Roméo was one of the first people I consulted when I decided to seek the nomination in Huron-Bruce, and he pledged then he would come and spend a day with me on the campaign trail.

I picked him up in Toronto at 6:30 a.m. on May 15 and then began the journey to Huron-Bruce. We stopped for tea and some campaigning at a diner just north of Clifford. Our day included two scheduled stops at Legion halls, a major speaking engagement with seven hundred high-school students bused in from across the riding to a school in Clinton, and the final event, a speech by Dallaire to a capacity crowd of more than three hundred at the Legion hall in Kincardine. Like Martin before him, Dallaire delivered a substantive message about Canada's place in the world, a critique of the Harper government, and also provided a strong endorsement for my campaign. I worked late into the night, going over my recordings of Dallaire's media scrums and speeches, then issued a press release written in a journalistic, non-partisan tone, documenting the day. Once again, several outlets published the release verbatim as a news report.[18]

To be honest, I felt some qualms as a career journalist, now working on the other side, seeking to get out my message and cultivate positive coverage. But I got over it. In the resource-strapped media environment dominated by small-town weeklies, outlets would often publish a press release verbatim, or report nothing at all. This is not to say there was no original reportage. But over the course of eighteen months, I had few sustained encounters with journalists. I did conduct several interviews in studios with radio reporters and also took part in short media scrums at the nomination meeting and after my events with Martin and Dallaire. But, with a few exceptions, there were precious few requests for formal interviews. At one point a reporter at the *Huron Expositor* in Seaforth conducted a lengthy interview and produced an extensive and flattering candidate profile,[19] which was ultimately featured in other Sun Media weeklies. The *Exeter Times Advocate* also published a full-page profile, based on a detailed in-person interview. Later, during the writ, the *Huron Expositor* again spent an hour or so with me on the campaign trail and published a feature about my experiences knocking on doors under the headline, "The Life of a Candidate Campaigning on Foot."[20] National media, after reporting on my initial bid for the nomination, ignored my candidacy for the duration. I appeared on television only twice, in a brief report by the correspondent for CTV London when I launched my nomination bid, and in a riding profile on Huron-Bruce broadcast toward the end of the campaign.

Of course, reaching the media was not nearly as important as interacting with voters. To better accomplish this, we took the major pre-writ step of opening the first of what would eventually be five campaign offices across the vast riding. These offices were billed as "Volunteer Centres" and were fully decked out with signage and our campaign branding. The first and primary office opened in May in Kincardine, my home base and the centre of operations for my campaign manager. We opened the second office in June in Goderich as a hub for the full-time volunteer managing Huron County operations. A third office was opened during the writ in Exeter, a fourth in Port Elgin, and the final storefront on the main street in Walkerton in late September. All of these centres were staffed by volunteers.

By June, the full slate of federal candidates had fallen into place. Kincardine-area farmer and environmental activist Jutta Splettstoesser would represent the Greens, and a reporter who had worked at weekly papers in Goderich and Clinton, Gerard Creces, would carry the NDP banner.

And my campaign team was now fully formed, with a core committee of more than twenty and close to three hundred volunteers across the riding. My campaign manager had by now been working full-time for close to a year. Two regional coordinators managed operations in Huron and Bruce counties and two volunteers kept my schedule, which we shared through my Gmail account. A communications lead, a candidate's aide, and several others had all ramped up to full-time, unpaid work.

The pace was relentless.. We would usually door-knock in three-hour bursts. At times I would actually run from door to door, in part to pick up speed but often to lead by example and motivate the volunteers who were helping out that day. I realized early on that it is not only important to work hard but also to be seen to be working hard. Word of mouth is a powerful force, particularly in a rural community.

By now, the consensus was that Harper would stick with the fixed election date. All that remained to be seen was the exact timing of the writ drop. My personal view was that he would call the election early to maximize his spending power. In the meantime, of course, the relentless, negative, American-style attack ads aimed at Trudeau were taking their toll. More than once, I ran into children — little kids — who would begin to parrot the famous Tory attack ad once they heard I was a Liberal. "Justin Trudeau, he's just not ready," one ten-year-old chirped at a beef supper in Brussels. Another day, as I walked past a group of kids assembled in front of a TV at the McDonald's restaurant in Kincardine, they too began to parrot the ad in unison when they saw Trudeau's face on TV. And it wasn't just children who were echoing the messaging of the Tory attack ads. Frequently on the doorsteps, I'd hear from voters who expressed some doubts about Trudeau, reciting almost verbatim some of the points in the attack ads.

For all intents and purposes, the campaign was on once the House of Commons rose in late June. On July 14, the first anniversary of my campaign launch, we posted a new video message to YouTube,[21] recorded on my iPhone at the farm in Glammis, our old barn in the background. My daily schedule now included canvassing door-to-door as well as an ongoing stream of events. This included a dozen or more appearances in parades at country fairs and festivals, major events in rural communities. Typically, we would use a volunteer's convertible — preferably red — with me perched up on the back seat. When possible, Roula and Laith would join me. Indeed, Laith gave up most of his summer holiday to help on the campaign.

"Look like you are already the MP," my campaign manager counselled.

Quoting the famous penguins from the movie *Madagascar*, my advice under my breath to Laith was simple: "Smile and wave, boy, smile and wave."

It is a strange experience to put yourself forward as a public figure, especially when doing it for the first time. It always felt a bit audacious to be sitting in the back of a convertible in a parade, waving at the crowd. Introducing myself to voters on the street or in restaurants and public places felt more natural, a conversation. And while it seemed awkward at first just walking up to people and extending a hand, time and again people would say that they appreciated me saying hello and asking what was on their mind. And as often as possible, we recorded what I was doing in photos and video clips posted to social media.

As a result, we did succeed in creating a public image, grounded in reality, of a hard-working candidate who was willing to put in long hours to meet people across the riding, most often from morning until night. Some days that meant underlining the point by posting pictures of photogenic sunrises in the morning and shots of me planting campaign signs in the dark that evening.

The impact of my social media presence is hard to gauge without further research, but we know that it reached tens of thousands of voters over the course of the campaign, with different audiences subscribing to different platforms. And the impact of the coverage I received on radio and in the weeklies cannot be overestimated. After a while, I found myself being recognized while out in public, and people often said they'd seen me in the paper.

In the months leading up to the writ, we also produced a series of pieces of campaign literature, most branded with a photo of me in shirt sleeves, leaning on a farm gate, a dirt road leading off in the background. My personal campaign catchphrase remained consistent throughout and was woven through my stump speech: *Integrity. Fairness. A Rural Voice.*

Virtually every house in the riding received a "door-hanger" piece, a two-sided flyer with a hole to hang it on the doorknob. To keep costs down, in the towns these door-knockers were hand-delivered by volunteers, who wrote their names on the front and encouraged neighbours to get involved in the campaign. Another version was mailed to rural routes. We also produced thousands of copies of several iterations of a candidate card, with my picture, a short message, and links to all of our contacts and social media platforms. These cards were delivered by me door to door and at events. Later, as the party platform took shape, we began to use a trifold flyer, with more detailed information on policy positions.

On policy I focused on advancing the positions set out by Trudeau and the national team, for example, the detailed blueprint for democratic reform released in May. And where a party position had not been taken on an issue of keen local interest — such as the Ontario Power Generation proposal for a deep geological repository (DGR) to bury low- and intermediate-grade nuclear waste from the Bruce site — I conferenced with key team members and agreed on a stance, which was released on the campaign website and through a news release.

The strategic considerations of the campaign were relatively obvious: we needed to gain support from across the spectrum. I entered politics out of a determination to counter the Harper agenda and to bring his regime to an end, and that message was the focus of my campaign. Our goal was to start from the 2011 numbers and reach out to "progressive" Conservatives who had no home in Harper's party, to bring back the Liberals who'd bled to either the Conservatives or the NDP last time, and also appeal to NDP supporters who realized that to get rid of Harper the Liberals were the only real alternative.

To that end, my messaging was clear: it was time for a change across Canada and in Huron-Bruce and I was the best person to accomplish change locally. I framed every speech around three themes — fairness, integrity in politics, and the need for a strong rural voice, committing myself to being a voice at the table in Ottawa for those who live on farms, on country roads, and in small towns.

My communications lead developed an advertising strategy based primarily on Facebook, using ads and sponsored posts to push our campaign messaging and reach out to tens of thousands of voters at relatively low cost. Late in the writ period, we placed a week's worth of radio ads[22] and also placed display ads in the weeklies, but this kind of traditional advertising was very costly. And in what would become the longest election in modern history, after Harper dropped the writ on Sunday, August 2, cost was always a factor.

## THE WRIT PERIOD

In anticipation of the August 2 writ drop, we had a press release ready to launch, the first campaign blog entry pre-written for release at 11:01 a.m., and new photos taken with my first campaign sign, which we pounded in at 7 a.m. on the front lawn in Glammis. We took pictures for release once the writ dropped, then covered the sign with a blanket in the interim. To signal my intention to continue covering the riding from top to bottom, we planned a writ-day schedule that would begin at 8 a.m. in the southernmost corner of Huron-Bruce at a diner in Centralia (more than an hour's drive from Glammis). The rest of the day included stops in Goderich, in Kincardine, at the northernmost boundary in Southampton, close to Clifford in the east, and finally, on the shores of Lake Huron at a beef supper in Port Albert. At day's end a menacing purple cloud oozed in over the lake and a devastating windstorm took down most of the campaign signs that my team had erected within hours of the writ drop. Day one was complete.

The remaining seventy-seven days are now a blur. In the mornings, I would often work the phones from home in Glammis, or at one of our campaign offices, making my way through phone banks to contact rural voters who would be difficult to reach in person. Most afternoons and evenings were taken up with door-to-door canvassing, often in two or three different locations per day. And of course, outside of the bubble I was operating in, scores of campaign volunteers continued to fan out across the riding, knocking on doors or calling their neighbours to solicit support. From day one, our sign team had blanketed the riding with large signs at key locations on roadsides and increasingly on people's front lawns. Before running, I'd never fully understood the impact of lawn signs, which my campaign manager referred to as the "silent salesmen." But time and again, when I'd introduce myself, people would say they'd seen my name on the signs.

Routinely, I was joined in the car by my candidate's aide, in this case a young volunteer from Exeter who had been working full-time since the spring. At each stop a volunteer from the community would join us so that there would be a familiar face at the doorsteps. And when possible, Roula and Laith would be with me as well. I would knock, introduce myself as the Liberal candidate and extend my hand, ask people directly for their support, and make clear I was available to answer any questions. Whenever possible, we snapped photos and posted them to Facebook, Twitter, and Instagram.

My sidekick would be collecting data, entering responses into the "Liberalist" voter database loaded on his smartphone. We would record if voters expressed outright support, or seemed to be "possible Liberals," undecided, or supporters of another party. This information would be used on election day to follow up and get supporters out to vote. It also helped us to gauge support. We also had categories for "won't say" or "hostile." All candidates can share stories of hilarious, memorable, or sometimes frightening moments on the doorstep. Door-knocking was my favourite part of campaigning by far.

Of course, no matter what time of day you came, many people weren't home. In those cases, I would write, "Sorry to miss you — Allan," on my canvass card and slide it on an angle into the crack of the door. I didn't put my flyer in mailboxes because I wanted people to know I'd delivered it in person.

When there was someone at home, we found considerable outright support or those who seemed to be leaning our way. In the end, that would explain how I managed to garner more than twenty-three thousand votes. I also encountered many, many people whom I'd met in the year prior at one event or another, bolstering my view that months of event-based campaigning had been effective. But there were also many who would not indicate their choice, or who said they were undecided. On instinct, we came to label some of those undecideds as PCs — "polite Conservatives." Others were not at all polite. At least once a day, it seemed, a voter would slam the door, tell me to F-off, or make crystal clear using some other expletive that Trudeau was not the man.

But on the whole, canvassing was an overwhelmingly positive and enriching experience — an education and a privilege. Many people delved into detail on policy issues. The single most common issue to come up was health care, followed by services for seniors or those with some kind of special need. There were heartbreaking moments with some — often older women — who were struggling to deal with a partner suffering from dementia or Alzheimer's, women who would break down in tears when you asked them how they were doing. One of the most gut-wrenching encounters for me was with a woman in a low-income apartment who was wheelchair–bound because of advanced multiple sclerosis. She wanted to know my position on death with dignity, physician-assisted suicide. Our conversation will remain private, but the interaction will always stay with me.

I noticed a very positive trend about midway through the writ period. Fewer people were asking me to explain if Trudeau was ready to be prime minister. Particularly after his strong debate performances, more people began to express outright support. I remember vividly talking with one older fellow who admitted, in colourful language, that he'd underestimated Trudeau. "That little bugger is smarter than I thought," he said. While the "Just Not Ready" refrain had worried me months earlier, toward the end of the campaign, I concluded that Harper had made a critical error in putting so much focus on Trudeau, notably with the relentless airtime for the series of ads about the résumé committee, the one with the jab about Trudeau's "nice hair" and the tagline that he was "just not ready."

I remember as a graduate student doing research on agenda-setting by the media and coming across the famous maxim from Bernard Cohen. He wrote that the press "may not be successful much of the time in telling people what to think, but it is stunningly successful in telling its readers what to think about."[23] Harper set out to tell Canadians "what to think" about Justin Trudeau, but instead, was stunningly successful at convincing Canadians to simply "think about" Trudeau. And after thinking about him for a while, many reached the clear conclusion that not only was he ready to be prime minister but that his positive and "sunny" approach was the best alternative to the cold and negative Harper.

But another more disturbing sentiment also emerged on the doorsteps in every corner of the riding. The wedge issues that Harper's Conservatives had been pushing so hard — the niqab, a subtle anti-Muslim sentiment, cynicism about Syrian refugees, the move to change citizenship law to deport anyone convicted of a terrorist act — were resonating with a significant number of voters in Huron-Bruce. (*Toronto Star* reporter Tom Walkom picked up on this during a brief visit to the riding.[24] ) Some who self-identified as Liberal supporters told me they agreed with Harper's stance that a woman wearing a niqab face veil should not be allowed to take part in a citizenship ceremony. My arguments — that the issue was a distraction, that the women did in fact reveal their faces to officials before the ceremony, and that their numbers were miniscule anyway — often seemed to fall on deaf ears. At one door I was shocked to hear a middle-aged man ranting about the dangers of a "Muslim invasion." Others said we needed to push back and put immigrants in their place before our communities were taken over "the way Toronto had been." Political candidates are coached to argue but not to be argumentative, and in the effort to identify support to minimize the amount of time spent with those who are clearly not going to vote for you. But it was frustrating and worrying to realize that what could only be described as Harper's agenda of fear was resonating with some voters in my riding, even as it turned off voters in most urban centres.

In the final weeks of the campaign, candidates took part in a series of nine all-candidates meetings. Two were devoted specifically to agriculture issues. Others were hosted by chambers of commerce, schools, and service clubs, and followed a pattern of opening statements then questions. Where possible, we recorded the meetings to post video to YouTube. Because of my background in journalism and as a lecturer, I was confident I could hold my own in a debate format, but also nervous about being able to impart so much policy information and about the prospect of hecklers or off-the-wall questions.

As a campaign, we decided not to try to stack the debates with boisterous supporters or to plant questions. We just let things unfold. I also decided not to use prepared remarks or detailed notes, but instead to rely on simple bullet points or no notes at all. By contrast, the Conservative incumbent — who to his credit participated in all of the debates — spoke exclusively from party talking points and usually got a tepid audience response as a result. The Green candidate also relied on her policy book, while the

NDP candidate — also a journalist by training — was reasonably effective with his prepared remarks but seemed to flounder when answering questions off the cuff. In every case, the meetings were in a question-and-answer format, with limited opportunity for actual debate among the candidates. We posted recordings of a number of the debates to my YouTube channel.[25]

The most heated exchanges were between me and the Conservative incumbent, speaking in response to questions linked to Harper's wedge issues. In the Walkerton debate — held the day after the national Munk debate — a Conservative supporter who had been taunting me on Facebook raised the issue of Bill C-24 and Trudeau's opposition to the plan to revoke citizenship of those convicted of terrorism offences.

In posing his question, the man said he was proud of Stephen Harper's leadership, criticized Trudeau's opposition to the Conservative plan to strip those convicted of terrorism offences of their Canadian citizenship, and asked me what I thought of Trudeau's position.

My reply, echoing Trudeau, was unequivocal.

"A Canadian is a Canadian is a Canadian," I said to a round of applause. "And I am proud — I clapped last night when I watched Justin Trudeau saying those words because I think it defends a fundamental principle of our society, and I think when we start creating second-class citizens, everyone who was not born in this country but chose to join the Canadian family starts looking over their shoulder and wondering, am I next? What crime is now going to warrant stripping Canadian citizenship? A Canadian is a Canadian is a Canadian."

"Well, Allan, you're out to lunch on that one," Lobb replied. "If you've been out door-knocking, I'd try that line on the people of Huron-Bruce and you'll find out real quick you are at odds with the vast majority of people in this riding. If you have dual citizenship and you commit an act of terror, you're out of here and that's the bottom line."

After the debate, on the front steps of the Walkerton town hall, my campaign manager put his arm around my shoulder and said something that I'll never forget: "If we lose this election for stating 'a Canadian is a Canadian is a Canadian,' then so be it."

While knocking on doors in Goderich on a sweltering 30° C afternoon during an August heat wave, it dawned on me that I was with the same volunteer who had canvassed with me back in February, when it was a frosty −30° C. I predicted then that during this, the longest election campaign in modern history, we would inevitably sweat it out in the early days and trudge through snow before voting day. The snowstorm came on October 18, and my social media feed includes a great picture of me, bent against the wind and snow, door-knocking in Hensall.

In the final, frenetic days, we focused intently on visiting the main streets of many towns in the riding, traditional glad-handing in diners, businesses, and coffee shops. On the eve of the election, I ended my door-to-door canvassing where my campaign had begun, in my hometown of Glammis. At our campaign offices, volunteers zeroed in on our Get Out The Vote (GOTV) planning for election day.

On October 19, Roula and Laith and I undertook another marathon tour of the riding, stopping in every corner and visiting polling stations as well as all of our campaign offices and some of the home centres where volunteers were working on GOTV. By early evening, with no opportunity left to campaign, we settled in at my sister's house near Kincardine, with all of the extended family, to watch the results come in. My campaign manager was adamant a candidate should not watch the results in public at the hall we'd rented for the "election celebration," but rather wait with close family until the outcome was clear. I took his advice. He also told me it is standard practice to have two speeches ready, one for victory and one for defeat. This advice I ignored, although not because of some bravura sense of overconfidence. Going in, we knew it would likely be relatively close, but had no real sense whether I would win or lose. My decision to draft one speech — with optional opening lines for a win or loss — was based on my absolute confidence that Trudeau was going to become prime minister, a victory no matter what and something to celebrate. And win or lose in Huron-Bruce, I knew it would be close and that we should be celebrating a remarkable campaign, an amazing team, and for me, the most profound professional experience of my life.

Because of time zones, the first results were, as always, from Atlantic Canada. As it became clear that Trudeau and the Liberals were going to sweep the region, I began to think that I actually would win, on the crest of a Trudeau wave. When results in Ontario started to trickle in, the first reports had me in the lead, albeit with only a few polls reporting. For a few minutes at least, Huron-Bruce was an island of red in a blue sea across rural Ontario on the CBC-TV map. But gradually, the tide turned in Huron-Bruce, with Lobb pulling into the lead and his margin growing. Not long after 10 p.m., the phone rang, with my campaign manager advising me to brace myself, but to wait for a final call. A few moments later the phone rang again. We had lost.

Weeks later, at a campaign team post-mortem on the election, we pored over maps to look at detailed results poll-by-poll. As we had hoped, I won most of the polls in Bruce County, my home base and the riding's traditional Liberal heartland. In some areas, my margin of victory was quite decisive. But notably, I didn't win by huge margins across the board. And Lobb did win some polls in Bruce County and, notably, did much better in rural areas than he did in the towns. Along the lakeshore, I made real breakthroughs in Goderich — Huron's county seat — and in the affluent community of Bayfield, winning most of the polls in both towns. But in much of Huron County, I got hammered — to put it mildly — by the Tory incumbent. In a dynamic perhaps unique to my riding, I did well in Bruce County and, with a couple of notable exceptions, poorly in Huron County. And as was the case with many Liberal candidates across Ontario, generally speaking I fared poorly in rural areas. As I had feared, Harper's not-so-subtle fear tactics did resonate with some rural voters, many of whom were also clearly drawn to a solid, likeable incumbent.

On election night, I'd been providing updates to my family from Twitter and other sources, so the final phone call simply confirmed what we had all come to realize. After eighteen months of hard work, I had been defeated. While I am an emotional person at times, I have yet to shed a tear about the loss. Part of this is likely a personal defence mechanism and a determination to remain positive. But I meant every word of my concession speech delivered to crestfallen supporters at the Ainsdale golf course, the remarks I had prepared earlier about the significance of Trudeau's victory, what we had accomplished as a team in Huron-Bruce, and how proud we could all be of the campaign. Just before heading to the podium, I told my campaign manager how I intended to begin my speech: "The people of Huron-Bruce have spoken — and so have the people of Canada."

Months earlier, my campaign manager made clear to me he wouldn't work with a candidate who refused to go and shake his opponent's hand on election night. I was in full agreement. So after delivering my speech, Rod and I climbed into his van and headed out in pouring rain on the forty-minute drive to Goderich. On the way down Highway 21, a deer suddenly leapt in front of our vehicle. Rod, who once worked as an ambulance driver, calmly veered to the left and the buck grazed the front corner of the van, on my side, with a bit of a clunk. Saying barely a word, we continued on our journey, said congratulations to Ben, then returned to join the supporters who were still at my party in Kincardine.

There was a lot of disappointment and some tears. But words of encouragement as well. In the middle of the night, when we finally got back to Glammis, I decided to send out a message of thanks before turning off my campaign machinery. The message read as follows:

> The people of Huron-Bruce have spoken — and so have the people of Canada.
>
> ---
>
> It has been a privilege for me to stand as the Liberal Party of Canada candidate in Huron-Bruce and I have to thank the thousands of people who supported me, a simply remarkable campaign team and my family. In the end, we did not achieve the result we wanted in Huron-Bruce. But we more than restored the Liberal Party's standing.... And we can all celebrate Justin Trudeau's triumph across Canada. As I said in my speech to supporters last night at Ainsdale golf club in Kincardine, Trudeau's victory is a watershed in Canada's political culture, an end to a decade of cynicism and fear, and proof that once again, you can win in Canadian politics without negative attack ads and by putting forward a relentlessly positive and optimistic program. Last night was a great moment for our country, proof, that in Canada, better is always possible. After celebrating

the Liberal victory with my supporters in Kincardine, I drove with my phenomenal campaign manager Rod MacDonald to Goderich, to congratulate Ben Lobb in person on his victory. During the wet and windy drive to Goderich, a deer leapt onto the road in front of our vehicle. Rod managed to swerve so that in the end, we clipped the animal's antlers. It was a close call. But the buck survived and will live to see another day. — Allan

## NOTES

1. Elections Canada online publication: *Political Financing Handbook for Nomination Contestants and Financial Agents*, www.elections.ca/pol/nom/man/ec20182/ec20182_e.pdf.
2. My Facebook posts can be found in two locations, my personal Facebook page at Allan Thompson, www.facebook.com/prof.allanthompson, and my professional page, created for the campaign, at Allan Thompson, Journalist, www.facebook.com/allan2015.
3. Allan Thompson, Journalist, www.facebook.com/allan2015.
4. Allan Thompson, www.twitter.com/electallant.
5. https://web.archive.org/web/20151001190414/https://allanthompson.liberal.ca/.
6. Allan 2015: allanthompson.ca, http://archive.benchmarkemail.com/ElectAllan2015; and Allan 2015: News about Liberal candidate Allan Thompson's campaign in Huron-Bruce, http://burl.co/5872299.
7. Audio recordings of speeches and interviews were posted to SoundCloud.com: Allan 2015, https://soundcloud.com/electallanthompson.
8. All of the videos posted during the campaign can be found on my YouTube channel at "Allan Thompson," YouTube, www.youtube.com/channel/UC7JeAZnFYPdzbkbb9WqtlmQ.
9. "The Huron-Bruce Shuffle," www.youtube.com/watch?v=fM3PxDdlTeI.
10. Media coverage of my campaign launch was described in a July 15, 2015, blog entry on Allan2015.com titled "Day One — the 'Soft Launch,'" Allan2015: Reflections on Allan Thompson's election campaign in Huron-Bruce, http://allan2015.com/2014/07/15/day-one-the-soft-launch/.
11. "Campaign Launch Event Generates Media Coverage," Allan2015: Reflections on Allan Thompson's election campaign in Huron-Bruce, http://allan2015.com/2014/07/23/campaign-launch-event-generates-media-coverage/.
12. I documented my nomination victory in a blog posted later that evening under the heading, "The Candidate (Part 1)": http://allan2015.com/2014/10/21/the-candidate-part-1/. A few days later I posted a blog rounding up the media coverage: http://allan2015.com/2014/10/29/a-look-back-at-media-coverage-of-the-oct-20-nomination-victory/. We also posted to YouTube a recording of my speech to the October 20,

2014, Huron-Bruce Federal Liberal Association nomination meeting: www.youtube.com/watch?v=oQKhXs9BqvU. And a recording of my first media scrum as a candidate was posted to SoundCloud.com: https://soundcloud.com/electallanthompson/allan-thompson-media-scrum-after-oct-20-liberal-nomination-victory.

13. Typical blog entries from HaveYourSayCAFE events: Allan Thompson, "My First HaveYourSayCAFE Has to Be Called a Success," Allan2015: Reflections on Allan Thompson's election campaign in Huron-Bruce, http://allan2015.com/2014/11/28/my-first-haveyoursaycafe-has-to-be-called-a-success/; and Allan Thompson, "Questions and Comments Aplenty at Janet's Country Donut Cafe," Allan2015: Reflections on Allan Thompson's election campaign in Huron-Bruce, http://allan2015.com/2015/02/24/questions-and-comments-aplenty-at-janets-country-donut-cafe/.
14. Typical blog entries from a Pub&Politics event: Allan Thompson, "Back on My Old Stomping Grounds at Walker's Landing," Allan2015: Reflections on Allan Thompson's election campaign in Huron-Bruce, http://allan2015.com/2015/02/21/back-on-my-old-stomping-grounds-at-walkers-landing/; and Allan Thompson, "Getting an Earful at the Black Dog," Allan2015: Reflections on Allan Thompson's election campaign in Huron-Bruce, http://allan2015.com/2015/01/25/getting-an-earful-at-the-black-dog/.
15. Allan Thompson, "Jim Munson Hears Gut-Wrenching Testimony from Families with Autism," Allan2015: Reflections on Allan Thompson's election campaign in Huron-Bruce, http://allan2015.com/2014/11/16/sen-jim-munson-hears-gut-wrenching-testimony-from-families-dealing-with-autism/.
16. A blog about campaigning through a snowstorm: Allan Thompson, "Huron-Bruce Dreaming — on Such a Winter's Day," Allan2015: Reflections on Allan Thompson's election campaign in Huron-Bruce, http://allan2015.com/2015/02/14/huron-bruce-dreaming-on-such-a-winters-day/.
17. Two blogs were posted about Paul Martin's visit to Huron-Bruce: Allan Thompson, "Paul Martin's New Mission in Life," Allan2015: Reflection's on Allan Thompson's election campaign in Huron-Bruce," http://allan2015.com/2015/02/26/paul-martins-new-mission-in-life/; and Allan Thompson, "Former Prime Minister Paul Martin Takes Huron-Bruce by Storm — Literally," Allan2015: Reflections on Allan Thompson's election campaign in Huron-Bruce, http://allan2015.com/2015/02/26/former-prime-minister-paul-martin-takes-huron-bruce-by-storm-literally/.
18. Two blogs were posted about the Dallaire visit: http://allan2015.com/2015/05/17/an-epic-day-on-the-campaign-trail-with-my-friend-romeo-dallaire/; and http://allan2015.com/2015/05/17/romeo-dallaire-visit-dominates-front-pages-and-the-airwaves/.
19. www.seaforthhuronexpositor.com/2015/04/19/former-journalist-looks-to-win-huron-bruce-for-liberals.
20. www.seaforthhuronexpositor.com/2015/09/17/the-life-of-a-candidate-campaigning-on-foot.
21. "Allan Thompson, Liberal Candidate in Huron-Bruce, Counts Down to the October Election," YouTube.com, July 14, 2015, www.youtube.com/watch?v=KiR4nH76hxs.
22. "Allan Thompson. Huron-Bruce Liberal candidate, radio ad # 2," SoundCloud.com,

https://soundcloud.com/electallanthompson/allan-thompson-huron-bruce-liberal-candidate-radio-ad-2; and "Allan Thompson: Huron-Bruce Liberal Candidate, Radio Ad # 1," SoundCloud.com, https://soundcloud.com/electallanthompson/allan-thompson-huron-bruce-liberal-candidate-radio-ad-1.

23. Bernard Cohen, *The Press and Foreign Policy* (Princeton, NJ: Princeton University Press, 1963).
24. The *Toronto Star* noted how wedge issues were resonating in Huron-Bruce: "Stephen Harper's Muslim Issue Comes to a Rural Riding: Walkom," *Toronto Star*, October 10, 2015, www.thestar.com/news/federal-election/2015/10/10/stephen-harpers-muslim-issue-comes-to-a-rural-riding-walkom.html.
25. Recordings of some of the debates were posted to my YouTube channel: "Allan Thompson," YouTube.com, www.youtube.com/channel/UC7JeAZnFYPdzbkbb9WqtlmQ.

# CHAPTER 9

## Like, Share, Vote: The CTV/Facebook Partnership and the 2015 Canadian Election

Mary Francoli, Josh Greenberg, and Christopher Waddell[1]

The proliferation of online media, the continuing move of legacy news outlets to social and mobile platforms, steeply declining advertising revenue, fragmenting audiences, and an extraordinary eleven-week campaign made the 2015 election like no other for Canadian media. It provided an opportunity to move away from traditional questions about how news media cover a federal election campaign, namely: What were the dominant news frames? How much of the coverage was driven by the "horse race" narrative? Which sources were most frequently quoted, and in what ways? Which issues garnered front-page or lead-story attention?

Important as these questions may be, they presume that the reportage and commentary of a few media outlets determine what the electorate knows of the contest as it unfolds, and that their coverage is instrumental in both contributing to and reflecting the campaign dynamic, thus setting the agenda of concern for voters. This may have been true when members of the public had to turn to newspapers and newscasts for information about election campaigns, but lacked any effective means of circulating information and conversing among themselves beyond their immediate social circles. Now, however, the legacy media's election coverage is not the only way by which voters inform themselves, and may no longer even be the dominant way. Rather, voters follow the campaign through multiple sources made possible by social media platforms, in which the events of the campaign are taken up, interpreted, refracted, discussed, and disputed — with voters themselves contributing to this churn of election content through their own public comments, posts, reposts, likes, and online activity feeding into algorithms that influence how content appears and is presented to them via their digital portals. Crudely, in the late twentieth century, most members of the electorate saw the same campaign for the most part. In the early twenty-first century, each potential voter can know a different campaign, and if they choose, they can view one tailored to their preferences and those of their friends and followers in the digital mediascape.

As a result, measuring what appeared in print or on television newscasts now seems somewhat antiquated and, dare we say, irrelevant, as audiences have fractured and news organizations spread their coverage across multiple platforms at all hours of the day. There is less and less of a shared audience experience in reading or watching campaign coverage, or any sort of news.

The changes in both the news environment and how Canadians consume news are driving media to use different platforms to display content. Facebook, for example, has emerged as a significant platform for news media to present stories and engage audiences.

Indeed, in March 2015 Facebook inked a deal that would see it host content from prominent media outlets like the *New York Times*, *National Geographic*, and Buzzfeed.[2] Facebook's 1.4 billion users would have access to this content within Facebook itself — clicking on a news item does not redirect the user to the news organization's site but instead to a new page on the Facebook site. According to the terms of these deals, Facebook and the news organizations split advertising revenue, while Facebook gains access to ever more user data, which it can monetize and sell back to advertisers. The deals may expand the reach of news coverage, particularly to younger audiences; equally important, though, they provide new opportunities to track engagement through the number of likes, the range of user comments, and the extent to which stories are shared on Facebook and other platforms.

In 2015 there was another reason for examining Facebook as a distribution platform for election content. In June, CTV News announced it would become "the first [media organization] to broadcast exclusive Facebook content, providing voters with an added layer of insight throughout the campaign."[3] The partnership was meant to establish CTV News as the "premier source for election insights" — it would be provided with "first access to Facebook experts throughout the campaign and exclusively during election night coverage."[4] As the campaign unfolded, it became clear this also involved promoting rudimentary analytics, such as the cumulative number of likes, shares, and comments about each of the federal party leaders on individual Facebook pages, the number of people who "friended" each of the leaders, and the cumulative number of interactions with the Facebook pages of each of the parties.

Then, in September, the social media giant announced a partnership with Elections Canada. To celebrate International Day of Democracy and encourage first-time voters and those who had moved since 2011, a prompt would be sent to the Facebook pages of all those aged eighteen and older to register or update their voter information to ensure they could vote on October 19. These developments illustrate the efforts by Facebook to insert itself more deeply into the everyday social and political lives of the electorate, and thus present an opportunity for researchers of digital media and political communication to consider new questions about how social media may be transforming both elections and election journalism at a time when traditional voter turnout has been in a state of fairly steady decline, news organizations have been shedding jobs, and more reporters are finding themselves precariously employed.

Focusing on CTV's partnership with Facebook, this chapter asks whether CTV was able to leverage this partnership in a way that distinguished its election coverage from other media organizations. To answer this question, we focus on not just CTV but also CBC, Global Television, the *Globe and Mail*, the *Toronto Star*, and the *National Post*. Did the CTV-Facebook partnership lead to innovations in use of social media that, in turn, allowed for the telling of different kinds of election stories? Was CTV's use of Facebook more effective in generating different types or levels of user engagement? In answering these related questions, the chapter draws on a corpus of original data collected from the Facebook pages of these media outlets during the final four weeks of the federal election, from September 19 to October 19, 2015. In particular, we look at three major issues:

- the amount, type, and timing of content used on the Facebook pages of these news outlets;
- voter/user engagement through likes, comments, and shares;
- the nature of the content posted to Facebook by news organizations.

Ultimately, we found variations in quantity and content, but little evidence to show that the CTV-Facebook partnership led to any distinctly novel uses of the platform to engage Canadians in what was described as an election that would bring a new generation of Canadians into positions of political leadership and participation.[5]

## FACEBOOK, MEDIA, AND ELECTIONS

The partnership between CTV and Facebook during the 2015 Canadian election was a new development, although the play of Facebook in electoral politics has been the subject of academic and journalistic attention since the 2008 U.S. presidential election,[6] when the Obama campaign knew that its success, particularly in swing states, hinged on the mobilization of young voters who did not have listed telephone numbers. These voters lived in what *Time* magazine called the "cellular shadows," where they were "immune to traditional get-out-the-vote efforts." The Obama team turned to Facebook to support targeted sharing of video, news, and other campaign materials. As Teddy Goff, Obama's campaign digital director, stated, Facebook became "the most groundbreaking piece of technology" they could have possibly used.[7]

As illustrated by the myriad studies of the Obama campaign's social media activities, a great deal of scholarly attention has been dedicated to examining how candidates or political parties use social media to engage and persuade voters. Grow and Ward, for example, look at how candidates employ social media in a manner that allows them to demonstrate authenticity.[8] In a study of municipal campaigns, Raynauld and Greenberg identified how Twitter, in particular, was used for both town hall–style question-and-answer sessions and for smear campaigns against opponents.[9] Small and others have questioned the inherent "newness" of campaign activities on the Internet, and in the Canadian context have often argued that there tends to be a mirroring of online and offline campaign activities, where the online activities are simple extensions of those that take place offline and are not fundamentally new or innovative.[10] Finally, in the U.S. context, Carlisle and Patton argue that in the case of the 2008 presidential campaigns, while social media was significant, popular media accounts may have overstated the amount and scope of actual political activity on Facebook.[11]

Many news stories during the 2015 Canadian election looked at candidates' use of social media, but in rather banal ways. At times, this was simply done as a means of reporting who had the most friends, followers, or likes on a given social media platform. CP24, a Toronto-area broadcaster, noted that while Liberal leader Justin Trudeau was the most popular individual candidate, the Conservative Party was, for a time, still the most talked-about party in social media rankings.[12] Many other stories emphasized the social media "gaffes of the day" as a way of highlighting the risks and vulnerabilities that increased visibility and openness on social media sites present to candidates and parties. Several news outlets reported how social media can be the "Achilles heel" of many candidates or aides. Even the *Guardian* — reporting on Canada's election from afar — took delight in reporting that twelve candidates from all major parties had been ceremoniously dumped for their stupid, offensive, or bizarre statements on Facebook or Twitter, some of which had been posted years earlier and well before they ever imagined running for office.[13]

An aspect of social media that has received significant scholarly attention is the link between digital activism, citizen engagement, and elections. Often this work is grounded in debates over the democratic potential of technology.[14] Numerous studies advance variations of the claim that Internet-enabled technologies lower the transaction costs associated with political participation, and thus facilitate more engaged citizenship.[15] Others suggest that the novelty of digital technologies can potentially convert disaffected voters who have become disillusioned with traditional modes of political participation.[16] Optimists argue that the simple availability of technology that allows for the potential enhancement of the public voice and organization of like-minded persons will reinvigorate democracies afflicted by declining voter turnout and political participation.

More skeptical scholars insist that digital media have neither revitalized democracy nor led to citizens rushing to cast election-day ballots. Here, the argument is that technology is neutral at best,[17] and at worst perpetuates the democratic deficit by taking citizens away from "real world" physical venues that have traditionally provided spaces for engagement.[18] Along the same line, these skeptics have pointed to problems, such as information overload, which they argue make it increasingly difficult for citizens to navigate the online environment. Instead of embracing the democratic potential afforded by digital concourses, people shun or ignore opportunities for engagement, opting instead to revel in the entertainment activities these platforms provide. They are more likely to be fixated on sharing cat memes or playing Candy Crush than they are to be politically attentive, attuned to current affairs, and participant in civic discourse.

As the literature on social media and elections continues to grow and becomes more nuanced, one facet that has remained relatively understudied is the relationship between legacy news and social media, and the potential impact this has on elections and electoral coverage.

We have seen various media outlets engaging with social media in different ways during elections. In 2008, CBC partnered with Ryerson University's Infoscape Research Lab to provide coverage of the federal election, including analysis of social media activities, such as the popularity of political Facebook groups.[19] In 2011, Canadian Press partnered with Mark Blevis, CEO of Full Duplex, an Ottawa-based public affairs consultancy, to provide analysis of how campaigns were using digital technologies and platforms, from social media sites to mobile devices, how social media itself was shaping the public and media narratives of the campaign, and whether it would influence election results.

This most recent election showed how news outlets looked to leverage social media in other ways. In addition to the CTV-Facebook partnership that is explored in this chapter, Toronto's City featured Facebook data during breaks in the August 6, 2015, *Maclean's* party leaders' debate.

City described the material on air as data from polls. The broadcast of these entirely unscientific results appeared to violate sections 326 and 327 of the Canada Elections Act. The act specifies that the methodology must be included in reporting the results of any survey. As well, if the survey is not based on any recognized statistical methods this must be stated plainly. City made no mention of either the methodology used or of its utility as a statistical tool. However, other media throughout the remainder of the campaign described Facebook data more carefully. Perhaps that was because Facebook was very quick to clarify its activities. As Kevin Chan, head of public policy for Facebook Canada, explained to the *Toronto Star*, "Facebook is not in the business of political analysis." Chan suggested that its data only show "important political conversations are happening among Canadians as they're watching and engaging with each other."[20]

## RESEARCH DESIGN AND METHODS

A consideration of how social media may afford new opportunities for audience and voter engagement provides the context for the questions informing this research. Where many other studies of digital media and elections examine how politicians and parties use social media to engage voters, this study focused on the use of Facebook by news organizations. We pay special attention to CTV News, given its partnership with Facebook, and provide comparative analysis to Global National, CBC, the *National Post*, the *Globe and Mail*, and the *Toronto Star*. While this is not an entirely representative sample of all media outlets in Canada, it captures a range of editorial positions and perspectives, includes both public and private media, and examines what are arguably the country's major national agenda-setting news organizations.

We focus on Facebook for several reasons, some of which were noted above:

1. Facebook is worthy of analysis given its ubiquitous presence and use by many different kinds of Canadians (older and younger, urban and rural, liberal and conservative, et cetera)

for everything from socializing to information gathering. Facebook is far more prevalent in Canada than other social media platforms, such as LinkedIn, Twitter, and Instagram. In 2015, approximately 60 percent of Canadians used Facebook, compared to the 30 percent who used LinkedIn, 25 percent who used Twitter, and 16 percent who used Instagram.[21] Facebook is becoming increasingly important in shaping the information flows during election campaigns. Today, it is more common than not for a political candidate, or elected representative, to have a Facebook presence.[22]

2. Facebook's use of text, image, audio, and video content also enables users to participate in many different kinds of conversations and in different ways. Indeed, its very infrastructure provides multiple tools to foster and promote engagement. As Carlisle and Patton argue, Facebook is "uniquely positioned to facilitate online engagement because its feature-set (e.g., the 'newsfeed' and user 'wall') act as mechanisms to support the individual's voice in broadcasting political content to a networked audience or online public sphere."[23]
3. Facebook is transforming journalism in ways that are still unclear but certain to be important. The launch of its native video player in 2015 has the potential to provide new opportunities for media organizations to engage viewers and promote more content sharing and discussion. News organizations are already beginning to produce content specifically for Facebook users. Al Jazeera's AJ+ division, which features news tailored specifically for a global youth market, creates stories exclusively using video and shares them only on its social and mobile platforms. To illustrate, on December 13, 2015, Al Jazeera posted a Facebook-only video from the global climate change conference in Paris announcing the results of the historic international agreement. Within one hour, the video had been viewed 43,000 times, generated nearly 50 user comments, been liked more than 1,000 times, and shared on 377 walls. Facebook is also set to launch a new "spherical video" service into its newsfeed that will allow users to change their viewing angles for more

immersive multimedia experiences. This will certainly have an impact on future live news reports of all kinds of events, from sports to protests and election campaign stops.

While Facebook is an important platform, deserving of further attention, it can be notoriously difficult to research. The newsfeeds move quickly, and since the architecture can be personalized to some degree, it is virtually impossible to know what individuals are actually exposed to via their personal profiles. Recognizing these challenges, this study focused solely on the *public* Facebook pages of media outlets. The authors worked with a team of five senior undergraduate research assistants to examine the Facebook timelines of CTV, Global National, CBC[24], the *National Post*, the *Globe and Mail*, and the *Toronto Star* from September 19 until October 19, 2015. A codebook was developed to identify the topics of the stories (both election- and non-election–related), the focus on different parties, and different measures of user engagement (number of likes, shares, and comments). Research assistants collected all raw data and compiled them into a master file to allow for a comparison of the news outlets' Facebook pages over the sample period. We wanted to know how frequently each news organization posted content to its Facebook pages, the proportion of election-related stories, the time of day material was posted, the types and levels of engagement it generated, as well as the overall thematic focus of the content posted.

We present the findings of the research below, organized in response to the following analytical questions:

1. How did the volume and timing of CTV's election related posts on Facebook compare to those of other news organizations?
2. Were users more engaged with CTV's Facebook content, through use of the like, comment, and share features, than they were with other news organizations?
3. How did the content on the CTV Facebook page diverge or align with that of other media Facebook pages in the final four weeks of the election?

## FINDINGS

### Timing and Volume

The most obvious manifestation of the partnership between CTV and Facebook during the election campaign was the volume of election-related material posted on the CTV News Facebook page. CTV had many more stories than its competitors. It almost seemed that anything election-related being produced by CTV was placed on its Facebook page. As a result, someone following its coverage could do it almost as well from Facebook as from the network's own website. How did this differ from the way other news organizations used Facebook during the election? To discover this, we tabulated: the amount of election coverage placed on the page, the balance between election and non-election coverage, the time of day the material was posted to Facebook, and the substantive nature of those posts.

As can be seen in Figure 9.1, CTV did post more election stories to its Facebook page than any of its five competitors, garnering more than one-third (34 percent) of all election-focused coverage. However, as can be seen in Figure 9.2, CTV also had a higher number of non-election–related stories on its Facebook page, meaning that its election coverage was not as central to its Facebook activities as that of other media.

In contrast, and taken as a proportion of its Facebook posts, CBC Politics had the highest concentration of election-focused coverage. However, this is not unexpected given the specific focus of the CBC Politics page and the high likelihood that most of its content during the campaign would have been election-focused. CTV, by contrast, did not create a separate Facebook page devoted exclusively to its political coverage. Also noteworthy was the strong proportion of *Toronto Star* election stories on its Facebook page. At 80 percent, this far surpassed the other media sites we examined (except the specialty CBC site).

There were some similarities among the news outlets studied when it came to the time of day that they posted content on their Facebook pages. As can be seen in Figure 9.3, the majority of outlets tended to post content more frequently in the morning. Little content was posted in the afternoon compared to morning and evening. CBC Politics and the

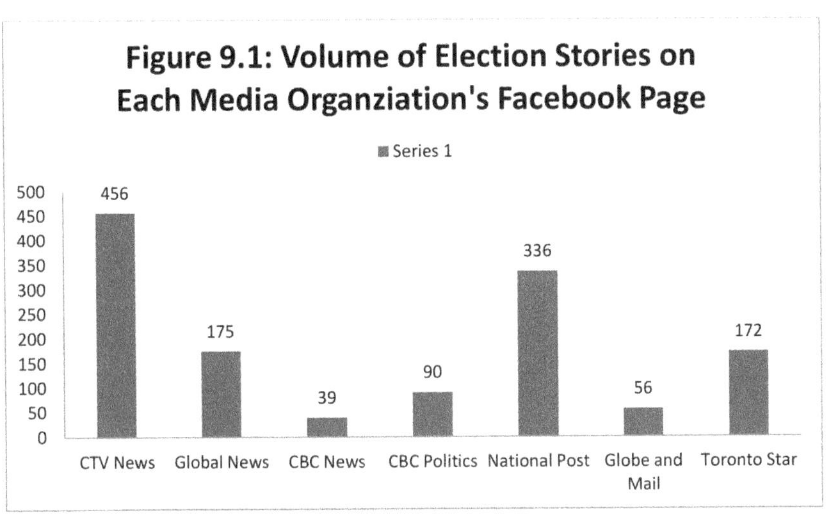


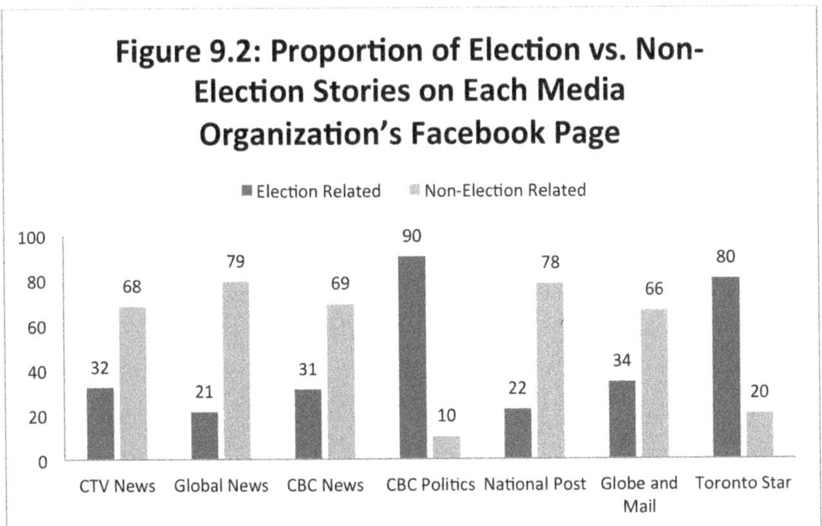


*Percentages have been rounded.

*Toronto Star* were outliers with the highest number of posts in the evening.

There were also some similarities among the media outlets when comparing the proportion of stories posted at different times during the last four weeks of the campaign. As can be seen in Figure 9.4, the second last week of the campaign saw either relative stability in the proportion of stories posted to Facebook, or some degree of decline. CBC

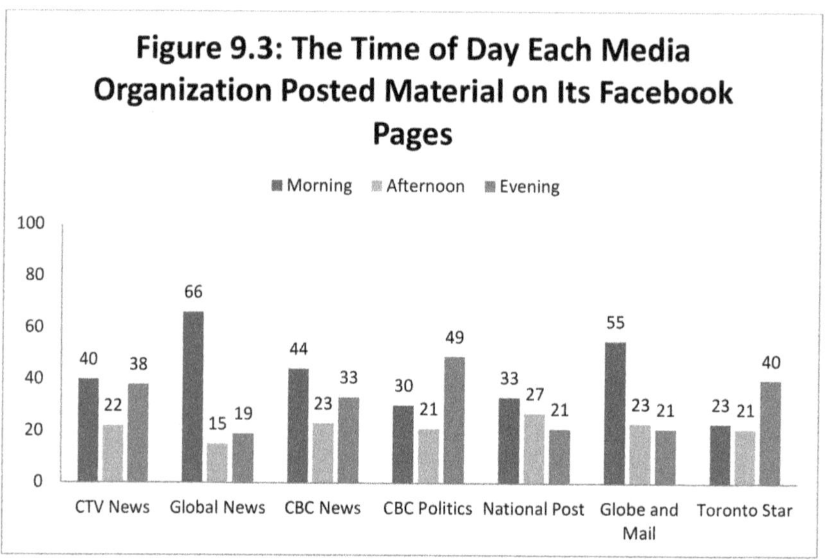


**Figure 9.3: The Time of Day Each Media Organization Posted Material on Its Facebook Pages**

*Percentages have been rounded.

Politics and the *National Post* were two exceptions, with notable increases seen in that second-last week. The *Toronto Star* also experienced some minimal growth.

A spike in the proportion of stories published in the final week of the campaign was identified across the sample, which is hardly surprising. The *Globe and Mail* is particularly noteworthy with a significant increase. Again, CBC Politics and the *National Post* were exceptions with a decreased proportion of stories seen in the final week of the campaign.

Collectively, the data reveal some similarities and differences in how media outlets used Facebook.

**CTV News:** While CTV posted more stories on the election to its Facebook page than any other media outlet, these stories still accounted for only one-third of the total material posted to the CTV Facebook page in the final month of the campaign. This means a reader looking specifically for election stories would have had to search through a lot of other material to find election-specific content.

CTV also posted material fairly evenly during the day. Data collection shows a pattern in how CTV posted to Facebook, with some three or four

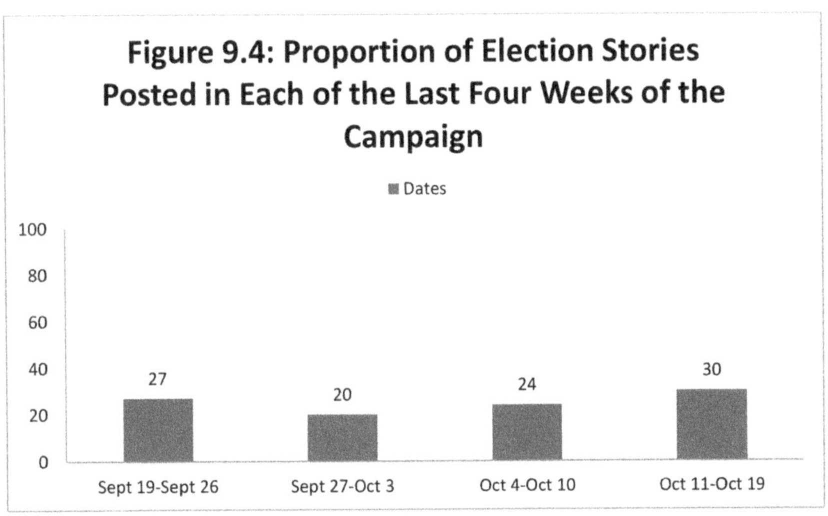


stories in the morning, the same number at noon, and then again about the same in the evening.

Spreading its posting that way, CTV kept the site up-to-date. In the morning, it posted stories from the previous evening, then continued building during the day with new stories that reflected a real-time view of the campaign as it unfolded daily. Not surprisingly, the evening stories would be end-of-day material that might have gone to supper-hour newscasts or *CTV National News* in the evening.

While some posted material originated with wire services, CTV had the benefit of its own news channel collecting and broadcasting election material all day from which it could choose for its Facebook page.

CTV produces *Power Play*, a daily, supper-hour parliamentary politics program on its television news channel. During the campaign, the program focused on the election; however, material from that program was not featured more prominently than other CTV content on CTV's Facebook page, perhaps missing an opportunity to promote the program among Facebook users.

CTV did post a lot of video on its Facebook page that could be viewed directly without leaving the page. There were also links in stories posted on the Facebook page that redirected users from Facebook to the CTV website. CTV also posted weekly summaries and campaign blog posts produced by its reporters following the party leaders.

Finally, like some of its competitors, CTV increased its volume of campaign coverage in the last week leading up to election day. While CTV featured poll results on the Facebook page throughout the campaign, perhaps not surprisingly polling had increased prominence on the Facebook page in the campaign's final week. That made some sense, for as the eventual results demonstrated, many voters were deciding in that week which of the two main opposition parties they would support.

**Global News:** Global posted only about a third as many election-related stories as CTV. This is presumably because, unlike CTV and CBC, Global has no news channel operation generating and broadcasting material all day that can be easily copied or adapted to Facebook. Its posts were mostly stories done initially for Global local newscasts or *Global National*, with supplemental stories derived from material produced for Global's websites or by Canadian Press.

The fact that two-thirds of Global's Facebook content was posted in the morning indicates that it was largely using the page to recirculate older material. Readers looking for election content could catch up on the previous day's news first thing in the morning, but if they wanted to follow the campaign's daily developments through Facebook, Global News really was not doing much of note. Most of the content on its Facebook page tended toward entertainment rather than hard news or political analysis. This was true even in its election-focused coverage, where much of it was geared toward a younger audience, focusing on issues such as marijuana legalization and Liberal leader Justin Trudeau's celebrity status.

**CBC News:** Of all the news organization pages surveyed, CBC News had the smallest number of election stories on its regular Facebook page. That likely reflects the presence of a stand-alone CBC Politics Facebook page, which collected CBC's election coverage in one place for those looking specifically for campaign news and commentary.

Similar to Global News, almost half of the CBC News election stories were posted to Facebook in the morning, meaning they were yesterday's news. Like CTV, CBC also has a news channel that followed campaign developments during each day. More than Global, CBC used Facebook to update readers during the day, while still posting a larger share of its material in the evening rather than the afternoon.

A significant share of CBC News' Facebook posts consisted of the vignettes of individual voters from across the country that its main news program, *The National*, featured most nights during the campaign.

On the main CBC News Facebook page, the election was just one of many stories covered during the sample period for this study. It had to compete with everything else in the news cycle, including the October appearance of the Toronto Blue Jays in major league baseball's playoffs for the first time in two decades. That could account for the fact that almost half the election coverage on the site was in the last week of September, unlike the content of the other two networks' Facebook pages.

**CBC Politics:** While almost half of the election stories on the CBC News site were posted in the morning, the evening was the prime time for Facebook election posts on the CBC Politics page. A major source for material for this page was the supper-hour political program *Power and Politics* on CBC News Network. It included daily interviews, campaign updates, and panel discussions, providing a significant amount of election-related material for the Facebook page.

As noted above, it is no surprise that 90 percent of the stories on the site during the period were related to the election, given the focus of CBC Politics. However, unlike most other news organizations, the CBC Politics Facebook page had the fewest number of election stories in the week leading up to the vote.

***National Post*:** The *National Post* had the second-highest number of election-related stories on its Facebook page, but like CTV News, the *Post*'s Facebook page included all sorts of content. As a result, the election material made up less than one-quarter of all content on the site during the last four weeks of the campaign.

One-third of the stories on the *Post*'s Facebook page appeared in the morning, likely as a way of pushing material from the morning paper (which focused on events of the previous day) into the social mediascape. Like its national newspaper competitor, the *Globe and Mail*, only a fifth of the *Post*'s Facebook election stories were posted in the evening, suggesting that Facebook was used primarily as an additional distribution outlet for stories that first appeared in the paper or perhaps on the *National Post*'s website.

The *Post*'s Facebook page spent considerable space covering political developments in the United States, particularly Donald Trump's pursuit of the 2016 Republican presidential nomination. The Facebook page also devoted a lot of attention to stories about candidates in the Canadian election who had made offensive statements in the past or committed gaffes on social media, several of whom were forced to withdraw after their comments were publicized.

With the campaign's last week dominated by a sense that the Conservatives were headed for defeat, perhaps it wasn't surprising that the *National Post*, a proudly Conservative newspaper, had relatively little campaign coverage on its Facebook page in the last few days leading to the vote. Only 15 percent of all the election stories on the *Post*'s Facebook page during the campaign's four weeks were posted in that final week prior to October 19.

***Globe and Mail***: The *Globe and Mail* had the fewest number of election-related Facebook posts, despite its self-description as "Canada's national newspaper" and its long history of national political coverage. Non-election stories dominated the *Globe*'s Facebook page throughout the campaign.

The comparatively sparse election content suggests the paper does not yet see Facebook as a method to promote coverage, to drive newspaper readers to its own online sites, or as a valuable tool for engaging audiences. Its readers are indeed engaged with the *Globe*, as demonstrated by the outraged response to the paper's late-campaign editorial endorsement of the Conservatives, but not Stephen Harper — although this is perhaps not the sort of engagement the paper might prefer.

To the extent that it did use Facebook, the *Globe and Mail* backloaded the majority of its content to the last week of the campaign. Almost 60 percent of the total number of election stories it posted to Facebook over the course of the final month appeared in those last seven days. Stephen Harper and Justin Trudeau were the focus of a lot of that coverage, but the *Globe* also devoted space on its Facebook page to the niqab debate that emerged during the campaign.

That 55 percent of its Facebook posts appeared in the morning suggests that the *Globe and Mail* saw the social media site as primarily a way to republish stories about campaign developments of the preceding day that appeared in that morning's paper and on its website.

***Toronto Star***: Of all the media organizations studied, the *Toronto Star* was the one that was most obviously using its Facebook page as a way to promote its election coverage. In total, it ran an almost identical number of election stories as the *National Post*. But while the *Post*'s election coverage made up just 22 percent of the stories on its Facebook page, election stories accounted for 80 percent of the stories on the *Star*'s page during the last four weeks of the campaign. This is almost triple the amount of Facebook space devoted to the election on any of the main pages of the other news organizations.

The *Toronto Star* also matched CBC Politics in posting the largest proportion of its stories in the evening, after 4 p.m. That increased as the campaign unfolded, with more attention to evening postings as election day approached. In the same way but not as extensively as the *Globe and Mail*, the *Toronto Star* backloaded its election postings, with 40 percent of the four-week total occurring in the campaign's last week. This was not a surprise, considering the *Toronto Star*'s editorial endorsement of the Liberal Party. As the final week unfolded, it seemed more and more likely that the Liberals would finish in first place, although many thought a majority was out of reach. The fact that the party it backed was headed for victory could have given the *Toronto Star* an added incentive to post stories to Facebook.

The focus on evening posts may reflect other events at the *Toronto Star*. In mid-September, it launched a new tablet publication, *Star Touch*, with an evening deadline for a daily 5 a.m. online distribution. That meant a lot of the newsroom was working to evening deadlines, perhaps making some stories available for Facebook publication prior to coming out the next morning in addition to picking up Canadian Press and *Star* stories filed during the day for online distribution.

---

Returning to the main question about CTV's potentially distinct contribution as a result of its partnership with Facebook, we can see some similarities and differences with other news outlets in terms of the volume of content and timing of publication. In an effort to further tease out potential variations in Facebook use between CTV and its competitors, the study also looked at the manner in which media outlets were engaging with audiences.

## Engagement with Audiences

The number of stories posted by each news organization during the last four weeks of the campaign is one indicator of how seriously they view Facebook as a key "partner" for delivering audience views. Equally important is what those audiences do with the stories they see on the news organizations' Facebook pages. As such, it is interesting to look at the extent to which audiences like, share, and comment on individual stories. This can be seen as a measure of the degree of engagement they have with the election issue and with the news organizations themselves.

It is commonly argued that social media encourage new levels of connection and interactivity between content and audiences.[25] The 2015 campaign, in particular, captured voters' interest from the outset, which was surprising given the launch of the campaign in the dog days of summer. Polling consistently showed that high numbers of voters wanted

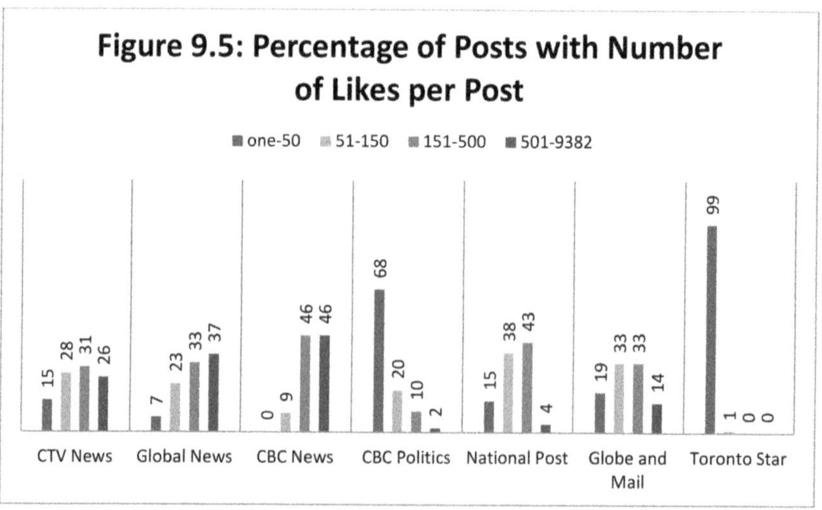


*Percentages have been rounded.

change and were monitoring the election.[26] The electorate's engagement with the campaign yielded a voter turnout on election day of 69.1 percent, the highest since 1993.

However, in spite of high interest in the campaign and relatively high voter turnout, the findings from our study do not suggest that Canadians turned to the Facebook pages of the media outlets we studied to actively engage with campaign issues or to get others involved in electoral politics.

Figure 9.5 reveals the extent to which Facebook users were commenting on content posted by the media outlets.

As can be seen by Figure 9.6, similar engagement is seen in the percentage of posts with comments.

Engagement declines further if looking at the percentage of posts that are shared. As can be seen in Figure 9.7, four of the pages examined had minimal shared content.

Looking at engagement through the lens of likes, comment, and shared content, it appears that the promoted relationship between CTV News and Facebook did not appreciably affect how engaged the CTV audience was with material on its Facebook page. While a quarter of the posts were liked by more than five hundred users, 44 percent of the posts had ninety comments or less, and none of them were shared by more than one hundred users, even though the site had almost three times the

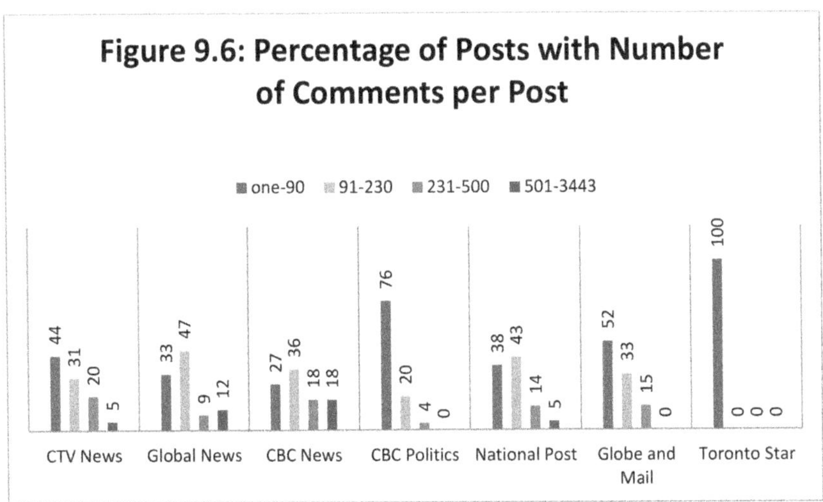


*Percentages have been rounded.

number of stories posted during the four weeks as any of the other pages we examined. In fact, Global News and the *National Post* both had a greater percentage of their stories liked by a larger number of Facebook users than CTV. The number of likes received by the *Globe and Mail* was similar to those recorded by CTV News.

In terms of comments, CBC had the largest percentage of stories with more than 500 comments per story. However, as was noted at the start of this section, it published the smallest number of stories by far. On the CBC Politics Facebook page, where one might expect to find the most engaged readers, three-quarters of the stories had fewer than ninety comments. Slightly more than 50 percent of the *Globe and Mail* stories had fewer than ninety comments while no stories on the *Toronto Star*'s page generated more than ninety comments.

As noted above, and shown in Figure 9.7, there was also limited sharing of material posted on the Facebook pages of these media organizations. CTV News, CBC News, and CBC Politics had no posts that were shared by more than one hundred people. The same was true for 98 percent of the content posted on the *Toronto Star*'s Facebook page. Only Global News had more than 50 percent of its Facebook posts shared by more than one hundred people and it was also the only site where more than 5 percent of posts were shared by more than five hundred people. These are minuscule numbers in

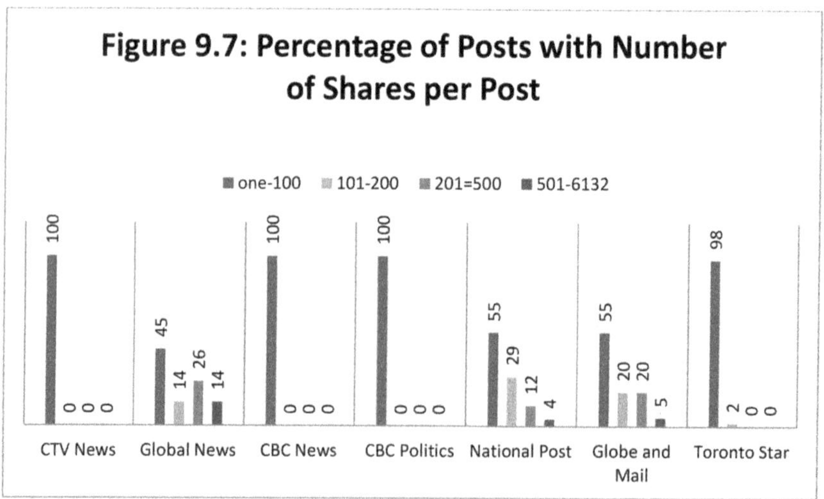


**Figure 9.7: Percentage of Posts with Number of Shares per Post**

*Percentages have been rounded.

the context of newspaper circulation figures in the hundreds of thousands and television newscast audiences of 500,000 or more. Even the two news channels get audiences for their political programs of about sixty thousand.

There are, of course, other methods that can gauge how voters are engaged during political events aside from looking at the Facebook pages of news organizations. Likes, comments, and sharing all occur on the websites of these media as well. Sharing also takes place through Twitter and other social media platforms. And sharing takes place on Facebook in ways that are not easily captured through basic Facebook analytics. For example, rather than using the share button to distribute content, people can copy the hyperlink from a news organization's website and then paste it into the comment box of their own Facebook page, thereby sharing material without that process being directly captured by a Facebook on-page counter. Such sharing techniques are difficult to measure for a variety of reasons, not the least of which includes privacy protection (however limited and problematic privacy protection may be on Facebook).

The architecture of Facebook and the way that stories are displayed on a news organization's Facebook page may also limit the ability of users to engage with and share material. Stories are presented on a continuous feed with the most recent story posted appearing at the top of the timeline, pushing all the others down. Posts are not currently ranked according to levels of engagement. In some cases, as with the *National Post*, which updated its site with new stories on all subjects about every thirty minutes, nothing would appear for long on the first screen a viewer read, limiting the opportunity to see a given story without sometimes endless scrolling. This practice may have also affected the extent of engagement as well, particularly on the *Post*'s Facebook page. Featuring a story or video in the left-hand column of the Facebook page (where it may stay on the initial screen longer than in the timeline) also appears to increase the number of likes and comments.

---

While the CTV-Facebook partnership did not seem to lead to any significant variations or advantages when it came to the volume of content posted, or interactivity with users, it is interesting to see whether it may have led to notable differences in the type of content posted.

## Content Variation

There is some differentiation between the content of the stories on the individual news organizations' Facebook pages. Opinion poll results drove almost a third of the stories on the CTV News page while more than half the stories related to election promises and campaign strategy. As can be seen in Figure 9.8, this was much higher than on any other organization's page.

At various points in the election campaign, Canada's economy was reported to be either in recession or heading to surplus. Of course, this also depended on whose numbers voters were prepared to believe. Either way, many pundits expected that the 2015 election would be about jobs and wider issues relating to the economy.[27] Yet, interestingly, no news organization gave the economy a significant degree of prominence on the content posted to its Facebook page. Despite the fact a global climate change conference

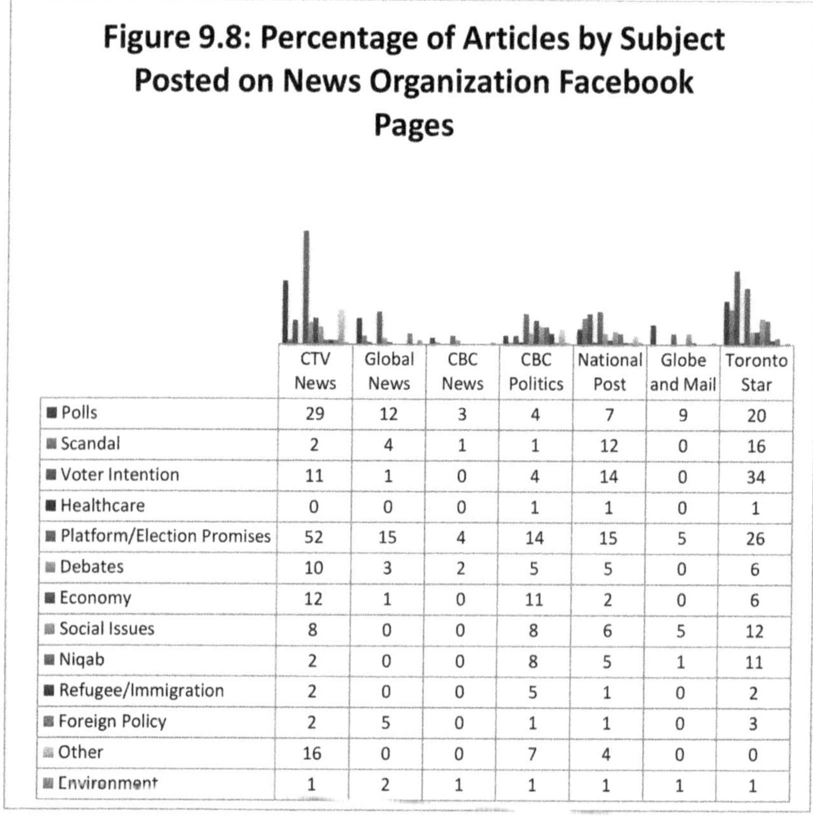

**Figure 9.8: Percentage of Articles by Subject Posted on News Organization Facebook Pages**

| | CTV News | Global News | CBC News | CBC Politics | National Post | Globe and Mail | Toronto Star |
|---|---|---|---|---|---|---|---|
| Polls | 29 | 12 | 3 | 4 | 7 | 9 | 20 |
| Scandal | 2 | 4 | 1 | 1 | 12 | 0 | 16 |
| Voter Intention | 11 | 1 | 0 | 4 | 14 | 0 | 34 |
| Healthcare | 0 | 0 | 0 | 1 | 1 | 0 | 1 |
| Platform/Election Promises | 52 | 15 | 4 | 14 | 15 | 5 | 26 |
| Debates | 10 | 3 | 2 | 5 | 5 | 0 | 6 |
| Economy | 12 | 1 | 0 | 11 | 2 | 0 | 6 |
| Social Issues | 8 | 0 | 0 | 8 | 6 | 5 | 12 |
| Niqab | 2 | 0 | 0 | 8 | 5 | 1 | 11 |
| Refugee/Immigration | 2 | 0 | 0 | 5 | 1 | 0 | 2 |
| Foreign Policy | 2 | 5 | 0 | 1 | 1 | 0 | 3 |
| Other | 16 | 0 | 0 | 7 | 4 | 0 | 0 |
| Environment | 1 | 2 | 1 | 1 | 1 | 1 | 1 |

was to be held in Paris within weeks of the election, the environment also assumed its usual fate, getting virtually no campaign coverage. And how did health care and foreign policy fare? These issues also got little to no attention on the Facebook pages of the media organizations we examined.

Scandal, by contrast, was a more popular topic for both the *National Post* and the *Toronto Star*'s Facebook pages, which included several stories recounting the social media outbursts, past and recent, from candidates of all parties.

The leaders' debates also appeared to be a more popular topic among news organizations, but here the focus was less on substantive themes or issues than the identification of key moments — so-called zingers — that some felt might move the electorate in one direction or another. With five leaders' debates in the campaign, as opposed to the conventional two debates in both official languages, this was perhaps to be expected.

It is no surprise, considering the scale of his victory and the fact that the Liberals came from a very distant third place in 2011 to win a majority in 2015, that Justin Trudeau garnered the largest share of coverage of any of the party leaders on all the media Facebook pages (except CBC Politics). As can be seen in Figure 9.9, Stephen Harper had a 1 percent advantage over Trudeau on the CBC Politics page. These findings might have varied had the study been conducted for the full duration of the campaign.

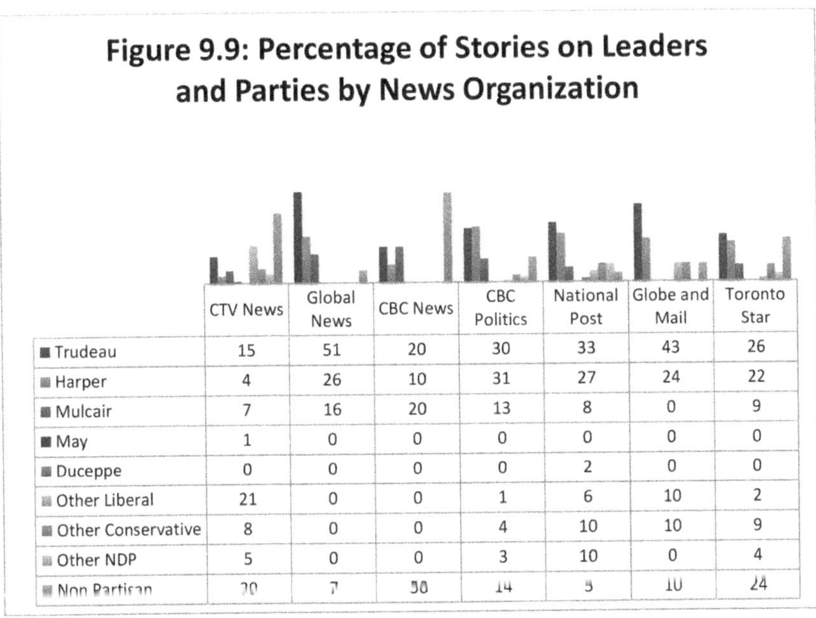

**Figure 9.9: Percentage of Stories on Leaders and Parties by News Organization**

| | CTV News | Global News | CBC News | CBC Politics | National Post | Globe and Mail | Toronto Star |
|---|---|---|---|---|---|---|---|
| Trudeau | 15 | 51 | 20 | 30 | 33 | 43 | 26 |
| Harper | 4 | 26 | 10 | 31 | 27 | 24 | 22 |
| Mulcair | 7 | 16 | 20 | 13 | 8 | 0 | 9 |
| May | 1 | 0 | 0 | 0 | 0 | 0 | 0 |
| Duceppe | 0 | 0 | 0 | 0 | 2 | 0 | 0 |
| Other Liberal | 21 | 0 | 0 | 1 | 6 | 10 | 2 |
| Other Conservative | 8 | 0 | 0 | 4 | 10 | 10 | 9 |
| Other NDP | 5 | 0 | 0 | 3 | 10 | 0 | 4 |
| Non Partisan | [illegible] | 7 | 50 | 14 | 5 | 10 | 24 |

The data do highlight that in the crucial final weeks of the campaign, as voters made their decisions, the NDP and leader Thomas Mulcair received much less coverage than either Stephen Harper or Justin Trudeau. While the NDP was at the top of the polls for the first half of the campaign, and was even publicly readying itself for government,[28] several news organizations treated them as little more than a sideshow as October 19 approached. This minimal-to-non-existent coverage can be seen clearly in Figure 9.9, particularly in the data captured for the *Globe and Mail.*

## DISCUSSION AND CONCLUSIONS

When announcing its partnership with Facebook for the 2015 election, CTV appeared to be promising its users enhanced content and engagement, stating that: "Facebook is the biggest social platform in Canada and CTV News properties will tap into it in a way no other media organization can."[29] To tease out the differences between CTV's Facebook content during the election and that of its competitors, this study posed three analytical questions:

1. How did the volume and timing of CTV's election-related posts on Facebook compare to those of other news organizations?
2. Were users more engaged with CTV's Facebook content, through use of the like, comment, and share features, than they were with other news organizations?
3. How did the content on the CTV Facebook page diverge or align with that of other media Facebook pages in the final four weeks of the election?

Ultimately, this chapter has demonstrated that while there are some minor variations in the type and volume of content that was offered by CTV, it did not afford users any novel or unique opportunities for interactivity and engagement during the 2015 election. It is unclear what benefits actually accrued to CTV as a result of its partnership with Facebook. One could very well imagine that the big winner in the partnership was Facebook, which no doubt collected a trove of data to better understand the psychological profiles of its users. Yet, it is curious that at a time when Facebook has command of such a vast and interconnected population, and seems to be expanding its reach into the environment formerly owned by legacy news organizations,[30] its Canadian media partner would not look to take better advantage of the opportunities to grow its audience. And this is arguably true for all media we examined in this study. The future of political journalism will have to accommodate the powerful role of Facebook in the media ecology of today.

This study focused specifically on the public presence and content of media organizations' Facebook pages. We believe that this makes an important contribution to political communication research and studies of social media and elections. Future research should build on our findings by looking more closely at the nature of such partnerships, including issues relating to data and ad revenue sharing. Facebook's native video player and the future of immersive multimedia storytelling also provide opportunities to examine how Facebook's media architecture may change the nature of political journalism broadly, and election storytelling in particular. Indeed, as news organizations move increasingly toward a "digital first" strategy, it will be important to monitor whether patterns change in terms of when content is posted, and whether these changes are also reflected in the cycle of campaign events over which media organizations arguably have little control.

## NOTES

1. We thank Erin Fagan, Mitchell White, Veronica Araujo, Mimi Husseini, Meagan Massad, Taylor Hewitt, and Victoria Gawronska for their assistance with data collection and analysis.
2. See, for example, Matt Kwong, "Facebook, New York Times Deal Could Change News Business." CBC News Online, March 27, 2015. www.cbc.ca/news/technology/facebook-new-york-times-deal-could-change-news-business-1.3011073.
3. Renee Dupuis and Patricia Garcia, "CTV News Partners with Facebook for Federal Election Coverage," Business News Network, June 16, 2015, www.bnn.ca/News/2015/6/16/CTV-News-partners-with-Facebook-for-federal-election-coverage.aspx.
4. Ibid.
5. See, for example, Mark Sutcliffe, "A New Generation Is Leading Canada, the Boomers Have Had Their Day," *Montreal Gazette*, November 2, 2015, http://montrealgazette.com/

opinion/columnists/opinion-a-new-generation-is-leading-canada-the-boomers-have-had-their-day.

6. See, for example, Thomas J. Johnson and David D. Perlmutter, eds., *New Media, Campaigning and the 2008 Facebook Election* (London: Routledge, 2011).
7. Michael Scherer, "Friended: How the Obama Campaign Connected with Young Voters," *Time*, November 20, 2012, http://swampland.time.com/2012/11/20/friended-how-the-obama-campaign-connected-with-young-voters/.
8. Gabrielle Grow and Janelle Ward, "The Role of Authenticity in Electoral Social Media Campaigns," *First Monday* 18, no. 4 (2013), http://firstmonday.org/article/view/4269/3425.
9. Vincent Raynauld and Josh Greenberg, "Tweet, Click, Vote: Twitter and the 2010 Ottawa Municipal Election," *Journal of Information Technology & Politics* 11, no. 4 (2014): 412–34.
10. See, for example, Tamara Small, "Still Waiting for an Internet Prime Minister," in *Elections*, ed. Heather MacIvor (Toronto: Emond Montgomery, 2010); Kenneth Kernaghan, "Moving Beyond Politics as Usual? Online Campaigning," in *Digital State at the Leading Edge*, ed. Sandford Borins et al. (Toronto: University of Toronto Press, 2007); and Darin Barney, *Communication Technology* (Vancouver: University of British Columbia Press, 2005).
11. Juliet E. Carlisle and Robert C. Patton, "Is Social Media Changing How We Understand Political Engagement? An Analysis of Facebook and the 2008 Presidential Election," *Political Research Quarterly* 66, no. 4 (2013): 883–95.
12. Joshua Freeman, "Trudeau Best Liked Federal Leader on Facebook, but Conservatives Lead as a Party," CP24, June 16, 2015, www.cp24.com/news/trudeau-best-liked-federal-leader-on-facebook-but-conservatives-lead-as-a-party-1.2425113.
13. Jessica Murphy, "Canadian Politicians' Social Media Blunders Cost Them in Election Campaign." *Guardian*, October 5, 2015, www.theguardian.com/world/2015/oct/05/social-media-gaffes-canada-election.
14. Martha McCaughey and Michael Ayers, eds., *Cyberactivism: Online Activism in Theory and Practice* (London: Routledge, 2003).
15. See, for example: Clay Shirky, *Here Comes Everybody: The Power of Organizing Without Organizations* (New York: Penguin, 2008).
16. Shelley Boulianne, "Does Internet Use Affect Engagement? A Meta-Analysis of Research," *Political Communication* 26, no. 2 (2009): 193–211.
17. Michael Margolis and David Resnick, *Politics as Usual: The Cyberspace "Revolution"* (London: Sage, 2000).
18. Robert Putnam, *Bowling Alone: The Collapse and Revival of the American Community* (New York: Simon and Schuster, 2000).
19. "Canada Votes 2008: Top 5 Facebook Groups," CBC, www.cbc.ca/news2/canadavotes/campaign2/ormiston/2008/09/facebook_24_9_2008.html.
20. www.thestar.com/news/federal-election/2015/08/09/social-media-activity-measured-after-leaders-debate.html.
21. Melody McKinnon, "2015 Canadian Social Media Usage Statistics." 2015, http://canadiansinternet.com/2015-canadian-social-media-usage-statistics/.
22. See PoliTwitter for some statistical analysis on Facebook use by politicians and parties in Canada over time: http://politwitter.ca/page/statistics_facebook.
23. Carlisle and Patton, op. cit.

24. Unlike all other news organizations, CBC administers a distinct Facebook page for its political coverage, running stories that also appear on its regular news page. To ensure we were able to capture all CBC posts about the election, we coded the two pages separately.
25. See, for example: Rena Bivens, *Digital Currents: How Technology and the Public Are Shaping Television News* (Toronto: University of Toronto Press, 2014).
26. Bruce Anderson and David Coletto, "The Battle for the Change Vote," Abacus Data, September 29, 2015, http://abacusdata.ca/the-battle-for-the-change-vote/.
27. Doug Saunders, "The Question of Election 2015: Can Government Create Jobs and Growth?" *Globe and Mail,* September 11, 2015, www.theglobeandmail.com/news/politics/on-the-economy-what-next-when-the-election-is-over/article26335844/.
28. See for example: James Cudmore, "Tom Mulcair's NDP Seeks Advice on Preparing to Govern After Election." CBC News Online, July 15, 2015, www.cbc.ca/news/politics/tom-mulcair-s-ndp-seeks-advice-on-preparing-to-govern-after-election-1.3151650.
29. Renee Dupuis and Patricia Garcia, "CTV News Partners with Facebook for Federal Election Coverage," Business News Network, June 16, 2015, www.bnn.ca/News/2015/6/16/CTV-News-partners-with-Facebook-for-federal-election-coverage.aspx.
30. Vindu Goal and Ravi Somaiya, "Facebook Begins Testing Instant Articles from News Publishers." *New York Times,* May 13, 2015, www.nytimes.com/2015/05/13/technology/facebook-media-venture-to-include-nbc-buzzfeed-and-new-york-times.html.

# CHAPTER 10

## A Debate About *The Debates*

André Turcotte

On the evening of September 26, 1960, two men vying for the most powerful political office in the world squared off in the first of four televised debates. Australia had held its own televised debate between political leaders in 1958,[1] but in 1960, as John F. Kennedy and Richard M. Nixon argued the main issues of the day, few at the time knew they were witnessing the creation of what would become a permanent fixture in modern electioneering. It would take almost two decades for this innovation to fully establish itself in modern campaigning, but after that gestation period there would be no turning back. Today, countries as diverse as France, Kenya, Germany, and Malta, among others, have adopted the tradition.[2]

Canada followed a similar pattern. The first federal leaders' debate was held on June 9, 1968,[3] but as a campaign event the debates did not become a regular occurrence until the 1984 election. While political parties and the media have tinkered with the format since, with that election it became generally accepted that staged, televised debates were inevitable. It was also expected that party leaders would participate in one English and one French debate, both organized through a consortium of major Canadian TV broadcasters. Just as regular as the debates themselves were complaints from party officials about the format of the debates, the number of participants, the length of the telecasts, the topics to be discussed, and other related items. For their part, broadcasters complained about the intransigence of party representatives and the loss of revenue associated with relinquishing advertising during prime time. But because it was understood that the network-televised debates were a necessary part of the electoral process, parties and leaders always eventually fell in line and a compromise was reached

Therefore, when Conservative strategists announced that Stephen Harper would not participate in a consortium-led debate in the 2015 election, the news was greeted with a general shrug. After all, such threats had been issued several times in the past. But this time there were platforms and means of public address other than those provided by the traditional broadcasters by which debates might be staged. In explaining the Conservative decision, party spokesman Kory Teneycke declared, "We believe the diversity and innovation inherent in different debate sponsors and approaches is valuable."[4] He upped the ante, declaring: "We won't participate in any [consortium debates]. It's a hard No. We have many, many offers from other credible media outlets."[5] And to everyone's surprise, the Harper Conservatives remained true to their word — something different was in store for the party leaders.

In the end, a total of five debates were held over the duration of the 2015 campaign. Originally, the Conservatives insisted they would only take part in independently organized events, but in the end they agreed to participate in one consortium-led debate in French, mainly because of self-interest. By the time of the French TV consortium debate, Harper's re-election prospects were dim and he needed a debate with a potentially large audience.

This chapter examines the unusual course of the leaders' debates in 2015 with a view to answering one of the perennial questions in the study of elections: "Do debates matter?" With five instead of the typical two debates occurring in the 2015 election, it is possible to analyze in greater depth the extent to which debates move voting intentions and what impact they might have — if any — on the election outcome. We will first review the theoretical debate about the debates, providing an overview of the existing literature on the Canadian context. This will set the stage for the analysis of the 2015 experience. The chapter will conclude with some reflections on the future of the debates as election events.

## THE THEORETICAL DEBATE

Leaders' debates have been studied from different perspectives. One approach examines the debates through the lenses of political communication and media studies. Scholarly works such as *Presidential Debates: Fifty Years of High Risk TV* by Alan Schroder,[6] *Inside the Presidential Debates:*

*Their Improbable Past and Promising Future* by Newton N. Minnow and Craig L. Lamay,[7] as well as *Political Communication in Britain: The Leader Debates, the Campaign and the Media in the 2010 General Election* by Dominic Wring et al.[8] are recent and important examples. This approach considers the debates as a communication tool and a media event and offers a "behind-the-scenes" look at the different components of how debates actually occur. Such studies dissect the process, examining the pre-debate negotiations and preparations, the debates themselves, their subsequent media coverage, and the very important post-debate communication efforts.

Others have examined the extent to which debates can contribute to a more informed electorate. Kathleen Hall Jamieson began her academic career focusing on this issue and concluded that presidential debates, despite their limitations, remain the best available vehicle to inform the electorate.[9] In the same vein, Owen,[10] as well as Lanoue and Schrott,[11] suggested that presidential debates constitute a perfect opportunity for voters to compare and contrast candidates' positions and personal styles and become better informed about their vote choice. As we will see later in this chapter, the knowledge dissemination function of the debates was one of the key discussion points of a colloquium on the future of leaders' debates held at Carleton University soon after the election.

There is also a comparative body of research that offers international perspectives on televised election debates.[12] This includes studies of debates in Australia, Israel, Great Britain, and New Zealand, among others. Another approach looks at debates within a broader study of elections and how they fit within the evaluation of campaign events and dynamics. Such works often take the form of an examination of a particular election campaign and speculate about the impact of the debates on the outcome. Others have tried to look at patterns over several elections.[13] Finally, and more directly pertinent to this chapter, an expansive literature has been devoted to gauging the extent to which debates have an impact on key determinants of vote choice. This chapter's analysis of the 2015 debates is squarely within that tradition.

The impact of debates on vote choice can be evaluated from two complementary angles. One straightforward analysis examines how aggregate vote support fluctuates in the aftermath of televised debates. This type of analysis tends to focus on the perceived winners and losers of the contests.

The TV watchers are asked which of the candidates "won" and how this might affect voting intentions. As is the case with several issues related to the study of voting behaviour, seminal works on debates have centred on U.S. presidential elections. The general consensus about the aggregate impact of debates is that "there is a tendency for the apparently victorious debater to experience some degree of surge in public support following the debate."[14] However, it would appear that much of this increase tends to disappear within a few days. Nevertheless, as Holbrook concluded, "generally speaking, the winning debater stands to make a modest gain in the polls"[15] and debates have at least the potential to act as effective persuasive tools.

A second approach looks at how individual attitudes are impacted by the debates. It assumes a more indirect impact on vote choice. This perspective looks beyond vote support and focuses on perceptions of leaders, voters' evaluation of performance, and impact on key leadership attributes. It supposes that the reason debate performance affects vote choice is because they have an impact on how voters perceive the candidates and their attitudes toward them. While this question seems straightforward, finding an answer has proven to be a complex operation.

One key obstacle in isolating a clear relationship between debate performance evaluation and individual impact on vote choice is that the assessment of "who won?" is strongly affected by party identification and political predispositions.[16] Specifically, Holbrook demonstrated that "pre-debate political predispositions are strongly related to post-debate vote choice, [and that] this is especially true for pre-debate vote choice, candidate assessment, and to a lesser degree, presidential approval."[17] However, debates appear to have an impact on the perception of the leaders on key attributes such as leadership strength, understanding of the issues, and overall personal evaluation. Even when controlling for political predispositions and party identification, evidence suggests that leaders' debates can have a significant influence on candidate evaluations.[18]

Thus, the general consensus emerging from the American literature suggests that debates have limited impact on the electoral outcome itself. This is not to say that they are not important. With a significant proportion of the electorate tuning in to watch, they influence the election process. They mobilize the attention of the electorate and the resources of the campaign. Leaders have to allocate considerable time to prepare for the debates, and as media events they can change the dynamics of the campaign. However, their influence is felt mainly through a short-term surge in support for the perceived winner, and this impact is limited both in scope and in time. This consensus extends to the Canadian context.

## DEBATES IN CANADIAN FEDERAL ELECTIONS

Considering the importance currently given to the leaders' debates in Canadian elections, it is hard to imagine a time when participating in such an event was optional and left to the discretion of party leaders and their advisers. As Leduc once wrote, "debates have assumed such prominence in elections that it sometimes appears as if nothing else matters."[19]

After taking part in the "National Debate" in 1968 alongside Robert Stanfield and Tommy Douglas, Pierre Elliott Trudeau decided to avoid debating his opponents in 1972 and 1974. By 1979, Trudeau was more open to the idea especially since he was convinced that he would fare favourably against his comparatively inexperienced PC adversary Joe Clark and the new NDP leader Ed Broadbent. While Trudeau performed well and probably "won" the debate, it became clear that there was more to debate dynamics than being the one with the winning performance. While Clark "received more negative than positive mentions in a post-debate questionnaire,"[20] he appeared to have done better than expected. Besting expectations is an important dimension of debate performance, and subsequent Canadian leaders benefitted from this important factor. Another derivative of debate performance is exposure, and NDP Leader Ed Broadbent took advantage of it in 1979. As LeDuc and his colleagues pointed out:

> For Ed Broadbent, the leadership debates were a heaven-sent opportunity to place the NDP on an equal footing with the other two parties, and to establish his image with the public. An experienced speaker, thoughtful and measured, Broadbent made the most of his opportunity, particularly in the lead-off pairing with Clark. Positioning the NDP as a viable opposition to the

> Liberals was particularly important to Broadbent because the party was fearful that voters might feel it necessary to vote Conservative in order to defeat the Liberals.[21]

Perhaps because he was perceived as having won the 1979 debates and yet still lost the election, Trudeau decided once again not to square off against his opponents in 1980.

The debates between John Turner and Brian Mulroney in 1984 and 1988 were consequential for three main reasons. First, they "ushered a new era in Canada much as the Carter-Reagan and Reagan-Mondale debates had done in the U.S."[22] Second, they both produced high drama and the interest they generated made it almost impossible for future leaders to avoid this media event. In 1984, a heated exchange between Turner and Mulroney over the issue of patronage concluded with the PC leader lecturing his Liberal counterpart by telling him, "You had an option, sir." This one-liner was viewed as a "knockout punch" that caused irreparable damage to Liberal electoral chances. Four years later it was Turner who delivered the "knockout" punch by accusing Mulroney of "selling us out" to the United States with the Free Trade Agreement (FTA). From then on, the search for "unforgettable one-liners" became an intrinsic part of post-debate analysis, although memorable one-liners themselves remain rare occurrences. Third, the 1984 campaign was also the first campaign in which the leaders agreed to take part in a separate debate conducted exclusively in French. Moreover, the 1984 election campaign also showcased another leaders' debate on women's issues. It was the first time until 2015 that more than two debates were held during the same election campaign.

By the 1988 election, it was expected that party leaders would participate in one English and one French debate, organized through a consortium of major Canadian TV broadcasters. These encounters created unforgettable — and some eminently forgettable — moments. For instance, five party leaders took part in the 1993 debates in what was more akin to a cacophonous shouting match than a serious discussion about the issues of the day. The same thing occurred in 1997, but this time it was the moderator of the French debate who stole the show when she fainted right in the middle of a key encounter between Jean Chrétien and Jean Charest. There was a change in format in 1993, with the introduction of "citizens' segments" when ordinary Canadians were given the opportunity to ask questions of the leaders. In 2000, Canadian Alliance leader Stockwell Day broke the debate rules by holding up a hand-crafted sign declaring his opposition to two-tier health care; a deadpan Joe Clark asked Day if he was auditioning to become a game-show host.

Debates continued to be held in every election between 2004 and 2011 but lost some of their earlier appeal. For one, the "free-for-all" format with as many as five leaders was not conducive to substantive discussions. Moreover, leaders had become increasingly well prepared and risk-averse and were more likely to simply want to survive the encounter instead of taking any definite stance on issues. The TV broadcasters themselves were increasingly frustrated by the process. They were annoyed by the tone of the negotiations with the respective party representatives, resented the mounting costs associated with the production of the event, were frustrated by the resistance of the parties involved to accept innovative format changes, and rueful of the loss of advertising revenues that came with pre-empting prime time programming.[23] And perhaps more importantly, it was unclear what impact, if any, debates still had on the outcome of the election.

Still, the debates do play an important part in the course of a campaign if only "because of the massive audience that they draw."[24] They are also significant because "the leaders themselves attach overwhelming importance to the debates."[25] Moreover, some studies have shown that they can affect voters' perceptions of the leaders. For instance, the 1988 National Election Study isolated an important shift in public attitudes in favour of Turner following his debate performance.[26] It has also been suggested that debates "may have a particularly important [...] influence on public opinion when several of the leaders are new faces, as in 1993,"[27] because voters develop lasting "first impressions" as a result of debate performance. Studies have shown that the debates can have an impact on the important perception of which leaders would "make the best prime minister." In 1993, Kim Campbell was leading Jean Chrétien on "who would make the best prime minister" by 39 percent compared to 19 percent before the debates. After the event, 31 percent of Canadians favoured Chrétien compared to 24 percent for Campbell.[28] A similar pattern occurred in 1997. Prior to the debates, 36 percent of Canadians believed Chrétien would make the best prime minister, compared to 22 percent for Charest. Afterward, the gap narrowed considerably with 35 percent favouring Chrétien — only 8 percentage points ahead of Charest.[29] In both instances, Chrétien won the election handily despite his lacklustre performance in the debates. Such a trend had been identified in most debates ever since where the perceived winner of the contest does not necessarily win on election day.

Several explanations have been offered to explain the apparent disconnect between debate performance and electoral outcomes. First, Canadian elections are not presidential contests[30] and the realities of our electoral system with its "first-past-the-post, single-member constituencies" may contribute to diluting the impact of leaders' evaluations. This is not to say that leaders do not play a predominant role in our elections, but they are only one element — alongside others such as parties, candidates, regional divisions, and issues. Second, it appears that it is difficult to sustain a positive impact from a debate performance over the course of the campaign. This is in line with the evidence presented in the previous section and party strategists are cognizant of this fact. As a result, debates are scheduled well ahead of election day with a view to allow for enough time for the potential losers to control the damage. Third, "the possible direct effects of the debate are somewhat diluted by the fact that viewers are also more likely to watch other political programs over the course of the campaign."[31] Hence, the initial impact on attitudes can possibly be changed by the secondary coverage and analysis of the debates. As Waddell and Dornan pointed out, only 31 percent of Canadians identified the debates themselves as the most influential factor in shaping debate conclusions, with the remaining 69 percent divided between other influences such as newspaper coverage the day after, post-debate TV analysis, and Internet news sites among others.[32] Finally, in the run-up to the 2015 federal election, leaders' debates had become predictable and highly scripted events. Campaign strategists had become accustomed to the two-debate format. They understood that "the debates create a period of disruption and uncertainty in the middle of the campaign but seem to have had little effect on the results."[33] Strategists were able to remove uncertainty through careful planning and preparations. But things were different in 2015 and this offers a perfect opportunity to revisit the impact of the leaders' debates.

## THE 2015 DEBATES

The first of the five debates held in 2015 took place on August 6 and was sponsored by *Maclean's* magazine. Harper, Mulcair, Trudeau, and May participated in the two-hour debate that aired on Rogers stations, CPAC, and Facebook. This particular debate was supposed to be a pre-writ event since it was scheduled prior to the writ drop. Paul Wells, political editor for *Maclean's* magazine, was the driving force behind this debate. He had wanted to break what he saw as an unfair monopoly on leaders' debates by the TV consortium.[34] The fixed election date made it easier for him to plan ahead and since *Maclean's* was part of the Rogers media group, he had the advantage of being able to count on a TV broadcaster to air the event. Interest for this encounter heightened considerably when, on August 2, Prime Minister Stephen Harper asked Governor General David Johnston to dissolve Parliament and call a general election for October 19.

The *Maclean's* Debate was followed on September 17 by a debate on the economy. Sponsored by the *Globe and Mail* and Google Canada, this debate was restricted to Harper, Mulcair, and Trudeau. Next was a French Media Consortium debate on September 24, where all five party leaders squared off for the first time. Harper, Mulcair, and Trudeau were invited to participate in a bilingual debate on September 28, focused on foreign policy and held as part of the regular Munk Debates, held at Toronto's Roy Thomson Hall since 2008. This particular event had been identified in advance by Conservative strategists as a possible option for a non-consortium debate since it was already planned to occur during the campaign. Finally, the five leaders faced each other for the last time on October 2 in a French debate sponsored by the Quebec broadcaster TVA.

The impact of the debates will be examined from three perspectives. First, I will look at the impact of the new multi-debates format on audience. As we mentioned, one of the key reasons why debates matter is because of the large audience they draw. With five instead of two debates, did more Canadians tune in to watch the leaders? Was there heightened interest, or did Canadians lose interest in the debates as the campaign progressed? Second, I will trace the fluctuations in voting intentions in relation to the debates with a view to isolating movements in vote choice that can be attributed to them. Third, relying on data collected during the first part of the campaign,[35] I will look at the potential impact that watching the debates may have had on overall impression of parties and voters' perceptions of the three main party leaders.

---

If the motivation behind the multi-debate strategy was to increase the exposure of the leaders to the Canadian electorate, it missed the mark. Table 10.1 shows that only the first debate — on August 6 — broke the million viewers mark, with an average of 1.5 million Canadians tuning in. This pales in comparison with the previous three debates — in 2011, 2008, and January of 2006 — which had average audiences of three million. Even the pre-Christmas leaders' debate in December 2005 drew close to two million viewers, about 25 percent more than on August 6, 2015. While equivalent historical data is not readily available,[36] it is reasonable to suggest that this debate was probably the least watched in Canadian federal elections to that point. And things would only get worse.

**Table 10.1: Audience Ratings, 2006–2015**

| Debate | Audience |
|---|---|
| December 16, 2005 | 1,977,000 |
| January 9, 2006 | 3,152,000 |
| October 2, 2008 | 3,048,000 |
| April 12, 2011 | 3,662,000 |
| August 6, 2015 | 1,507,000 |
| September 17, 2015 | 780,000 |
| September 24, 2015 | 291,000 |
| September 28, 2015 | 491,000 |
| October 2, 2015 | 973,000 |

Source: Numeris — Average Minute Audience

Described as "bruising"[37] in a top-of-the front-page headline, the first debate provided a strategic roadmap for each of the main leaders. It became evident that Harper intended to use the debate platform to appear prime ministerial, trying to stay calm and to demonstrate his grasp of the issues. The open question in this preliminary contest was whether Trudeau or Mulcair could emerge as Harper's main challenger. The two opposition leaders chose drastically different approaches to grab the spotlight, perhaps because they faced dissimilar sets of expectations. For his part, Mulcair, struggling to appear "not quite the aggressive prosecutor he is reputed to be,"[38] tried to soften his image; throughout the evening he sported a forced, fixed, and, to political observers, entirely unfamiliar smile. In contrast, Trudeau set out to dispel his image as a weak and inexperienced leader with a pugnacious performance, ready to "land blows."[39] As a sign of things to come, Elizabeth May was barely mentioned in the post-debate coverage and was largely ignored throughout the campaign. She was excluded from the Munk Debate and her weak grasp of the French language rendered her irrelevant in the two French debates. While the first debate was a generally entertaining affair, the subsequent audience ratings suggest that it failed to create sustained interest.

The audience for the second debate dropped to 780,000 Canadians: a 48 percent decrease. (By comparison, a nightly episode of the *CTV National News*, at 11 p.m., typically draws more than a million viewers.) Nevertheless, the event remained top-headline news the following day, with the *Globe and Mail*, which sponsored the debate and whose editor moderated, devoting the whole of its front page to the encounter.[40] The Munk Debate on foreign policy was largely ignored — drawing a dismal audience (491,000). Even the media were losing interest as post-debate coverage was no longer top-headline news. Interest rebounded for the final debate — drawing a more respectable audience than the first French encounter — but audience numbers remained below those garnered for the first debate and far below historical standards.

Reaching Canadians is only one dimension of the potential impact of the leaders' debates. As noted previously, Waddell and Dornan clearly showed that the actual broadcast of the debates is only one way voters assess leaders' performances. Another, and arguably more important, potential impact is on vote choice. Looking at the evolution of voting intentions throughout the campaign and how the debates affected party support (Table 10.2), it is difficult to discern any clear associations.

Before the writ was dropped on August 2, support for the Conservatives hovered around the 30 percent mark. Specifically, on July 28, Forum Research suggested that 33 percent of Canadians would support the Conservatives. After the first debate, support for the Harper troops dropped marginally to 30.8 percent in the first poll released immediately after, and then to 28 percent by August 11. However, it moved back up to 30 percent and stayed there until the second debate.

The next two debates appear to have had no significant impact on Conservative support. One day before the September 17 debate, a Nanos poll showed support for the CPC at 30.1 percent. That support dropped 3.6 percentage points in the immediate aftermath of the Munk Debate, but the loss was short-lived as the Conservatives bounced back to 35 percent after the October 2 debate. In terms of relative party standings, the Conservatives began the campaign in a dead heat with the NDP and ahead of the Liberals. The three parties moved in and out of the lead throughout the early part of the campaign, with no change directly attributed to the first debate. The Liberals managed to overtake the NDP after the second debate and after that never trailed them again; however, they did not permanently pull ahead of the Conservatives until the last week of the campaign, more than nine days after the last of the five debates.

## Table 10.2: Voting Intentions and the Debates

| Date / Poll | CPC | NDP | LIB |
|---|---|---|---|
| July 24–30 / Innovative | 29.3 | 33.7 | 25 |
| July 27–28 / Forum | 33 | 33 | 25 |
| **August 6 Debate** | | | |
| August 7–10 / Ipsos | 30.8 (-2.2) | 33 (no change) | 27 (+2) |
| August 10–11 / Forum | 28 | 34 | 27 |
| August 26–28 / Abacus | 30 | 31 | 28 |
| September 9–11 / Abacus | 29 | 31 | 29 |
| September 14–16 / Nanos | 30.1 | 30.4 | 30 |
| **September 17 Debate** | | | |
| September 18–20 / Nanos | 31 (+0,9) | 29.1 (-1.3) | 29 (-1) |
| September 18–21 / Ipsos | 27 (-3.1) | 30 (-0.4) | 33 (+3) |
| September 21–23 / Nanos | 30.5 | 30.8 | 31 |
| September 24 Debate | | | |
| September 25–27 / Nanos | 33 (+2.5) | 26.9 (-3.9) | 31 (no change) |
| September 25–26 / Ipsos | 32 (+1.5) | 27 (-3.8) | 33 (+2.0) |
| **September 28 Debate** | | | |
| September 29–Oct. 1 / Innovative | 29 (-3.6) | 29 (+2) | 31 (no change) |
| September 29–Oct 1 / Nanos | 31.9 (-0.7) | 25.9 (-1.1) | 33 (+2.0) |
| **October 2 Debate** | | | |
| Oct. 3–5 / EKOS | 35.1 (+3.2) | 22.2 (-3.7) | 30 (-3) |
| Oct. 4–6 / Nanos | 32.1 (+0.2) | 23 (-2.9) | 34 (+1) |
| Oct. 11–14 / Nanos | 29.4 | 23.7 | 37 |
| Oct. 13–14 / Forum | 31 | 24 | 37 |
| Oct. 16–18 / EKOS | 31.9 | 20.4 | 40 |
| ELECTION RESULTS | 32 | 20 | 39 |

Source: CBC Poll Tracker — (change in brackets) indicates change from pre-debate poll.

The story is not as straightforward when it comes to the battle between the Liberals and the NDP and how the debates may have contributed to the emergence of Justin Trudeau as the main challenger to Stephen Harper. Table 10.2 shows that at the beginning of the campaign the Trudeau Liberals were trailing both the NDP and the Conservatives by 8 percentage points. Seventy-three days later, they emerged as the winners: comfortably ahead of the Conservatives (+7) and well ahead of the NDP (+19). Over that period of time, support for the Liberals went up by 14 percentage points while NDP support dropped by 13 points. In contrast, despite some fluctuations during the campaign (from a low of 27 percent in one Ipsos poll in mid-September to a high of 35 percent in a EKOS poll in early October), Conservative support was the same on election day as it was on the day when the campaign began.

Looking more closely at the NDP support, there was a significant decline after the third debate from which the party never recovered. Specifically, the NDP was steadily garnering about 30 percent of support until about September 23. By September 27, however, support for the Mulcair team had dropped below 30 percent — to 26.9 percent — and remained permanently below that mark for the rest of the campaign. There was yet another significant decline after the last debate on October 2 (a drop of 3.7 percentage points) and NDP support continued to decline slowly until it reached its lowest point (20 percent) on election day. While we cannot conclude that debate performance was directly responsible for the demise of the NDP, it would appear that the debates in general, and especially the two French debates, hurt Mulcair's electoral fortunes. What is less clear is the extent to which Mulcair's poor debate showing directly benefitted Justin Trudeau.

Explaining the rise in Liberal support and finding links with debate performance is a difficult task. According to Paul Wells, political editor of *Maclean's* magazine and moderator of the first debate, the Conservative multi-debate strategy was "to smoke Trudeau out and make him look bad."[41] We can be confident in stating that this strategy did not work. At no point in the campaign did we see a drop in Liberal support in the aftermath of a debate. And we have already established that most of the Liberal rise in support occurred well after the October 2 debate. So what can be said about Trudeau's performance in the leaders' debates?

Examining the post-debate impacts on Liberal support throughout the campaign, it is hard to see any significant defining moment. Specifically, support for the Trudeau Liberals went up marginally (+2 percentage points) after the August 6 debate and down 1 point after the September 17 event. Trudeau's performance during the third and fourth debates had no impact on Liberal support while that support dropped marginally after the last debate (-3 points). The Liberals did pull ahead of the NDP after the third debate, but this was more the result of a poor showing by Mulcair. If we are to find any links between the debates and the rise of the Trudeau Liberals, we will need to look at some indirect links and rely on attitudinal data.

A third angle from which to analyze the effects of the leaders' debates on the outcome of the 2015 federal election is to examine the extent to which they may have altered the voting public's perceptions of the party leaders. Relying on data collected at three separate points during the campaign and immediately following the first three debates, changes in leaders perception can be examined along specific dimensions. As noted above, this line of inquiry is based on the assumption that one way debate performance affects vote choice is indirectly through an impact on how voters perceive and feel about the candidates.

Canadians were asked to evaluate the three main party leaders on the following six dimensions:

1. Overall impression.
2. Who would make the best prime minister?
3. Who would make the worst prime minister?
4. Which leader impressed you the most?
5. Which leader impressed you the least?
6. Which party leaders offer the best solutions to Canada's problems?

Furthermore, since "change" was the main message for both the Liberals and the NDP, sentiment about "time for a change" was also tracked in the early part of the campaign. The exact wording of the questions can be found in Appendix A.

The data in Table 10.3 suggest that the debates had some impact on leaders' image, mainly for Mulcair and Trudeau. For instance, while Mulcair was slightly ahead of both Harper (by 6 points) and Trudeau (by 8 points) after the August 6 debate in terms of "who would make the best prime minister," the three leaders were in a virtual tie in the aftermath of the second encounter. But this was the result of a decline of 5 points for Mulcair on that important attribute and a 4-point increase for Trudeau (with virtually no change for Harper). Throughout that period, half (50 percent) believed Harper would make the worst prime minister. In Quebec, Mulcair was still perceived as the one who would make the best PM after the first French debate on September 24 (39 percent), well ahead of Harper (26 percent) and Trudeau (16 percent).

There was very little movement on two of the other dimensions. Specifically, there was virtually no change with regard to the percentage of Canadians who strongly or somewhat agreed that it was "time for a change," presumably because that sentiment was already high when the writ was dropped. Similarly, impression scores varied very little during the early part of the campaign.

**Table 10.3: Leader Performance Evaluation**

| Determinant | August 7–10 N=1099 | September 18–20 N=1081 | September 25, N= 300 (Quebec only) |
|---|---|---|---|
| Time for a Change (% agree) | 71% | 70% | 67% |
| **Impression Scores (0–10)** | | | |
| Harper | 3.03 | 3.25 | 3.55 |
| Trudeau | 4.45 | 4.84 | 3.87 |
| Mulcair | 5.08 | 5.15 | 4.90 |
| **Best PM** | | | |
| Harper | 28% | 29% | 26% |
| Trudeau | 26% | 30% | 16% |
| Mulcair | 34% | 29% | 39% |
| **Worst PM** | | | |
| Harper | 50% | 50% | 35% |
| Trudeau | 19% | 17% | 23% |
| Mulcair | 12% | 13% | 9% |
| **Impressed You the Most** | | | |
| Harper | 18% | 25% | 20% |
| Trudeau | 30% | 43% | 9% |
| Mulcair | 26% | 32% | 28% |
| **Impressed You the Least** | | | |
| Harper | 54% | 58% | 24% |
| Trudeau | 15% | 26% | 34% |
| Mulcair | 18% | 16% | 15% |
| **Best Solutions to Problems** | | | |
| Harper Conservatives | 21% | 29% | 31% |
| Trudeau Liberals | 21% | 30% | 18% |
| Mulcair NDP | 25% | 29% | 33% |

Source: Online interviews, Angus Reid Forum — see wording of questions in Appendix A

If there was an early turning point for Trudeau that can be related to debate performance, the data suggest that it was in the aftermath of the second debate. When asked which "leader impressed you the most," in the days after the September 17 debate, 43 percent chose Trudeau — up 13 percentage points from the period after the *Maclean's* debate — and ahead of both Mulcair (32 percent) and Harper (25 percent). The second debate was particularly difficult for Harper, since 58 percent identified him as "the leader who impressed them the least." Another positive development for the Trudeau campaign was that while the Liberals were trailing the NDP in terms of which party "offers the best solutions to deal with the most important issue facing Canada'" after the first debate, the gap was closed after September 17.

The first French debate did not appear to have the same impact. In specific terms, the sentiment for change was also high in Quebec after the debate (67 percent strongly or somewhat agreed that it was time for a change) and Mulcair was still in a good position. He garnered the highest impression scores and was seen as the leader "who would make the best PM." Mulcair was the most impressive of the three main leaders and his NDP was seen as the party with the best solutions. When looking at the evolution in voting intentions (Table 10.2), we can see erosion in NDP support after the first French debate but attitudinal data suggest that Quebecers still had a favourable impression of the NDP leader by the end of September. Arguably, it was the final debate that sealed the fate of the Mulcair team.

## CONCLUSION: LOOKING AHEAD

It is a cliché to describe an election as "unique" and "unlike any other," but the 2015 Canadian federal election was certainly different than recent contests. It was the longest in modern Canadian history, it was the first to be held under the fixed election date rule, and the outcome was surprising to many. For the purpose of this study, it was unique because it offered more debates between the leaders than any other in our political history. The fact that five debates were held in this election provided an opportunity to examine the impact of leaders' debates and determine the extent to which they matter. The evidence supports certain conclusions.

Based on the review of the body of academic work dealing with the leaders' debates, the 2015 situation was examined from three perspectives. First, with regard to a potential relationship between fluctuations in voting intentions and debate performance, the impact was concentrated on the Liberals and the NDP. Specifically, there was a significant drop in NDP support after the third debate and Mulcair was unable to turn the tide after that point. The NDP decline benefitted the Liberals, but most of the upturn in Liberal support occurred well after the last debate on October 2. Consequently, it must be concluded that, consistent with most of the literature, the main impact of the leaders' debates was indirect. In the 2015 federal election, the result was principally focused on perceptions of Justin Trudeau.

As mentioned earlier, Leduc suggested that debates are likely to have more impact on new party leaders, as they help the public form first impressions. This analysis provides some substantiating evidence for that assertion. Despite some fluctuations during the campaign, Conservative support was the same on election day as it was when the campaign began and impressions and attitudes toward Stephen Harper were largely unchanged. While support for the NDP went down during the campaign, the attitudinal data from the early part of the campaign do not point to any specific deterioration in Mulcair's image that can explain the subsequent NDP decline. While not as well known as Stephen Harper, Mulcair had been around the political scene for many years, as a provincial minister in Quebec and then as federal NDP leader since 2012. In contrast, newcomer Justin Trudeau impressed voters in the second debate and improved the perceived ability of his party to deal with the most important issue facing the country. This was important because that particular debate focused on the economy, a perceived strength for the Conservatives and the main concern of Canadians. This arguably set the stage for the late and definitive surge in Liberal support in the last ten days of the campaign.

Whatever impact the debates might have turns on the size of the audiences they can draw. In that regard, the multi-debate strategy must be judged a failure for it yielded audiences on each night far below viewership in previous elections. The first debate drew the largest audience of the campaign debates but that was still much below historical viewership levels. The four subsequent debates drew even lower audiences. One could argue that the five debates combined yielded a substantial overall audience, but typically there is a lot of duplication in viewership of current affairs programs in general and of political events in particular — the same people, the political or news junkies, tend to watch most, if not all, of the broadcasts.

The disappointing audience as well as the frustration associated with the debate negotiations throughout the campaign was sufficiently alarming to the newly elected Trudeau government that dealing with this issue in advance of the 2019 federal election was included in the mandate letter to the minister responsible for democratic reform. It also convinced the major stakeholders involved in the leaders' debates — from political parties, broadcasters and government officials — to begin a discussion about the future of this campaign event.

On December 5, 2015, many who will likely play a role in determining the future of the leaders' debates gathered for a one-day colloquium at Carleton University. This event was organized by Bill Fox — former *Toronto Star* reporter, press secretary and director of communications for Prime Minister Mulroney, and long-time Progressive Conservative insider — who was involved in numerous debate negotiations, including for the 2011 election; and Chris Waddell, former *Globe and Mail* Ottawa bureau chief and the CBC's senior producer with *The National* and *Sunday Report*. Among those present were representatives from the CBC, Bell Media, Shaw, Radio-Canada, political staffers from the office of the minister responsible for democratic reform, and representatives from the Privy Council, as well as officials from the CRTC and Elections Canada.[42] Representatives of the NDP and the Conservatives pulled out at the last minute without explanation.

With the next federal election still four years away, no one expected to emerge from the meeting with a clear plan on how not to repeat the experience of 2015. Despite conflicting perspectives and interests, however, most agreed on a few things. First, while 2015 may have been an aberration, because of the intransigence of the Harper team, going back to the old format is probably not an option. As Bill Fox commented: "There were deep dissatisfactions in previous elections about the debates and especially the negotiations."[43] Second, the media landscape is likely to be much different in 2019 and digital platforms will be occupying a more prominent place, demanding a new approach and format. There will likely be increased demands for citizen participation beyond the tradition of a few token questions directed at the leaders before a live studio audience. Third, negotiations should occur prior to the writ period. Last-minute negotiations stifle the potential for creative and open discussions about new formats.

There was no real consensus about what to do next, though. Since this issue was mentioned in the minister's mandate letter, some legislation is likely to be enacted. It is unclear, however, how far the government might go in forcing participation in the debates and requiring that they be broadcast on the public airwaves. There was no apparent willingness to be proactive in order to pre-empt potentially detrimental legislation. Most agreed that the TV Consortium will not reclaim its prominent place in the next election, but there was no clear idea of what might replace it. On the surface, the idea of letting the market forces dictate how many debates will be held and who will broadcast the events has some appeal, but if the next election campaign reverts to a thirty-five-day format, it is unclear whether the party leaders will agree to participate in multiple debates.

If there was a major obstacle in defining the future, it was a lack of agreement about what, precisely, is the role of the debates. While the literature and this analysis show that the debates do have some impact, they are not defining strategic or tactical moments in a campaign. Some colloquium participants reminded the audience that debates are more than media events. For some, they are meant to inform the electorate. They have a knowledge dissemination function that has been largely ignored in recent years. Therein may lie the solution to the future of the debates. An agreement about the importance of this information role would lead to fundamental change in the way debates are structured. This should be the starting point of the discussion.

## APPENDIX A — QUESTION WORDING

On a scale of 0 to 10 where 0 is "not at all impressed" and 10 is "very impressed," how would you rate each of the following federal party leaders?

Which of the following federal party leaders would make the BEST prime minister?

Which of the following federal party leaders would make the WORST prime minister?

Which of the following federal party leaders impressed you the most?

Which of the following federal party leaders impressed you the least?

Which of the federal political parties, the Harper Conservatives, the Trudeau Liberals, the Mulcair NDP, or the May Green Party, would be best to provide solutions to deal with (MOST IMPORTANT ISSUE)?

Do you strongly agree, somewhat agree, somewhat disagree, or strongly disagree with the following statement: "It's time for a change in federal politics"?

## NOTES

1. Ian Ward and Mary Walsh, "Leaders' Debates and Presidential Politics in Australia," in Stephen Coleman ed., *Televised Election Debates: International Perspectives* (London: Macmillan, 2000), 48.
2. Martin Kettle, "All Eyes on the Leaders' Debates," *Guardian*, April 7, 2010, www.theguardian.com/commentisfree/2010/apr/07/debates-leaders-media (accessed October 28, 2015).
3. Lawrence LeDuc, et al., *Dynasties and Interludes* (Toronto: Dundurn, 2010), 258.
4. Canadian Press, "Conservatives Say Harper Won't Participate in Traditional Election Debates Run by Broadcasters," *National Post*, May 12, 2015, http://news.nationalpost.com/news/canada/conservatives-say-harper-wont-participate-in-traditional-election-debates-run-by-broadcasters (accessed on November 29, 2015).
5. Ibid.
6. Alan Schroeder, *Presidential Debates: Fifty Years of High-Risk TV*, 2nd ed. (New York: Columbia University Press, 2008).
7. Newton N. Minow and Craig L. LaMay, *Inside the Presidential Debates: Their Improbable Past and Promising Future* (Chicago: University of Chicago Press, 2008).
8. Dominic Wring, Roger Mortimore, and Simon Atkinson, eds., *Political Communication in Britain: The Leader's Debates, the Campaign and the Media in the 2010 General Election* (London: Palgrave Macmillan, 2011).
9. Kathleen Hall Jamieson, *Presidential Debates: The Challenge of Creating an Informed Electorate* (New York: Oxford University Press, 1988). See also, William L. Benoit, *Political Election Debates: Informing Voters About Policy and Character* (Lanham, MD: Lexington Books, 2015).
10. D. Owen, *Media Messages in American Presidential Elections* (Westport, CT: Greenwood Press, 1991).
11. D.J. Lanoue and P.R. Schrott, *The Joint Press Conference: The History, Impact, and Prospects of American Presidential Debates* (New York: Praeger, 1991).
12. Stephen Coleman, ed., *Televised Election Debates: International Perspectives* (London: Macmillan, 2000).
13. There are numerous examples of this approach. See for instance, Abramson, Paul et al., *Change and Continuity in the 2012 and 2014 Elections* (Washington: CQ Press, 2015); Richard Johnston, *Letting the People Decide* (Montreal and Kingston: McGill-Queen's University Press, 1992); and Dennis Kavanagh and Philip Cowley, *The British General Election of 2015* (London: Palgrave Macmillan, 2015).
14. Thomas M. Holbrook, *Do Campaigns Matter?* (Thousand Oaks, CA: SAGE

Publications 1996), 108.

15. Ibid., 114.
16. See Owen, *Media Messages*; Lanoue and Schrott, *The Joint Press Conference*; and Holbrook, *Do Campaigns Matter?*
17. Holbrook, *Do Campaigns Matter?* 116.
18. Ibid., 120.
19. Lawrence LeDuc, "The Leaders' Debates: Critical Event or Non-Event?" in *The Canadian General Election of 1993*, ed. Alan Frizzell et al. (Ottawa: Carleton University Press, 1994), 127.
20. Lawrence LeDuc et al., *Dynasties and Interludes: Past and Present in Canadian Federal Elections* (Toronto: Dundurn, 2010), 315.
21. Ibid., 316.
22. LeDuc, "The Leaders' Debates: Critical Event or Non-Event?" 129.
23. Bill Fox, speech, December 5, 2015, Carleton University Colloquium.
24. Lawrence LeDuc, "The Leaders' Debates (... And the Winner Is ...), in *The Canadian General Election of 1997*, ed. Alan Frizzell and Jon H. Pammett (Toronto: Dundurn, 1997), 212.
25. Paul Attallah, "Television and the Canadian Federal Election of 2004," in *The Canadian Federal Election of 2004*, ed. Jon H. Pammett and Christopher Dornan (Toronto: Dundurn, 2004), 275.
26. See full analysis in Johnston et al., *Letting the People Decide*, 180–91.
27. LeDuc, "The Leaders' Debates: Critical Event or Non-Event?" 131.
28. Ibid., 137.
29. LeDuc, "The Leaders' Debates (... And the Winner Is...), 219.
30. Ibid., 208.
31. Ibid., 213.
32. Christopher Waddell and Christopher Dornan, "The Media and the Campaign," in *The Canadian Federal Election of 2006*, ed. Jon H. Pammett and Christopher Dornan (Toronto: Dundurn, 2006), 248.
33. LeDuc, "The Leaders' Debates: Critical Event or Non-Event?" 130.
34. Paul Wells, speech, December 5, 2015 Carleton University Colloquium.
35. Three separate waves of online interviews were conducted between August 7 and September 25. The first wave was conducted with 1,099 adult Canadians between August 7 and 10, 2015; the second wave followed the second debate (September 18–20 with 1,081 adult Canadians); and the last wave took place on September 25 with 300 adult Quebecers.
36. Comparison looking at archival Numeris data is difficult because of restricted access and the fact that methodology has changed dramatically since the first debate in 1968.
37. Steven Chase, "Leaders Set Tone in Bruising First Debate," *Globe and Mail*, August 7, 2015, A1.
38. Campbell Clark, "Game Plans," *Globe and Mail*, August 7, 2015, A1.
39. Ibid.
40. "Three Visions for Prosperity," *Globe and Mail*, September 17, 2015, A1.
41. Paul Wells, speech, December 5, 2015, Carleton University Colloquium.
42. The author was also present and participated in the discussions. The event was open to the media and quotes and descriptions herein are from the preoceedings.
43. Bill Fox, speech, December 5, 2015 Carleton University Colloquium.

# CHAPTER 11

## "Because It's 2015": Gender and the 2015 Federal Election

Brenda O'Neill and Melanee Thomas

There was little reason to believe at the start of the campaign that the 2015 federal election would provide any kind of focused attention on gender. Previous elections had certainly not underscored the importance of women's political representation, and women's issues had not been a particular preoccupation of any one party in the lead-up to the election. Gender, and a specific focus on women, has flown under the radar in federal politics for quite some time.

One incident that identified the degree of silence on these questions took place in November 2014. Liberal leader Justin Trudeau suspended two members from caucus as a result of complaints against them from a female member in the NDP caucus. While the appropriateness of his actions was debated, what was also telling about the incident was that it brought to light the fact that Parliament had no policy or procedure in place for addressing sexual harassment between MPs. It wasn't until this particular incident that such a code of conduct was eventually introduced in June 2015.[1] The incident also precipitated the introduction of a harassment policy to cover the conduct of MPs toward political staff.[2] That such policies were absent while being commonplace in other workplaces in the country is indicative of the degree to which Parliament Hill has lagged behind in its attention to issues of particular concern to women.

The lack of explicit attention to gender in the 2015 election campaign does not mean that there was little related to gender in it. Instead, we argue, gender always has been of importance in federal election campaigns in spite of the "deafening silence." We will identify in this chapter some of the ways that gender played itself out in the 2015 campaign. Specifically, we focus on women's issues, women's political representation in both the House of

Commons and in Cabinet, and gender gaps in voting. While some elements of the campaign offered optimism for the future, the overall conclusion is that the election offered more of the same where women are concerned.

## ATTENTION TO WOMEN'S ISSUES

Women's issues are those that matter disproportionately for women. This occurs for two reasons: because women make up a greater share of those affected by the issue or policy, and/or because the issue has a more profound effect on the quality of women's lives compared to men. Issues cannot be defined as "women's" simply because a political party claims them to be. Instead, an issue becomes a "women's" issue when women's experiences broadly identify it as one.

For example, child care has been increasingly framed as a family issue or as a children's issue. Yet, women have been underscoring its importance for their ability to access the labour market since at least the Royal Commission on the Status of Women was tabled in 1970. Parties may choose to discuss child care as concerning families or children, but the same policy could be pitched in very different ways by different parties depending on whose votes they are trying to capture. Given this, it can be difficult to identify which issues disproportionately affect women from election campaigns alone.

The potential for women's issues to receive attention during the 2015 campaign was high. Up For Debate, an alliance of over 175 women's organizations, attempted to organize a leaders' debate during the campaign on the issues of violence against women, women's economic inequality, and women in leadership.[3] In addition to this, women ran the three most competitive campaigns: Katie Telford for the Liberals, Jenni Byrne for the Conservatives, and Anne McGrath for the NDP.[4] And, two of the leaders of those competitive campaigns — Justin Trudeau and Thomas Mulcair — publicly identified themselves as feminists. Given this context, it seemed reasonable to expect that gender and women's issues might have been treated with more importance than they had been in the past.

This ultimately was not the case. Women's issues were given relatively little attention during the campaign. The most prominent example is the Up For Debate leader's debate on women's issues noted above. On August

2, the organization announced that Justin Trudeau had confirmed his participation in the event. The event was cancelled, however, in late August when Stephen Harper declined the invitation and Thomas Mulcair, who had initially agreed to attend, eventually declined as well, saying that a debate without Stephen Harper "wouldn't make much sense." On the one hand, it makes some strategic sense for an opposition party leader to refuse to participate when the incumbent government's leader refuses to be present to be held accountable for his performance on women's issues. Yet, the NDP is also known as the party of progressive policies on women's issues, as well as for its commitment to increasing women's political representation. Given this, Mr. Mulcair's refusal to participate may have hurt the party among some Canadian women. Up For Debate did conduct lengthy interviews with four of the party leaders, Trudeau, Mulcair, May, and Duceppe, and hosted a panel late in September. They also posted transcripts and videos of the interviews online following the event. As impressive as this use of social media was, the impact would have been far more wide-reaching had a full leaders' debate been held as planned.

Another group of women organized the #WomenVote Day of Action on September 20, 2015. They encouraged women to engage in a social media campaign to stimulate greater dialogue about gender equality during the election campaign. Their chosen strategy was to use hashtags on Twitter for a three-hour period to correspond with the anniversary of the 1917 election that first gave (some) women the right to vote at the federal level in Canada. Like the Up For Debate panel, this initiative received muted press coverage.

A third example of a missed opportunity to discuss women's issues during the 2015 election campaign involved a report from Status of Women Canada. This report, which was released during the campaign, noted that in the developed world Canada had not only failed to achieve equality between women and men but was actually backsliding on several key dimensions, including poverty, pay equity, and violence against women.[5] Given the magnitude and severity of these issues, many of which could be directly addressed by the federal government, it is reasonable to expect that the parties and their campaigns would address the report and its content seriously during the campaign. They did not, and the media did not make it a campaign issue.

While the campaign may have been largely devoid of explicit discussions of gender and women's issues, we can nevertheless identify three specific issues about gender and women that were prominent in the 2015 campaign: child care, the niqab, and gender parity in Cabinet.

## CHILD CARE

Child care is of specific importance for women's equality in at least two ways. First, gender differences in the division of child-rearing work persist in Canada. In 2010, for example, women spent on average more than double the time taking care of children as did men.[6] Similarly, women are much more likely to head a lone-parent family than men, resulting in greater child-care responsibilities; in 2006, the ratio of lone-mother to lone-father families was nearly 4 to 1.[7] Second, child-care policies create incentives around family structures. Universal plans are seen to promote women's participation in the workforce, while tax rebates and incentives are viewed as incentivizing mothers to stay at home.[8] In light of this, how did the parties address child care in 2015?

Some background is in order. After their 2006 victory, the Conservatives introduced the Universal Child Care Benefit (UCCB) — a universal taxable direct transfer to parents for every child under six. Available to all families with young children, including those with a stay-at-home parent, and providing only a fraction of annual child-care costs, the policy was less about funding access to child-care spaces than it was about assisting parents with the costs of raising a family. The Conservatives increased the UCCB payment just prior to the start of the 2015 election campaign — from $100 to $160/month for each child under six — and the program expanded to include a payment of $60/month for every child between six and seventeen years old.

Dubbed "Christmas in July," these changes resulted in families across Canada receiving these cheques just before the start of the campaign, undoubtedly a strategic move for the Conservatives. In addition to this, the party introduced limited income splitting for families with children under eighteen years and pitched it as a "family tax cut."[9] Clearly, the Conservatives' strategic calculation focused on two-parent families generally, and two-parent families with a single-income earner specifically. Two-parent families are much more likely to vote than single-parent families, and more traditional nuclear families with a single male breadwinner are more predisposed to the Conservatives.

The Liberals, on the other hand, promised during the campaign to eliminate Conservative child-care policies and income splitting and to introduce a new tax-free child-care benefit. The benefit would not be universal, but would instead rest on a sliding scale of payments for families with combined incomes under $200,000. In addition, the Liberals promised to introduce greater flexibility in the receipt of Employment Insurance benefits to match the needs of new parents, including allowing them to take a longer leave period with lower benefits. And unlike the Conservatives, who avoided as much as possible intergovernmental social plans, the new Liberal government has announced that it intends to work with the provinces to introduce a National Early Learning and Child-Care Framework — a plan reminiscent of that introduced under the Martin government — that would include core infrastructure spending.

Like the Liberals, the NDP also campaigned against income splitting, but they promised to retain the UCCB. Notably, the NDP was the only competitive party in 2015 to commit to create or maintain one million $15/day child care spaces over eight years across Canada — a plan modelled after Quebec's child-care program. It also promised to create 110,000 child-care spaces in British Columbia alone — where costs are especially high. The cost for the plan would be shared between the federal government and the provinces.

On balance, the discussion of child-care policy in the 2015 election rested more with tax policy and what is "good" for families. Though every party discussed child care throughout the campaign, the way they chose to frame these discussions was rarely about women or gender equality. This shows how an issue that disproportionately affects women can, in fact, be presented in a manner that does not meaningfully address these differing, gendered effects.

## THE NIQAB

Unlike child care, the niqab was a gendered issue that inserted itself into the campaign quite outside parties' set platforms. Prior to the 2015 election, the Conservative government implemented a ban on the wearing of the niqab — an article of clothing that covers every part of a woman's face but her eyes — during citizenship ceremonies. One woman — Zunera Ishaq — fought this ban in court, claiming that it infringed on her religious beliefs. She was willing to reveal her face in private to a government official prior to the ceremony but objected to having to reveal her face at the public ceremony. The Federal Court overturned the ban, and when the federal government appealed, the Federal Court of Appeal upheld the lower court's ruling. The latter decision occurred during the 2015 election campaign, explaining why significant attention was devoted to the issue. The Conservatives appealed the Court of Appeal's ruling to the Supreme Court of Canada, and Stephen Harper added that if re-elected the Conservatives would expand the ban to include federal public servants.

The Conservatives pitched the policy as one designed to protect women from being told what to wear, and as an issue of Canadian values. A Conservative Party ad featured the prime minister declaring, "I will never tell my young daughter that a woman should cover her face because she is a woman. That's not our Canada."[10] This is arguably a deliberate misrepresentation of the issue, implying it is forced on women by men. The Liberals, NDP, and Greens, on the other hand, indicated that they would drop the appeal, supporting the right of women to wear face coverings during the ceremony provided that they privately uncovered their face to officials prior to the official public ceremony. The Bloc supported the ban, in line with Quebec legislation requiring that any woman accessing public services, or working for the provincial government, remove their niqabs.

According to a government poll, Canadians were overwhelmingly in support of the niqab ban (82 percent), with support especially high in Quebec (93 percent).[11]

The Conservatives expanded the issue, announcing a proposed RCMP hotline that would allow Canadians to report the existence of "barbaric cultural practices" in the country. Practices such as polygamy, forced or early marriage, and honour killings were identified in the Zero

Tolerance for Barbaric Cultural Practices Act that received Royal Assent in June 2015. The party connected face veils to practices identified in the Act, and framed its position as a defence of Canadian values and of women's equality. Immigration Minister Chris Alexander declared, "This practice of face covering reflects a misogynistic view of women which is grounded in medieval tribal culture."[12]

The Liberals, on the other hand, invoked religious freedom and freedom of expression in defence of a woman's right to choose to wear the niqab. In a speech in May, Trudeau stated. "It is a cruel joke to claim you are liberating people from oppression by dictating in law what they can and cannot wear."[13] He, and Mulcair, criticized the Conservatives for using identity politics to win votes.

Of all the parties, the NDP was arguably in the toughest position on the niqab. Its competitive position in the polls rested primarily on its base of support in Quebec, and while Quebecers were solidly in favour of the niqab ban, progressive voters in the rest of Canada would have been expecting the party to oppose the ban. Even though the Liberals and the NDP took the same position on the issue, it appears to have hurt the NDP more than the Liberals.

The issue is clearly a women's issue, as the niqab is worn only by women. But in this case, parties differed in which rights they chose to emphasize: equal rights for women, or equal rights for religious minorities. It is difficult to escape the conclusion that, at least on some level, the Conservatives and the Bloc were motivated more by political benefits that could be gained from Canadians' fear of an "other" rather than a genuine concern for women's equality per se. Instead, the language of women's equality was used to put a veneer on the niqab ban that might make it more palatable to some who might otherwise object to the violation of freedom of religion for a minority group.

## GENDER PARITY IN CABINET

In a very bold move, the Liberal Party platform promised that Cabinet appointments would embody gender parity, consisting of equal numbers of women and men. No other party made a comparable promise in its platform. It is difficult to argue that this was a strategic move to garner votes, as there was significiant negative media coverage directed at the proposal. The most common critique of the promise was that to ensure gender parity required ignoring merit as a key criterion for Cabinet appointments.[14] This focus on merit is interesting as a basis for a critique of women's presence in Cabinet, as Cabinet has typically been used to ensure representation of groups, most notably groups defined according to regional or provincial origin. Few argue that Cabinet ministers fulfilling the goal of representing a region struggle with "merit," and yet this argument was used routinely to critique gender parity in Cabinet.

Unlike the Conservatives' apparent defence of women's equality through the adoption of a ban of the wearing of the niqab in citizenship ceremonies, the Liberals' promise of gender parity in Cabinet was a move likely designed to position the party as the most progressive among the three main contenders for power and to court women voters directly. When asked for an explantion for his decision to prioritize gender, Trudeau responded simply, "Because it's 2015."

## WOMEN AS CANDIDATES

Given that "it's 2015," and that the year alone was deemed enough, by some, to ensure equal numbers of women and men were selected to Cabinet, did parties carry that same sentiment through to their candidate selection for the 2015 federal election? In short, the answer is no.

To be sure, the 2015 election saw more women candidates than any other federal election in history. A total of 533 women were nominated to run and 88 (or 16.5 percent) of them were elected.

Women now comprise 26 percent of members sitting in the House of Commons, not a significant change from the situation at the dissolution of the previous Parliament. In the forty-first Parliament, women made up 25 percent of the members of Parliament (MPs) in the House of Commons. The proportion of women elected to Parliament in 2015 is about the same as in 2011, 2006, 2004, and 2000.[15] Thus, though the 2015 election was broadly about change, as shown elsewhere in this volume, that change did not meaningfully extend to women's presence as candidates or as elected members in the House.

If we compare the three parties that led in the polls at some point during the campaign, a similar picture emerges (see Table 11.1). The Conservative Party of Canada (Conservatives), the New Democratic Party of Canada (NDP), and the Liberal Party of Canada (Liberals) collectively nominated 315 women as candidates, and elected 85, or 27 percent of them.

**Table 11.1: Women Candidates and MPs, 2015 Election**

| | Number of Women Candidates | % Women Candidates | Number of Women Elected | % Women in Caucus |
|---|---|---|---|---|
| Conservatives | 65 | 19% | 17 | 17% |
| NDP | 145 | 43% | 18 | 41% |
| Liberal Party | 105 | 31% | 50 | 27% |
| Green Party | 135 | 40% | 1 | 100% |
| Bloc Québécois | 21 | 27% | 2 | 20% |

However, there is considerable variation across these parties. The NDP historically nominates more women than the other parties due to an internal gender quota that stipulates that it nominate a gender-balanced candidate slate.[16] In 2015, the party came close to, but did not quite achieve, this goal; 43 percent of their nominated candidates were women. Despite unexpected losses, the NDP's caucus is comprised of roughly the same proportion of women as its candidate slate (41 percent). The Conservatives, by contrast, historically nominate fewer women as candidates than the other parties. And in 2015, the party extended the trend by nominating a smaller percentage of candidates than it did in 2011. This is in spite of the fact that thirty new ridings were added to the House of Commons, removing to some extent the problem of incumbency. The Liberals are, perhaps, the most interesting case. Just under one-third of their candidates were women in 2015; despite their unexpected seat gains, women nevertheless comprise a smaller proportion of their caucus (27 percent) than of their nominated candidates.

## WOMEN, REPRESENTATION, AND SUPPLY AND DEMAND

Women are a historically underrepresented political group in Canada. Once fully barred from participating in Canadian elections as both candidates and voters, Canadian women have had full access to federal democratic rights for decades. Women are actually slightly more likely than men to vote in Canada, and have been for quite some time. This is due, in part, to women's stronger sense of duty to vote.[17] Research shows, too, that Canadians are typically as likely, if not slightly more likely, to vote for a woman candidate than they are to vote for a man.[18] Given this, it is somewhat surprising that women are so much less likely than men to be nominated as candidates and elected to public office.

Women's presence as nominated candidates for public office is typically framed in terms of supply and demand.[19] This frame asks if the most powerful reasons why women remain underrepresented in Canadian politics are because women are not coming forward as candidates (i.e., supply), or if political parties are reluctant to nominate women as candidates (i.e., demand). There are compelling arguments on both sides of the supply-and-demand debate.

With respect to supply, it is well known that Canadian women possess fewer of the psychological factors that promote political participation, compared to men. Women are significantly less interested in politics, less knowledgeable about politics, and less confident in their political abilities than are men.[20] Research from the United States suggests that this lack of political confidence translates into a gender gap in political ambition, leading women to be less likely than men to seek a candidacy for public office.[21] This suggests that psychological barriers may limit the number of women available to parties to nominate as candidates.

Socio-economic barriers may also limit the supply of potential women candidates to political parties. In Canada, each electoral district association (EDA) of each political party is required to hold some form of nomination contest to select its candidate for a general election. This means that potential candidates may need to conduct a campaign to be selected as the party's candidate before the general election. These nomination contests are expensive: each candidate can spend up to 20 percent of their electoral district's election spending cap. For most districts in

Canada, this ranges anywhere from $14,000 to $24,000.[22] Though nomination contestants can solicit donations, some candidates rely on their personal finances to fund their nomination campaigns. Given the high spending limit, this potential requirement to self-fund a nomination campaign may be daunting for some women, particularly since the gender gap in pay in Canada was twice the global average in 2015.[23]

Another factor that may negatively affect the supply of women available to be candidates is family responsibilities. Research suggests that, on average, women's marital and parental status do not negatively affect their political participation.[24] Despite this, it may be that women in Canada *perceive* that their family status may harm or hinder a political career. This is reflected in how MPs display their parental status to constituents: in the forty-first Parliament, over 70 percent of male MPs, but only 55 percent of female MPs communicated their parental status to constituents via their websites.[25] News coverage of candidates disproportionately focuses on women's, but not men's, parental status.[26] MPs reported that, at least for men, "it is usually accepted and understood that the business of being an MP involves your whole family."[27] Women, by contrast, were more likely to receive comments from constituents about "who's looking after the children?"[28] This double standard may create a chilling effect on women who might otherwise be keen to volunteer as a potential candidate.

The factors that limit the supply of female candidates can be formidable, especially for some individual women. But what about factors that affect demand? Here, we address two: the public and political parties.

Notably, public opinion is *not* a factor that suppresses the demand for women as candidates for elected office. Evidence shows that Canadians are as willing to vote for a woman as they are to vote for a man, and that at times, men are even more likely to vote for a female candidate than are women.[29] A majority of Canadians agree that gender equality has *not* been achieved in Canada, and that one of the best ways to protect women's interests is to increase their presence in the House of Commons.[30] Yet, when asked directly if women's current, low levels of representation in electoral politics were a problem, a majority of Canadians said it was a minor problem, if a problem at all.[31] Thus the public is willing to vote for women, but does not prioritize solving the problem of women's chronic underrepresentation in politics.

Political parties present a more formidable barrier to women's election. Though federal parties set the rules for candidate nominations centrally, the actual process of nominating candidates is typically left to the discretion of local party associations. These procedures vary considerably across parties, from the NDP's affirmative action policy noted above, to the Conservatives' approach that requires that local associations simply find the "best possible" nominee.[32] This difference may be predicated on parties' differing views of equality. Arguably, parties such as the NDP evaluate equality in terms of results or outcomes, while the Conservatives explicitly see equality predominantly in terms of opportunities.[33] This helps explain why some parties appear to be more willing than others to explicitly recruit women as candidates.

Other party-specific factors affect women's nomination as candidates. For example, when women are active within political parties as local association presidents, they are more likely to recruit women as candidates than are male association presidents.[34] And between 2004 and 2011, the Conservatives, Liberals, and NDP all were more likely to nominate men as candidates in ridings where their support was stable over time. Women, by contrast, were more likely to be nominated in areas dominated by *another* party. It might be tempting to assume this is primarily due to the fact that more men are already MPs seeking re-election than are women. Yet, women who are MPs seeking re-election are most likely to be found in a riding where *another* party other than her own has high, stable levels of support.[35] This suggests that women remain more likely than men to be nominated as sacrificial-lamb candidates, with less chance of winning the elections or holding their seats than men.

Does this mean that Canada's federal parties are deliberately biased against women candidates? That conclusion may be too strong, in that it rests on the assumption that parties know in advance which seats they are likely to win or lose. Parties may have a good idea which seats are safe prior to an election, but the 2015 election also shows that parties can lose seats that had, in the past, been guaranteed wins. A fairer conclusion may be that, like the Canadian public, Canada's federal parties do not prioritize recruiting women as candidates in numbers that reflect women's presence in the population, nor do they prioritize nominating the women that are recruited in winnable ridings. The voluntary measures put in place by parties such as the NDP and Liberals (at times) are not enough, on their own, to overcome this.[36]

The balance of evidence suggests that the demand-side factor of political party inaction presents the greatest barrier to women's participation in Canadian democracy as candidates and elected officials. In 2015, any political party fielding a candidate in every electoral district needed to nominate a total of 338 people. Any party that wished to present voters with an equal number of men and women as candidates would have had to recruit, vet, and nominate 169 women. It is implausible to suggest that women's lower levels of political engagement and income, or their perception of difficulties balancing politics with their families, creates such a severe undersupply of political aspirants that this number could not be found.[37] What is plausible, though, is that organizers and activists within political parties do not prioritize recruiting equal numbers of women and men as candidates.

## WOMEN IN THE HOUSE

Would Canadian politics change much if more women were elected to the House of Commons? Research shows that even with their low numbers, women in Canadian politics do indeed advocate for gendered policy considerations and women's concerns more than do their male peers.[38] This may continue or increase if more women were elected as MPs. Yet, even if this were not the case, increasing the proportion of women MPs carries two additional benefits. First, diverse representatives bring experiences to Parliament that may be useful for deliberation and policy processes.[39] Increasing the proportion of women MPs toward 50 percent could reflect the diversity among Canadian women, as white women have different experiences than do women from visible minority groups, who, in turn, have different experiences than Aboriginal women, who all have different experiences from different groups and types of men.

It may be that women's continued underrepresentation in Canadian electoral politics rests, in part, on stereotypes informed by historical legal restrictions on women's voting rights, as these muted women's political participation for decades even after the barriers were removed. This informs the suggestion that women are not "as good" at politics compared to men. Thus, women's presence in politics now may help reset these stereotypical assumptions. Certainly, the Trudeau government's appointment of a parity Cabinet with equal numbers of women and men — a first in Canadian federal politics — may provide evidence that the conventional definition of "merit" requires expansion.

## GENDER GAPS IN VOTE CHOICE

Gender gaps in vote choice refer to the differences in support given to political parties by women and men. When it comes to ideology, contemporary Canadian women generally vote to the left of men, with variation in the size of the gaps determined by the particular context of any one election, including the nature of the campaign, the leaders involved, and the campaign's partisan makeup.[40] This particular pattern of realignment emerged in the 1990s and was most evident in the gap in voting for the Reform Party and then the Canadian Alliance.[41]

Recent elections suggest that gender gaps at the federal level in Canada have been largest on the right.[42] In the 2000 election, men were more likely to support the Alliance than women, with a gap of 11 percentage points. The merging of the Canadian Alliance and the Progressive Conservative Party into the Conservative Party of Canada in 2003 muted gaps in voting on this side of the ideological spectrum temporarily in 2004. However, the gap reappeared in the 2006 and 2008 elections. Gaps are also present on the left, but are smaller in size than those on the right. Women were 5 percentage points more likely to vote NDP than men in 2000, and 7 points more likely to vote for them in 2008.

Research shows that gender has to be cued for it to have a significant effect on vote choice, as both women's and men's vote choice is determined by a considerable number of pressures and considerations beyond gender. These cross-cutting cleavages tend to diminish the independent effect of gender on the vote. Furthermore, the issues that cue gender need not be those typically considered to be "women's issues" for them to shape the size of the gap. For example, in the 1988 federal election, there was a 16 percentage point gap between women and men in support of the Canada-United States Free Trade Agreement.[43]

Just as it would be a mistake to assume that gender acts as the primary factor that shapes vote choice, it is also important to note that women ought not to be considered a cohesive voting block. Canadian women are politically divided, too, and this is reflected in their vote choices.[44] The analysis presented here takes this into account, in part, by analyzing socio-demographic differences and their effect on the vote.

Using Abacus online survey data collected during the federal campaign, Table 11.2 provides a breakdown of vote and vote intention by gender.[45] The findings largely mirror trends in previous elections: the largest gender gap in voting is found for the Conservatives, with women nearly 7 percentage points less likely to vote for them than men. A slightly smaller, but nevertheless statistically significant gap is also found on the left: women are 4 points more likely to vote for the NDP than men. Note that there is no gender gap in support for the Liberals, Greens, or Bloc Québécois.

**Table 11.2: Gender Gaps in Voting and Voting Intention (National), 2015**

| | Female | Male | Gap |
|---|---|---|---|
| Conservative Party | 22.7 | 29.4 | -6.7*** |
| Liberal Party | 29.8 | 31.3 | -1.5 |
| New Democratic Party | 21.4 | 17.3 | 4.1** |
| Green Party | 4.0 | 3.6 | 0.4 |
| Bloc Québécois | 5.0 | 5.4 | -0.4 |
| Another Party | 1.7 | 1.7 | 0.0 |
| Undecided | 15.4 | 11.3 | 4.1 |
| Number | 1,610 | 1,459 | |

Source: Abacus, 2015 election online survey.
Note: *** p<.000, **p<.01, *p<.05, [l]p<.10.

There are also gender gaps among undecided voters, despite the late date at which the survey was undertaken in the campaign. These data were collected two days away from election day, and 15 percent of women reported being uncertain about how they would cast their vote. Only 11 percent of men reported being similarly unsure how to vote.

Any analysis of the gender gap in voting in Canada must examine Quebec voters separately from voters in the rest of the country. With the arrival of the Bloc Québécois in the 1993 federal election, voters in Quebec have had a different slate of parties and candidates to choose from than other Canadian voters. Similarly, the issue of sovereignty shapes voting in Quebec in a manner unmatched elsewhere. Table 11.3 shows that, with respect to the gender gap in vote choice, the findings in the rest of the country do not parallel those in Quebec. There are no statistically significant gender gaps in voting for any party in Quebec, despite the fact that women in Quebec have been somewhat less likely than men to support the Conservatives in the past.[46] The Conservatives' position on the niqab, matched only by the Bloc, may provide part of the answer. Given this, our further analysis of the gender gap confines itself to voters outside of Quebec. Restricting the analysis to voters outside of Quebec increases the size of the gaps in the rest of the country: a negative 8 point gap and positive 6 point gap separate women and men in support for the Conservatives and NDP respectively.

---

Two sets of explanations are generally identified as lying behind gender gaps in voting: structural/situational and attitudinal/values. Structural/situational explanations highlight gender differences in occupation, income, and educational opportunities that offer the potential for understanding women's greater propensity to support parties on the left. Factors such as women's greater likelihood to be engaged in precarious part-time work with fewer benefits, their dominance in pink-collar occupations with lower pay (i.e., nursing, teaching, secretarial work) which are often found within the public sector, and differences in their educational choices have been emphasized for their role in shaping voting gender gaps. The economic instability women often face as a result of divorce, tied to their continued high numbers among single parents, might also lie behind their support for the policies endorsed by left-of-centre parties.

Table 11.3: Gender Gap in Voting and Voting Intention (Rest of Canada and Quebec), 2015

| | Rest of Canada | | | Quebec | | |
|---|---|---|---|---|---|---|
| | Female | Male | Gap | Female | Male | Gap |
| Conservative Party | 26.1 | 33.7 | -7.6*** | 12.7 | 16.7 | -4.0 |
| Liberal Party | 30.3 | 32.9 | -2.6 | 28.5 | 27.0 | 1.5 |
| New Democratic Party | 20.5 | 15.0 | 5.5** | 23.9 | 24.0 | -0.1 |
| Green Party | 4.2 | 4.2 | 0.0 | 3.3 | 1.6 | 1.7 |
| Bloc Québécois | -- | -- | -- | 19.4 | 21.3 | -1.9 |
| Another Party | 1.7 | 1.8 | -0.1 | 1.7 | 1.6 | 0.1 |
| Undecided | 17.1 | 12.5 | 4.6** | 10.5 | 7.8 | 2.7 |
| Number | 1,192 | 1,089 | | 418 | 371 | |

Source: Abacus, 2015 election online survey.
Note: *** p<.001, **p<.01, *p<.05, ˡp<.10.

Explanations focusing on attitudinal and value differences between women and men have, however, offered greater purchase in understanding voting gender gaps. The significant societal and economic changes that women have experienced arguably have made women more likely to support state provision of services, regardless of their own personal circumstances. Similarly, women's entry into the workforce has made them more supportive of government policies designed to promote women's equality.[47] Both help to explain women's greater support for parties on the left. Men's greater support for issues of security and defence, on the other hand, helps to explain their greater support for parties on the right of the ideological spectrum. Tied to this, the rise of feminism has also been shown to have played a significant role in shifting women's political attitudes to the left, as has post-materialism. And, though they remain more religious than men, women's overall levels of religiosity are declining, accounting for part of this shift to the left. Thus, women's continued (though waning) religiosity — tied to a greater likelihood for voting for parties on the ideological right — likely masks what would otherwise be larger gaps in voting for parties on the left and right.

The context of any one single election is also important for understanding gender differences in vote choice. For example, leader evaluations are a key determinant of vote choice, and women and men are known to differ in their evaluation of party leaders.[48] In 2015, it is plausible that women and men could have evaluated the party leaders differently, contributing to the gender gaps in vote choice seen in Tables 11.2 and 11.3. In this campaign, issues and events may also hold the potential for explaining gender gaps in vote choice. This is especially the case if women and men respond to the issue or leader differently and/or if it matters differently to the vote decision for women and men.

Tables 11.4 and 11.5 analyze gender gaps in voting for the Conservatives and the NDP outside of Quebec. The first step in each table reports the unmediated relationship between gender and vote choice. The second step introduces a set of structural/situational, cultural/values, and more proximate campaign factors hypothesized to explain the gender difference in vote choice, or put differently, to reduce the size of the coefficient reported for gender.[49]

All variables are coded to range between 0 and 1. The dependent variables are simple dichotomous variables coded 1 for voted for the party, and 0 otherwise. Dummy variables include gender (1 for woman), marital status (1 for married or common law), education (1 for university graduate), union membership (1 for union member), employment status (1 for employed full-time), feminism (1 for strong or moderate feminist), religiosity (1 for religion very important), and subjective evaluation of the state of the economy (1 for poor or very poor). Annual household income ranges from 0 "less than $35,000" to 1 "over $100,000."

An additional set of factors specific to this campaign was created to assess their importance for gender differences in voting. The Harper, Trudeau, and Mulcair leader evaluations are a score derived from responses to a list of eighteen positive and negative leader attributes (e.g. tough, smart, a leader, hard-working, mean, tired). Respondents gave each leader a score according to how well they believed each attribute described him or her from 0 "not at all" to 10 "very well." These were recoded so that more positive evaluations corresponded to higher scores, an average score across these eighteen attributes calculated for each leader, and then this average score was recoded to range between 0 and 1.

The Abacus survey includes several questions tapping issues of particular importance in the campaign. These were included to evaluate their potential role in shaping gender gaps in voting. A dummy variable for opinions on the wearing of face coverings was created with 1 corresponding to those who believed that "Women should be allowed to wear a face covering during the public ceremony provided they remove the face covering and prove their identity to a citizenship officer before the ceremony begins" and 0 otherwise. A dummy variable for opinions on the funding of daycare was created with 1 corresponding to those who believed "The government should fund public daycare spaces" and 0 "otherwise." A dummy variable for opinion on how many refugees Canada should take in was also created with 1 corresponding to "a lot more than now" and 0 "otherwise."

**Table 11.4: Gender and Voting for the CPC outside Quebec — Impact of Structural, Ideological, and Campaign Variables on the Gender Gap** (logistic regression estimates)

| Step | | CPC |
|---|---|---|
| 1: No controls | Gender (without controls) | -.376 (.100)*** |
| 2: Includes controls for structural/situational, attitudinal/values and campaign factors | Gender | -.320 (.185)† |
| | Married/Common Law | .025 (.202) |
| | University Graduate | .216 (.207) |
| | Union Member | -.116 (.239) |
| | Working Full-Time | .166 (.199) |
| | Household Income | .518 (.307) |
| | Religion — Very Important | .280 (.219) |
| | Feminist — Strong or Moderate | .010 (.209) |
| | Economy Poor | -.170 (.192) |
| | Leader Evaluation — Harper | 12.946 (.791)*** |
| | Leader Evaluation — Trudeau | -6.005 (.649)*** |
| | Leader Evaluation — Mulcair | -5.604 (.687)*** |
| | Support Face Veils | -0.25(.185) |
| | Fund Public Daycare | -.471 (.185)* |
| | Accept More Refugees | -.377 (.284) |
| | Constant | -1.492 (.455)** |
| | Nagelkerke R Square (full model) | 0.781 |
| | Number | 1,920 |

Source: Abacus, 2015 election online survey.
Note: ***p<.001, **p<.01, *p<.05, †p<.10.

In Table 11.4, the introduction of the various controls reduces the gender gap in Conservative vote choice to a level of significance outside of normal standards ($p<0.10$). The results suggest that the standard explanations highlighting structural/situational and cultural/values factors play very little, if any role in shaping gender differences in voting for the CPC. Coefficients for these variables do not come close to standard levels of statistical significance. The various campaign variables that are included in the regression offer greater purchase. The leader evaluations offer by far the strongest explanation for the gap in Conservative voting. Positive evaluations of Harper significantly increase the probability of voting for the CPC. Positive evaluations of Mulcair and Trudeau, not surprisingly, significantly decrease the probability of voting for the CPC.

Leader evaluations can affect the gender gap in vote choice in two ways: if women and men factor in leader evaluations differently for their vote choice, or if women and men view the leaders differently. In 2015, the latter appears to have been the case. Results suggest that leader evaluations may have mattered less to women's votes than men's, but only for evaluations of Justin Trudeau, not Stephen Harper (analysis not shown). Instead, women and men in our sample offered significantly different evaluations of Stephen Harper. The gender gap in Conservative voting is at least partly due to men's more positive evaluations of Harper compared to women's.

Two additional factors offer the potential for helping to explain the gender gap in support for the CPC: attitudes toward child care and toward the economy. Respondents who indicated that they preferred the government to publicly fund child care rather than provide funding directly to parents were significantly less likely to vote Conservative. Subsequent analysis suggests that this matters for the gender gap in Conservative support in two ways. First, women and men take very different positions on this issue: 70 percent of women prefer public over private financing for child care, compared to only 60 percent of men. Second, opposition to public funding for child care had a significantly larger effect on men's support for the Conservatives than it did for women. Approximately 50 percent of men opposed to public child care voted Conservative compared to 36 percent of women

($p<0.05$). The effect of perceptions of the economy are similar: women (60 percent) are more likely than men (54 percent) to report that the economy is poor. But, among Canadians who think that the economy was performing well, 53 percent of men but only 43 percent of women ($p<0.05$) voted Conservative. Though the effect of these issues on vote choice is dwarfed by leader evaluations, they nonetheless play a role in the gender gap in Conservative support.

---

The findings for the gender gap in NDP voting are less clear. As shown in Table 11.5, controlling for situational/structural and campaign factors cannot explain why women are more likely to vote NDP than men.

Feminism does, however. As was the case with university graduates, strong and moderate feminists were more likely to vote Liberal in 2015 than they were to vote NDP. However, this feminist gap is much larger for men than it is for women. Of men who identified as feminists, only 15 percent voted NDP. A full 45 percent, however, voted Liberal. By contrast, feminist women were significantly more likely to vote NDP (23 percent) and significantly less likely to vote Liberal (36 percent) than their male counterparts ($p<0.05$). One reason why this feminist gender gap exists may be that the NDP nominated considerably more women as candidates than did the other parties. Similarly, the NDP took policy positions (e.g., child care noted above) more in line with women's preferences than the other parties. Still, these results suggest that the 2015 election result would have been worse for the NDP if not for feminist women.

### Table 11.5: Gender and Voting for the NDP Outside Quebec — Impact of Structural, Ideological, and Campaign Variables on the Gender Gap (logistic regression estimates)

| Step | | NDP |
|---|---|---|
| 1: No controls | Gender (without controls) | .325 (.121)** |
| 2: Includes controls for structural/situational, attitudinal/values and campaign factors | Gender | .354 (.161)* |
| | Married/Common Law | -0.27 (.173) |
| | University Graduate | -.380 (.181)* |
| | Union Member | .189 (.200) |
| | Working Full-Time | .184 (.169) |
| | Household Income | .218 (.265) |
| | Religion — Very Important | -.108 (.217) |
| | Feminist — Strong or Moderate | -.398 (.173)* |
| | Economy Poor | .309 (.175)† |
| | Leader Evaluation — Harper | -3.708 (.419)*** |
| | Leader Evaluation — Trudeau | -5.089(.494)*** |
| | Leader Evaluation — Mulcair | 10.051 (.610)*** |
| | Support Face Veils | .009 (.164) |
| | Fund Public Daycare | .112 (.176) |
| | Accept More Refugees | -.005 (.190) |
| | Constant | -3.635 (.450)*** |
| | Nagelkerke R Square (full model) | 0.478 |
| | Number | 1,921 |

Source: Abacus, 2015 election online survey.
Note: *** p<.001, **p<.01, *p<.05, †p<.10.

The remaining findings are more in line with expectations. Those who thought the economy was doing poorly were more likely to vote NDP, and women were more likely than men to believe that the economy was doing poorly. And, as was the case for the Conservatives, leader evaluations played a strong role in shaping votes for the NDP; voters who did not like Harper were more likely to vote NDP, and as noted above, Canadian women did not especially like Harper in 2015. This helps explain, at least in part, women's greater support for the NDP at the polls.

## GENDER, STRATEGIC VOTING, AND THE "CHANGE" ELECTION

As noted elsewhere in this chapter and in this volume, the 2015 election was generally seen to be about change. Even though this view is common, it is also gendered. Women (64 percent) were more likely than men (56 percent) to think that "it's definitely time for a change in government," while men (23 percent) were more likely than women (17 percent) to think that it was "best to keep the Conservatives in office" ($p<0.05$). This suggests that while the majority of Canadians may have been open to strategic voting, women may have been more open to it than men. That said, women were *not* considerably more likely than men to have said that beating the Conservatives was the main reason why they voted the way they did.

In order for women to be more likely than men to be strategic voters, it follows that women would have had to have made their vote decision later on the campaign, after the national polls turned in the Liberals' favour. The Abacus survey asked Canadians (including Quebecers) who had decided how they were going to vote when they had made up their minds about who they were going going to vote for. The results suggest small but significant differences between women and men. Men were more likely than women to have made up their mind about their vote before the campaign started (52.6 versus 43.3 percent). By contrast, women were more likely to say that they made up their mind near the beginning of the campaign: 22.8 versus 14.7 percent ($p<0.10$). Those who made up their minds later in the campaign — "soon after Labour Day" or "in the past day or two" — were equally likely to be women or men. Importantly, when these data were collected — two days from election day — women remained much more likely than men to be undecided (see Table 11.2).

This suggests two things. First, the campaign, at least in its early stages, mattered more for women's votes than it did for men's. This may have been too early in the campaign for many of these women to have decided to be strategic voters, swinging from one party to another. However, a second point supplements the first: because women were more likely than men to be undecided at the very end of the campaign, those women — small in number though they may be — may have been most likely to be strategic voters.

To evaluate this possibility, we identified which party voters identified as being closest to their own positions (Table 11.6) and then asked whether that party differed from the party they voted for, or planned to vote for (Table 11.7).

As expected, gender differences in platform preferences largely mirror those found for vote and vote intention. As shown in Table 11.6, men were almost 10 points more likely to identify the Conservatives than women and more likely by a gap of a little over 4 points to select the Liberal Party. Women were about 3 percentage points more likely to identify the NDP than men. The gaps are small for the remaining parties. Importantly, the gender gap in percentage who selected "unsure" is considerable: almost a third of women chose this option (32.0 percent) compared to just under one in five of the men. The tendency for women to reveal greater levels of uncertainty that has been identified in research in political knowledge is mirrored in these data, even this late in the campaign.[50]

**Table 11.6: Gender Differences in Party Platform Closest to Own Positions, 2015**

| | Female | Male | Gap |
|---|---|---|---|
| Conservative Party | 21.2 | 31.0 | -9.8*** |
| Liberal Party | 22.0 | 26.2 | -4.2* |
| New Democratic Party | 16.1 | 13.1 | 3.0* |
| Green Party | 4.5 | 4.2 | 0.3 |
| Bloc Québécois | 4.0 | 5.2 | -1.2 |
| Another Party | 0.2 | 0.8 | -0.6ᵗ |
| Unsure | 32.0 | 19.6 | 12.4*** |
| Number | 1,610 | 1,460 | |

Source: Abacus, 2015 election online survey.
Note: *** p<.000, **p<.01, *p<.05, ᵗp<.10.

Given the narrative of the campaign, it is perhaps surprising that Table 11.7 shows that most respondents voted for the party whose platform was closest to their own position on the issues. Or, to put it differently, most of these respondents were *not* strategic voters. Roughly the same proportion of women and men who thought the Conservative platform was closest to their own also voted for the party (83 percent). The same is true for those who thought the Liberal platform was closest to their own positions on the issues: about 84 percent of these men and women cast their vote for the Liberals.

Where evidence for strategic voting becomes apparent is when the focus is on voters who thought the NDP had a platform that was closest to their own position on the issue. In fact, most who identified the NDP platform as closest to their own views voted for them (78 percent of men and 77 percent of women). Despite this, respondents who thought that the NDP had the platform closest to their own were more likely to move their vote to another party than were those closest to the Liberal or Conservative platforms. These movers are, in our view, strategic voters. Second, and more important for us, women appear to be more likely than men to have voted strategically. A full 14 percent of women and 10 percent of men whose position on issues was closest to the NDP nevertheless voted instead for the Liberals.

This is due, at least in part, to the fact that these voters thought the Liberals had a better shot at beating the Conservatives than did the NDP. Those who preferred the NDP's platform but voted Liberal were more likely to report that it was "definitely time for a change in government" than were voters who voted for the party running on their preferred platform. As before, this pattern is gendered, too. A staggering 88 percent of women who preferred the NDP but voted Liberal reported that it was time for a change of government. By contrast, only 63 percent of women who did not vote strategically reported it was time for a change. A similar, though less stark pattern appears for men: 72 percent who preferred the NDP but voted Liberal said it was time for a change, compared to 56 percent of men who did not vote strategically.

**Table 11.7: Platform Closest to Own Compared to Vote/Vote Intention by Gender**

| Platform Closest to Own | Vote/Vote Intention | | | | | |
|---|---|---|---|---|---|---|
| *Men* | CPC | Liberal | NDP | Other | Undecided | N |
| CPC | 82.7% | 6.4% | 3.1% | 3.1% | 4.7% | 451 |
| Liberal | 2.9% | 83.5% | 8.1% | 1.8% | 3.7% | 381 |
| NDP | 1.6% | 9.4% | 77.5% | 4.2% | 7.3% | 191 |
| Other | 2.0% | 16.7% | 12.0% | 66.0% | 3.3% | 150 |
| Unsure | 13.3% | 23.4% | 14.7% | 10.1% | 38.5% | 286 |
| *Women* | | | | | | |
| CPC | 83.9% | 5.6% | 3.8% | 2.3% | 4.4% | 341 |
| Liberal | 1.4% | 83.9% | 7.1% | 4.0% | 3.7% | 354 |
| NDP | 1.5% | 13.5% | 76.5% | 3.8% | 4.6% | 260 |
| Other | 2.9% | 12.9% | 20.7% | 55.7% | 7.9% | 140 |
| Unsure | 12.8% | 21.5% | 15.3% | 12.4% | 38.0% | 516 |

Source: Abacus 2015 election online survey.

Clearly, the Liberal campaign rhetoric was effective at reaching voters who preferred the NDP's platform but were prepared to vote for a different party out of their desire for change. Notably, this strategy appears to have been more effective with women than men. And yet, we cannot note without some irony that these votes for "change" occurred in a campaign context that, as noted above, offered very little real change in how gender is addressed in Canadian electoral politics.

## CONCLUSION

The 2015 federal election provided much in the way of continuity vis-à-vis gender. Women's numbers in the House of Commons increased only marginally, as parties failed to nominate considerably more women as candidates, despite the addition of thirty seats to the House, and, in a number of cases, also failed to nominate women in winnable ridings. The campaign provided very little in the way of spontaneous discussion of women's issues. The competitive parties contending for power were all led by men. Unlike elections conducted over thirty years ago, party leaders did not all agree to participate in a debate on women's issues. And, the women's issues raised during the campaign were debated and framed as ones dealing with families or security rather than women.

At its worst, the campaign offered examples of parties using women as strategic fodder to further their electoral chances. At its best, it promised women that they would share equally in the seats allocated to Cabinet. Overall, it provided remarkably little in the way of progressive or real change for women from previous elections.

This lack of attention belies gender's importance to Canadian federal election campaigns, including this most recent one. Gender continues to matter for vote choice in a manner that appears to be largely overlooked by parties and pundits alike. The Conservatives held less appeal for women than men, in part because women were more desirous of change and in part because the Conservative positions on key women's issues, such as child care, were out of step with the view of the majority of Canadian women. By contrast, the NDP has greater appeal among women than men, and this gender gap appears to be especially large for Canadians who self-identify as feminists. As was the case with the Conservatives, this gender gap in NDP voting appeared to be driven in 2015 in part by a desire for change across the electorate. And though there was no gender gap in support for the Liberals, it appears as though women may have been more likely than men to be strategic Liberal supporters.

What, then, are we to make of Justin Trudeau's bold assertion that gender equality in politics is just a matter of natural justice, because "it's 2015"? On one hand, we are heartened that new barriers were broken down for women after the 2015 election, especially with respect to powerful appointments to the federal Cabinet. But on balance, it is difficult to view the "it's 2015" assertion without skepticism. If "it's 2015," then why are women still underrepresented as candidates? Why are women's unique voting patterns broadly ignored, and the issues that disproportionately affect them discussed in gender-neutral terms, if at all? Indeed, even in 2015, the more things change, the more they stay the same.

## NOTES

1. CBC News, "MPs' Sexual Harassement Code of Conduct Outlined in House Report," June 8, 2015, www.cbc.ca/news/politics/mps-sexual-harassment-code-of-conduct-outlined-in-house-report-1.3105023.
2. Jordan Press, "New Parliament Hill Harassment Policy Unveiled to Cover MPs' Conduct with Their Employees," *National Post*, December 10, 2014, news.nationalpost.com/news/canada/new-parliament-hill-harassment-policy-unveiled-to-cover-mps-conduct-with-their-employees.
3. See upfordebate.ca.
4. See Anne Kingston, "The Surprising End of a Depressing Campaign for Women," *Maclean's* October 20, 2015, www.macleans.ca/politics/ottawa/the-surprising-end-of-a-depressing-campaign-for-women/.
5. CBC News, "Secret Status of Women Report Paints Grim Picture for Canada," September 7, 2015, www.cbc.ca/news/politics/status-of-women-internal-report-1.3214751.
6. Statistics Canada and Status of Women Canada, *Women in Canada: A Gender-Based Statistical Report*, 6th ed. (Ottawa: Minister of Industry, 2012), 42.
7. Statistics Canada and Status of Women Canada, *Women in Canada,* 34.
8. "Election Issues 2015: A *Maclean's* Primer on Child Care," *Maclean's,* September 10, 2015, www.macleans.ca/politics/ottawa/child-care-primer/.
9. Andy Blatchford, "Family Tax Cut: Tories Introduce Legislation to Enact Income-Splitting Plan." *Huffington Post*, May 27, 2015, www.huffingtonpost.ca/2015/03/27/tories-introduce-family-t_n_6957054.html.
10. "Conservative Cultural Practice," VibNews, October 4, 2015, www.vibnews.com/trouble-with-neighbors-wearing-the-niqab-canadian-conservatives-propose-rcmp-barbaricculturalpractices-tip-line/.
11. Dean Beeby, "Poll Ordered by Harper Found Strong Support for Niqab Ban at Citizenship Ceremonies," CBC News, September 24, 2015, www.cbc.ca/news/politics/canada-election-2015-niqab-poll-pco-1.3241895.
12. Bruce Cheadle, "Tories Promise RCMP Tip Line for People to Report Neighbours for 'Barbaric Cultural Practices,'" *National Post,* October 2, 2015, news.nationalpost.com/news/canada/tories-promise-rcmp-tip-line-for-people-to-report-neighbors-for-barbaric-cultural-practices.
13. Aaron Wherry, "Justin Trudeau and the Niqab," *Maclean's,* March 10, 2015, www.macleans.ca/politics/justin-trudeau-and-the-niqab/.
14. Andrew Coyne, "Trudeau Cabinet Should Be Based on Merit, Not Gender," *National Post,* November 2, 2015, news.nationalpost.com/news/canada/canadian-politics/andrew-coyne-trudeau-cabinet-should-be-built-on-merit-not-gender.
15. Parliament of Canada, "Women Candidates in General Elections — 1921 to Date," n.d., www.parl.gc.ca/About/Parliament/FederalRidingsHistory/hfer.asp?Search=WomenElection&Language=E.
16. William Cross, *Political Parties* (Vancouver: UBC Press, 2004).
17. Elisabeth Gidengil, André Blais, Neil Nevitte, and Richard Nadeau, *Citizens* (Vancouver: UBC Press, 2004). See also André Blais, *To Vote or Not to Vote: The Merits*

and Limits of Rational Choice Theory (Pittsburgh: University of Pittsburgh Press, 2000).

18. Elizabeth Goodyear-Grant, "Who Votes for Women Candidates and Why? Evidence from Recent Canadian Elections," in *Voting Behaviour in Canada*, ed. Cameron D. Anderson and Laura B. Stephenson (Vancouver: UBC Press, 2010).
19. Brenda O'Neill, "Unpacking Gender's Role in Political Representation in Canada," *Canadian Parliamentary Review* 38, no. 2: 22–30.
20. Gidengil et al., *Citizens*. See also Melanee Thomas, "The Complexity Conundrum: Why Hasn't the Gender Gap in Subjective Political Competence Closed?" *Canadian Journal of Political Science* 45, no. 2: 337–58.
21. Jennifer Lawless and Richard Fox, *It Still Takes a Candidate: Why Women Don't Run for Office* (Cambridge: Cambridge University Press, 2010).
22. Elections Canada. "Nomination Contests Held to Select a Candidate for the 42nd General Election," October 2013, www.elections.ca/content.aspx?section=pol&document=index&dir=limits/limitnom42&lang=e.
23. Mary Beach, "Gender Pay Gap in Canada More Than Twice Global Average, Study Shows," *Globe and Mail*, May 5, 2015, www.theglobeandmail.com/news/british-columbia/gender-pay-gap-in-canada-more-than-twice-global-average-study-shows/article24274586/.
24. Nancy Burns, Kay Lehman Schlozman, and Sidney Verba, *The Private Roots of Public Action* (Cambridge, MA: Harvard University Press, 2001). See also Thomas, "The Complexity Conundrum" and Lawless and Fox, *It Still Takes a Candidate.*
25. Melanee Thomas and Lisa Lambert, "Private Moms vs. Political Dads? Communications of Parental Status in the 41st Canadian Parliament," Paper presented at the 2013 Meeting of the Canadian Political Science Association.
26. Elizabeth Goodyear-Grant, *Gendered News: Media Coverage and Electoral Politics in Canada* (Vancouver: UBC Press, 2013).
27. Thomas and Lambert, "Private Moms vs. Political Dads," 9.
28. Ibid., 10.
29. Goodyear-Grant, "Who Votes for Women Candidates and Why?"
30. *2011 Canadian Election Study*, author's calculations.
31. *2004 Canadian Election Study*, author's calculations.
32. Cross, *Political Parties.*
33. Conservative Party of Canada, *Policy Declaration*, 2014, www.conservative.ca/media/documents/Policy-Declaration-Feb-2015.pdf.
34. Christine Cheng and Margit Tavits, "Informal Influences in Selecting Female Political Candidates," *Political Research Quarterly* 64, no. 2: 460–71.
35. Melanee Thomas and Marc André Bodet, "Sacrificial Lambs, Women Candidates, and District Competitiveness in Canada," *Electoral Studies* 32, no. 1: 153–66.
36. Ibid.
37. Jeanette Ashe and Kennedy Stewart, "Legislative Recruitment: Using Diagnostic Testing to Explain Underrepresentation," *Party Politics* 18, no. 5: 687–707.
38. Manon Tremblay, "Do Female MPs Substantively Represent Women? A Study of Legislative Behaviour in Canada's 35th Parliament," *Canadian Journal of Political Science* 31, no. 3: 435–65.
39. Jane Mansbridge, "Should Blacks Represent Blacks and Women Represent Women? A Contingent 'Yes.'" *Journal of Politics* 61, no. 3: 628–57.

40. See Lynda Erickson and Brenda O'Neill, "The Gender Gap and the Changing Woman Voter in Canada," *International Political Science Review* 23 (2002): 373–92.
41. See Elisabeth Gidengil, Matthew Hennigar, André Blais, and Neil Nevitte, "Explaining the Gender Gap in Support for the New Right: The Case of Canada," *Comparative Political Studies* 38 (2005): 1171–195.
42. Elizabeth Goodyear-Grant, "Women Voters, Candidates and Legislators: A Gender Perspective on Recent Party and Electoral Politics," in *Parties, Elections and the Future of Canadian Politics*, ed. Amanda Bittner and Royce Koop (Vancouver: UBC Press, 2013).
43. Elisabeth Gidengil, "Economic Man-Social Women? The Case of the Gender Gap in Support for the Canada-United States Free Trade Agreement." *Comparative Political Studies* 28 (1995): 384–408.
44. Elisabeth Gidengil, "Beyond the Gender Gap." *Canadian Journal of Political Science* 40 (2007): 815–31.
45. The Abacus survey was conducted online with a sample of 3,070 Canadians from a large representative panel of over 500,000 Canadians between October 15 and 17, 2015. We wish to thank David Coletto of Abacus Data for sharing these data with us. Thirty percent of respondents had voted in advance polls prior to completing the survey.
46. Elisabeth Gidengil, Neil Nevitte, André Balis, Joanna Everitt and Patrick Fournier, *Dominance and Decline: Making Sense of Recent Canadian Elections* (Toronto: Univeristy of Toronto Press, 2012), 198–201.
47. Bernadette Hayes, Ian McAllister, and Donley T. Studlar, "Gender, Post-Materialism, and Feminism in a Comparative Context," *International Political Science Review* 21, no. 4: 425–39.
48. See Brenda O'Neill, "The Relevance of Leader Gender to Voting in the 1993 Canadian Federal Election," *International Journal of Canadian Studies* 17 (1998): 39–65.
49. The analysis employs logistic regressions rather than multinomial logistic regressions to evaluate the relative effects of various factors on the gender gap in voting. We adopted this strategy in order to simplify the analysis. A test of these same regressions using multinomial logistic regression, one that compares the impact of factors on the probability of voting for one party versus one other party, reveals substantively comparable results. The multinomial logistic regression analyses are available from the authors.
50. Kathleen Dolan, "Do Women and Men Know Different Things? Measuring Gender Differences in Political Knowledge," *Journal of Politics*, 73, no. 1: 97–107.

# CHAPTER 12

## Polling and the 2015 Federal Election

David Coletto

From the beginning of the campaign, the major political parties were almost evenly split in terms of popular support: no more than 7 points separated the three in national opinion polls, with the NDP fractionally ahead. Although most therefore anticipated a minority government, there were no confident predictions of which party would win the greatest number of seats. Indeed, over the course of the campaign each of the three parties would occupy the lead in at least one publicly released national poll measuring vote intentions or in a horse-race poll— a historical first. And in the end, this was the first Canadian election since the dawn of modern polling in which a party that began the campaign in third place in public polls would go on to form the government.

As has become the norm in modern elections, polls — and in particular the horse-race numbers — dominated much of the media coverage. When the Conservatives fell to third place early in the campaign, news stories seized on the impact of these declining poll numbers on the party's campaign organization and leadership.[1] Near the end of the campaign, with polls still showing a tight race and no party seemingly positioned to win an outright majority, media coverage turned to speculation about how the leaders might respond, scenarios by which the different parties might be able to form a minority government, and how the governor general was obliged to act, and what latitude he might have in the event that no single party could command the confidence of the House.[2] As late as the eve of the vote, few in the media or in the public anticipated that the outcome would be a majority government.

Beyond the horse-race, polls released during the formal campaign period told us much more than simply which political parties were leading and which were trailing. They demonstrated a desire for change among the Canadian electorate so intense and widespread that re-election for Stephen Harper and the Conservative Party would be very difficult. The polls provided insight into how Canadians viewed the party leaders and in particular the impact of the campaign in changing people's impressions of Justin Trudeau, whose personal numbers, along with Liberal support, had been slumping heading into the election. The polls also told us that, while the economy remained the most important issue for voters, the ballot question was not about the economy but about change and which alternative to the Conservative Party had the best chance of replacing it in government. In these ways, the polls were instrumental in helping us to understand the dynamics of the campaign and what voters were thinking. But they also served as a beacon, guiding those voters looking for change to the alternative best positioned to defeat the Conservative Party.

This chapter will place the polls in context by examining what they told us before the campaign began, and how they captured public opinion dynamics over the next seventy-eight days. It will also consider how accurately the polls estimated the eventual outcome — important, since the provincial elections in Alberta in 2012 and British Columbia in 2013 had been disastrous for the polling industry. In both cases, every polling firm estimated the share of popular vote that each competing party could expect on election day. And they were all conspicuously wrong. The 2015 Canadian general election also came on the heels of a general election in the United Kingdom, in which polls severely underestimated support for the Conservative Party, and were criticized for hijacking the narrative of the campaign.[3] Just as the fortunes of the competing parties hinged on the results of the vote, so did the credibility of Canadian polling firms.

## THE MOST POLLED CANADIAN ELECTION IN HISTORY?

Although the 2015 Canadian general election was preceded by the longest election campaign in modern Canadian history, it was not the most polled election. Despite the length of the campaign, there were actually fewer national horse-race polls released in 2015 than there were in

2006, and only two more released than in 2008. When we control for the length of the campaign, the number of national horse-race polls released per campaign day was 1.47 compared with 2.19 in 2011, and 2.20 in 2006. In fact, the 2008 Canadian general election was the most polled in the past decade, with 3.05 horse-race polls released per day of that campaign.

**Table 12.1: National Horse-Race Polls Released During Canadian General Elections, 2006 to 2015**

| Election | Number of National Horse-Race Polls Released | Polls Released per Campaign Day |
|---|---|---|
| 2015 | 115 | 1.47 |
| 2011 | 81 | 2.19 |
| 2008 | 113 | 3.05 |
| 2006 | 122 | 2.2 |

Source: CBC Poll Tracker,4 Wikipedia.

Nanos Research was the most prolific pollster during the 2015 election, releasing forty-five national horse-race polls thanks to its daily tracking surveys commissioned by CTV News and the *Globe and Mail.* The daily tracking from Nanos, released every day at 6 a.m. ET, began in earnest after Labour Day weekend. EKOS Research and Forum Research were also quite active, with more than a dozen national horse-race polls being released by each firm.

As in past elections, polling firms employed a range of methodologies. Nanos Research exclusively used live telephone surveys to conduct its three-day tracking surveys. EKOS, Forum, and Mainstreet used automated telephone surveys, also known as Interactive Voice Response, although EKOS included live telephone interviews in its sample near the end of the campaign. Abacus Data, Leger Marketing, and Angus Reid Institute exclusively used Internet-based methods, while Ipsos and Innovative Research used a hybrid survey method, a combination of live telephone and online interviews.

**Table 12.2: National Horse-Race Polls Released During 2015 Election by Firm**

| Firm | Number of National Horse-Race Polls Released | Methodology |
|---|---|---|
| Nanos Research | 45 | Live Telephone |
| EKOS Research | 19 | IVR (Automated Telephone) / Live Telephone |
| Forum Research | 14 | IVR |
| Ipsos | 9 | Live Telephone/Internet |
| Innovative Research | 7 | Live Telephone/Internet |
| Leger Marketing | 6 | Internet |
| Abacus Data | 5 | Internet |
| Mainstreet Research | 5 | IVR |
| Angus Reid Institute | 4 | Internet |
| Environics Research | 1 | Live Telephone |

Source: CBC Poll Tracker.

A number of news organizations entered into formal relationships with polling firms. Nanos Research was the official pollster for CTV News and the *Globe and Mail*. Ipsos was the pollster of record for Global News, while Forum Research provided extensive results to the *Toronto Star*. Innovative Research published its results in the *Hill Times*, Mainstreet Research was the pollster for the Postmedia chain of newspapers, and EKOS Research continued its long-standing partnership with *i*Politics.ca. Abacus Data self-published its polls, which also appeared on news aggregator NationalNewswatch.com.

Although national horse-race polls were not as frequent as in past elections, there were also extensive regional, provincial, and electoral district polls. For example, Mainstreet Research conducted a number of province-wide surveys and targeted polling in the markets of many Postmedia newspapers.

This election also saw extensive polling conducted by third-party organizations, like Leadnow and the Dogwood Institute. These were polls conducted for the purpose of strategically advising voters determined to unseat the Conservative Party. The results were used to recommend the local constituency candidate who had the best chance of defeating the Conservative candidate. Leadnow commissioned Environics Research to conduct fifty-seven electoral district surveys using IVR polling methodology, possibly the largest publicly released third-party polling operation ever in Canada.

## HOW DID THE POLLS DO?

Throughout the campaign, headlines warned readers about the unreliability of polls. Certainly, the provincial elections in Alberta (2012) and British Columbia (2013) were major setbacks for the industry. Since then, however, the industry had performed well in a number of other provincial and municipal elections.[5] Many questioned whether polls could accurately measure voting intention as survey response rates and landline telephone use declined, while Internet access was not yet so common as to make online surveys completely reliable.[6] But, in fact, like the majority of recent provincial and federal elections, the 2015 Canadian general election was a good election for the polling industry in Canada.

The estimates of the seven firms that released horse-race polls in the final days of the campaign did a good job of anticipating the popular vote percentages. Note, I refrain from using the term "predicting," as I am quite skeptical about a survey's ability to predict a result. On average, the absolute error for the five party estimates was 6.7.[7] Forum Research's final poll, released the day before the election, was the most accurate with an error score of only three. Polls that were released closer to election day were more accurate, as they were able to pick up what appears to have been a last-minute shift toward the Liberals at the expense of the NDP. Heading into the final days of the campaign, the polls agreed that the Liberals had taken a clear lead, but it was not until the final weekend that the possibility of a majority government became apparent.

### Table 12.3: Final National Horse-Race Poll Estimates by Firm

| Firm | Liberal | CPC | NDP | GPC | BQ | Polling Error* |
|---|---|---|---|---|---|---|
| Forum Research | 40% | 30% | 20% | 3% | 6% | 3 |
| Nanos Research | 39% | 31% | 20% | 5% | 6% | 5 |
| EKOS Research | 36% | 32% | 20% | 6% | 5% | 7 |
| Ipsos | 38% | 31% | 22% | 4% | 4% | 7 |
| Mainstreet Research | 39% | 32% | 21% | 5% | 3% | 7 |
| Leger Marketing | 38% | 30% | 22% | 4% | 6% | 8 |
| Angus Reid Institute | 35% | 31% | 22% | 5% | 5% | 10 |
| **Average** | | | | | | **6.7** |
| | | | | | | |
| **Election Result** | **40%** | **32%** | **20%** | **4%** | **5%** | |

* The absolute error of the firm's final poll for the five major parties.

Compared to the polling done for the Canadian general elections in 2011 and 2008, the 2015 estimates were more accurate on average. For context, the average error in the now famous polling "misses" in Alberta in 2012 and British Columbia in 2013 were 23 and 17 respectively, much higher than the error in any of the last four federal elections.

### Table 12.4: Average Absolute Polling Error (Five-Party) by Canadian General Election, 2006–2015

| Election | Average Polling Error |
|---|---|
| 2015 | 6.71 |
| 2011 | 8.29 |
| 2008 | 8.75 |
| 2006 | 5.50 |

So Canadian pollsters breathed a sigh of relief. Every firm that released a poll in the final few days of the election did a good job at estimating the final popular vote. Those who were in the field until the day before the election were even more accurate — a lesson that pollsters learned from their experience in Alberta. Increasingly, many voters are making up their minds in the final days of the campaign or on election day itself. A post-election survey conducted by EKOS Research found that 55 percent of voters made up their minds during the election campaign and 29 percent said they made up their minds in the final week of the campaign or on election day.[8]

Despite their success at accurately forecasting the final popular vote totals, the extent of the Liberal victory was still a surprise to many. Going into the final days of the campaign, many commentators still believed that the Liberals would have a difficult time winning a majority government, even with close to 40 percent of the vote.

While pollsters think in terms of votes, election outcomes are decided by the number of seats a party wins in the House of Commons. And it is people's expectations about how many seats the Liberals would win that made the returns on election night so surprising. This view was informed by seat projections that use public polling results to estimate how the vote breakdown would translate into seats. Only one of these projections, that conducted by Forum Research, projected a Liberal majority.

---

While the 2015 election was not the most polled campaign in history, it may have had more active seat projections than ever before. Almost every major media outlet had its own model, and a number of individuals had developed models that were regularly cited by commentators. Éric Grenier, founder of the website threehundredeight.com, perhaps the best known seat projector in Canada, was contracted with CBC News. Global News, *Le Journal de Montréal*, the *Toronto Star*, and the *Globe and Mail* each had its own seat projection model. David Akin with the Sun Media newspaper chain had his own prediction model he called the "Predictionator." Forum Research was the only polling firm to include seat projections as part of its polling results. Andrew Coyne, a columnist with the Postmedia newspaper chain, frequently tweeted a compilation of all the seat projections posted online.

Most of the models were, however, well off the mark. All predicted the Liberals would win the most seats, but only Forum Research's final projection of 171 Liberal seats predicted a majority, and even then it still fell thirteen short of the actual result. The average of the final projections predicted the Liberals would win 149 seats, thirty-five fewer than they actually won.

If Canadians were surprised by the results as ballots were counted the night of October 19, much of the reason lay with the seat projections, not the polls.

**Table 12.5: Final Seat Projections**

| Seat Projection | Liberal | CPC | NDP | GPC | BQ |
|---|---|---|---|---|---|
| Forum Research | 171 | 109 | 46 | 1 | 11 |
| *Toronto Star* | 160 | 120 | 50 | 1 | 7 |
| Predictionator (D. Akin) | 149 | 105 | 81 | 1 | 2 |
| 308.com (CBC) | 146 | 118 | 66 | 1 | 7 |
| LISPOP (Global) | 140 | 115 | 79 | 1 | 3 |
| Too Close to Call | 137 | 120 | 72 | 1 | 8 |
| Le Calcul Electoral (JdM) | 137 | 117 | 76 | 1 | 6 |
| **Average** | **149** | **115** | **67** | **1** | **6** |
| **Election Result** | **184** | **99** | **44** | **1** | **10** |

## WHAT DID THE POLLS TELL US?

### The Pre-Campaign: June 2011 to August 2015

Much happened in federal politics from the May 2011 election to the start of the official campaign in August 2015. As they did during the campaign, all three major parties had at one point led in publicly released polls over the previous four years.

From May 2011 until March 2012, the Conservative Party held a sizable lead over the NDP and the Liberal Party. Jack Layton, who had led the NDP to their status as Official Opposition, passed away from cancer on August 22, 2011. Despite this loss, the NDP maintained its second-place standing in the polls throughout this period, while the NDP's interim leader Nicole Turmel and the Liberal Party's interim leader Bob Rae worked to hold the Conservative government to account in the House of Commons.

In March 2012, Tom Mulcair was elected as the new NDP leader, after which NDP poll numbers improved for the remainder of 2012. In June 2012, soon after Mulcair's win, the campaign for leadership of the Liberal Party began, although Justin Trudeau, the eventual winner, did not declare until

October 2. It is at this point that Liberal poll numbers begin to improve. After Trudeau was elected as Liberal leader on April 14, 2013, the Liberal Party's support increased again and the party sustained its lead in the polls for almost two years. During this period, NDP support eroded as the party fell into third place while Conservative Party support in the polls hovered around 30 percent.

From early 2015 until the start of the campaign, there were significant shifts in vote intention. With the Mike Duffy affair off the agenda and a renewed focus on security issues following the attacks in Ottawa and Quebec in late 2014, Conservative support improved to the point where it was tied with the Liberals in most publicly released polls through the first quarter of 2015.

Two events occurred that impacted party support in the final five months before the campaign began in early August. On May 5, the Alberta NDP won a stunning majority victory in the provincial election, decisively ending the forty-two-year continuous reign of the Alberta Progressive Conservative Party. Second, on May 25, the Conservative Party released the first set of its "Interview" ads, targeting Trudeau by insisting he was "just not ready" to be prime minister.

These two events changed the dynamics of public opinion leading into the 2015 Canadian general election. NDP support jumped across the country to the point where it led in public polling from mid-June until the start of the campaign. Before the Alberta provincial election in May, NDP support sat at 21 percent to 23 percent in most public polls. Soon after, the federal NDP was in the low to mid-30s in most snapshots of public voting intentions.

At the same time as the NDP was rising in the polls, Liberal support began to erode. In May, Liberal support averaged around 33 percent in horse-race polls. By July, that had dropped to 25 percent.

More importantly, the public's expectation of who was going to win had changed substantially. More than a year before the campaign began, polling by Abacus Data in August 2014 found that a large plurality of eligible voters (39 percent) expected the Liberal Party would win the next election. A year later, in August 2015 — in the run-up to the official campaign — that number had dropped to 17 percent. The numbers of those who thought or hoped the NDP would win climbed 15 points over the same period (from 7 percent to 22 percent). Notably, a plurality (26 percent) still believed the Conservatives would win the election at the start of the campaign.

And so, heading into the official campaign period, the NDP held a small lead over the Conservatives with the Liberals in third. However, only 4 to 7 points separated the first- and third-placed parties in most publicly available survey research. The 2015 Canadian general election would start with an unprecedented level of competition — unlike at any point since public polling was available.

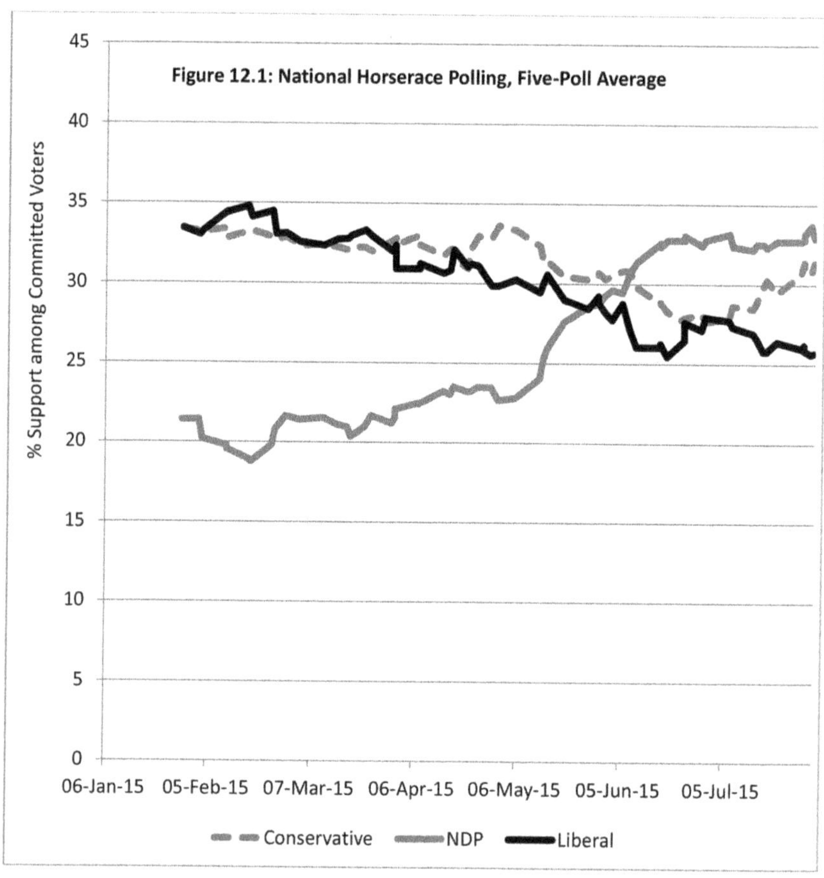


## The Official Campaign Period

When Stephen Harper visited the governor general and asked him to dissolve Parliament the prospect of Harper winning a fourth straight election looked dim, but not impossible. In most polls, the Conservatives trailed the NDP by only 2 or 3 points. Although the prospect of winning a majority government seemed slim, many projections at the time estimated that it was still possible that the Conservatives could win the most seats in the House, even if the party came second in the popular vote.[9]

For the NDP, the start of the 2015 Canadian general election was historic for the party. The NDP and its leader Tom Mulcair were well positioned to win a national election, something the party had never accomplished. Having led in the polls for most of the summer, the NDP was the front-runner, and its campaign strategy reflected this.[10]

As for the Liberal Party and leader Justin Trudeau, they started third in the polls. However, separated by only 5 to 7 points from the NDP, and with a majority of eligible voters indicating that they would consider voting Liberal[11] (Abacus Data, 2015), reversing this trend over a long, seventy-eight-day campaign was not impossible. Yet, at least in modern Canadian general elections, where substantial public polling was available, never has a political party that started in third in the polls won the election. And not since Arthur Meighen and the Progressive Conservatives won the 1926 election had the third party in the House of Commons won a general election.

**Figure 12.2: National Horserace Polling, Canadian General Election 2015 (Three-Poll Average)**

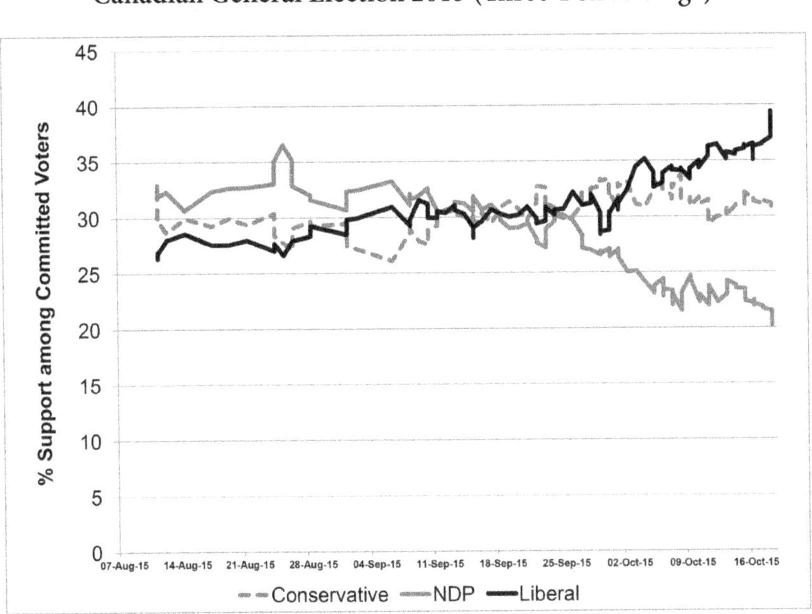


Source: Individual poll results from CBC Poll Tracker, aggregated by author.

## WHAT DID CANADIANS THINK ABOUT THE PARTY LEADERS?

The election campaign changed both voting intentions and impressions of the party leaders.

For Prime Minister Stephen Harper, the election campaign further eroded the already weak personal numbers he had heading into the start of the campaign. Soon after the writ was issued for the election, Harper's net personal impression numbers stood at -19 (those with a negative impression subtracted from those with a positive impression), with less than three in ten eligible voters saying that they had a positive impression of the Conservative Party leader. In contrast, NDP leader Tom Mulcair started the campaign as the most popular leader, with a net impression score of +25. Forty-one percent of eligible voters viewed Mulcair favourably compared with only 16 percent who viewed him negatively. Liberal leader Justin Trudeau also started the campaign with a net positive score, albeit lower than Mulcair's at +6 with 35 percent viewing him positively and 29 percent viewing him negatively.

By the end of the campaign, impressions of Trudeau improved the most, with his positive rating increasing by 9 points and his negatives only marginally increasing. The same cannot be said for his two primary opponents. Harper's negatives increased by 9 points while Mulcair's negatives increased by 12 points by the end of the campaign. And it is worth noting that although the NDP lost a substantial amount of support over the course of the campaign, Mulcair ended the campaign with a net positive rating: 35 percent viewed him favourably while 28 percent had a negative impression.[12]

**Table 12.6: Change in Public Impressions of Political Party Leaders**

| Leader | Start of Campaign | | End of Campaign | | Change in Net Impression |
|---|---|---|---|---|---|
| | Positive | Negative | Positive | Negative | |
| Stephen Harper | 28% | 47% | 27% | 56% | -10 |
| Justin Trudeau | 35% | 29% | 44% | 30% | +8 |
| Tom Mulcair | 41% | 16% | 35% | 28% | -18 |
| Elizabeth May | 25% | 15% | 28% | 16% | +2 |

Source: Abacus Data.

It was not just overall impressions that changed over the campaign; the image of each leader in the minds of voters also evolved. In Abacus Data surveys conducted at the start and end of the campaign, respondents were asked to rate how well a series of statements or words described each of the three main party leaders. For Harper, by the end of the campaign fewer eligible voters said that he had a good heart, had good ideas, was honest, empathetic, and was ready to be prime minister. The polling suggests that the election campaign further damaged an already weak image of the prime minister.

Mulcair's image was also impacted by the dynamics of the campaign. Although a plurality still believed he had a good heart and was honest, fewer believed that he was tough and that he had good ideas. The shift in perceptions for Harper and Mulcair provides evidence that neither the NDP nor the Conservative campaigns was able to improve the image of their respective leaders, perhaps explaining why neither was able to make much progress in gaining support throughout the election.

Survey data, however, provide substantial evidence that the Liberal campaign and Trudeau's performance had a crucial effect on how voters perceived the Liberal leader. By the end of the campaign, voters' perceptions about whether he had a good heart, had good ideas, and, perhaps most importantly, his readiness to be prime minister, all improved. Perceptions about his readiness to be prime minister alone increased 9 points over the campaign from 29 percent in August to 38 percent in the final weekend of the election. If the secondary ballot question, apart from the desire for change, was whether Trudeau was capable of being the prime minister, evidence from public polling indicates that he was successful in changing the perceptions of sufficient numbers of voters on this question to win.

The relative importance to the Liberal Party's success of Trudeau's competence cannot be overstated. Among the 38 percent of decided voters who believed that Trudeau was "ready to be prime minister," 70 percent said they planned to vote Liberal in the final days of the campaign, 56 points higher than those who did not feel he was ready. Had the Liberal campaign, and in particular Trudeau himself, not demonstrated that he was competent and able to be prime minister, a Liberal victory, certainly a majority victory, would have been unlikely.

### Table 12.7: Change in Public Image of Party Leaders

| Conservative Leader Stephen Harper | Start of Campaign | End of Campaign | Change |
|---|---|---|---|
| Tough | 43% | 46% | +3 |
| Good heart | 25% | 20% | -5 |
| Good ideas | 27% | 23% | -4 |
| Honest | 22% | 19% | -3 |
| Understands people like you | 23% | 19% | -4% |
| Ready to be prime minister | 42% | 38% | -4% |

| Liberal Leader Justin Trudeau | Start of Campaign | End of Campaign | Change |
|---|---|---|---|
| Tough | 25% | 27% | +2 |
| Good heart | 46% | 49% | +3 |
| Good ideas | 34% | 41% | +7 |
| Honest | 37% | 40% | +3 |
| Understands people like you | 33% | 37% | +4% |
| Ready to be prime minister | 29% | 38% | +9% |

| NDP Leader Tom Mulcair | Start of Campaign | End of Campaign | Change |
|---|---|---|---|
| Tough | 38% | 34% | -4 |
| Good heart | 40% | 42% | +2 |
| Good ideas | 38% | 35% | -3 |
| Honest | 37% | 37% | - |
| Understands people like you | 34% | 32% | -2% |
| Ready to be prime minister | 39% | 38% | -1% |

Source: Abacus Data.

## THE ISSUES

### The Economy and Fiscal Policy

The economy was supposed to be the dominant issue of the election campaign — that, at least, was the intention of Conservative Party campaign strategists. The party started the campaign with the slogan, "Proven leadership for a safer Canada and stronger economy." Later, its slogan changed to "Protect our Economy."

Polling found that the economy and jobs were the top issues for voters throughout the campaign.[13] An Abacus Data survey released near the start of the campaign found that 57 percent of eligible voters described the state of the Canadian economy as poor or very poor, while for 43 percent the Canadian economy was good or very good. In a similar vein, 64 percent believed the Canadian economy was in a recession.[14] Yet, when asked whether the Canadian economy was doing better or worse than most of Canada's major competitors, most respondents to the same survey (66 percent) felt that the economy was doing better, or at least no better or worse than other countries like Canada. This was an indicator that few blamed the Conservative government directly for the state of the economy, but that confidence in its ability to improve economic conditions was starting to deteriorate.

Along with economic management, fiscal policy also featured prominently during the campaign. On August 25, Mulcair promised that his government would balance the federal budget in its first year, even with all the commitments it had made in its platform. A few days later Trudeau announced that a Liberal government would not balance the budget in its first three years so that it could spend new money on infrastructure.[15] This policy distinction was one of many that would define the NDP and Liberal campaigns as both sought the support of voters who wanted a change in government.

Public opinion on balancing the federal budget or running deficits was mixed, but data indicate that Trudeau and the Liberal Party tapped into a wedge issue that put them on one side of an issue with their two main opponents on the other. For example, a survey by Abacus Data in September found that respondents were split when asked their opinion about deficits to stimulate the economy. Thirty-seven percent believed the Government of Canada should spend money to ensure the economy grows, even if it meant going into deficit, while 38 percent believed that the government should keep the budget balanced, even if the economy weakened. In a Nanos Research survey conducted in August, 54 percent said they supported or somewhat supported a "new round of deficit spending by the federal government to simulate the economy."[16]

Many assumed that the Conservative Party had an advantage on the economy and fiscal policy as election issues — yet on both, thanks to a policy stand by the NDP, the Liberals found themselves alone in calling for deficit spending to finance infrastructure investment so as to stimulate the economy. This was not the last time the NDP would find that one of its policy positions would put it offside with a large portion of its potential supporters.

## The Niqab and Citizenship Ceremonies

Perhaps more than any other issue, attitudes about the niqab and whether a woman can cover her face during citizenship ceremonies had the greatest effect on the outcome of the election.

Public opinion on the question released during and prior to the campaign pointed to overwhelming support for the Harper government's position that a woman should not be able to cover her face during the public citizenship ceremony. A survey conducted by the Privy Council Office by Leger Marketing in March 2015 found that 82 percent of respondents supported the requirement that people show their faces while taking the oath of citizenship. In Quebec, support was highest at 93 percent.[17]

It should be noted that no data were released on public attitudes on the issue if a respondent knew that a new citizen would still have to verify her identity in front of an immigration officer before swearing the oath. The questions that guided media coverage of the issue were too simplistic to effectively measure the nuances of attitudes and perceptions of the issue.

That said, it is clear the debate on the niqab did affect perceptions of the parties, most significantly the NDP in Quebec. Figure 12.3 shows the average horse-race poll results in Quebec in four periods over the course of the formal campaign. Until the middle of September, the NDP was well ahead of all three of the other major political parties in the province, averaging 45 percent support in polls conducted between September 9 and 15.

On September 15, the Federal Court of Appeal ruled that the Government of Canada's policy banning the wearing of face veils at citizenship ceremonies was illegal, placing the issue back onto the agenda of public concern. The Conservative Party and Bloc Québécois seized the opportunity to use the issue as a wedge against the NDP. During the first French-language debate on Radio-Canada on October 2, Mulcair once again had to defend his position on the citizenship ceremony issues.

Public polling data indicate that NDP support in Quebec fell around 16 points over a two-week period, the equivalent of 4 percentage points in national polls. This drop in Quebec was soon followed by a drop of support in other parts of the country as it became clear to voters looking to change the government that the NDP was not the alternative most likely to defeat the Conservatives.

**Figure 12.3: Quebec Horse-Race Polling, Six-Poll Average by Time Period**

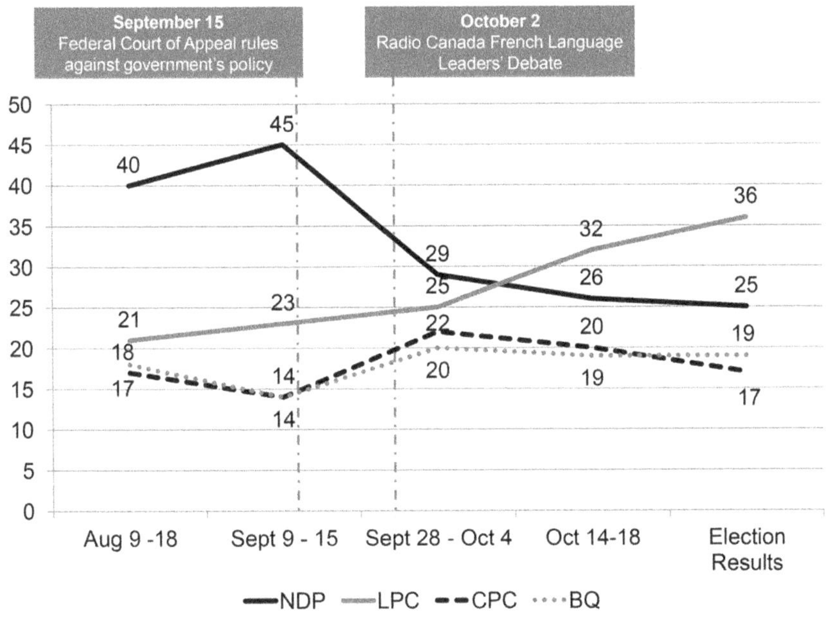

Source: Author's calculation, six-poll average of Quebec horse-race numbers for polls released between these dates.

Putting so much focus on the niqab and the NDP's position on the issue might have won the Conservatives a few seats in Quebec but it certainly contributed to their defeat at the national level. It weakened the NDP and allowed the Liberals to consolidate more of the "change" vote in the final weeks of the campaign. In the end, it may have been only one of many strategic errors on the part of the Conservative campaign but it was perhaps the most costly. It turned the election from one primarily about the economy to one in which voters were evaluating the parties in terms of their values.

## Desire for Change

While the party leaders, values issues, and the economy were the focus for much of the campaign, polling suggests that the desire for change, more than anything else, was the driving factor in the election's outcome. If nothing else, the NDP and Liberal Party campaign slogans of "Ready for Change" and "Real Change" announced what the opposition parties wanted the campaign to be about.

At the start of the campaign, an Abacus Data poll conducted in mid-August found that more than three-quarters of eligible voters wanted a change in government, with 59 percent saying they thought it was definitely time for a change. Other polls confirmed this intense desire for change, which did not dissipate over the course of the campaign. In an Innovative Research poll conducted from August 24 to 26, 62 percent of respondents said it was time for a change. By early September, those agreeing it was time for a change had increased to 66 percent in Innovative Research's polling, and by the end of the campaign,[18] 67 percent of respondents to an Ipsos survey said it was time for another federal party to take over.[19] Clearly, the Conservative campaign was unable to weaken the desire for change among two-thirds of the electorate.

Meanwhile, a parallel election plot was about which alternative to the Conservatives best represented the kind of change voters wanted. Polling conducted during the campaign gave us insights into how that story unfolded.

In Abacus Data's first survey of the formal campaign period, 51 percent of those who definitely wanted a change in government were planning to vote NDP, compared with 35 percent who said they would vote Liberal. By the final weekend of the campaign, in Abacus Data's final survey, the Liberals had opened up a 15-point lead over the NDP among this key group of the electorate, reversing a similar deficit from the start of the campaign.

Why were the Liberals so successful at consolidating these change voters? Along with the impact of the niqab debate on NDP support in Quebec, evidence from another Abacus Data poll conducted in the middle of the campaign found that voters distinguished between the type of change being offered by Mulcair and Trudeau. Of those who wanted a change over government, 63 percent said that Trudeau represented “ambitious change” compared with 37 percent who selected Mr. Mulcair. In contrast, when asked which leader best represented “moderate change,” Mulcair came ahead of Trudeau by 20 points, with 60 percent choosing Mulcair and 40 percent selecting the Liberal leader.

The distinction between the moderate and steady change being offered by Mulcair and the ambitious, more speedy change being proposed by Trudeau was, in the end, a crucial factor in determining the outcome of the election. Voters, particularly those looking for change, recognized the difference in policy and campaign rhetoric and when it came to casting their ballots more chose the ambitious version of change offered by the Liberals.

Publicly released polling beyond the horse race helped us to better understand how the electorate was reacting to each party’s messaging and policy promises and how this ultimately influenced their individual voting decisions.

## FINAL THOUGHTS

The 2015 Canadian general election was remarkable, not least for the way in which the parties’ fortunes shifted over the course of the long campaign, and the publicly released polling conducted throughout the campaign offers insight into how and why voters responded as they did to the competing policy platforms, the performance and personae of the leaders, and the events that marked the contours of the contest.

Polls registered the state of the “horse race,” but a lot of polling also examined why the horse race was changing. Polling told us that voters’ impressions of Justin Trudeau improved markedly over the campaign. It helped us to understand that while the economy was the top issue on people’s minds, it was not likely as important in driving votes as the desire for change and the response of voters to the different versions of change being offered by the Liberal Party and NDP.

Those who advocate for a ban on public polling during election campaigns point to the influence it has on media coverage and on the decisions voters make. And there is little doubt that polls influence how journalists cover elections. A focus on the horse race may crowd out coverage of substantive issues and policy differences during a campaign. But imagine an election campaign without any publicly released polls. How would journalists frame the state of the race? How would voters know which alternative has the best chance of defeating a party they dislike the most? Had the public not been aware that NDP support was rising in Quebec during the 2011 Canadian general election, would its support have grown in other regions of the country?

Despite concern that political polling had become unreliable, the 2015 federal election was a good one for the polling industry in Canada. A large number of firms participated. Different methodologies and perspectives produced varied insights into what voters were thinking. And the final snapshots of voting intent captured by the firms in the field on the final days of the campaign very closely approximated how voters ultimately cast their ballots. There were no embarrassing repudiations of the polling industry's claims to reliability and authority, as in the case of the 2012 Alberta and 2013 B.C. elections.

But despite this, many were surprised by the results when votes were tallied on election day. This was because almost all of the seat projections using public polls were far off the mark. Only one predicted a Liberal majority and that did so by only two seats.

Public opinion researchers around the world face formidable challenges in accurately measuring the perceptions, attitudes, and anticipated behaviour of the people they study. Canadian researchers are no exception. The lessons learned from the high-profile "polling failures" exemplified by the 2012 Alberta and 2013 B.C. elections[20] were such that the industry as a whole performed well during the 2015 federal election. Its survey data provided an accurate account of how voting intention — and voters' deliberations — changed over the course of the campaign. Its surveys captured what was top of mind for voters and what was driving voting intention, thus revealing the contours of the campaign dynamic. And in the end its snapshots of the national electoral mood were extremely close approximations of how the country actually voted.

## NOTES

I thank my colleague Maciej Czop at Abacus Data for his helpful assistance in preparing this chapter.

1. CTV News, "Campaign Woes, Poll Numbers Rattle Conservative Campaign" September 8, 2015, online edition.
2. Kathleen Harris, "Minority Government Could Force Governor General to Flex Constitutional Muscle" October 17, 2015, CBC News, online edition.
3. Mick Temple, "Lies, Damned Lies and Opinion Polls," in *UK Election Analysis 2015: Media, Voters, and the Campaign* ed. Daniel Jackson and Einar Thorsen (Bournemouth, UK: Centre for the Study of Journalism, Culture & Community, 2015); Suzanne Franks, "How Could the Polls Have Been So Wrong?" in *UK Election Analysis 2015.*
4. "Éric Grenier's Poll Tracker," CBC News, www.cbc.ca/news2/interactives/poll-tracker/2015/.
5. David Coletto and Bryan Bregeut, "The Accuracy of Public Polls in Provincial Elections," *Canadian Political Science Review* 9, no. 1 (2015): 41–54.
6. Murad Hemmadi, "How Pollsters Fight for Relevance in the Age of Big Data," *Canadian Business*, October 16, 2015, www.canadianbusiness.com/innovation/how-pollsters-fight-for-relevance-in-the-age-of-big-data/.
7. The error measure is calculated by adding up the total absolute difference between a firm's final vote estimate from the actual results for each of the main five parties.
8. EKOS Research Associates. "Great Expectations," November 11, 2015, www.ekospolitics.com/index.php/2015/11/great-expectations/.
9. "Éric Grenier's Poll Tracker," CBC News.
10. David McGrane, "The NDP's 'Government in Waiting' Strategy," in *Canadian Election Analysis 2015: Communication, Strategy, and Democracy*, ed. Alex Marland and Thierry Gisasson (Vancouver: UBC Press, 2015). Accessed from www.ubcpress.ca/CanadianElectionAnalysis2015.
11. Bruce Anderson and David Coletto, "Race Narrows as NDP Support Dips," Abacus Data, August 31, 2015, http://abacusdata.ca/race-narrows-as-ndp-support-dips/.
12. Abacus Data — Data provided by author.
13. "Vote Compass: Economy and Environment Rate as Top Issues," CBC News, September 10, 2015, www.cbc.ca/news/politics/vote-compass-canada-election-2015-issues-canadians-1.3222945.
14. Bruce Anderson and David Coletto, "The Mood of the Electorate Worsens as Perceptions About the Economy Deteriorate" Abacus Data, August 20, 2015, http://abacusdata.ca/mood-of-the-electorate-worsens-as-perceptions-about-the-economy-deteriorate/.
15. "Justin Trudeau Says Liberals Plan 3 Years of Deficits to Push Infrastructure," CBC News, August 27, 2015, www.cbc.ca/news/politics/canada-election-2015-liberals-infrastructure-deficits-1.3205535.
16. Campbell Clark,"Canadians Believe Economy in Recession, OK with Deficit: Poll," *Globe and Mail*, August 31, 2015, www.theglobeandmail.com/news/politics/canadians-believe-economy-is-in-recession-okay-with-deficit-poll/article26119298/.

17. Stephanie Levitz, Canadian Press, "Majority of Canadians Agree with Conservatives Over Niqab Ban, Poll Finds," Canadian Press, September 24, 2015, http://news.nationalpost.com/news/canada/majority-of-canadians-support-conservatives-niqab-ban-poll-finds.
18. Innovative Research Group, "2015 Election Polling Wave 6: Core Tracking Deck," www.innovativeresearch.ca/sites/default/files/pdf%2C%20doc%2C%20docx%2C%20jpg%2C%20png%2C%20xls%2C%20xlsx/151009_IRG29%20Wave%206%20Hill%20Times%20Oct%209%20Release.pdf. Accessed November 3, 2015.
19. Ipsos, "End of an Era: For a Second Time, a Trudeau Is Headed to 24 Sussex as Liberals Poised to Win Election" www.ipsos-na.com/download/pr.aspx?id=14991. Accessed November 4, 2015.
20. Coletto and Bregeut, 2015.

## CHAPTER 13

### It's Spring Again! Voting in the 2015 Federal Election

Harold D. Clarke, Jason Reifler, Thomas J. Scotto, and Marianne C. Stewart

For Canadians of a certain age, the outcome of the 2015 federal election seemed very familiar. The election produced a Liberal majority government, with the party capturing the majority of the seats in several provinces, including both Ontario and Quebec. Turnout was 69.1 percent, down from the twentieth-century norm, but well above the discouraging numbers of the past two decades. Most interesting, the victorious party leader was someone named Trudeau. The new prime minister promised to use deficit spending to invigorate the economy, strike new and productive relationships with the provinces, help minorities protect their cultures, and generally practise the "sunny ways" of fairness and justice. In foreign affairs, the country would once again act as a benign middle power, returning to old ways such as participating in peacekeeping under the auspices of the United Nations. For Canadians old enough to remember Expo 67, political nostalgia was definitely the order of the day. And for younger Canadians, a junior version of Trudeaumania was an invigorating tonic.

In this chapter, we employ national survey data[1] to analyze voting behaviour in the 2015 election. The results of these analyses are similar to those from studies of earlier elections.[2] In 2015, a familiar combination of partisanship, judgments about party performance, and party leader images did much to shape the choices voters made. Evaluations of the government's handling of the economy and voters' reactions to the party leaders were especially important in this election. During his lengthy tenure as Conservative leader, Stephen Harper had failed to generate positive emotional reactions from large numbers of voters, and many now questioned his competence to manage the country's economy effectively. In contrast, Liberal leader Justin Trudeau showed that he had political game as well as a famous name. Over the course of the 2015 campaign, he favourably impressed many Canadians, convincing them that he was "ready" to govern and that it was time to restore a Liberal government to power in Ottawa. On October 19, 2015, the voters did exactly that.

## ISSUES

Over the past half century, research in Canada and other mature democracies has established that what political scientists call *valence issues* have very strong effects on the choices voters make.[3] Unlike *position issues* such as the use of the Canadian military to combat ISIS, admitting large numbers of Syrian refugees, or the gun registry, on which sizable numbers of voters hold opposing views, valence issues are ones for which there is broad consensus on the goals of public policy. The canonical example is the economy — virtually everyone agrees about the desirability of a healthy economy characterized by low rates of inflation and unemployment, coupled with vigorous, sustainable growth. When it comes to the economy and other valence issues, such as the delivery of cherished public services in areas such as health care, education, and national security, political debate focuses not on "what to do" but rather on "how to do it" and, especially, "who can do it best."

Under Stephen Harper's leadership, the Conservative Party of Canada (CPC) had made the maintenance of a healthy economy the centrepiece of its political agenda. Pointing to his graduate degree in economics at the University of Calgary, Harper had argued repeatedly that he had the knowledge, experience, and competence needed to deliver the sustained prosperity that everyone wanted. In earlier elections, the argument had served him and his party well. However, this was not the case in 2015 — as the federal election campaign began in early August, the economy had sputtered into a mild recession after several years of steady, if unspectacular, growth. Other widely watched indicators were trending in negative directions as well, with joblessness ticking upward to 7 percent and the value of the Canadian dollar falling sharply, concomitant with a precipitous decline in the price of oil on world markets.

The Canadian public took notice of the bad news. As Figure 13.1 shows, evaluations of the state of the economy just before the 2015 election were quite different than they had been four years earlier. At that time, fully 68 percent of those participating in the Political Support in Canada pre-election survey indicated that the economy was doing either "very" or "fairly" well and only 26 percent said that it was doing "fairly" or "very" poorly. In 2015, a pre-election survey conducted by Abacus Data revealed that the former number had fallen to 40 percent and the latter had increased to 56 percent. The precise timing of the increase in negativity about the economy is not known, but what is important is that it occurred early enough to influence voting in the 2015 election and was widespread across the country. Specifically, the percentages saying that the economy was either "poor" or "very poor" ranged from a low of 50 percent in the Prairies to a high of 71 percent in Quebec. In the Atlantic provinces, 61 percent voiced negative opinions about economic conditions, as did 53 percent of those living in British Columbia and 54 percent of those living in Ontario. The breadth of the economic pessimism meant that its effect on the election outcome was potentially very large.

Figure 13.2 indicates that judgments about the federal government's performance had become much more negative as well. In 2011, 53 percent stated that the government was doing a "very good" or a "good" job on the economy, but in 2015 the Local Parliament pre-election survey indicated that positive judgments of federal government performance on the economy had fallen to 39 percent, with a majority saying that the government was doing either a "poor" or a "very poor" job.

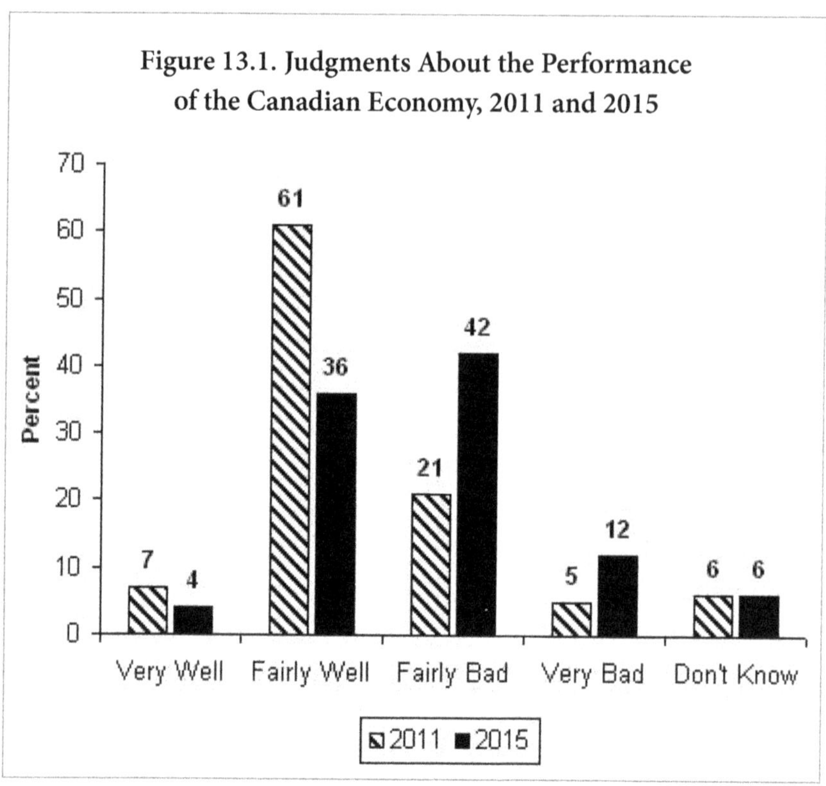


**Figure 13.1. Judgments About the Performance of the Canadian Economy, 2011 and 2015**

Source: 2011 Political Support in Canada pre-election survey, 2015 Abacus pre-election survey.

The importance of these pessimistic economic judgments is suggested by responses to an open-ended question in the 2015 Abacus pre-election survey on the most important issue in the election. The responses, summarized in Figure 13.3, demonstrate that concerns about the economy were dominant, with nearly 47 percent citing jobs or the economy generally, and an additional 6.9 percent mentioning taxes or the government debt. No other issue was mentioned by more than 10 percent of those surveyed. In particular, although the media had given great play to the controversy about whether Muslim women should be allowed to wear a veil (the niqab) during the Canadian citizenship ceremony, only 4 percent mentioned this issue or related cultural concerns. Other issues receiving relatively little emphasis from the public included health care (6.4 percent), the environment (4.4 percent), crime and terrorism (3.6 percent), and the quality of governance and the desirability of change (8.2 percent).

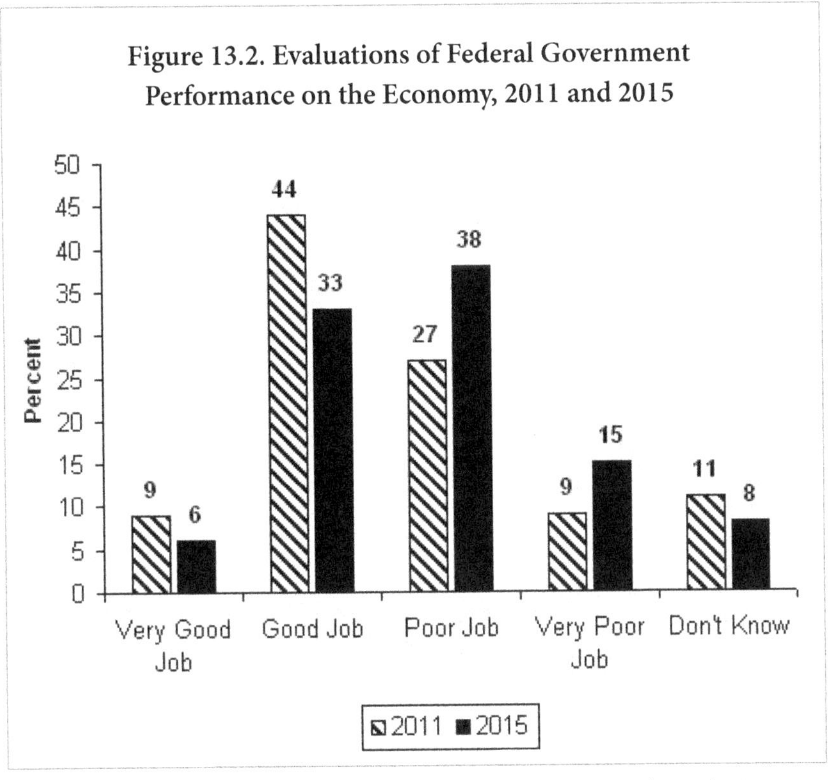


Source: 2011 Political Support in Canada pre-election survey, 2015 Local Parliament Project pre-election survey.

Given the dominance of the economy as an issue in 2015 and the unhappiness of many Canadians with the government's performance on it, it is not surprising that far fewer people chose the governing Conservatives as the party most competent to deal with the issue they deemed most important. This was a big change from 2011. Specifically, as Figure 13.4 illustrates, only one-quarter (26 percent) of those in the 2015 Abacus pre-election survey chose the Conservatives as the party "best able to handle" the most important issue. Four years earlier, fully 40 percent had done so. The NDP's "party best" share also decreased considerably — from 24 percent in 2011 to 16 percent in 2015 — while the percentage choosing the Greens inched upward slightly (from 3 to 5 percent) and the BQ percentage remained stable (at 3 percent). Only the Liberals enjoyed a big increase, with many more respondents

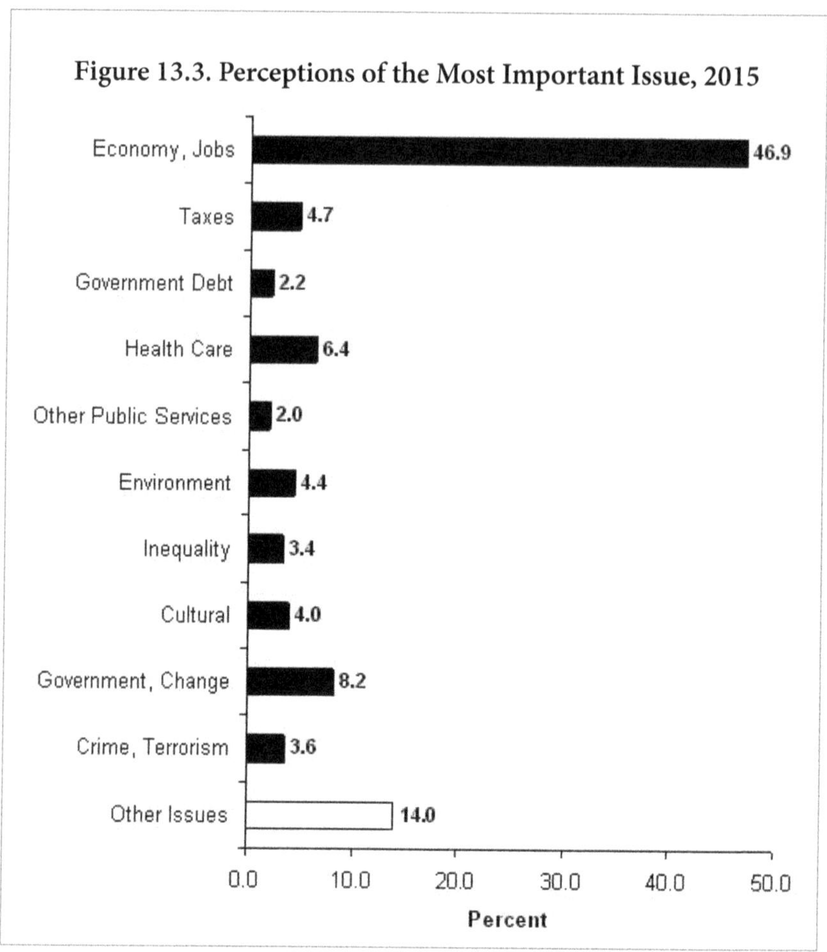


Source: 2015 Abacus pre-election survey.

stating that they viewed the party as competent to address the issue they identified as the most important. Indeed, the Liberal share of responses to the "party best able to handle" question surged from a dismal 11 percent in 2011 to 28 percent in 2015. Although the latter figure was not spectacular, it was sufficient to give the Liberals a slight edge over the Conservatives as the best party on issues of paramount concern to the electorate in 2015.

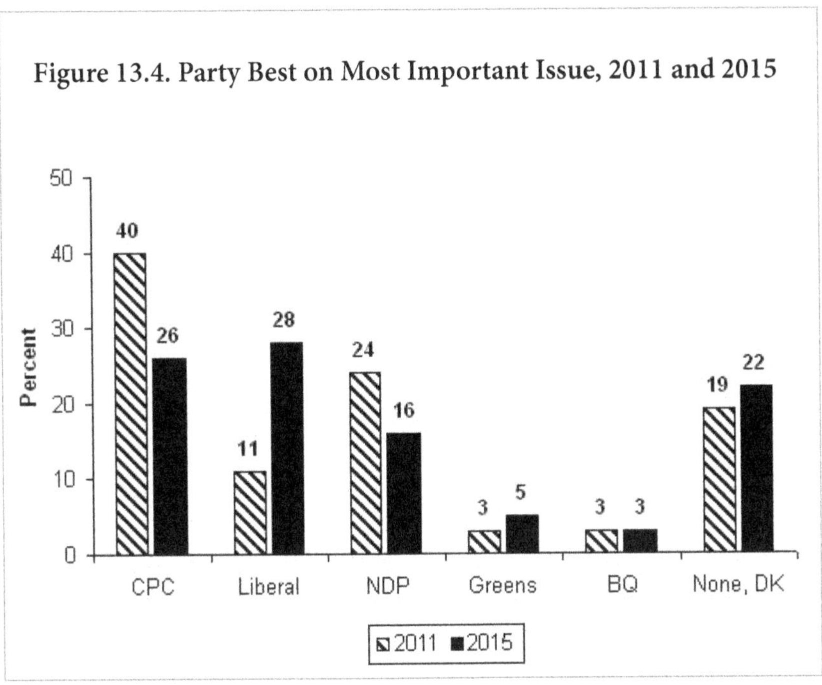


Source: 2015 Abacus pre-election survey.

## PARTIES

When the first Canadian national election studies were conducted in the 1960s, they were heavily influenced by theoretical and methodological developments pioneered in research on voting in American presidential elections at the University of Michigan.[4] One of the key theoretical concepts imported from these Michigan election studies was *party identification*, a voter's sense of psychological attachment to a political party. According to the Michigan theory, party identification was akin to the sorts of identification people form with ethnic, racial, or religious groups. Similar to these social identifications, partisan attachments developed during childhood or adolescence, largely as a result of socialization processes occurring in families and other close-knit groups. Once formed, party identifications typically did not change, except to grow stronger over the life cycle as a result of behavioural reinforcement, i.e., by voting for the same party in successive elections.

In addition to influencing electoral choice directly, party identification had indirect effects on the vote; it was a "perceptual screen" that helped to shape how people reacted to issues, party leaders, and local candidates. Besides exerting powerful effects on individual voting behaviour, the widespread existence of party identifications across the electorate helped to anchor party systems over time and stabilize the processes of democratic governance.

However, results from the early Canadian election studies conducted in the 1960s did not support important elements of this story. Although many Canadians indicated that that they identified with a political party, these identifications appeared to have considerable individual-level flexibility, with sizable minorities reporting that they previously had identified with one or more other parties. By interviewing the same people at multiple points in time, subsequent studies confirmed the presence of substantial instability in party identification.[5] In addition, these studies have revealed that many Canadians do not maintain consistent partisan attachments across levels of the federal system; rather, they identify with different parties in federal and provincial politics, with large numbers identifying only weakly with a party at either level of governance.[6] Partisan attachments in the Canadian electorate thus lack the durability, cross-level consistency, and strength needed to shelter parties from negative performance evaluations on salient issues and adverse reactions to their leaders.

That said, research does indicate that at any point in time party identifications, short-term as they may be, are widespread in the electorate and that they function as significant heuristics — cueing devices voters use to help them decide how to cast their ballots in political contexts characterized by high stakes and considerable uncertainty. Accordingly, the distribution of party identifications is always important. Figure 13.5, which displays the distribution of federal party identifications from 1988 to 2015, indicates that the cohorts of Liberal and Conservative partisans have varied widely in size. The Liberal group shows the most variability — reaching as high as 40 percent in 2000 and as low as 18 percent in 2011. Four years later, Liberal partisanship had rebounded modestly, with 26 percent of those in the 2015 Abacus pre-election survey saying they identified with the Liberals.

The Conservative partisan share was exactly the same size, 26 percent. This Conservative percentage, however, was 4 percent below where it had been in 2011. Figure 13.5 also documents that the NDP partisan cohort was 14 percent in 2015, 3 points lower than it had been in 2011. Thus, as is typical in federal elections, both the Liberals and the Conservatives had considerably more identifiers than did the NDP. However, similar to judgments about which party was most competent to address key issues, the Liberals and the Conservatives were neck-and-neck on party identification in 2015. The growth of Liberal partisanship was an indicator that the party had increased its acceptability in the run-up to the election.

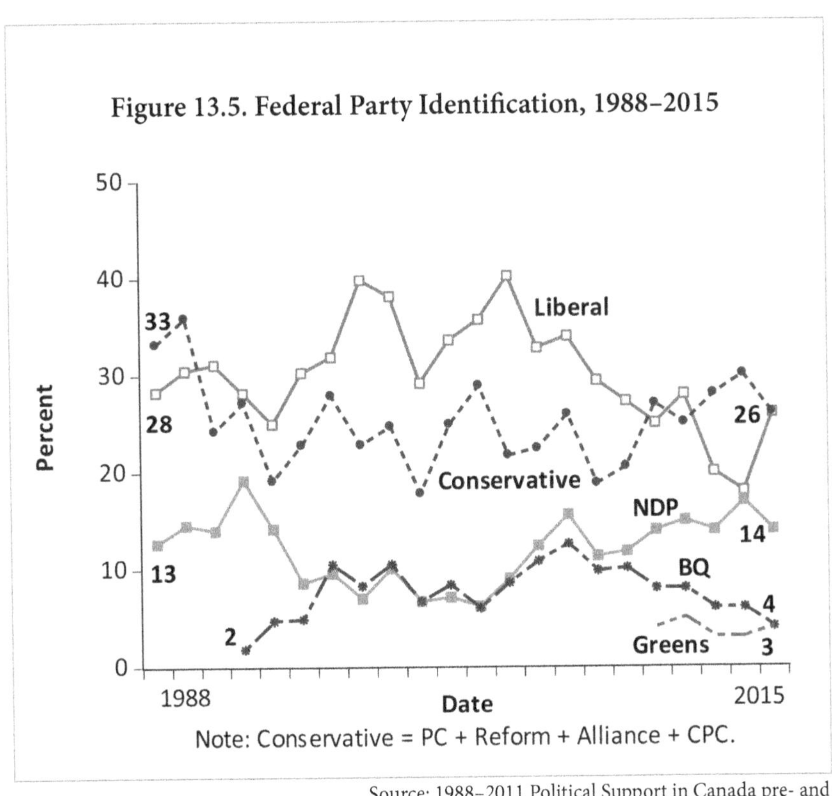


Figure 13.5. Federal Party Identification, 1988–2015

Note: Conservative = PC + Reform + Alliance + CPC.

Source: 1988–2011 Political Support in Canada pre- and post-election surveys, 2015 Abacus pre-election survey.

## LEADERS

Leader images are the third factor in the set of explanatory variables emphasized in the valence politics theory of electoral choice. Like party identification, leader images serve as key heuristics, cueing voters about how they should make decisions about which party to support.[7] Given that it is difficult, indeed oftentimes impossible, to assess the consequences of competing policy proposals for addressing major problems, such as how to deliver stable economic growth, ensure a reliable supply of high-quality health care, or guard against security threats posed by terrorists and rogue regimes, voters rely heavily on their impressions of party leaders for guidance. Perceptions of competing leaders' competence, responsiveness, and trustworthiness are key to determining their images, and previous research has shown that these perceptions are conveniently summarized by simple affective (like-dislike) reactions.

Figure 13.6 displays data on how Canadians felt about the rival party leaders just before the 2011 and 2015 federal elections. In 2011, people had not been particularly enthusiastic about Conservative leader Stephen Harper, giving him an average score of 4.7 on a 0–10 dislike-like scale. This was far below the score accorded former NDP leader Jack Layton, who recorded an impressive 6.2 score in 2011. Harper's rating was also just slightly below the 4.8 given to Green leader Elizabeth May. However, Harper's 2011 score was well above that for ex-Liberal leader Michael Ignatieff, whose 3.0 average rating was one of the lowest ever recorded since the first Canadian election studies were conducted in the 1960s. As Figure 13.6 also shows, much had changed by 2015. Especially noteworthy was the fact that Harper's average rating had decreased to a decidedly mediocre 3.7, substantially less than the 5.2 and 5.1 ratings given to Justin Trudeau and Thomas Mulcair, respectively. Indeed, Harper's 2015 rating was the lowest of any of the five party leaders, with Elizabeth May of the Greens scoring 4.4 and Gilles Duceppe of the Bloc Québécois recording 4.0 (Quebec only).

Figure 13.6. Feelings About the Party Leaders, 2011 and 2015

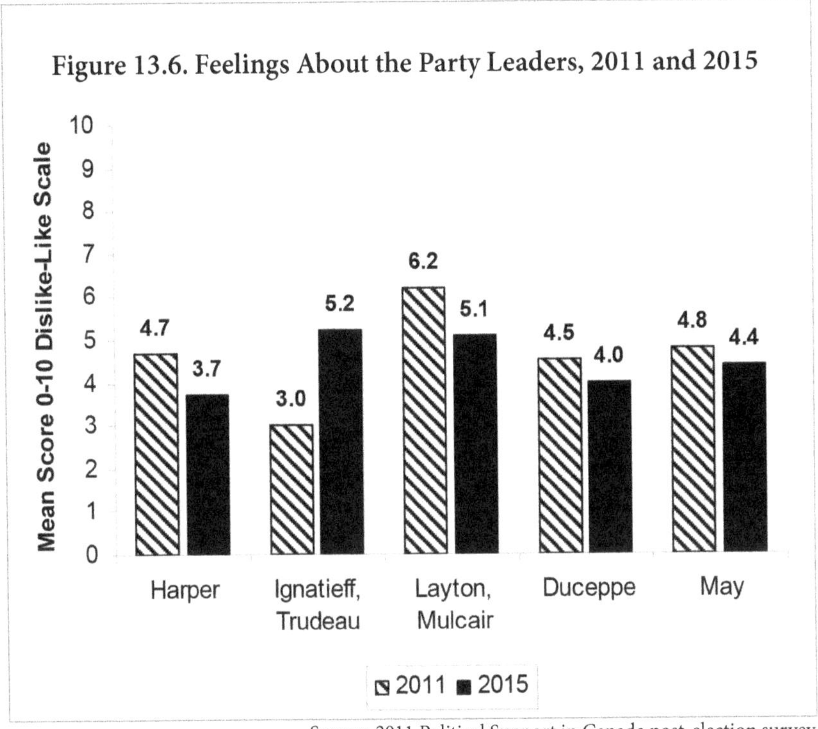


Source: 2011 Political Support in Canada post-election survey, 2015 Local Parliament Project pre-election survey.

The conclusion that many Canadians were unenthusiastic about Harper is reinforced by the data presented in Figure 13.7. When asked a general question about whether they had positive or negative impressions of the five party leaders, only 27 percent of those surveyed in the 2015 Abacus survey reported that they had a positive impression of Harper, whereas a clear majority (56 percent) said they had a negative impression. The ratio of these two numbers is decidedly different than it is for any of the other leaders, each of whom garnered more favourable than unfavourable impressions. A preponderance of positive evaluations was especially noticeable in Justin Trudeau's case — his favourable rating was 44 percent and his unfavourable rating was 30 percent. In contrast, the ratios of favourable to unfavourable scores for Thomas Mulcair, Elizabeth May, and Gilles Duceppe were 35:28, 28:16, and 37:33 (Quebec only), respectively. In summary, the 2015 survey data testify that Trudeau had the most positive image and Harper had the most negative one.

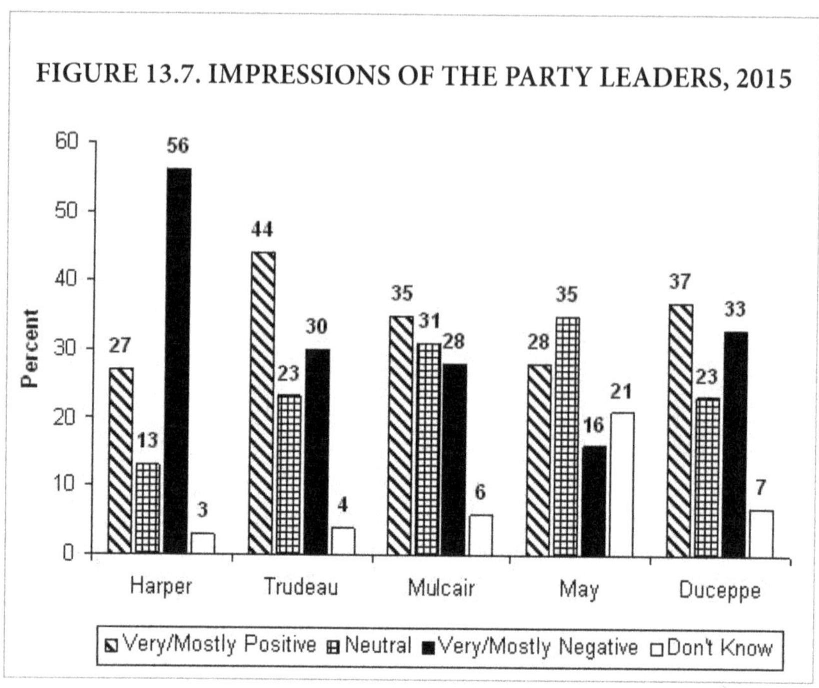


Source: 2015 Abacus pre-election survey.

Harper had more specific image problems as well. When the campaign began, the media were full of stories about the trial of former Conservative senator Mike Duffy, who was facing thirty-one criminal charges involving fraud, breach of trust, and bribery. The Duffy scandal hit close to home, as it involved individuals in the Prime Minister's Office. Heightened publicity about the scandal was coming at exactly the wrong time and it had potential to erode public confidence in the honesty and trustworthiness of the prime minister. Although it is not possible to know if the scandal was an important contributing cause, the Local Parliament Project pre-election survey shows that only 31 percent of those interviewed thought that Harper was either "very" or "somewhat" honest. Fully 54 percent thought he was either "somewhat" or "very" dishonest. Opinion about Justin Trudeau was very different, with fully 56 percent rating him honest and only 25 percent saying he was dishonest. Similarly, 50 percent rated Thomas Mulcair honest and 26 percent thought he was dishonest. Comparable figures for Elizabeth May were 50 percent and 14 percent, respectively. Clearly, Conservative strategists, disheartened by their leader's failure to generate positive feelings across much of the electorate, could not take solace in survey data showing that many voters were impressed by his probity or, at a minimum, that voters believed he was not different in this regard than the other leaders. The data gainsaid such interpretations.

A second, specific aspect of a leader's image merits consideration as well. As noted earlier, when making his case to lead the country, Harper relied heavily on the argument that he was the most competent on the economy. In previous elections, many voters had accepted the claim. For example, as Figure 13.8 illustrates, in 2011 more than one-third (37 percent) designated Harper as the best leader on the economy. In contrast, 21 percent cited Jack Layton and only 11 percent opted for Michael Ignatieff. These public impressions of the various leaders' competence on the economy shifted markedly in 2015. Figure 13.8 shows that those citing a belief in Harper fell to 28 percent, whereas nearly as many, 26 percent, opted for Justin Trudeau. And, despite his strenuous efforts to assure Canadians that he was a "safe pair of hands" when it came to managing the economy, Thomas Mulcair received the endorsement of only 14 percent — 7 percent less than Jack Layton had garnered four years earlier. Mulcair failed to make his case to lead the country on the economy, whereas Trudeau — castigated as "just not ready" in Conservative attack ads — was only 2 points behind Harper. The gap had narrowed both because Trudeau scored much better than his predecessor and because Harper's reputation for economic competence had been badly tarnished. Taken together, the leader image data painted a bleak picture of Prime Minister Harper. He was disliked by many voters, many thought he was less than honest, and many questioned his ability to manage the nation's economic affairs.

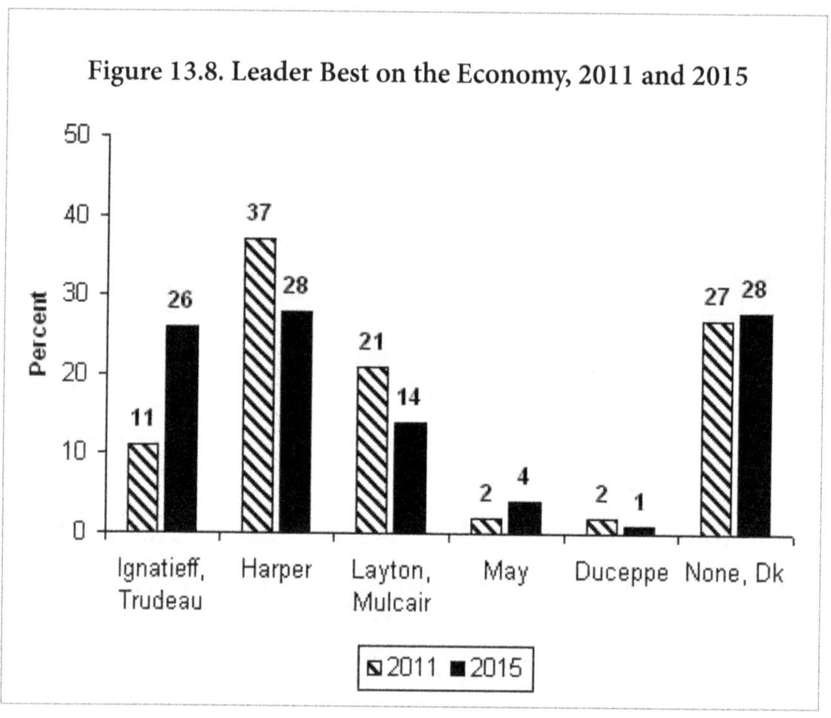


Source: 2011 Political Support in Canada post-election survey, 2015 Local Parliament Project pre-election survey.

## THE 2015 CAMPAIGN: DYNAMICS AND DEBATES

Although much of the data we are using for this chapter came from surveys at the very end of the campaign, there is evidence that party support exhibited consequential dynamics over the course of the 2015 election campaign. Extraordinarily long by Canadian standards, the campaign officially began on August 4 and ended on October 18. During this two-and-one-half-month period there were an unusually large number of leader debates, with Canadians being given five opportunities to learn about the leaders and their proposals to improve the lives of Canadians. From the viewpoint of political strategy, the length of the campaign and the governing Conservatives' willingness to participate in five debates merit comment. If given a choice, governing parties typically prefer short campaigns and as few leader debates as possible. Long campaigns and multiple debates give opposition parties numerous chances to introduce their leaders and policies to voters and exploit unforeseen events for partisan advantage. If at all possible, governing parties should not give their rivals these opportunities, or so the conventional wisdom goes.

A key premise underlying this belief is that governing parties are ahead in the polls when the election campaign begins. As Figure 13.9 shows, this was not the case in 2015. When the election writs were issued in early August, the CPC had a 31 percent vote intention share as compared to 33 percent for the NDP and 27 percent for the Liberals. Thirty-one percent was not a majority government number; indeed, it might not even be a minority government number. The Conservatives needed a long campaign to give themselves time to rebuild public support. Holding several debates would provide multiple opportunities for Harper to refurbish his image as the most competent leader and for his chief rivals, Mulcair and Trudeau, to make costly mistakes.

It was not to be. Soon after the campaign began, the NDP began to lose support — a downward trend that continued with only a minor pause right up to election day. In contrast, the Liberals inched upward, running neck-and-neck with the Conservatives until early October, when they started to move decisively ahead. When the campaign ended on October 18, polls showed the Liberals with 38 percent as compared to the NDP's dismal 20 percent. The Conservatives' 31 percent was exactly the same number with which they had started. Their attempt to benefit from a long campaign had failed (see Chapter 2).

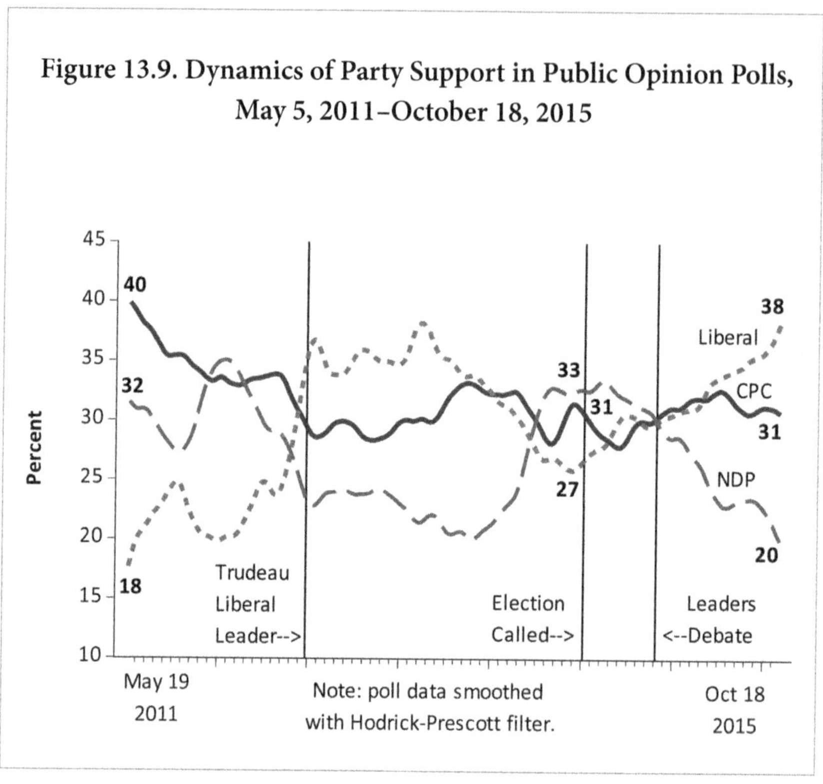


**Figure 13.9. Dynamics of Party Support in Public Opinion Polls, May 5, 2011–October 18, 2015**

Source: 359 public opinion polls published between May 5, 2011 and October 18, 2015.

Recognizing the importance of leader image, the Conservatives prepared for the election by crafting an attack ad on Justin Trudeau. Similar to ads used against Stéphane Dion in 2008 ("Not a Leader") and Michael Ignatieff in 2011 ("Just Visiting"), the anti-Trudeau ad questioned his credentials to lead Canada — noting that although he had "nice hair," he was "just not ready." The not-so-subtle message was that Trudeau was a "lightweight"; he may have inherited his father's famous name, but he lacked the experience and intellectual acumen required to lead the country. By framing their Liberal rival this way, Conservative strategists hoped to tarnish his image before the election began and create conditions that would magnify any miscues he might commit as the campaign unfolded. In particular, exposing Trudeau to five debates meant that there would be five chances for him to demonstrate that he was unsuited to be prime minister.

Of course, there was a danger. By casting Trudeau as junior varsity material, the Conservatives were setting the bar very low; if he defied predictions and performed reasonably well, voters might conclude that he was indeed ready to lead. Viewed in this light, five debates provided five opportunities for Trudeau to introduce himself to the electorate and make his case (see Chapter 3). NDP leader Thomas Mulcair would have the same opportunities.

Evidence from the Abacus pre-election survey shows that 39 percent watched or heard one or more of the debates.[8] This is not a huge number by historical standards, but, nevertheless, it represents a large share of the electorate. Analyses show that outside of Quebec, exposure to the debates had virtually no relationship with holding a favourable impression of Harper. The net balance of favourable versus unfavourable impressions for the Conservative leader in the rest of Canada was −1.6 percent, indicating that, when compared to the group of voters who had not seen or heard any of the debates, those who had seen or heard one or more debates were slightly more negatively disposed toward him. However, the net balance of positive impressions of Mulcair and, especially, Trudeau, moved in a positive direction among non-Quebecers exposed to one or more debates. In Mulcair's case, the balance was +5.8 percent and in Trudeau's it was a sizable +14.4 percent. The Quebec pattern was different. Harper's net balance of favourable and unfavourable impressions was negative, −5.2 percent, and Mulcair joined him with −7.0 percent. In sharp contrast, Trudeau's net balance in Quebec was highly positive, an impressive +21.7 percent.

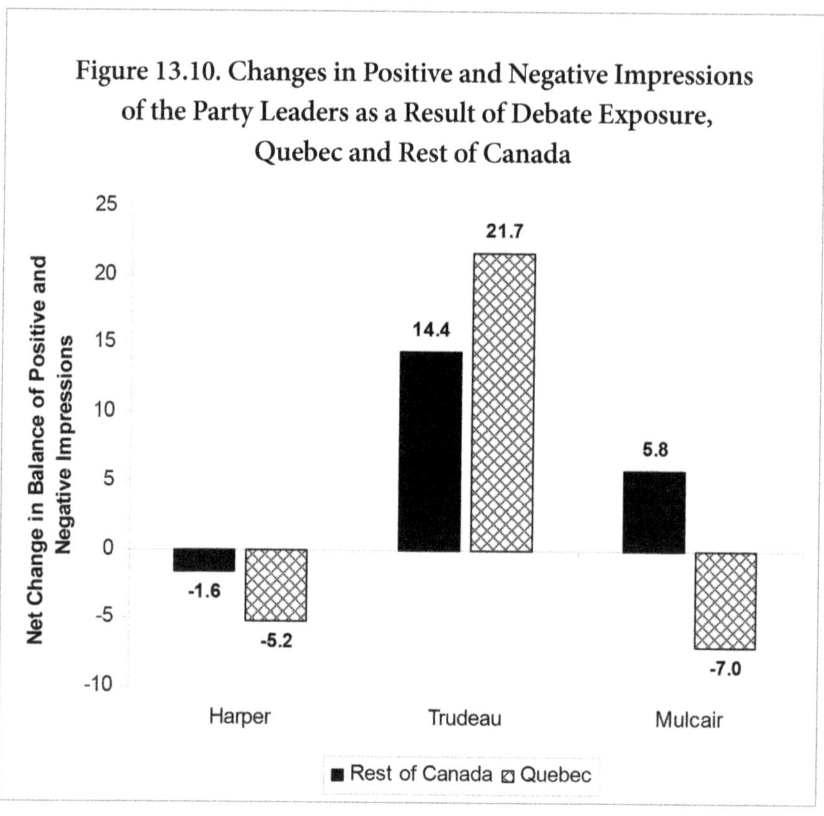


Source: 2015 Abacus pre-election survey.

Note: Numbers in the figure are percentage changes in favourable minus unfavourable impressions of party leaders among survey respondents seeing or hearing one or more debates compared to those not seeing or hearing any debates.

Although debate exposure is not the kind of randomized treatment extolled in research methodology texts, these numbers suggest that Trudeau used his debate opportunities to excellent advantage both in Quebec and the rest of Canada. In contrast, the result for Mulcair was mixed; he benefitted modestly outside of Quebec, but experienced a net loss in that province. For his part, Harper found no relief in the debates — debate exposure was associated with erosion in his net balance of favourable to unfavourable impressions among both Quebecers and other Canadians who watched or heard one or more debates as compared to people who did not view or listen to any of these events. Any hopes

Conservative strategists might have had that the debates would help to restore their leader's image while damaging the images of his opposition rivals went unfulfilled.

The long campaign also enhanced the potential for unexpected events to happen — events that could help or hurt one or more of the parties. On September 15, such an event occurred when an appeals court ruled that a Muslim woman did not have to remove her veil, or niqab, during the Canadian citizenship ceremony. The federal government quickly replied that it would appeal the decision to the Supreme Court and, if re-elected, would introduce a bill to make it binding to remove veils when a citizenship oath was administered. However, both the NDP and the Liberals supported the appeal court decision and, by so doing, put themselves at odds with the preponderance of public opinion. As Figure 13.11 illustrates, across Canada as a whole, 72 percent favoured making women remove veils during the citizenship ceremony. In Quebec, opinion was especially one-sided — fully 88 percent wanted the niqab removed — and New Democratic Party support in the province soon eroded. Interestingly, the Liberals, whose stance on the niqab was essentially the same as the NDP's, did not suffer a similar loss of support. In the aftermath of the niqab incident, both the Liberals and the Conservatives moved up slightly in national polls.

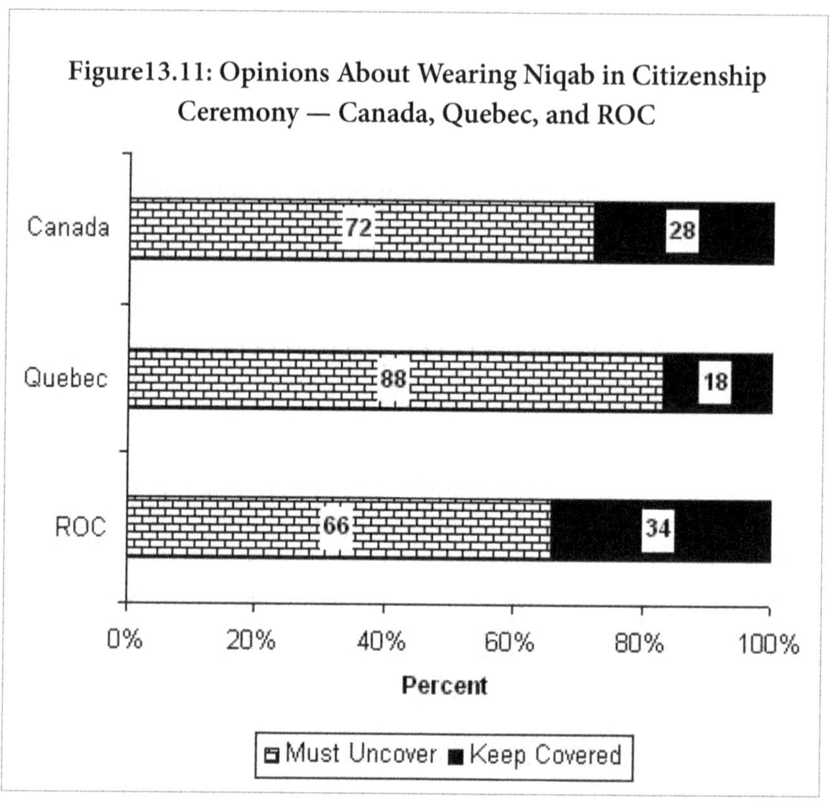


Source: 2015 Abacus pre-election survey.

Anxious to refocus the campaign narrative from the sluggish economy to issues that might prove more favourable to their party, Conservative strategists concluded that cultural concerns might be a good bet. In addition to wide opposition to the niqab, polls showed that many people, while sympathetic to Syrian refugees, did not want large numbers of them to settle in Canada. In the Abacus pre-election survey, only 21 percent wanted to admit a "lot more" refugees; 35 percent wanted to admit fewer, and 45 percent favoured the status quo. More general sentiments about helping minority cultures were more one-sided, with only 9 percent calling for the government to do more, 35 percent wanting to keep things as they are, and 55 percent desiring to give higher priority to building Canadian culture. There appeared to be a complex of cultural issues that, if they became salient, might benefit the CPC.

To focus public attention on these issues, the Conservatives announced in early October that they would establish a hotline where people could tip off the RCMP about "barbaric cultural practices." The ploy gained precious little traction. This is not surprising — as discussed above, only 4 percent of those in the Abacus pre-election survey mentioned the niqab or other cultural issues as their primary concern. Among those, a plurality designated the Conservatives as best able to handle the issue. However, this was only about 1.4 percent of the electorate — not anywhere close to what was needed to turn around the party's flagging campaign.

In the last two weeks of the campaign, numerous polls reported that the Liberals were pulling away from the pack. CPC strategists reacted by "jumping the shark," arranging for their leader to appear at two rallies with former Toronto mayor Rob Ford.[9] Having Harper on the same platform with someone who had gained notoriety for substance abuse while mayor of Canada's largest city was clearly an act of desperation. It did not work — the Conservatives continued to lose ground to the Liberals as the campaign drew to a close.

## MAKING POLITICAL CHOICES — 2015

Valence politics theory designates three explanatory variables — party identification, party competence on important issues, and leader image — as the key drivers of electoral choice. As noted earlier, the 2015 survey data indicate that the Conservatives and the Liberals were essentially tied in terms of their numbers of party identifiers. Similarly, only 2 points separated the two parties in terms of which one would do the best job on important issues. However, the Liberals had a decisive lead over the CPC when it came to leader image. NDP leader Thomas Mulcair also had a less positive image than Trudeau, and his party trailed both the Liberals and the Conservatives in terms of the size of its partisan cohort and perceptions of competence on key issues.

Multivariate statistical analyses enable us to determine how big the effects of these valence politics variables were on the choices voters made in 2015.[10] We examined voting for each of the parties in turn, with leader image, judgments about party competence on important issues, and party identification as predictors. The voting models also included controls for economic evaluations, a cultural issues index, left-right ideological orientations, and several socio-demographic characteristics (age, education, gender, income, region of residence). Results of the analyses were used to calculate how much the probability of voting for a particular party changed if a predictor variable moved from its lowest to its highest value while all other predictors were held at their means. These probabilities are displayed in Table 13.1.

**Table 13.1. Impact of Changes in Significant Predictors on Change in Probability of Voting Conservative, Liberal or NDP in the 2015 Federal Election**

| Predictor | Change in Probability of Voting Conservative | Change in Probability of Voting Liberal | Change in Probability of Voting NDP |
|---|---|---|---|
| **Party Identification:** | | | |
| Conservative | 0.20 | – 0.27 | – 0.11 |
| Liberal | | 0.17 | – 0.11 |
| NDP | – 0.13 | – 0.18 | 0.20 |
| Green | | –.27 | |
| BQ | – 0.23 | – 0.27 | – 0.12 |
| **Party Best Most Important Issue:** | | | |
| Conservative | 0.24 | – 0.34 | – 0.14 |
| Liberal | – 0.28 | 0.32 | – 0.19 |
| NDP | – 0.32 | – 0.33 | 0.38 |
| Green | – 0.23 | | |
| BQ | | | |
| **Leader:** | | | |
| Harper | 0.60 | – 0.28 | – 0.15 |
| Trudeau | – 0.32 | 0.68 | – 0.26 |
| Mulcair | – 0.16 | – 0.37 | 0.48 |
| May | – 0.16 | | – 0.11 |
| Duceppe | – 0.42 | – 0.25 | – 0.20 |
| McKelvey $R^2$ | 0.87 | 0.78 | 0.70 |
| Percentage of Party's Voters Correctly Classified | 96.5 | 90.2 | 92.0 |

Note: Voting models also include variables measuring economic evaluations, opinions about cultural issues, general left-right ideology, and controls for socio-demographic characteristics, including age, gender, education, income, and region of residence (Atlantic, Quebec French, Quebec Non-French, Prairies, British Columbia, with Ontario as reference category).

As shown, leader image, judgments about party performance on important issues, and party identification all had sizable effects on voting in 2015. Thus, as impressions of Harper moved from very negative to very positive, the probability of voting Conservative rose by 0.60 points on the 0-1 probability scale. As feelings about Mulcair moved from negative to positive, comparable increases in the likelihood of voting NDP were also substantial: 0.48 points. For the Liberals, the effects of changes in Trudeau's image were especially large, with the probability of voting Liberal going up by fully 0.68 points as his image moved from negative to positive.

Effects of perceived party competence on important issues and party identification were substantial as well. Shifts in trust from the Conservatives to the Liberals regarding which party was best able to effectively deal with the most important issue decreased the probability of voting CPC by 0.52 points (0.24 to −0.28). Similarly, such a shift increased the likelihood of voting Liberal by 0.66 points. As a third example, changing from NDP to Liberal on the question of which party was best able to deal with the most important issue boosted the chance of a Liberal vote by 0.57 points. As for party identification, Table 13.1 illustrates that, all else being equal, a shift from the NDP to the Liberals increased the likelihood of voting for the latter party by 0.35 points (−0.18 to 0.17). A shift from Liberal to New Democrat raised the probability of casting an NDP ballot by 0.31 points. Overall, although the effects of changes in partisanship were somewhat smaller than those associated with judgments about issue competence and leader image, the influence of party identification was important.

Viewed generally, the multivariate voting analyses testify to the importance of all three of the valence politics variables. Their joint explanatory power, as indexed on a 0–1 scale by the McKelvey $R^2$ statistic, varies from 0.70 to 0.78 to 0.87 in the NDP, Liberal, and CPC analyses, respectively. Percentages of voters classified correctly are also impressive, ranging from 90.2 percent for the Liberal model to 92.0 percent for the NDP model and to 96.5 percent for the Conservative one.

Overall, it is evident that leader image, evaluations of party performance on major issues, and partisan attachments combined in familiar ways to drive voting behaviour in 2015. Although the distributions of party identification and party performance judgments put the Conservatives and the Liberals in a virtual tie with the NDP trailing well behind, this was not true for leader image. When it came to feelings about the leaders, Justin Trudeau ranked ahead of Mulcair and, especially, Harper, who was heartily disliked by many voters. Given the demonstrated power of leader images to drive the vote, these positive feelings about Trudeau gave the Liberals the edge they needed to achieve a decisive electoral victory.

## FROM 2011 TO 2015: MAKING A MAJORITY

To learn more about the sources of party support in 2015, we conclude our empirical analyses by using the Abacus survey data to examine the distribution of the electoral choices Canadians made in terms of what they had done in the previous federal election. Table 13.2, Panel A, displays the percentages of people voting for various parties in 2015 in terms of how they voted in 2011. The votes of people who did not cast a ballot in 2011 are also included. Examining these numbers shows that the Liberals were most successful in retaining their support, with 80.7 percent of those who voted for the party in 2011 doing so again in 2015. The Conservatives were somewhat less successful, retaining 74.4 percent of their 2011 voters, while the NDP fared poorly, keeping only a small majority, 54.8 percent, of their 2011 supporters. Among 2011 non-voters, a substantial plurality, 38.3 percent, voted Liberal in 2015, with 25.2 and 24.9 percent, respectively, casting their ballots for the Conservatives or the NDP. Thus, the Liberals did considerably better than both of their major rivals in terms of holding on to previous supporters and attracting new ones.

## Table 13.2. The Flow of the Vote, 2011 to 2015

A. Where the 2011 Vote Went in 2015

| | 2011 Vote | | | | | |
|---|---|---|---|---|---|---|
| *2015 Vote* | CPC | Liberal | NDP | Greens | BQ | Non-Voter |
| CPC | 74.4 | 6.4 | 5.0 | 1.7 | 3.1 | 25.2 |
| Liberal | 17.4 | 80.7 | 30.9 | 39.7 | 10.8 | 38.3 |
| NDP | 5.9 | 11.2 | 54.8 | 22.4 | 16.2 | 24.9 |
| Greens | 1.9 | 1.0 | 3.2 | 34.5 | 0.8 | 7.8 |
| BQ | 0.4 | 0.8 | 6.1 | 1.7 | 69.2 | 3.8 |

B. Combinations of Party Support in 2011 and 2015 as Percentages of Everyone Voting in 2015

| | 2011 Vote | | | | | |
|---|---|---|---|---|---|---|
| *2015 Vote* | CPC | Liberal | NDP | Greens | BQ | Non-Voter |
| CPC | 21.1 | 1.0 | 1.0 | 0.0 | 0.2 | 7.4 |
| Liberal | 4.9 | 12.2 | 6.2 | 0.9 | 0.5 | 11.2 |
| NDP | 1.7 | 1.7 | 11.0 | 0.5 | 0.8 | 7.3 |
| Greens | 0.5 | 0.2 | 0.7 | 0.8 | 0.0 | 2.3 |
| BQ | 0.1 | 0.1 | 1.2 | 0.0 | 3.5 | 1.1 |

Panel B of Table 13.2 displays the percentage of all those voting in 2015 in terms of combinations of behaviour in the two elections. These percentages help us to calibrate the importance of various sources of Liberal support in 2015. Specifically, Panel B shows that 12.2 percent of all those voting in 2015 were people who had voted Liberal four years earlier. This total, well below the Conservatives, emphasizes the importance of new supporters for Liberal success. As Panel B also indicates, 4.9 percent of the 2015 voters were Conservatives moving to the Liberals and another slightly larger group (6.2 percent) was comprised of former New Democrats. Added together, these numbers indicate that 11.1 percent of everyone voting in 2015 cast Liberal ballots after supporting either the CPC or the NDP in 2011. Another 1.4 per cent of the 2015 Liberals were people who had cast Green or BQ ballots in 2011. In summary, the total flow to the Liberals in 2015 from former supporters of other parties was slightly larger than the size of the group of stable Liberal voters in the two elections.

Finally, Panel B shows that there was yet another important source of new Liberal support. As noted, in 2015 the Liberals gained a plurality of 2011 non-voters. This sizable group, 11.2 percent of everyone voting in 2015, was nearly equal to the percentages of stable Liberals and the total percentage coming to the Liberals from other parties. The 2015 Liberal coalition thus had three significant parts — 2011 Liberals, 2011 voters from other parties, and 2011 non-voters. Each of these three groups was sufficiently large to be crucial for giving the Liberals the vote total needed to obtain a parliamentary majority in 2015.

## CONCLUSION: SUNNY WAYS

As constituency results started to come in from the Atlantic provinces on the evening of October 19, it was quickly evident that a Liberal landslide was in the offing. When the ballots were counted, Justin Trudeau and his party had captured 39.5 percent of the vote, more than double the percentage the Liberals had won in 2011. Their win was impressive over much of the country, and enabled them to sweep all of the seats in the four Atlantic provinces and to capture the majority of seats in Ontario and Quebec. They also gained seat pluralities in Manitoba and British Columbia. Overall, the Liberals won 184 seats, sufficient to give them their first majority government in Ottawa since 2000.

In sharp contrast, both the Conservatives and the New Democrats suffered serious setbacks. The CPC's vote total fell from 39.6 to 31.9 percent, while the NDP's fell from 30.6 to 19.7 percent. Both parties lost large numbers of seats, with the Conservatives finishing with ninety-nine, sixty-seven fewer than they had won in 2011. For their part, the NDP won only forty-four seats, fifty-nine fewer than four years earlier. As in 2011, the Greens and the BQ remained decided also-rans, with the former keeping its only seat and the latter increasing its total from four to ten. Quite simply, everyone but the Liberals were losers.

In his election-night victory speech, Justin Trudeau, echoing Sir Wilfrid Laurier, spoke of the politics of "sunny ways." One hundred and twenty years earlier, Laurier had extolled the advantages of a politics of fairness and justice, and Trudeau claimed that running a campaign based on these themes and promising the real change needed to achieve them had enabled his party to sweep its rivals aside. Viewed in terms of issues, there is little evidence to support the new prime minister's assertion that fairness and justice mattered much. Rather, the sputtering economy was clearly the dominant concern in 2015. And, unlike the situation in the preceding election, many voters no longer believed that Conservative leader Stephen Harper was best qualified to manage Canada's economic affairs. Harper's "competence edge" on the economy over Trudeau was a mere 2 percentage points, far less than the 26-point lead Harper had enjoyed over Trudeau's predecessor, Michael Ignatieff, in 2011.

This is not to say that Trudeau enjoyed widespread confidence on the economy. One-quarter of the electorate endorsed him as the best economic manager, but three-quarters did not. Nevertheless, he did promise that help was on the way and he did sound credible. When asked about his economic policies, Trudeau articulated an orthodox Keynesian fiscal strategy involving modest deficits for three years to finance infrastructure projects and reduce unemployment, coupled with reduced taxes for the middle class and higher taxes for the wealthy. It may be that the Conservative "not ready" attack ad was correct and Trudeau really did not know Maynard Keynes (the renowned economist) from Milton Keynes (a city near London, England) but it did not matter — the electorate was receptive to an economic policy that promised action without gainsaying prudence. Trudeau argued that his party's plan would restore the country's economic good health without abandoning fiscal rectitude — deficits would be manageable and would end in three years. By changing the balance of the tax burden, the policy also enabled the Liberals to appeal to those voters, many of them potential NDP supporters, concerned about fairness and justice for working Canadians. Frightened of appearing fiscally irresponsible, the NDP had not coupled proposals for middle-class tax relief with deficit spending to create jobs. By doing both, Trudeau's plan reinforced the idea that the Liberals were the party of "real change."

Read in the context of events in the 2015 election campaign, Mr. Trudeau's "sunny ways" comments invite misinterpretation. Specifically, it might be concluded that that the Liberals attracted broad public support because of their stand on issues such as the niqab and Syrian refugees and their sympathetic attitudes toward cultural minorities more generally. Clearly, the Conservatives had tried to refocus the campaign away from the economy onto possible cultural and security threats posed by Muslim immigrants. Perhaps they played into the Liberals' hands by doing so.

There are two problems with this interpretation. First, as observed, survey data indicate that many Canadians opposed wearing the niqab in citizenship ceremonies, were reluctant to admit large numbers of Syrian refugees, and did not want to do more to support minority cultures. Second, cultural issues were not major concerns for most people. Less than one person in twenty ranked one of these issues as most important, and, of those who did, a plurality thought the Conservatives were the best party to address them. The Liberals' positions on issues such as the niqab may have been seen as a friendly and compassionate expression of the "sunny ways" Mr. Trudeau espoused, but they did not have much potential to help him harvest a large crop of votes, especially in Quebec. Equally, the Liberals' positions on these issues did not deter people from voting Liberal if they had other reasons to do so.

Leader image — a key heuristic in the valence politics model of electoral choice — did have that potential. As observed above, Trudeau's predecessor, Michael Ignatieff, had suffered a very chilly reception in 2011. Not only were Ignatieff's like-dislike scores low, but only about one person in ten thought that he would be the most competent leader on the economy. In contrast, although many voters were not enthusiastic about him, Conservative leader Stephen Harper was widely seen to have the "right stuff" needed to keep the country on a path to prosperity. In 2015, much had changed. Although, as discussed in Chapter 2, people had a variety of reasons to dislike Harper, the most significant negative for him was the flagging economy, which tarnished his image for competence, enabling Trudeau to almost match him in terms of perceived ability to handle this crucial issue. And, when it came to the affective dimension of leader image, Trudeau ran far ahead of his Conservative rival. Thomas Mulcair was much closer to Trudeau in this respect, but, unfortunately for him, his party trailed badly in terms of its number of party identifiers and judgments about its ability to handle important issues.

In the end, it was Justin Trudeau's superior image that provided the Liberals with the edge they needed to wrest power from Stephen Harper's

Conservatives. As the election campaign progressed, Trudeau demonstrated that he was, in fact, "ready" — he not only had name and fame, but game as well. Although Conservative attack ads had set a low bar by which to judge him, Trudeau performed well on the campaign trail by any reasonable standard. In his October 19 victory speech, Trudeau proudly argued that his success was a product of espousing "sunny ways." Certainly, voters' reactions to his candidacy were quite positive and, equally certain, they were highly consequential. Forty-seven years earlier, his father, Pierre Trudeau, had led the Liberals to a landslide victory in his initial campaign with the slogan "It's spring!" "Sunny ways" seems very suitable for a family encore.

## NOTES

1. The election survey data analyzed in this chapter were supplied by Abacus Data and the Local Parliament Project. The former data were gathered in a pre-election survey conducted immediately prior to the October 19, 2015, federal election. The latter were gathered in surveys conducted before and after that election. We wish to take this opportunity to thank David Coletto of Abacus Data and Peter Loewen and Daniel Rubenson of the Local Parliament Project for making their data available to us. Survey questionnaires are available at: www.thomasjscotto.co.uk
2. See, e.g., Harold D. Clarke, Jane Jenson, Lawrence LeDuc, and Jon Pammett, *Absent Mandate: Canadian Politics in an Era of Restructuring*, 3rd ed. (Toronto: Gage Educational Publishing, 1996); and Harold D. Clarke, Allan Kornberg, and Thomas J. Scotto, *Making Political Choices: Canada and the United States* (Toronto: University of Toronto Press, 2009).
3. See Donald E. Stokes, "Spatial Models of Party Competition," *American Political Science Review* 57 (1963): 368–77.
4. The basic statement of the "Michigan model" of voting behaviour is Angus Campbell, Philip E. Converse, Warren E. Miller, and Donald E. Stokes, *The American Voter* (New York: Wiley, 1960).
5. Harold D. Clarke and Allan McCutcheon, "The Dynamics of Party Identification Reconsidered," *Public Opinion Quarterly* 73 (2009): 704–28. See also Harold D. Clarke, Allan Kornberg, and Thomas J. Scotto, "The Valence Politics Model of Electoral Choice and Canadian Election Studies," in *Four Decades of Canadian Election Studies: Learning from the Past and Planning for the Future*, ed. Mebs Kanji and Thomas Scotto (Vancouver: UBC Press, 2012), ch. 10.
6. Harold D. Clarke, Jane Jenson, Jon Pammett, and Lawrence LeDuc, *Political Choice in Canada* (Toronto: McGraw-Hill Ryerson, 1979); Marianne C. Stewart and Harold D. Clarke, "The Dynamics of Party Identification in Federal Systems: The Canadian Case," *American Journal of Political Science* 42 (1998): 97–116.

7. See, e.g., Paul Whiteley, Harold D. Clarke, David Sanders, and Marianne C. Stewart, *Affluence, Austerity and Electoral Change in Britain* (Cambridge: Cambridge University Press, 2013); Harold D. Clarke, Euel Elliott, and Marianne C. Stewart, "Heuristics, Heterogeneity, and Green Choices: Voting on California's Proposition 23," *Political Science Research and Methods* 4 (2016): forthcoming.
8. For a detailed discussion of the 2015 leader debates and references to studies of the impact of debates on voting and election outcomes in Canada and elsewhere, see Chapter 10 in this volume.
9. The term "jump the shark" originated with the TV show *Happy Days*, which tried to revive flagging ratings by having one of the program's stars, Fonzie, jump a shark while water skiing. As now used, the term signifies an act of desperation that seems bound to fail.
10. Binomial logit analyses are conducted with voting for each of the five parties treated as dichotomies (e.g., vote Conservative = 1, vote for another party = 0). Predictor variables in the statistical models include leader image, party judged best on most important issue, party identification, economic evaluations, cultural issue index, left-right ideological orientations, and socio-demographic characteristics (age, education, gender, income, region of residence). Information regarding variable construction is available at www.thomasjscotto.co.uk. On logit analysis, see, e.g., J. Scott Long and Jeremy Freese, *Regression Models for Categorical Dependent Variables Using Stata*, 3rd ed. (College Station, TX: Stata Corporation, 2014).

# CHAPTER 14

## The Fall of the Harper Dynasty

Jon H. Pammett and Lawrence LeDuc

The 2015 election drew the Stephen Harper era in Canadian federal politics to a close. His Conservative Party was in government for almost ten years, having taken power in early 2006. Harper's Conservatives won three elections, achieving minorities of the seats in 2006 and 2008 and a majority in 2011. The Harper dynasty was established in a somewhat unusual manner, with a slow building of support rather than a dramatic initial victory. The dynasty also ended in an unusual manner, with a slow bleeding away of support during a campaign in which the Conservatives were widely perceived to be leading much of the time, only to be overcome with a surge of support for the Liberals as the long campaign moved into its final stages.

### DYNASTIES AND INTERLUDES

Having won three consecutive elections and held office for nearly a decade, Stephen Harper's Conservatives met all of the tests that we have applied in identifying other periods of dominance by parties and leaders over the course of Canadian history.[1] Harper's tenure in office was nearly equal to that of Jean Chrétien, who, together with Paul Martin, formed the preceding dynasty. The Harper dynasty formed the sixth such period of dominance so documented, and only the second Conservative dynasty in Canadian history. Whether the Liberals under Justin Trudeau will be able to establish a regime of comparable duration is a question beyond the scope of this chapter and can only be addressed following a subsequent federal election, which could provide a test of the durability of some of the trends observed in 2015. In this chapter, we will consider some of the factors that led to both the rise and the fall of the Harper dynasty. By examining not only the outcome of the 2015 election but also those of 2006, 2008, and 2011, we can identify some of the factors that led both to Harper's electoral successes and to his party's eventual defeat.

Canadian federal politics has repeatedly followed a pattern of long periods of political hegemony under electorally successful political leaders, sometimes punctuated by interludes of varying duration. The dynasties achieved their dominance and longevity not only as a result of the personal appeal of their leaders but also because of their ability to capture a degree of public trust on the three main issue areas that are nearly always present in Canadian electoral politics. These three "keys to victory" have been:

1. to be perceived by the public as the leader and party best able to deal with the key *economic* questions of the time;
2. to have the ability to ensure *national unity*;
3. and, (at least since the mid-twentieth century) to gain public confidence on the issue of expanding or preserving the *social safety net* provided by the key elements of the modern welfare state — e.g., health care, pensions, unemployment insurance — on which large numbers of Canadians depend.

It was never an easy task for Stephen Harper to reposition his party in these three critical areas and thus to gain power. But, following the merger of the Progressive Conservative and Canadian Alliance parties in 2003, the new party achieved modest gains in its first (2004) election, winning 30 percent of the vote and 99 of the 308 seats.

More importantly, the Liberals under Paul Martin were reduced to a minority in that election, thus assuring that another federal election would soon follow. Having learned a number of important lessons from the 2004 defeat, Harper continued to advance the repositioning of the party in each of the three core issue areas. Helped by the damage to the Liberals wrought by the sponsorship scandal, the Conservatives made short-term but realistic commitments in the economic realm (GST cuts) and the welfare area (money to cut hospital wait times and support child care). They also put forward an opening to Quebec that sought to reposition themselves as a party of national unity, and they avoided discussion of many potentially divisive social issues. These efforts bore fruit, and the party was able to achieve a minority government in 2006 with 36 percent of the vote and 124 seats. That total included a surprising 25 percent of the vote in Quebec, which yielded ten Conservative seats in that province. However tentatively, the Harper era in federal politics had begun.

The 2008 election provided the first electoral test of the Harper dynasty, but it was only a partial success for the Conservatives. Their share of the vote rose to 37.6 percent and they gained an additional nineteen seats. However, the government remained a minority, in part because it had fallen back somewhat in its positioning in all three of the key issue areas. While the economy appeared to continue to work to their advantage, the uncertainties introduced by the global economic crisis placed even that area at risk as the financial crisis in the United States accelerated during the 2008 campaign.[2] In the more successful 2011 election campaign, a modest economic recovery and the implementation of a program of fiscal stimulus (the "Economic Action Plan") positioned the Conservatives more favourably in this area. They also managed to at least neutralize any advantage that the other parties had held in the social welfare area with repeated commitments to protect the provincial transfers for health care. Only in the national unity area, as the 2006 breakthrough in Quebec receded, did the Conservatives fall short of meeting the standards established by other successful dynasties. But their dominance in two other regions — the West and Ontario, together with the Liberals' inability to re-establish their position in Quebec given the continued strength of the Bloc, at least neutralized this factor.

The Harper dynasty was similar to some others, particularly that of Chrétien/Martin, in that it depended in part for its success on a divided and relatively weak opposition. The Conservatives owed their majority outcome in 2011 largely to the party's substantial gains in Ontario, with a net gain in that province of twenty-one seats over the 2008 result. Most of these were in the Greater Toronto Area, a highly significant breakthrough in comparison with the party's rather dismal showing in urban areas in its three previous elections.[3] The result was an overall majority of 166 seats, but one achieved with less than 40 percent of the total vote.

FIGURE 14.1

Six Dynasties and Seven Interludes in Canadian Politics

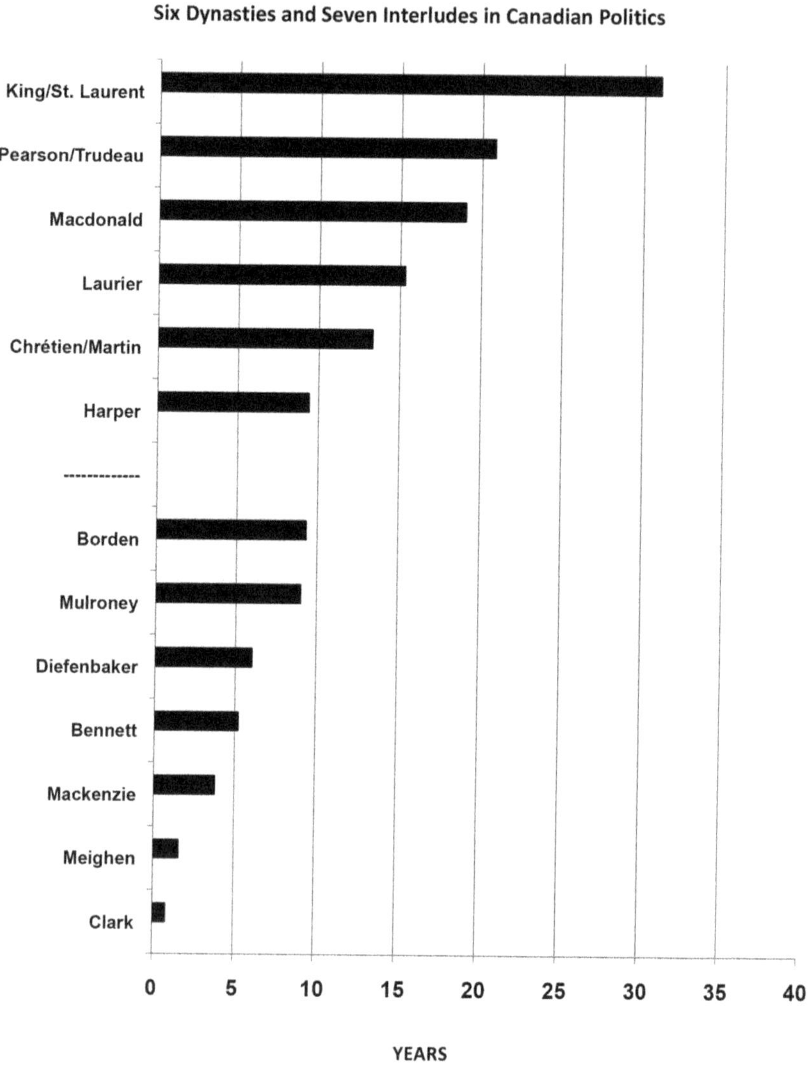


## ESTABLISHING A DYNASTY

The establishment of the six dynasties highlighted in Figure 14.1 was not a simple matter. While each began with an election victory — not always a decisive one — the new electoral pattern established in that election was tested in the one following. Often, given the inherent volatility of

Canadian electoral politics, the existence of a dynasty cannot be confirmed until a third election has demonstrated the staying power of both the party and its leader. In the cases of both Mackenzie King and Pierre Trudeau, the test that occurred after their initial election was a dramatic one. King, whose initial victory in 1921 was at the head of a minority government, lost the election of 1925, but managed to remain in power for eight months before yielding to Arthur Meighen, whom he defeated more decisively in the subsequent (1926) election. Pierre Trudeau's election victory in 1968 was followed by near defeat in 1972. Only after his political recovery in the 1974 election would it have been possible to discern the shape and durability of that dynasty. Such patterns suggest that, to understand electoral politics in Canada, it is essential not to put too much emphasis on the interpretation of a single election. Instead, it is important to place elections within the context of a somewhat longer and more complex process of political and social change.

These periods of electoral dominance, often identified with the fortunes of individual political leaders, are truly long ones by comparative standards. In the forthcoming edition of our book *Dynasties and Interludes*, we pose two questions to discover the reasons for these patterns in Canadian politics: What explains these patterns of enduring political success enjoyed by Canadian political leaders, and by the parties that they led? The stark contrast between the dynasties and the brief interludes that often intervened tells much of the story of Canadian federal politics as it has evolved over nearly a century and a half. A second question therefore is: Can we explain how and why these interludes occurred, even in some instances when the dynasties that they toppled appeared secure?

Part of the answer to these questions is found in the cases that do not fit quite so neatly into our typology of "dynasties and interludes." Lester Pearson served five years as prime minister, and his tenure in office is highly regarded by historians today, in part because of the significant policy achievements of his administration. But Pearson endured one of the worst electoral defeats in Canadian history at the hands of John Diefenbaker in 1958, and he never succeeded in obtaining a majority of parliamentary seats in the two elections that he won (1963 and 1965). Nevertheless, he managed to pass the reins of power to a successor who presided over one of the more enduring political dynasties of recent times.

Do we think then of a "Pearson interlude" or a "Pearson/Trudeau dynasty," as is suggested by the configuration employed in Figure 14.1 and as we have argued in *Dynasties and Interludes*? Neither term captures with total accuracy the high and low points, the successes and failures, of the Pearson and Trudeau eras. But, with the benefit of hindsight, we can see that the longevity of the Pearson/Trudeau dynasty rivals those of Macdonald and Laurier, even though neither Pearson nor Trudeau enjoyed unqualified political success over the course of his own political career.

The fortunes of two other political leaders who fell short of establishing dynasties can also help us formulate part of the answer to the questions posed above. John Diefenbaker and Brian Mulroney led the Progressive Conservative Party to two of its greatest electoral victories, in 1958 and 1984 respectively, but neither was able to found a political dynasty based on that initial success. Diefenbaker's six-year tenure as prime minister ended with his party's defeat in 1963. Mulroney's two terms culminated in the near destruction of his party in the 1993 election. But both leaders left a political legacy that endured long after their time in office had ended. Diefenbaker bequeathed to his successors a solidly Conservative West and Mulroney a more nationalist Quebec. In part, the huge and unwieldy electoral coalitions that these two leaders built explain both their initial success and their ultimate failure. In the longer term, holding these diverse coalitions together proved more difficult than constructing them in the first place.

---

The evolution of the Harper dynasty was more incremental. It was Preston Manning who established the Reform Party in the West, but he was unable to extend that success significantly beyond his regional base. Under the banner of Reform's successor party, the Canadian Alliance, Stockwell Day did somewhat better, obtaining 24 percent of the vote in Ontario in the 2000 federal election; however, that translated to only two seats in that province. With the merger of the Alliance and Progressive Conservative parties, Harper was well positioned to build on these previous efforts. Aided by the sponsorship scandal in 2004, the Conservatives' vote share in Ontario improved to 31 percent, yielding twenty-four parliamentary seats.

Nearly all of those were in rural areas of the province. The 2006 election, which brought the party to power, was partially a result of the party's breakthrough in Quebec. Thus, each election saw the Conservatives adding another building block, while at the same time retaining most of the gains realized previously. One of the weaknesses of the Conservatives in the 2006 and 2008 elections had been their failure to win a seat in any of Canada's three largest cities. This was overcome in 2011, when the party achieved a breakthrough in Toronto, taking a number of urban seats previously held by Liberals.

## THE KEYS TO VICTORY

The main argument in *Dynasties and Interludes* is not focused on partisan "alignments" per se; rather, it deals the various ways that Canadian political parties structure the choices available to the voter in an election. Canadian parties have always had considerable freedom in this regard because they have typically tended to eschew long-term ideological commitments and are thus better able to manoeuvre strategically in choosing issues and emphases in an election campaign. The particular ways in which parties attempt to structure the voting choice in any given election are often dependent on short-term, strategic choices of issues and the appeal of the current party leaders.[4] However, the parties are not totally free to structure electoral choice in any way that they wish. They are constrained by a set of factors traditionally associated with the Canadian political landscape, and which commonly recur in some form from one election to the next. They must be well positioned on the key economic questions of the time, have public confidence on issues of national integration, and, in modern times, be in favour of expanding, or at least preserving, the essential elements of the welfare state.

Lest we think that these three factors are of recent vintage, consider that André Siegfried, writing at the beginning of the twentieth century about elections in Canada, identified a remarkably similar set of essential issues, the first of which he described as "the prosperity of the country."[5] Today, we would refer to "the economy" in this context, but the meaning is essentially the same. While the specific issues arising in this area are not always the same ones in every election, the more general issue of economic performance is invariably central to any election campaign, particularly so for incumbent governments seeking re-election.

Siegfried's second issue cluster — "the defence of race or religion" — sounds antiquated today, yet divisions arising around matters of language, region, ethnicity, or religion must always be managed effectively in any federal election campaign in Canada. In practice, this has meant structuring a party's electoral appeal across regional and societal divisions. The accommodation of Quebec has been the most important of these historically, but in the multicultural Canada of today, other divisions and potential cleavages are equally important. The Reform Party of the 1990s was capable of achieving only limited electoral success with an appeal structured largely around Western grievances. In contrast, Harper's Conservative Party of Canada was successful in broadening its appeal beyond that region without sacrificing its solid support in the West.

The third factor that we identify as essential in successful electoral campaigns is the need to extend, maintain, improve, or defend the welfare state. This issue area represents a more modern extension of the emphasis that Siegfried, in the era in which he was writing, placed on "public works." The modern variation on this theme stems from the policy consensus forged after the Great Depression of the 1930s, which established the belief that it was a responsibility of the state to provide a "social safety net."[6] During and after the Second World War, a number of programs were put in place to create such a framework — unemployment insurance, welfare, health insurance, medicare, and pensions. Not all of these programs were established by the federal government, and their implementation often involved controversy. However, their popularity with the public meant that support for them has needed to be stated with assurance by political parties during election campaigns, regardless of any desires they might harbour for substantially changing or even replacing such programs. The incorporation of welfare-state measures into their election strategies is the price that mainstream parties have had to pay to prevent sharp class divisions from arising in Canadian elections.[7]

The accusation by the Liberals in the 2004 election campaign that the Conservative Party of Canada under Stephen Harper had a "hidden agenda" favouring tax cuts at the expense of social programs was meant to exploit a public perception that the Conservatives were hostile to such programs. Any attack on the welfare state, which might be in the policy plans of politicians, cannot easily be acknowledged in elections, even in the name of fiscal prudence, without serious electoral repercussions. The Harper Conservatives learned this lesson well following their experience in the 2004 election campaign. Thereafter, they sought to provide firm assurances of their commitments in the social welfare area, particularly with respect to health care and pensions.

Siegfried, as well as nearly all other analysts of Canadian electoral politics of the past two centuries, also recognized the central role that leaders play in this process of structuring a party's appeal and credibility in each of the three core issue areas. From the time of Macdonald and Laurier to the present, the leader has been the central figure by which the party communicates its message to voters over the course of an election campaign. Thus, a leader who appeals only to one region of the country, or who lacks credibility in the social welfare or economic areas, is less likely to be successful in the federal electoral arena. Stephen Harper managed to overcome both real and potential limitations in each of the three areas during his tenure as leader of the Conservative Party and prime minister. But, as we will argue in the following sections of this chapter dealing with each of the three core issue areas, both accumulated weaknesses and strategic missteps in each of the three areas contributed to his defeat in the 2015 election and to the end of the Harper dynasty.

## THE ECONOMY

Governing parties, although they must invariably defend their own economic policies and performance, are not always in full control of the economic agenda. In today's globalized world, external economic shocks, or problems emanating from trade imbalances or structural deficits, can easily derail even the most carefully planned campaign strategies. In the wake of the economic crisis of 2008–09, governing parties in Europe and elsewhere suffered substantial electoral losses in elections following, and a number of these parties were removed from office by the voters.[8] The extensive literature on "economic voting" considers both its "retrospective aspects, i.e., evaluating the performance of a governing party, *and* its "prospective" components, i.e., choosing among the alternative economic policies or programs put forward by competing parties.[9]

At the beginning of the 2015 campaign, the Conservatives believed that they had a substantial advantage over the other parties in both of these areas of economic performance. This was not because the economy was in particularly good shape but rather because they felt that their Economic Action Plan, brought in belatedly in the wake of the 2008–09 economic crisis, had effectively guided the Canadian economy through a period of severe recession. The Conservatives promoted the plan extensively in pre-election advertising, maintaining that their economic stewardship had indeed been successful, particularly in comparison to that of other G7 countries. They also believed that they could effectively isolate and demonize the other parties on the prospective side of the economic issue. The NDP was portrayed as a party of big spenders, whose policies would bankrupt the country, or who would impose large tax increases to pay for their social welfare programs such as subsidized daycare. The Liberals at first were not the primary target of these types of attacks, in part because of the perceived inexperience of their leader and their lower standing in the polls. However, the Liberals and NDP could both be denigrated in much the same way. If they chose to spend more without increasing taxes, they were irresponsible, and if they chose to tax, they would inflict damage on a fragile economy. The Conservatives made much of themselves as the party of balanced budgets and responsible economic management, going so far as to pass a piece of legislation making future balanced budgets mandatory and promising to extend this legislation to a prohibition on tax increases if re-elected.

The Liberals and NDP chose to counteract the Conservative dismissal of their credibility on the larger economic issues in different ways. The NDP insisted that they would balance the budget in each year, no matter what the circumstances — a position designed to outflank the Conservatives on the issue of economic responsibility and sound management. They did not just take that position with respect to their own proposals but also attacked the Conservatives for running deficits in seven of their eight budgets, despite the fact that they had urged them to do so in the first place, when the Conservatives' initial stand-pat position following the 2008 financial crisis was deemed inadequate.

The Liberals, in a move thought of at the time as risky, conceded that they would not try to balance the federal budget at all for three years but, rather, would run what they referred to as "modest deficits of $10 billion a year" in order to free up resources to fund their commitment to increased spending on infrastructure and a "middle-class tax cut." The Liberals calculated that this position would support an activist stance during the campaign, helping to counteract the claim that they were not ready to govern. But it also seemed, in ideological terms, to position the Liberals to the left of the NDP. If they could show that there was a lot that they wanted to do, they could portray themselves as the true progressives in a battle with the NDP over who could provide a clear alternative to the Harper Conservatives. They accompanied this positioning with an election slogan of "Real Change," which emphasized the "change" theme as well as a sense of genuineness (compared with the NDP, who they continually accused of "balancing Harper's budget").

The Conservatives campaigned on the premise that they were not just the party of fiscal responsibility when it came to spending but also the party of low taxes. However, the only major new tax proposal they put forward was a commitment to allow income splitting for couples with children — a technically complex plan that would benefit only families in certain situations. Their overall position on tax issues was in strong contrast to that of the Conservative campaign of 2006 in which they had come to power. In that election, the Conservatives promised a cut of 2 percent to the GST, an effective tactic that served to bring the issue home to a much wider cross-section of people. By 2015, however, any political credit that they may have received for this move was well in the past.

The trade agreements that had been negotiated by the Conservatives during the tenure of their majority were also cited as prominent examples of economic competence. But the free trade agreement with the European Union had not yet been ratified, and the Trans-Pacific Partnership (TPP) involving twelve countries was still in the process of negotiation. When the conclusion of the TPP negotiations was announced late in the campaign, the Conservatives' attempt to take credit for this achievement was quickly overtaken by controversies about the actual content of the agreement.

The Liberal strategy was aided substantially by the unprecedented length of the campaign, called at the beginning of August for an election in mid-October. The Conservatives' assumption in producing a campaign of this length was that voters would gradually come around to the conclusion that they were the best alternative, given the uncertain effects of the other parties' proposed policies on the economy. Unfortunately for them, however, this long campaign period provided an opportunity for the Liberals' activist campaign to slowly gain publicity and momentum, as many voters concluded that they did not want to stay the course with Harper and used the additional time to sort out which of the two opposition alternatives they might prefer. The initial Conservative judgment that the Liberals, not the NDP, were the main threat turned out to be accurate.

**Figure 14.2**
**Quarterly Percentage Growth in GDP, 2012–2015**

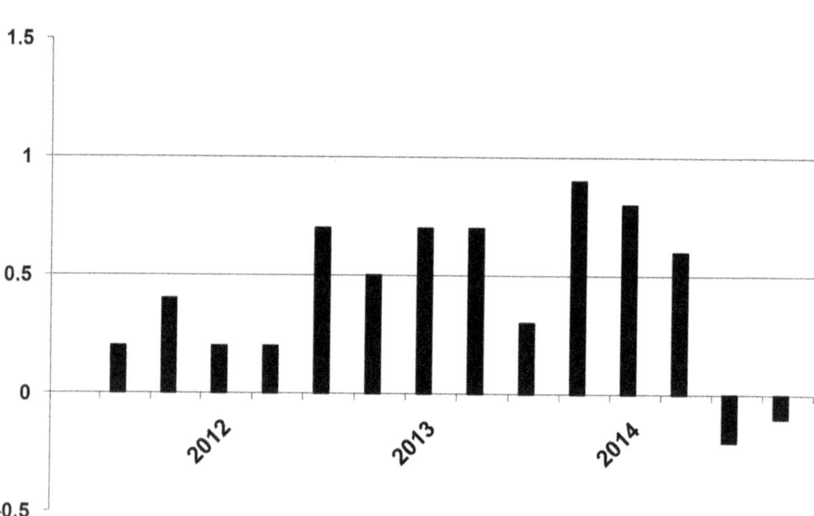


With hindsight, the Conservatives' belief that they held an advantage over other parties in both the retrospective and prospective areas of economic policy and performance proved to be something of a delusion. Because of the economic after-effects of the long and deep recession, the Harper era had proven to be a time of, at best, weak economic growth. By the onset of the campaign, the Canadian economy was once again teetering on the brink of recession, generally defined by economists as two consecutive quarters of negative GDP growth (Figure 14.2). The Conservatives' claim of superior economic management in the retrospective sense simply did not ring true, especially when coupled with seven consecutive budget deficits.

The health of the economy was also blindsided by the sudden fall in oil prices that occurred in the year prior to the election. This was particularly damaging, given the strong association of the governing party with the continued evolution of a resource-based economy. While the government could hardly be blamed for the collapse in oil prices, this development nevertheless undermined their claim that the economy was fundamentally in good shape and that the government deserved credit retrospectively for its economic success. Neither did the Conservatives have any specific policy proposals to put forward to deal with this new set of economic challenges. The announcement of the signing of the Trans-Pacific Partnership in the final days of the campaign simply introduced another element of economic uncertainty into an already disorienting set of new economic realities.

Accompanying the decline in oil prices was the rapid fall in the value of the Canadian dollar, which declined significantly in value over the course of the campaign. While a cheaper dollar can bring economic benefits to some sectors, it also brings hardship to others, and the Harper Conservatives made little or no attempt to put forward any policy arguments in this area. To the casual observer, as well as the voter, the deeply diminished dollar looked like one more area of dissonance in the Conservatives' continued assertion of greater economic competence.[10]

## NATIONAL UNITY

One of the keys to electoral success in Canadian federal politics has always been the ability of a party to capture the issue area we have called "national unity." This deceptively simple term can have multiple dimensions, and only occasionally emerges as an overt "most important issue" for large numbers of people. The most frequent association is with the territorial dimensions of the concept. The ability to bring diverse geographical parts of the country together so that they share a feeling of belonging to a national community is a skill that has rewarded some of Canada's most prominent political leaders.

As with the other important key issue areas in Canadian federal elections — the economy and social welfare — the process of building regional or linguistic inclusiveness has generally been supported in some form by all political parties that hope to form government. The main battle between the parties, therefore, has been over which one can claim "ownership" of the issue, in the sense of being perceived as the most likely to advance regional interests and/or be able to bring the country together. Specific investments in the economies of provinces or regions are often proposed during an election campaign in an attempt to position a party as the one most likely to gain public approval in the national unity area, while other parties will often mirror or even try to outdo such promises. Just as important are symbolic measures, such as the recognition of Quebec as a "distinct society" contained in the Mulroney government's Meech Lake and Charlottetown Accord proposals or the Harper government's resolution recognizing the Québécois as a nation within Canada in 2006.

The long-standing Liberal advantage on national unity issues over much of Canada's history originated with the prime ministership of Wilfrid Laurier and the negative images in Quebec of the Conservatives stemming from the First World War. In recent decades, however, the Liberal advantage in this area diminished and disappeared, partly due to fallout from failed constitutional initiatives and the 1995 Quebec sovereignty referendum. The Liberals under Jean Chrétien were unable to counteract continued support for the Bloc Québécois in federal elections or the Parti Québécois provincially. The federal sponsorship program was designed to promote the federal government in Quebec and repair some of the relations damaged by the referendum campaign. However, it erupted into a major financial scandal that dominated the political scene well into the mid-2000s. Any advantage that the Liberal Party once had in the area of Quebec-Canada relations was totally gone by 2011, an election that saw the party, then led by Michael Ignatieff, submerged in the province of Quebec by a tide of New Democratic Party MPs elected in areas that had formerly supported Liberals. In the 2011–2015 period, the NDP attempted to use its Official Opposition status, and its large number of new Quebec MPs, to stake out a position as the new champion of national unity. A key factor in the outcome of the 2015 election was its ultimate failure to accomplish this.

In its strategic plan for the 2015 campaign, the Liberal Party put forward several positions and promises designed to reassert its historic advantage in the national unity area, broadly defined. These advanced the party's claims in both the traditional regional and linguistic bases mentioned above and also several other dimensions that positioned the party as a more inclusive entity than the others.

On the general valence interpretation of national unity, the positive tone of the campaign, refraining from attacks that pitted individuals and groups against each other, presented the Liberals as different from not only Conservatives, who had defined this tone with a series of attack advertisements against Trudeau, but also from the NDP, which was desperate to hold on to its perceived status as the main alternative choice to the Conservatives. Trudeau was also determined not to respond to personal attacks in kind, but rather used them as a springboard for Liberal advertisements asserting that he was "ready" to accomplish the change that was the catchphrase of their campaign.

Alienated groups of people and their sympathizers (scientists, academics, advocacy groups, fans of public broadcasting, First Nations) were assured that their voices would be heard under a Liberal government. The "change" theme, which has been used by opposition parties on numerous occasions, was given a slightly different twist. People who had felt excluded during the Harper regime had a figure with whom they could identify with, and were encouraged to declare their readiness for change by supporting the Liberals. Trudeau was going to run an administration that countered the Conservatives' anti-intellectual policies of the previous nine years.

The relentless emphasis on the "middle class" by both the NDP and Liberal campaigns tried to portray this group, even though most of the population self-identified as members, as being left out of Conservative decision making. The Conservatives, of course, had featured benefits for the middle class in all their campaigns, including 2015. But in government they were unable to counter a feeling by many that the middle class had been left behind when various benefits were being distributed.

The traditional territorial dimension of national unity was further addressed by promises of consultation with provincial governments, particularly at the level of first ministers' meetings, which had been shelved during the Harper administration. Rather than simply imposing a payment to the provinces for health and education transfers, as the Conservatives had done, Trudeau promised to consult and negotiate with the provinces, starting with a new health-care agreement. In Quebec, these promises were interpreted as a recognition of the importance of provincial governments, and a potential commitment to an active role for government more generally, both directions downplayed under the Conservatives. In Ontario, in particular, the intergovernmental consultation included expansion of public pension programs, a subject on which the provincial government had decided to act unilaterally, partly because of the hostility of the Conservative federal government to any expansion in this area.

The intergovernmental consultation promised by the Liberals was nowhere more in evidence than in the field of environmental policy, an area of low priority for the Conservatives. Not only had Harper failed to act on the environment at the federal level in meaningful ways, he had refused to convene or attend meetings with the provinces on this subject and had downplayed Canadian co-operation in international initiatives. The Liberals were certainly not alone in castigating the Conservatives on the issue of environmental degradation; the NDP and Green parties had environmental platforms arguably stronger than the Liberal one. However, the Liberals positioned themselves on this issue better than the others, partly because their willingness to run a budget deficit allowed them to promise money for specific actions with more credibility. This area, like any in which money would have to be spent, was one in which the deficit plank in their platform freed them from attacks that any action would undermine the goal of attaining a balanced budget or require the imposition of new taxes. And the environment was a strategically chosen area of common interest and concern across the country.

Another example of issues important in the national unity area had to do with relations between the Canadian government and Aboriginal communities. Once again, these relations had deteriorated during the Harper period, as manifested most vividly by the seeming indifference of the government to the numerous instances of murders and disappearances of Aboriginal women in the western provinces. The Liberals promised to accede to requests to convene a public inquiry to investigate this situation, something that the Harper government had refused to do. The NDP made the same promise. However, in this area, the Liberals were building on a positive past reputation with Native groups established by both Jean Chrétien (who had been a well-liked minister of Indian affairs) and Paul Martin, who had negotiated the Kelowna Accord with Aboriginal groups prior to the 2006 election, an agreement that was promptly cancelled by Harper on assuming office.

In addition to these traditional areas of accommodation, two new issues emerged during the 2015 election campaign that we consider to be part of the national unity issue cluster. Once again, both the Liberals and the NDP took similar positions on them, diametrically opposed to the Conservatives, but it was the Liberals who managed to become associated with these in the public perception. The first involved refugees from the military conflicts in Syria. When the dramatic increase in refugees leaving Syria occurred toward the beginning of the campaign, and European countries began admitting large numbers of these, the Canadian government appeared largely indifferent to the seriousness of the situation and could be seen as lacking compassion and urgency. The Liberal promise to admit twenty-five thousand refugees by the end of the year if elected caught the public imagination and set the government scrambling. The Conservatives' response was to play up possible security problems, which they maintained were the real issue of national concern, but the public reaction characterized these as minor and petty and supported more direct and quicker action. Action to admit refugees involved a number of elements of national unity, including federal-provincial co-operation, work with churches and other sponsoring groups, recognition of multiculturalism, and a strengthening of the bonds of community. Added to this was the Liberal commitment to increasing immigration for purposes of family reunification, something that had been demanded by immigrant groups for a long time, and which had been downplayed by the Conservatives.

The second issue was the position that the Liberals and NDP both took with regard to a court decision allowing Muslim women to wear the niqab at citizenship ceremonies. The Conservatives and Bloc Québécois argued that the full face of these women needed to be visible during the ceremony, not just during the identification process that took place earlier. They presented this as a requirement for equality, and as somehow relating to security, but the court decision ruled that veiling was acceptable. By supporting the women's rights, the Liberals were invoking the spirit of the Charter of Rights and Freedoms (established by Trudeau's father), the rights of women, the right of religious expression, and a commitment to the diversity of Canadian society. This issue, unlike most other national unity issues, was a more controversial one, as public opinion was supportive of required unveiling. But in Quebec, where the issue received more attention, it was the NDP that most suffered from this controversy, and the Liberals managed to still gain votes there for other reasons.

Ironically, the Conservatives, although they lost the election, did manage to regain some of their previous support in Quebec, winning twelve seats, albeit with only 15 percent of the vote in the province. The Bloc Québécois also enjoyed something of a resurgence, winning ten seats, even though its total vote (19 percent) was four percent less than it had received in 2011. But surface evidence suggests that the Liberals' positioning on many of the national unity issues discussed here was more successful, as they won some seats in every province, including four in Alberta. In Quebec, their total of forty of the seventy-eight seats, achieved with 36 percent of the vote in the province, demonstrated that the party could once again assert its claim to be the preferred party of national unity.

## SOCIAL WELFARE

The third issue area in which political parties regularly compete in Canadian federal elections is the one that we have broadly termed "social welfare." Prominent in this area in recent years has been the health-care system, with its ancillary subjects of elder care, maternal health, drug costs, et cetera. This issue area also includes other social programs, such as pensions, poverty reduction, child care, housing, and education. Initiatives in these areas are prominent parts of party campaign platforms, so that the ideas can be regarded by voters in both valence and specific position terms. That is, one political party may be generally seen as more concerned with social welfare programs than others and therefore as the one to be supported in case that area is uppermost in mind during the campaign. But even if the more important campaign issues lie elsewhere, social policy questions always arise during a government's time in office, and parties can benefit or lose support depending on how their likely performance in this area is evaluated. The specific proposals of the parties may also cause voters to evaluate them during the campaign, and the platforms of all parties are often full of social policy ideas.

The social welfare issue area, predominantly health care, was the most important one in voters' minds during a series of elections in the 2000s, namely those of 2000, 2004, and 2006.[11] Emphasis on social programs was a major pillar of the Chrétien/Martin dynasty during those years. The fact that this was a successful electoral strategy, despite the draconian cuts to financial transfers to the provinces for these programs in the 1995 budget, is a tribute not only to the way subsequent campaign promises were developed by the Liberals but also to the negative associations voters had developed toward the Alliance and Conservative parties, the main opposition in those elections. In 2000, the Alliance was subjected to allegations that they supported two-tier health care, which would undermine the public health system; and in 2004, the Conservatives had to deal with public skepticism about their proposal to increase health-care funding, which many felt wasn't credible in the face of a companion proposal for substantial tax cuts. Only in 2006 were the Conservatives able to neutralize the health-care issue. They did this by proposing targeted expenditures for wait-time reductions, at the same time that the Liberals were promising massive increases in health-care spending.

The Conservatives' handling of the health-care issue was more complex in 2015, given the budgetary constraints. Starting in 2014, they moved to limit health-care transfer payments to the provinces. With little publicity, the budget of that year changed the formula for transferring money to a per capita model from one involving equalization calculations. Critics charged that this meant that smaller and less populous provinces would have greater difficulty in providing equivalent health services.[12] A second Conservative change involved planning a shift in 2017 from the annual increase of 6 percent in health transfers to the provinces that had been the norm for a number of years to one tying the increase to growth in the GDP. With any economic slowdown, the increases would therefore be substantially reduced, perhaps to a level half that of the previous norm. Under such a formula, the provinces would not be able to cope with the increasing demands on the health system of an aging population, or so they maintained. In the 2015 campaign, the Conservatives chose not to bring up these details of funding formulas, but nevertheless maintained that more money was continuing to go into health care. The public, however, had not forgotten about the health care issue. A survey that received media attention during the campaign provides some basis for thinking that the opposition may have gained electorally from the health-care issue, if only indirectly, because of the overall image of the Conservatives as being neglectful of it.[13]

With the Conservative campaign emphasis on the economy and security issues, the NDP and Liberals saw opportunities to stress the social welfare area, if they could manage to draw voter attention toward it. The NDP promised that, if elected, they would continue the 6 percent funding level provided for in the health-care transfer agreement in effect at the time. The NDP also felt it could build on the image of the Quebec government in the area, given the Quebec base of the party and Mulcair's involvement with the provincial government under which welfare services such as Quebec's daycare program were established. The signature NDP policy commitment was a national daycare program costing $15 per day, which was modelled on Quebec's subsidized program. Finally, the party proposed to expand aspects of federal support for the coverage of public expenses on drugs and promised expanded treatment for dementia patients. The party that had established medicare, as it styled itself, would be the one to trust in government for maintenance and expansion of the social safety net.

Going a step farther than the NDP, the Liberals proposed to negotiate a new health-care agreement with the provinces, something that would take effect after 2017. This would be a negotiation, they stressed, as opposed to the current plan, which had been unilaterally imposed by the federal government. In taking this position, they were reinforcing their general campaign stance of meeting and co-operating with provincial governments to build national unity. They also proposed an overhaul of the Universal Child Care Benefit introduced by the Conservatives in 2006 and increased substantially by the Harper government prior to the onset of the 2015 election campaign. The Liberal proposal would have increased the benefit for lower-income families and removed it from taxation, but also imposed a means test for its receipt. Other social program initiatives were included in the Liberal manifesto, such as increased support for home care for seniors and support for improvements in the Canada

Pension Plan. This latter idea melded with an initiative from the Ontario government to introduce a government pension at the provincial level, a plan denigrated by Harper. The federal Liberal commitment to improving pensions reinforced the determination of Ontario's provincial Liberals to campaign openly for the federal party.

## CONCLUSION

Canadian voters were initially hesitant about the new Conservative Party of Canada, and about its low-key leader, but ultimately were satisfied by 2011 that Stephen Harper was the most desirable among the competing group of potential prime ministers. By 2015, a dedicated group of Conservative partisans remained (the party achieved 31.5 percent of the vote), but many others had had enough. Still, it was only toward the end of the lengthy 2015 campaign that opinion crystallized regarding which of the alternatives, Liberal or NDP, could achieve the goal of defeating the Harper government. The decline of the NDP over the course of the campaign, particularly in Quebec, and the slow but steady rise in Liberal support, worked in tandem to position the Liberals as the clear alternative for these voters.

The lacklustre Conservative campaign definitely contributed to the party's unsatisfactory result. But the reasons for the lack of success of their campaign had much to do with the fact that they did not have real command of *any* of the three key issue areas that were essential to sustain continuation of the dynasty. The sputtering economy made it difficult for the party to get mileage out of claiming credit for past performance, or to make a persuasive argument that they were the only ones to promote future economic growth. The focus on balanced budgets and deficit reduction made it impossible for the Conservatives to propose new social programs, or even to promise to support the existing ones at current levels, and gave the ring of truth to opposition charges that the party was not really committed to sustaining those programs in their current form. And finally, the Conservative Party found itself on the wrong side of a number of national unity issues, in particular respect for universal human rights and welcoming refugees.

The demise of the Harper dynasty was not particularly dramatic, despite the unexpected scope of the Liberal victory. Harper himself was personally re-elected and the party was left with a core of ninety-nine MPs, a reasonable base on which to rebuild. However, as the new Liberal government quickly embarked on a series of activities designed to replace Conservative policies, it was unclear what kind of Conservative Party would emerge from the period of self-examination and leadership contention that began immediately after the election. Canadian dynasties have never been exact replications of previous ones, even when created by the same party.

Despite their rapid decline in the latter part of the campaign, the NDP may still have the potential to once again become a real alternative governing party, as it had appeared to be at the beginning of the 2015 campaign. Whether the future of Canadian electoral politics will be one of genuine three-party competition, which would make the establishment of any new dynasty more problematic, or some other possible configuration, remains a matter of pure speculation.

**Table 14.1: Party Vote Percentages, 2015 and 1965**

| | 2015 | 1965 |
|---|---|---|
| Liberal | 39.5 | 40.2 |
| Conservative | 31.9 | 32.4 |
| NDP | 19.7 | 17.9 |
| Other | 9.1 | 9.5 |

Future dynasties can only be formed from within the volatile electoral environment that is a well-documented feature of our political system. But despite this volatility, there are certain continuities that regularly recur. The electoral system, which makes it difficult for third parties (other than regional ones) to establish themselves competitively, is a constant factor, notwithstanding a 2015 Liberal commitment to consider institutional changes. Thus, the two major parties, despite their historic setbacks and reconfigurations, remain the major governing alternatives available to Canadian voters in most elections. It is indeed remarkable that, over a period longer than two generations, the party system, as it presents itself to voters in Canada, looks remarkably similar to that of fifty years ago (Table 14.1). This is not to suggest that nothing has changed over such a long period. Only that, given the institutional constraints, there is a natural tendency for the Canadian party system, even with its inherent volatility, to periodically reconfigure itself in ways that are well known and understood by scholars, politicians, and voters alike.

## NOTES

1. Lawrence LeDuc, Jon H. Pammett, Judith I. McKenzie, and André Turcotte, *Dynasties and Interludes: Past and Present in Canadian Electoral Politics*, 2nd ed. (Toronto: Dundurn, 2016).
2. See Jon H. Pammett and Christopher Dornan, eds., *The Canadian Federal Election of 2008* (Toronto: Dundurn, 2009), especially 45–55, 237–49, and 259–66.
3. See Jon H. Pammett and Christopher Dornan, eds., *The Canadian Federal Election of 2011* (Toronto: Dundurn, 2011), especially 325–27.
4. On this theme, see Lawrence LeDuc and Richard G. Niemi, "Voting Behavior: Choice and Context," in *Comparing Democracies 4: Elections and Voting in a Changing World*, ed. Lawrence LeDuc, Richard G. Niemi, and Pippa Norris (London: Sage, 2014), 133–49.
5. André Siegfried, *The Race Question in Canada* (London: Eveleigh Nash, 1907), 207. See also the discussion of Siegfried in *Dynasties and Interludes*, 35–40.
6. See Raymond Blake, Penny Bryden, and J. Frank Strain, eds., *The Welfare State in Canada: Past, Present and Future* (Concord, ON: Irwin, 1997).
7. Janine Brodie and Jane Jenson, *Crisis, Challenge and Change: Party and Class in Canada Revisited* (Ottawa: Carleton University Press, 1988).
8. Lawrence LeDuc and Jon H. Pammett, "The Fate of Governing Parties in Times of Economic Crisis," *Electoral Studies* 32 (2013): 494–99.
9. For a review of these concepts in the Canadian context, see Cameron D. Anderson, "Economic Voting in Canada: Assessing the Effects of Subjective Perceptions and Electoral Context," in *Voting Behaviour in Canada*, ed. Cameron D. Anderson and Laura B. Stephenson (Vancouver: UBC Press, 2010), 139–62.
10. The dollar declined from a position of parity with the U.S. dollar in mid-2012 to $0.75 at the time of the election. Oil prices declined even more sharply — from more than $100 (U.S.)/boe in 2014 to about $45/boe a year later.
11. *Dynasties and Interludes*, 534.
12. Michael McBane, *Hill Times*, February 17, 2014.
13. Amir Attaran and Frank Graves, "Health Care Has Potential to Take Down Harper," *Toronto Star*, October 12, 2015.

## Key to Appendices/Political Affliations

| | |
|---|---|
| BQ | Bloc Québécois/Bloc Québécois |
| CHP | Christian Heritage Party of Canada/Parti de l'Héritage Chrétien du Canada |
| COMM | Communist Party of Canada/Parti communiste du Canada |
| Cons | Conservative Party of Canada/Parti conservateur du Canada |
| DAPoC | Democratic Advancement Party of Canada/Parti pour l'Avancement de la Démocratie au Canada |
| FeDC | Forces et Démocratie – Allier les Forces de Nos Régions |
| GP | Green Party of Canada/Le Parti Vert du Canada |
| Liberal | Liberal Party of Canada/Parti libéral du Canada |
| Libert | Libertarian Party of Canada/Parti Libertarien du Canada |
| ML | Marxist-Leninist Party of Canada/Parti marxiste-léniniste du Canada |
| NDP | New Democratic Party/Nouveau Parti démocratique |
| RP | Rhinoceros Party/Parti Rhinocéros |
| IND | Independent/Indépendant |
| No Affiliation | No Affiliation/Aucune appurtenance |

# APPENDIX A: The Results in Summary

| | Canada | | N.L. | | P.E.I. | | N.S | | N.B. | | Que. | | Ont. | | Man. | | Sask. | | Alta. | | B.C. | | Y.T. | | N.W.T. | | Nun. | |
|---|---|---|---|---|---|---|---|---|---|---|---|---|---|---|---|---|---|---|---|---|---|---|---|---|---|---|---|---|
| | # seats | % votes | # seats | % votes | # seats | % votes | # seats | % votes | # s eats | % votes | # seats | % votes | # s eats | % votes | # seats | % votes | # seats | % votes | # seats | % votes | # s eats | % votes | # seats | % votes | # seats | % votes | # seats | % votes |
| BQ | 10 | 4.7 | | 0 | | 0 | | 0 | | 0 | 10 | 19.4 | | 0 | | 0 | | 0 | | 0 | | 0 | | 0 | | 0 | | 0 |
| CHP | 0 | 0.1 | | 0 | | 0.3 | | 0 | | 0 | | 0 | | 0.1 | | 0.3 | | 0 | | 0.1 | | 0.1 | | 0 | | 0 | | 0 |
| COMM | 0 | 0 | | 0.1 | | 0 | | 0 | | 0 | | 0 | | 0 | | 0 | | 0 | | 0 | | 0.1 | | 0 | | 0 | | 0 |
| Cons | 99 | 31.9 | | 10.3 | | 19.3 | | 17.9 | | 25.4 | 12 | 16.7 | 33 | 35.1 | 5 | 37.4 | 10 | 48.5 | 29 | 59.6 | 10 | 29.9 | | 24.3 | | 18.3 | | 24.8 |
| DAPoC | | 0 | | 0 | | 0 | | 0 | | 0 | | 0 | | 0 | | 0 | | 0 | | 0.1 | | 0 | | 0 | | 0 | | 0 |
| FeDC | 0 | 0 | | 0 | | 0 | | 0 | | 0 | | 0.2 | | 0 | | 0 | | 0 | | 0 | | 0 | | 0 | | 0 | | 0 |
| GP | 1 | 3.4 | | 1.1 | | 6 | | 3.4 | | 4.7 | | 2.2 | | 2.8 | | 3.2 | | 2.1 | | 2.5 | 1 | 8.2 | | 2.6 | | 2.8 | | 1.5 |
| Liberal | 184 | 39.5 | 7 | 64.5 | 4 | 58.3 | 11 | 62 | 10 | 51.6 | 40 | 35.7 | 80 | 44.8 | 7 | 44.7 | 1 | 23.9 | 4 | 24.5 | 17 | 35.1 | 1 | 53.7 | 1 | 48.3 | 1 | 47.1 |
| Libert | 0 | 0.2 | | 0 | | 0 | | 0 | | 0 | | 0.1 | | 0.2 | | 0.2 | | 0.1 | | 0.5 | | 0.3 | | 0 | | 0 | | 0 |
| ML | 0 | 0.1 | | 0 | | 0 | | 0 | | 0 | | 0.1 | | 0 | | 0 | | 0 | | 0 | | 0.1 | | 0 | | 0 | | 0 |
| NDP | 44 | 19.7 | | 21.1 | | 16 | | 16.3 | | 18.4 | 16 | 25.4 | 8 | 16.6 | 2 | 13.6 | 3 | 25.1 | 1 | 11.6 | 14 | 26 | | 19.4 | | 30.5 | | 26.6 |
| RP | 0 | 0 | | 0 | | 0 | | 0 | | 0 | | 0.1 | | 0 | | 0 | | 0.1 | | 0 | | 0 | | 0 | | 0 | | 0 |
| IND | 0 | 0.2 | | 0 | | 0 | | 0.3 | | 0.1 | | 0.1 | | 0.2 | | 0.6 | | 0.2 | | 0.9 | | 0.1 | | 0 | | 0 | | 0 |
| No Affiliation | 0 | 0.1 | | 2.9 | | 0 | | 0 | | 0 | | 0 | | 0 | | 0 | | 0 | | 0 | | 0 | | 0 | | 0 | | 0 |
| | 338 | | 7 | | 4 | | 11 | | 10 | | 78 | | 121 | | 14 | | 14 | | 34 | | 42 | | 1 | | 1 | | 1 | |

+ PARTIES WITH LESS THAN 0.05% IN ANY PROVINCE OMITTED

# APPENDIX B

## The Results by Constituency

| District and Party | Vote % |
|---|---|
| **NEWFOUNDLAND** | |
| AVALON | |
| Liberal | 55.9 |
| No Affiliation | 17.8 |
| NDP-New Democratic Party | 14.4 |
| Conservative | 11.1 |
| Green Party | 0.5 |
| Forces et Démocratie — Allier les forces de nos régions | 0.2 |
| BONAVISTA—BURIN—TRINITY | |
| Liberal | 81.8 |
| Conservative | 10.1 |
| NDP-New Democratic Party | 7.3 |
| Green Party | 0.9 |
| COAST OF BAYS—CENTRAL—NOTRE DAME | |
| Liberal | 74.8 |
| Conservative | 18.3 |
| NDP-New Democratic Party | 6.1 |
| Green Party | 0.8 |
| LABRADOR | |
| Liberal | 71.8 |
| NDP-New Democratic Party | 14.4 |
| Conservative | 13.9 |
| LONG RANGE MOUNTAINS | |
| Liberal | 73.9 |
| Conservative | 12.2 |
| NDP-New Democratic Party | 11.3 |
| Green Party | 2.7 |
| ST. JOHN'S EAST | |
| Liberal | 46.7 |
| NDP-New Democratic Party | 45.3 |
| Conservative | 6.6 |
| Green Party | 1.1 |
| Communist | 0.3 |
| ST. JOHN'S SOUTH—MOUNT PEARL | |
| Liberal | 57.9 |
| NDP-New Democratic Party | 36.8 |
| Conservative | 4.6 |
| Green Party | 0.8 |
| **PRINCE EDWARD ISLAND** | |
| CARDIGAN | |
| Liberal | 65.0 |
| Conservative | 16.2 |
| NDP-New Democratic Party | 11.1 |
| Green Party | 6.4 |
| Christian Heritage Party | 1.3 |
| CHARLOTTETOWN | |
| Liberal | 56.3 |
| NDP-New Democratic Party | 23.1 |
| Conservative | 14.8 |
| Green Party | 5.8 |
| EGMONT | |
| Liberal | 49.3 |
| Conservative | 29.0 |
| NDP-New Democratic Party | 19.2 |
| Green Party | 2.6 |

| District and Party | Vote % |
|---|---|
| MALPEQUE | |
| Liberal | 62.1 |
| Conservative | 17.6 |
| NDP-New Democratic Party | 11.2 |
| Green Party | 9.2 |
| **NOVA SCOTIA** | |
| CAPE BRETON—CANSO | |
| Liberal | 74.4 |
| Conservative | 14.5 |
| NDP-New Democratic Party | 8.2 |
| Green Party | 3.0 |
| CENTRAL NOVA | |
| Liberal | 58.5 |
| Conservative | 25.8 |
| NDP-New Democratic Party | 10.2 |
| Green Party | 4.1 |
| Independent | 1.3 |
| CUMBERLAND—COLCHESTER | |
| Liberal | 63.7 |
| Conservative | 26.5 |
| NDP-New Democratic Party | 5.7 |
| Green Party | 3.6 |
| Independent | 0.4 |
| Independent | 0.2 |
| DARTMOUTH—COLE HARBOUR | |
| Liberal | 58.2 |
| NDP-New Democratic Party | 24.4 |
| Conservative | 14.0 |
| Green Party | 3.4 |
| HALIFAX | |
| Liberal | 51.7 |
| NDP-New Democratic Party | 36.1 |
| Conservative | 8.6 |
| Green Party | 3.3 |
| Marxist-Leninist | 0.3 |

| District and Party | Vote % |
|---|---|
| HALIFAX WEST | |
| Liberal | 68.6 |
| Conservative | 15.6 |
| NDP-New Democratic Party | 11.8 |
| Green Party | 3.9 |
| KINGS—HANTS | |
| Liberal | 70.7 |
| Conservative | 18.6 |
| NDP-New Democratic Party | 6.4 |
| Green Party | 3.4 |
| Rhinoceros | 0.4 |
| Independent | 0.3 |
| Independent | 0.2 |
| SACKVILLE—PRESTON—CHEZZETCOOK | |
| Liberal | 48.0 |
| NDP-New Democratic Party | 34.4 |
| Conservative | 14.9 |
| Green Party | 2.8 |
| SOUTH SHORE—ST. MARGARETS | |
| Liberal | 56.9 |
| Conservative | 22.6 |
| NDP-New Democratic Party | 16.8 |
| Green Party | 2.9 |
| Independent | 0.5 |
| Communist | 0.3 |
| SYDNEY—VICTORIA | |
| Liberal | 73.2 |
| NDP-New Democratic Party | 13.1 |
| Conservative | 10.6 |
| Green Party | 2.5 |
| Libertarian | 0.6 |
| WEST NOVA | |
| Liberal | 63.0 |
| Conservative | 26.1 |
| NDP-New Democratic Party | 6.8 |
| Green Party | 4.2 |

| District and Party | Vote % |
|---|---|
| **NEW BRUNSWICK** | |
| ACADIE—BATHURST | |
| Liberal | 50.7 |
| NDP-New Democratic Party | 39.4 |
| Conservative | 7.6 |
| Green Party | 2.3 |
| BEAUSÉJOUR | |
| Liberal | 69.0 |
| NDP-New Democratic Party | 15.1 |
| Conservative | 11.4 |
| Green Party | 4.5 |
| FREDERICTON | |
| Liberal | 49.3 |
| Conservative | 28.4 |
| Green Party | 12.4 |
| NDP-New Democratic Party | 9.9 |
| FUNDY ROYAL | |
| Liberal | 40.9 |
| Conservative | 37.1 |
| NDP-New Democratic Party | 17.5 |
| Green Party | 3.9 |
| Independent | 0.6 |
| MADAWASKA—RESTIGOUCHE | |
| Liberal | 55.7 |
| NDP-New Democratic Party | 25.9 |
| Conservative | 16.5 |
| Green Party | 1.9 |
| MIRAMICHI—GRAND LAKE | |
| Liberal | 47.3 |
| Conservative | 34.3 |
| NDP-New Democratic Party | 15.4 |
| Green Party | 3.0 |

| District and Party | Vote % |
|---|---|
| MONCTON—RIVERVIEW—DIEPPE | |
| Liberal | 57.8 |
| Conservative | 21.5 |
| NDP-New Democratic Party | 16.2 |
| Green Party | 4.6 |
| NEW BRUNSWICK SOUTHWEST | |
| Liberal | 43.9 |
| Conservative | 38.6 |
| NDP-New Democratic Party | 12.6 |
| Green Party | 4.9 |
| SAINT JOHN—ROTHESAY | |
| Liberal | 48.8 |
| Conservative | 30.5 |
| NDP-New Democratic Party | 17.5 |
| Green Party | 3.1 |
| TOBIQUE—MACTAQUAC | |
| Liberal | 46.6 |
| Conservative | 37.0 |
| NDP-New Democratic Party | 11.3 |
| Green Party | 5.1 |
| **QUEBEC** | |
| ABITIBI—BAIE-JAMES—NUNAVIK—EEYOU | |
| NDP-New Democratic Party | 37.0 |
| Liberal | 32.1 |
| Bloc Québécois | 18.5 |
| Conservative | 9.3 |
| Green Party | 2.3 |
| Rhinoceros | 0.7 |
| ABITIBI—TÉMISCAMINGUE | |
| NDP-New Democratic Party | 41.5 |
| Liberal | 29.6 |
| Bloc Québécois | 19.4 |
| Conservative | 6.9 |
| Green Party | 1.7 |
| Rhinoceros | 0.9 |

| District and Party | Vote % |
|---|---|
| AHUNTSIC—CARTIERVILLE | |
| Liberal | 46.8 |
| NDP-New Democratic Party | 30.0 |
| Bloc Québécois | 13.2 |
| Conservative | 7.3 |
| Green Party | 2.1 |
| Rhinoceros | 0.5 |
| ALFRED—PELLAN | |
| Liberal | 44.5 |
| NDP-New Democratic Party | 24.0 |
| Bloc Québécois | 17.8 |
| Conservative | 11.3 |
| Green Party | 2.0 |
| Independent | 0.4 |
| ARGENTEUIL—LA PETITE-NATION | |
| Liberal | 43.3 |
| NDP-New Democratic Party | 24.8 |
| Bloc Québécois | 18.7 |
| Conservative | 11.1 |
| Green Party | 2.2 |
| AVIGNON—LA MITIS—MATANE—MATAPÉDIA | |
| Liberal | 39.5 |
| Bloc Québécois | 21.0 |
| NDP-New Democratic Party | 20.2 |
| Forces et Démocratie — Allier les forces de nos régions | 11.6 |
| Conservative | 6.1 |
| Green Party | 1.0 |
| Rhinoceros | 0.5 |
| BEAUCE | |
| Conservative | 58.9 |
| Liberal | 22.3 |
| NDP-New Democratic Party | 9.7 |
| Bloc Québécois | 7.4 |
| Green Party | 1.7 |

| District and Party | Vote % |
|---|---|
| BEAUPORT—CÔTE-DE-BEAUPRÉ—ÎLE D'ORLÉANS—CHARLEVOIX | |
| Conservative | 33.5 |
| Liberal | 26.9 |
| Bloc Québécois | 19.1 |
| NDP-New Democratic Party | 18.4 |
| Green Party | 1.7 |
| Forces et Démocratie — Allier les forces de nos régions | 0.4 |
| BEAUPORT—LIMOILOU | |
| Conservative | 30.6 |
| NDP-New Democratic Party | 25.5 |
| Liberal | 25.4 |
| Bloc Québécois | 14.8 |
| Green Party | 2.4 |
| Libertarian | 0.8 |
| Forces et Démocratie — Allier les forces de nos régions | 0.3 |
| Marxist-Leninist | 0.2 |
| BÉCANCOUR—NICOLET—SAUREL | |
| Bloc Québécois | 40.0 |
| Liberal | 24.3 |
| NDP-New Democratic Party | 22.1 |
| Conservative | 11.4 |
| Green Party | 2.3 |
| BELLECHASSE—LES ETCHEMINS—LÉVIS | |
| Conservative | 50.9 |
| Liberal | 20.7 |
| NDP-New Democratic Party | 13.6 |
| Bloc Québécois | 11.5 |
| Green Party | 3.2 |
| BELOEIL—CHAMBLY | |
| NDP-New Democratic Party | 31.1 |
| Liberal | 29.3 |
| Bloc Québécois | 27.7 |
| Conservative | 9.3 |
| Green Party | 2.3 |
| Libertarian | 0.4 |

| District and Party | Vote % |
|---|---|
| BERTHIER—MASKINONGÉ | |
| NDP-New Democratic Party | 42.2 |
| Bloc Québécois | 25.8 |
| Liberal | 20.3 |
| Conservative | 10.2 |
| Green Party | 1.6 |
| BOURASSA | |
| Liberal | 54.1 |
| Bloc Québécois | 17.1 |
| NDP-New Democratic Party | 14.9 |
| Conservative | 9.3 |
| Green Party | 2.2 |
| Independent | 1.6 |
| Marxist-Leninist | 0.6 |
| Forces et Démocratie — Allier les forces de nos régions | 0.2 |
| BROME—MISSISQUOI | |
| Liberal | 43.9 |
| NDP-New Democratic Party | 24.5 |
| Bloc Québécois | 17.5 |
| Conservative | 11.5 |
| Green Party | 2.3 |
| Forces et Démocratie — Allier les forces de nos régions | 0.3 |
| BROSSARD—SAINT-LAMBERT | |
| Liberal | 50.3 |
| NDP-New Democratic Party | 24.6 |
| Conservative | 12.6 |
| Bloc Québécois | 10.6 |
| Green Party | 1.9 |
| CHARLESBOURG—HAUTE-SAINT-CHARLES | |
| Conservative | 42.2 |
| Liberal | 23.2 |
| NDP-New Democratic Party | 20.1 |
| Bloc Québécois | 12.3 |
| Green Party | 2.2 |

| District and Party | Vote % |
|---|---|
| CHÂTEAUGUAY—LACOLLE | |
| Liberal | 39.1 |
| Bloc Québécois | 24.4 |
| NDP-New Democratic Party | 23.1 |
| Conservative | 11.2 |
| Green Party | 1.9 |
| Marxist-Leninist | 0.3 |
| CHICOUTIMI—LE FJORD | |
| Liberal | 31.1 |
| NDP-New Democratic Party | 29.7 |
| Bloc Québécois | 20.5 |
| Conservative | 16.6 |
| Green Party | 2.1 |
| COMPTON—STANSTEAD | |
| Liberal | 36.9 |
| NDP-New Democratic Party | 27.4 |
| Bloc Québécois | 20.7 |
| Conservative | 12.5 |
| Green Party | 1.9 |
| Rhinoceros | 0.6 |
| DORVAL—LACHINE—LASALLE | |
| Liberal | 54.9 |
| NDP-New Democratic Party | 21.6 |
| Conservative | 11.1 |
| Bloc Québécois | 9.8 |
| Green Party | 2.3 |
| Independent | 0.4 |
| DRUMMOND | |
| NDP-New Democratic Party | 30.5 |
| Liberal | 26.5 |
| Bloc Québécois | 22.8 |
| Conservative | 17.7 |
| Green Party | 2.4 |

| District and Party | Vote % |
|---|---|
| GASPÉSIE—LES ÎLES-DE-LA-MADELEINE | |
| Liberal | 38.7 |
| NDP-New Democratic Party | 32.5 |
| Bloc Québécois | 20.9 |
| Conservative | 6.1 |
| Green Party | 1.0 |
| Rhinoceros | 0.8 |
| GATINEAU | |
| Liberal | 53.8 |
| NDP-New Democratic Party | 26.6 |
| Bloc Québécois | 9.4 |
| Conservative | 8.2 |
| Green Party | 1.6 |
| Independent | 0.3 |
| Marxist-Leninist | 0.2 |
| HOCHELAGA | |
| NDP-New Democratic Party | 30.9 |
| Liberal | 29.9 |
| Bloc Québécois | 27.7 |
| Conservative | 6.8 |
| Green Party | 3.2 |
| Rhinoceros | 0.8 |
| Communist | 0.3 |
| Marxist-Leninist | 0.3 |
| HONORÉ—MERCIER | |
| Liberal | 56.5 |
| NDP-New Democratic Party | 16.4 |
| Bloc Québécois | 12.9 |
| Conservative | 12.1 |
| Green Party | 1.6 |
| Forces et Démocratie — Allier les forces de nos régions | 0.3 |
| Marxist-Leninist | 0.2 |

| District and Party | Vote % |
|---|---|
| HULL—AYLMER | |
| Liberal | 51.4 |
| NDP-New Democratic Party | 31.5 |
| Conservative | 7.7 |
| Bloc Québécois | 6.5 |
| Green Party | 1.9 |
| Christian Heritage Party | 0.5 |
| Independent | 0.3 |
| Marxist-Leninist | 0.2 |
| JOLIETTE | |
| Bloc Québécois | 33.3 |
| Liberal | 28.2 |
| NDP-New Democratic Party | 25.7 |
| Conservative | 10.1 |
| Green Party | 2.4 |
| Forces et Démocratie — Allier les forces de nos régions | 0.4 |
| JONQUIÈRE | |
| NDP-New Democratic Party | 29.2 |
| Liberal | 28.5 |
| Bloc Québécois | 23.3 |
| Conservative | 16.9 |
| Green Party | 1.4 |
| Rhinoceros | 0.8 |
| LA POINTE-DE-L'ÎLE | |
| Bloc Québécois | 33.6 |
| Liberal | 28.6 |
| NDP-New Democratic Party | 26.8 |
| Conservative | 8.0 |
| Green Party | 2.1 |
| Rhinoceros | 0.6 |
| Forces et Démocratie — Allier les forces de nos régions | 0.2 |
| Marxist-Leninist | 0.2 |

| District and Party | Vote % |
|---|---|
| LA PRAIRIE | |
| Liberal | 36.5 |
| Bloc Québécois | 26.2 |
| NDP-New Democratic Party | 22.9 |
| Conservative | 11.9 |
| Green Party | 2.1 |
| Marxist-Leninist | 0.4 |
| LAC-SAINT-JEAN | |
| Conservative | 33.3 |
| NDP-New Democratic Party | 28.5 |
| Liberal | 18.4 |
| Bloc Québécois | 18.4 |
| Green Party | 1.5 |
| LAC-SAINT-LOUIS | |
| Liberal | 64.1 |
| Conservative | 17.4 |
| NDP-New Democratic Party | 12.8 |
| Green Party | 2.9 |
| Bloc Québécois | 2.7 |
| LASALLE—ÉMARD—VERDUN | |
| Liberal | 43.9 |
| NDP-New Democratic Party | 29.0 |
| Bloc Québécois | 17.0 |
| Conservative | 6.9 |
| Green Party | 3.2 |
| LAURENTIDES—LABELLE | |
| Liberal | 32.1 |
| Bloc Québécois | 29.7 |
| NDP-New Democratic Party | 26.3 |
| Conservative | 9.8 |
| Green Party | 2.0 |

| District and Party | Vote % |
|---|---|
| LAURIER—SAINTE-MARIE | |
| NDP-New Democratic Party | 38.3 |
| Bloc Québécois | 28.7 |
| Liberal | 23.7 |
| Conservative | 4.1 |
| Green Party | 3.5 |
| Libertarian | 1.1 |
| Independent | 0.3 |
| Communist | 0.2 |
| Marxist-Leninist | 0.2 |
| LAVAL—LES ÎLES | |
| Liberal | 47.7 |
| NDP-New Democratic Party | 19.8 |
| Conservative | 18.1 |
| Bloc Québécois | 12.4 |
| Green Party | 1.7 |
| Marxist-Leninist | 0.3 |
| LÉVIS—LOTBINIÈRE | |
| Conservative | 50.1 |
| Liberal | 21.7 |
| NDP-New Democratic Party | 14.8 |
| Bloc Québécois | 11.4 |
| Green Party | 1.8 |
| ATN | 0.2 |
| LONGUEUIL—CHARLES-LEMOYNE | |
| Liberal | 35.4 |
| Bloc Québécois | 27.0 |
| NDP-New Democratic Party | 24.1 |
| Conservative | 9.6 |
| Green Party | 2.9 |
| Rhinoceros | 0.6 |
| Marxist-Leninist | 0.3 |

| District and Party | Vote % |
|---|---|
| LONGUEUIL—SAINT-HUBERT | |
| NDP-New Democratic Party | 31.2 |
| Liberal | 30.0 |
| Bloc Québécois | 27.3 |
| Conservative | 8.7 |
| Green Party | 2.5 |
| Forces et Démocratie — Allier les forces de nos régions | 0.3 |
| LOUIS-HÉBERT | |
| Liberal | 34.8 |
| Conservative | 27.2 |
| NDP-New Democratic Party | 20.8 |
| Bloc Québécois | 14.4 |
| Green Party | 2.5 |
| Christian Heritage Party | 0.2 |
| LOUIS-SAINT-LAURENT | |
| Conservative | 50.5 |
| Liberal | 21.4 |
| NDP-New Democratic Party | 15.9 |
| Bloc Québécois | 10.3 |
| Green Party | 1.9 |
| MANICOUAGAN | |
| Bloc Québécois | 41.3 |
| Liberal | 29.4 |
| NDP-New Democratic Party | 17.5 |
| Conservative | 10.3 |
| Green Party | 1.6 |
| MARC-AURÈLE-FORTIN | |
| Liberal | 40.9 |
| NDP-New Democratic Party | 23.5 |
| Bloc Québécois | 21.7 |
| Conservative | 11.9 |
| Green Party | 1.9 |

| District and Party | Vote % |
|---|---|
| MÉGANTIC—L'ÉRABLE | |
| Conservative | 35.4 |
| Liberal | 28.1 |
| NDP-New Democratic Party | 22.0 |
| Bloc Québécois | 12.3 |
| Green Party | 2.1 |
| MIRABEL | |
| Bloc Québécois | 31.5 |
| NDP-New Democratic Party | 30.1 |
| Liberal | 26.1 |
| Conservative | 10.1 |
| Green Party | 2.2 |
| MONTARVILLE | |
| Liberal | 32.5 |
| Bloc Québécois | 28.4 |
| NDP-New Democratic Party | 24.7 |
| Conservative | 10.9 |
| Green Party | 2.4 |
| Libertarian | 1.1 |
| MONTCALM | |
| Bloc Québécois | 36.6 |
| Liberal | 27.3 |
| NDP-New Democratic Party | 23.5 |
| Conservative | 9.6 |
| Green Party | 1.8 |
| Forces et Démocratie — Allier les forces de nos régions | 1.2 |
| MONTMAGNY—L'ISLET—KAMOURASKA—RIVIÈRE-DU-LOUP | |
| Conservative | 29.0 |
| Liberal | 28.4 |
| NDP-New Democratic Party | 24.2 |
| Bloc Québécois | 16.1 |
| Green Party | 1.7 |
| Rhinoceros | 0.6 |

| District and Party | Vote % |
|---|---|
| MONT-ROYAL | |
| Liberal | 50.3 |
| Conservative | 37.9 |
| NDP-New Democratic Party | 8.1 |
| Bloc Québécois | 1.9 |
| Green Party | 1.6 |
| Marxist-Leninist | 0.3 |
| NOTRE-DAME-DE-GRÂCE—WESTMOUNT | |
| Liberal | 57.7 |
| NDP-New Democratic Party | 21.8 |
| Conservative | 14.4 |
| Green Party | 3.1 |
| Bloc Québécois | 2.5 |
| Marxist-Leninist | 0.4 |
| Independent | 0.3 |
| OUTREMONT | |
| NDP-New Democratic Party | 44.1 |
| Liberal | 33.5 |
| Conservative | 9.5 |
| Bloc Québécois | 8.4 |
| Green Party | 3.6 |
| Libertarian | 0.5 |
| Communist | 0.4 |
| PAPINEAU | |
| Liberal | 52.0 |
| NDP-New Democratic Party | 25.9 |
| Bloc Québécois | 12.2 |
| Conservative | 4.7 |
| Green Party | 2.8 |
| Independent | 1.0 |
| Rhinoceros | 0.6 |
| Marxist-Leninist | 0.3 |
| Independent | 0.3 |
| No Affiliation | 0.2 |

| District and Party | Vote % |
|---|---|
| PIERRE-BOUCHER—LES PATRIOTES—VERCHÈRES | |
| Bloc Québécois | 28.6 |
| Liberal | 28.3 |
| NDP-New Democratic Party | 24.3 |
| Conservative | 10.2 |
| Green Party | 8.5 |
| PIERREFONDS—DOLLARD | |
| Liberal | 58.7 |
| Conservative | 20.0 |
| NDP-New Democratic Party | 16.4 |
| Bloc Québécois | 3.5 |
| Green Party | 1.5 |
| PONTIAC | |
| Liberal | 54.5 |
| NDP-New Democratic Party | 22.5 |
| Conservative | 13.9 |
| Bloc Québécois | 6.9 |
| Green Party | 1.7 |
| Forces et Démocratie - Allier les forces de nos régions | 0.2 |
| Marxist-Leninist | 0.2 |
| PORTNEUF—JACQUES-CARTIER | |
| Conservative | 44.0 |
| NDP-New Democratic Party | 22.1 |
| Liberal | 21.5 |
| Bloc Québécois | 10.7 |
| Green Party | 1.8 |
| QUÉBEC | |
| Liberal | 28.9 |
| NDP-New Democratic Party | 27.0 |
| Conservative | 21.8 |
| Bloc Québécois | 18.8 |
| Green Party | 2.9 |
| Marxist-Leninist | 0.3 |
| Forces et Démocratie — Allier les forces de nos régions | 0.2 |

| District and Party | Vote % |
|---|---|
| REPENTIGNY | |
| Bloc Québécois | 34.7 |
| Liberal | 27.3 |
| NDP-New Democratic Party | 23.3 |
| Conservative | 10.8 |
| Forces et Démocratie — Allier les forces de nos régions | 2.0 |
| Green Party | 1.9 |
| RICHMOND—ARTHABASKA | |
| Conservative | 31.6 |
| Liberal | 24.7 |
| NDP-New Democratic Party | 24.3 |
| Bloc Québécois | 17.2 |
| Green Party | 1.7 |
| Rhinoceros | 0.7 |
| RIMOUSKI-NEIGETTE—TÉMISCOUATA—LES BASQUES | |
| NDP-New Democratic Party | 43.1 |
| Liberal | 28.0 |
| Bloc Québécois | 19.3 |
| Conservative | 7.5 |
| Green Party | 1.5 |
| Rhinoceros | 0.6 |
| RIVIÈRE-DES-MILLE-ÎLES | |
| Liberal | 32.4 |
| NDP-New Democratic Party | 29.5 |
| Bloc Québécois | 25.4 |
| Conservative | 10.5 |
| Green Party | 2.0 |
| Independent | 0.3 |
| RIVIÈRE-DU-NORD | |
| Bloc Québécois | 32.0 |
| NDP-New Democratic Party | 30.1 |
| Liberal | 26.4 |
| Conservative | 8.5 |
| Green Party | 2.5 |
| Rhinoceros | 0.5 |

| District and Party | Vote % |
|---|---|
| ROSEMONT—LA PETITE-PATRIE | |
| NDP-New Democratic Party | 49.2 |
| Bloc Québécois | 21.1 |
| Liberal | 20.7 |
| Conservative | 4.3 |
| Green Party | 3.1 |
| Rhinoceros | 0.8 |
| Libertarian | 0.6 |
| Marxist-Leninist | 0.3 |
| SAINT-HYACINTHE—BAGOT | |
| NDP-New Democratic Party | 28.7 |
| Liberal | 27.6 |
| Bloc Québécois | 24.3 |
| Conservative | 16.7 |
| Green Party | 2.3 |
| Independent | 0.5 |
| SAINT-JEAN | |
| Liberal | 33.2 |
| NDP-New Democratic Party | 29.1 |
| Bloc Québécois | 24.8 |
| Conservative | 10.8 |
| Green Party | 2.1 |
| SAINT-LAURENT | |
| Liberal | 61.6 |
| Conservative | 19.5 |
| NDP-New Democratic Party | 11.5 |
| Bloc Québécois | 4.7 |
| Green Party | 2.4 |
| Marxist-Leninist | 0.3 |
| SAINT-LÉONARD—SAINT-MICHEL | |
| Liberal | 64.7 |
| NDP-New Democratic Party | 14.8 |
| Conservative | 11.1 |
| Bloc Québécois | 7.2 |
| Green Party | 1.8 |
| Marxist-Leninist | 0.3 |

| District and Party | Vote % |
|---|---|
| SAINT-MAURICE—CHAMPLAIN | |
| Liberal | 41.5 |
| NDP-New Democratic Party | 20.8 |
| Bloc Québécois | 19.2 |
| Conservative | 16.3 |
| Green Party | 1.9 |
| Marxist-Leninist | 0.3 |
| SALABERRY—SUROÎT | |
| NDP-New Democratic Party | 30.4 |
| Liberal | 29.2 |
| Bloc Québécois | 28.4 |
| Conservative | 10.0 |
| Green Party | 1.4 |
| Independent | 0.4 |
| Forces et Démocratie — Allier les forces de nos régions | 0.3 |
| SHEFFORD | |
| Liberal | 39.0 |
| NDP-New Democratic Party | 23.7 |
| Bloc Québécois | 22.2 |
| Conservative | 12.8 |
| Green Party | 2.4 |
| SHERBROOKE | |
| NDP-New Democratic Party | 37.4 |
| Liberal | 29.8 |
| Bloc Québécois | 20.4 |
| Conservative | 9.4 |
| Green Party | 2.0 |
| Independent | 0.5 |
| Rhinoceros | 0.5 |
| TERREBONNE | |
| Bloc Québécois | 33.0 |
| Liberal | 28.0 |
| NDP-New Democratic Party | 25.6 |
| Conservative | 11.3 |
| Green Party | 1.7 |
| Forces et Démocratie — Allier les forces de nos régions | 0.3 |

| District and Party | Vote % |
|---|---|
| THÉRÈSE-DE BLAINVILLE | |
| Liberal | 32.5 |
| Bloc Québécois | 27.1 |
| NDP-New Democratic Party | 24.9 |
| Conservative | 12.4 |
| Green Party | 2.4 |
| Libertarian | 0.6 |
| TROIS-RIVIÈRES | |
| NDP-New Democratic Party | 31.8 |
| Liberal | 30.2 |
| Conservative | 18.6 |
| Bloc Québécois | 17.0 |
| Green Party | 1.7 |
| Libertarian | 0.6 |
| VAUDREUIL—SOULANGES | |
| Liberal | 46.6 |
| NDP-New Democratic Party | 22.3 |
| Bloc Québécois | 15.0 |
| Conservative | 13.8 |
| Green Party | 2.2 |
| VILLE-MARIE—LE SUD-OUEST—ÎLE -DES-SŒURS | |
| Liberal | 50.8 |
| NDP-New Democratic Party | 23.4 |
| Conservative | 11.9 |
| Bloc Québécois | 8.6 |
| Green Party | 4.8 |
| Rhinoceros | 0.3 |
| Communist | 0.2 |
| VIMY | |
| Liberal | 46.2 |
| NDP-New Democratic Party | 21.0 |
| Bloc Québécois | 16.7 |
| Conservative | 13.4 |
| Green Party | 2.4 |
| Christian Heritage Party | 0.5 |

| District and Party | Vote % |
|---|---|
| ONTARIO | |
| AJAX | |
| Liberal | 55.9 |
| Conservative | 34.4 |
| NDP-New Democratic Party | 8.2 |
| Green Party | 1.4 |
| United Party | 0.1 |
| ALGOMA—MANITOULIN—KAPUSKASING | |
| NDP-New Democratic Party | 39.9 |
| Liberal | 34.1 |
| Conservative | 23.7 |
| Green Party | 2.2 |
| AURORA—OAK RIDGES—RICHMOND HILL | |
| Liberal | 47.3 |
| Conservative | 45.2 |
| NDP-New Democratic Party | 5.7 |
| Green Party | 1.3 |
| Animal Alliance/Environment Voters | 0.5 |
| BARRIE—INNISFIL | |
| Conservative | 46.4 |
| Liberal | 37.1 |
| NDP-New Democratic Party | 11.8 |
| Green Party | 4.0 |
| Christian Heritage Party | 0.4 |
| CAP | 0.3 |
| BARRIE—SPRINGWATER—ORO—MEDONTE | |
| Conservative | 41.7 |
| Liberal | 41.6 |
| NDP-New Democratic Party | 10.3 |
| Green Party | 5.2 |
| Libertarian | 0.8 |
| Independent | 0.4 |

| District and Party | Vote % |
|---|---|
| BAY OF QUINTE | |
| Liberal | 50.7 |
| Conservative | 34.3 |
| NDP-New Democratic Party | 12.1 |
| Green Party | 2.2 |
| Independent | 0.6 |
| BEACHES—EAST YORK | |
| Liberal | 49.4 |
| NDP-New Democratic Party | 30.8 |
| Conservative | 16.4 |
| Green Party | 2.6 |
| Independent | 0.5 |
| Marxist-Leninist | 0.2 |
| Independent | 0.1 |
| BRAMPTON CENTRE | |
| Liberal | 48.6 |
| Conservative | 33.7 |
| NDP-New Democratic Party | 15.1 |
| Green Party | 2.1 |
| Marxist-Leninist | 0.4 |
| BRAMPTON EAST | |
| Liberal | 52.3 |
| Conservative | 23.5 |
| NDP-New Democratic Party | 23.0 |
| Green Party | 1.1 |
| BRAMPTON NORTH | |
| Liberal | 48.4 |
| Conservative | 33.0 |
| NDP-New Democratic Party | 16.5 |
| Green Party | 1.9 |
| Communist | 0.2 |
| BRAMPTON SOUTH | |
| Liberal | 52.1 |
| Conservative | 35.0 |
| NDP-New Democratic Party | 10.7 |
| Green Party | 2.2 |

| District and Party | Vote % |
|---|---|
| BRAMPTON WEST | |
| Liberal | 55.9 |
| Conservative | 30.1 |
| NDP-New Democratic Party | 12.4 |
| Green Party | 1.6 |
| BRANTFORD—BRANT | |
| Conservative | 40.9 |
| Liberal | 30.7 |
| NDP-New Democratic Party | 24.8 |
| Green Party | 2.5 |
| Libertarian | 0.8 |
| Independent | 0.3 |
| BRUCE—GREY—OWEN SOUND | |
| Conservative | 46.7 |
| Liberal | 38.8 |
| NDP-New Democratic Party | 11.1 |
| Green Party | 3.3 |
| BURLINGTON | |
| Liberal | 46.0 |
| Conservative | 42.5 |
| NDP-New Democratic Party | 9.1 |
| Green Party | 2.4 |
| CAMBRIDGE | |
| Liberal | 43.2 |
| Conservative | 38.6 |
| NDP-New Democratic Party | 13.9 |
| Green Party | 3.2 |
| Independent | 0.9 |
| Marxist-Leninist | 0.2 |
| CARLETON | |
| Conservative | 46.9 |
| Liberal | 43.7 |
| NDP-New Democratic Party | 6.1 |
| Green Party | 3.3 |

| District and Party | Vote % |
|---|---|
| CHATHAM-KENT—LEAMINGTON | |
| Conservative | 41.7 |
| Liberal | 37.2 |
| NDP-New Democratic Party | 18.4 |
| Green Party | 2.7 |
| DAVENPORT | |
| Liberal | 44.3 |
| NDP-New Democratic Party | 41.4 |
| Conservative | 10.6 |
| Green Party | 3.1 |
| Communist | 0.5 |
| Independent | 0.2 |
| DON VALLEY EAST | |
| Liberal | 57.8 |
| Conservative | 29.2 |
| NDP-New Democratic Party | 10.4 |
| Green Party | 2.6 |
| DON VALLEY NORTH | |
| Liberal | 51.4 |
| Conservative | 37.8 |
| NDP-New Democratic Party | 8.5 |
| Green Party | 2.2 |
| DON VALLEY WEST | |
| Liberal | 53.8 |
| Conservative | 37.6 |
| NDP-New Democratic Party | 6.0 |
| Green Party | 1.7 |
| Libertarian | 0.6 |
| Communist | 0.2 |
| Independent | 0.1 |
| DUFFERIN—CALEDON | |
| Conservative | 46.3 |
| Liberal | 39.1 |
| Green Party | 7.3 |
| NDP-New Democratic Party | 7.3 |

| District and Party | Vote % |
|---|---|
| DURHAM | |
| Conservative | 45.1 |
| Liberal | 35.8 |
| NDP-New Democratic Party | 16.0 |
| Green Party | 2.5 |
| Christian Heritage Party | 0.6 |
| EGLINTON—LAWRENCE | |
| Liberal | 48.9 |
| Conservative | 42.6 |
| NDP-New Democratic Party | 6.3 |
| Green Party | 1.4 |
| Libertarian | 0.6 |
| Animal Alliance/Environment Voters | 0.2 |
| ELGIN—MIDDLESEX—LONDON | |
| Conservative | 49.2 |
| Liberal | 31.0 |
| NDP-New Democratic Party | 15.4 |
| Green Party | 3.1 |
| Christian Heritage Party | 0.9 |
| Rhinoceros | 0.3 |
| ESSEX | |
| NDP-New Democratic Party | 41.4 |
| Conservative | 35.7 |
| Liberal | 20.9 |
| Green Party | 1.9 |
| Marxist-Leninist | 0.1 |
| ETOBICOKE CENTRE | |
| Liberal | 52.8 |
| Conservative | 37.3 |
| NDP-New Democratic Party | 7.9 |
| Green Party | 1.4 |
| PC Party | 0.6 |

| District and Party | Vote % |
|---|---|
| ETOBICOKE NORTH | |
| Liberal | 62.4 |
| Conservative | 23.0 |
| NDP-New Democratic Party | 12.4 |
| Green Party | 1.3 |
| Marxist-Leninist | 0.6 |
| No Affiliation | 0.4 |
| ETOBICOKE—LAKESHORE | |
| Liberal | 53.7 |
| Conservative | 32.4 |
| NDP-New Democratic Party | 10.9 |
| Green Party | 2.3 |
| Animal Alliance/Environment Voters | 0.4 |
| Marxist-Leninist | 0.3 |
| FLAMBOROUGH—GLANBROOK | |
| Conservative | 43.5 |
| Liberal | 39.1 |
| NDP-New Democratic Party | 14.0 |
| Green Party | 3.4 |
| GLENGARRY—PRESCOTT—RUSSELL | |
| Liberal | 53.3 |
| Conservative | 36.4 |
| NDP-New Democratic Party | 7.9 |
| Green Party | 1.8 |
| Libertarian | 0.6 |
| GUELPH | |
| Liberal | 49.1 |
| Conservative | 26.3 |
| NDP-New Democratic Party | 12.0 |
| Green Party | 11.3 |
| Libertarian | 0.7 |
| Radical Marijuana | 0.3 |
| Communist | 0.2 |

| District and Party | Vote % |
|---|---|
| HALDIMAND—NORFOLK | |
| Conservative | 44.1 |
| Liberal | 36.6 |
| NDP-New Democratic Party | 13.6 |
| Green Party | 3.3 |
| Christian Heritage Party | 1.6 |
| Independent | 0.5 |
| Independent | 0.3 |
| HALIBURTON—KAWARTHA LAKES—BROCK | |
| Conservative | 44.8 |
| Liberal | 31.8 |
| NDP-New Democratic Party | 19.4 |
| Green Party | 4.0 |
| HAMILTON CENTRE | |
| NDP-New Democratic Party | 45.6 |
| Liberal | 33.4 |
| Conservative | 14.6 |
| Green Party | 4.3 |
| Radical Marijuana | 0.8 |
| Libertarian | 0.8 |
| Independent | 0.5 |
| HAMILTON EAST—STONEY CREEK | |
| Liberal | 39.0 |
| NDP-New Democratic Party | 32.7 |
| Conservative | 25.3 |
| Green Party | 2.6 |
| Communist | 0.3 |
| Marxist-Leninist | 0.1 |
| HAMILTON MOUNTAIN | |
| NDP-New Democratic Party | 35.9 |
| Liberal | 33.5 |
| Conservative | 25.7 |
| Green Party | 2.5 |
| Libertarian | 1.5 |
| Christian Heritage Party | 0.9 |

| District and Party | Vote % |
|---|---|
| HAMILTON WEST—ANCASTER—DUNDAS | |
| Liberal | 47.7 |
| Conservative | 31.8 |
| NDP-New Democratic Party | 16.3 |
| Green Party | 4.2 |
| HASTINGS—LENNOX AND ADDINGTON | |
| Liberal | 42.4 |
| Conservative | 41.9 |
| NDP-New Democratic Party | 12.7 |
| Green Party | 2.9 |
| HUMBER RIVER—BLACK CREEK | |
| Liberal | 66.9 |
| Conservative | 20.2 |
| NDP-New Democratic Party | 10.7 |
| Green Party | 1.6 |
| Marxist-Leninist | 0.6 |
| HURON—BRUCE | |
| Conservative | 44.9 |
| Liberal | 39.7 |
| NDP-New Democratic Party | 13.0 |
| Green Party | 2.4 |
| KANATA—CARLETON | |
| Liberal | 51.3 |
| Conservative | 39.2 |
| NDP-New Democratic Party | 6.8 |
| Green Party | 2.7 |
| KENORA | |
| Liberal | 35.5 |
| NDP-New Democratic Party | 33.9 |
| Conservative | 28.5 |
| Green Party | 1.6 |
| Independent | 0.5 |

| District and Party | Vote % |
|---|---|
| KINGSTON AND THE ISLANDS | |
| Liberal | 55.4 |
| Conservative | 22.7 |
| NDP-New Democratic Party | 17.0 |
| Green Party | 4.5 |
| Libertarian | 0.5 |
| KING—VAUGHAN | |
| Liberal | 47.4 |
| Conservative | 44.2 |
| NDP-New Democratic Party | 6.5 |
| Green Party | 1.9 |
| KITCHENER CENTRE | |
| Liberal | 48.8 |
| Conservative | 30.4 |
| NDP-New Democratic Party | 16.6 |
| Green Party | 3.1 |
| Libertarian | 1.0 |
| Marxist-Leninist | 0.2 |
| KITCHENER SOUTH—HESPELER | |
| Liberal | 42.3 |
| Conservative | 36.7 |
| NDP-New Democratic Party | 15.6 |
| Green Party | 3.7 |
| Libertarian | 1.6 |
| Marxist-Leninist | 0.2 |
| KITCHENER—CONESTOGA | |
| Conservative | 43.3 |
| Liberal | 42.8 |
| NDP-New Democratic Party | 9.8 |
| Green Party | 2.8 |
| Libertarian | 1.4 |
| LAMBTON—KENT—MIDDLESEX | |
| Conservative | 50.2 |
| Liberal | 29.4 |
| NDP-New Democratic Party | 17.0 |
| Green Party | 3.3 |

| District and Party | Vote % |
|---|---|
| LANARK—FRONTENAC—KINGSTON | |
| Conservative | 47.9 |
| Liberal | 33.8 |
| NDP-New Democratic Party | 14.1 |
| Green Party | 3.5 |
| Libertarian | 0.7 |
| LEEDS—GRENVILLE—THOUSAND ISLANDS AND RIDEAU LAKES | |
| Conservative | 47.4 |
| Liberal | 40.6 |
| NDP-New Democratic Party | 8.4 |
| Green Party | 3.7 |
| LONDON NORTH CENTRE | |
| Liberal | 50.5 |
| Conservative | 31.1 |
| NDP-New Democratic Party | 14.7 |
| Green Party | 3.6 |
| Marxist-Leninist | 0.2 |
| LONDON WEST | |
| Liberal | 45.8 |
| Conservative | 35.3 |
| NDP-New Democratic Party | 14.8 |
| Green Party | 2.8 |
| Libertarian | 1.1 |
| Communist | 0.1 |
| LONDON—FANSHAWE | |
| NDP-New Democratic Party | 37.8 |
| Liberal | 31.4 |
| Conservative | 27.2 |
| Green Party | 2.9 |
| Independent | 0.6 |
| MARKHAM—STOUFFVILLE | |
| Liberal | 49.2 |
| Conservative | 42.8 |
| NDP-New Democratic Party | 6.1 |
| Green Party | 1.9 |

| District and Party | Vote % |
|---|---|
| MARKHAM—THORNHILL | |
| Liberal | 55.7 |
| Conservative | 32.3 |
| NDP-New Democratic Party | 10.7 |
| Green Party | 1.2 |
| MARKHAM—UNIONVILLE | |
| Conservative | 49.4 |
| Liberal | 43.3 |
| NDP-New Democratic Party | 5.1 |
| Green Party | 2.2 |
| MILTON | |
| Conservative | 45.4 |
| Liberal | 40.4 |
| NDP-New Democratic Party | 10.9 |
| Green Party | 2.3 |
| Libertarian | 1.0 |
| MISSISSAUGA CENTRE | |
| Liberal | 54.7 |
| Conservative | 33.6 |
| NDP-New Democratic Party | 9.5 |
| Green Party | 2.2 |
| MISSISSAUGA EAST—COOKSVILLE | |
| Liberal | 54.2 |
| Conservative | 35.4 |
| NDP-New Democratic Party | 8.6 |
| Green Party | 1.5 |
| Marxist-Leninist | 0.3 |
| MISSISSAUGA—ERIN MILLS | |
| Liberal | 49.7 |
| Conservative | 39.2 |
| NDP-New Democratic Party | 9.4 |
| Green Party | 1.6 |

| District and Party | Vote % |
|---|---|
| MISSISSAUGA—LAKESHORE | |
| Liberal | 47.7 |
| Conservative | 41.2 |
| NDP-New Democratic Party | 8.0 |
| Green Party | 2.4 |
| Libertarian | 0.5 |
| Marxist-Leninist | 0.2 |
| MISSISSAUGA—MALTON | |
| Liberal | 59.1 |
| Conservative | 26.4 |
| NDP-New Democratic Party | 12.3 |
| Green Party | 1.7 |
| Independent | 0.5 |
| MISSISSAUGA—STREETSVILLE | |
| Liberal | 47.8 |
| Conservative | 40.4 |
| NDP-New Democratic Party | 9.0 |
| Green Party | 2.3 |
| Christian Heritage Party | 0.5 |
| NEPEAN | |
| Liberal | 52.4 |
| Conservative | 36.1 |
| NDP-New Democratic Party | 8.2 |
| Green Party | 2.3 |
| Independent | 0.6 |
| Independent | 0.1 |
| Independent | 0.1 |
| Marxist-Leninist | 0.1 |
| NEWMARKET—AURORA | |
| Liberal | 45.2 |
| Conservative | 42.6 |
| NDP-New Democratic Party | 8.5 |
| Green Party | 2.4 |
| PC Party | 1.3 |

| District and Party | Vote % |
|---|---|
| NIAGARA CENTRE | |
| Liberal | 35.7 |
| NDP-New Democratic Party | 31.5 |
| Conservative | 29.7 |
| Green Party | 2.4 |
| Animal Alliance/Environment Voters | 0.5 |
| Marxist-Leninist | 0.2 |
| NIAGARA FALLS | |
| Conservative | 42.1 |
| Liberal | 34.5 |
| NDP-New Democratic Party | 20.9 |
| Green Party | 2.5 |
| NIAGARA WEST | |
| Conservative | 48.8 |
| Liberal | 32.7 |
| NDP-New Democratic Party | 11.5 |
| Green Party | 3.0 |
| Christian Heritage Party | 2.4 |
| Libertarian | 1.6 |
| NICKEL BELT | |
| Liberal | 42.8 |
| NDP-New Democratic Party | 37.8 |
| Conservative | 16.7 |
| Green Party | 2.5 |
| Marxist-Leninist | 0.2 |
| NIPISSING—TIMISKAMING | |
| Liberal | 51.9 |
| Conservative | 29.3 |
| NDP-New Democratic Party | 16.2 |
| Green Party | 2.6 |
| NORTHUMBERLAND—PETERBOROUGH SOUTH | |
| Liberal | 42.5 |
| Conservative | 39.6 |
| NDP-New Democratic Party | 14.8 |
| Green Party | 3.1 |

| District and Party | Vote % |
|---|---|
| OAKVILLE | |
| Liberal | 49.4 |
| Conservative | 42.5 |
| NDP-New Democratic Party | 5.9 |
| Green Party | 2.2 |
| OAKVILLE NORTH—BURLINGTON | |
| Liberal | 46.7 |
| Conservative | 43.3 |
| NDP-New Democratic Party | 7.2 |
| Green Party | 1.6 |
| Libertarian | 1.1 |
| ORLÉANS | |
| Liberal | 59.7 |
| Conservative | 30.5 |
| NDP-New Democratic Party | 8.0 |
| Green Party | 1.8 |
| OSHAWA | |
| Conservative | 38.2 |
| NDP-New Democratic Party | 31.9 |
| Liberal | 27.3 |
| Green Party | 2.5 |
| Marxist-Leninist | 0.1 |
| OTTAWA CENTRE | |
| Liberal | 42.7 |
| NDP-New Democratic Party | 38.5 |
| Conservative | 14.5 |
| Green Party | 3.0 |
| Libertarian | 0.7 |
| Rhinoceros | 0.2 |
| Radical Marijuana | 0.2 |
| Communist | 0.2 |

| District and Party | Vote % |
|---|---|
| OTTAWA SOUTH | |
| Liberal | 60.1 |
| Conservative | 24.3 |
| NDP-New Democratic Party | 11.6 |
| Green Party | 2.9 |
| PC Party | 0.6 |
| Libertarian | 0.4 |
| Communist | 0.2 |
| OTTAWA WEST—NEPEAN | |
| Liberal | 55.9 |
| Conservative | 30.0 |
| NDP-New Democratic Party | 9.8 |
| Green Party | 2.8 |
| Christian Heritage Party | 1.2 |
| Marxist-Leninist | 0.2 |
| OTTAWA—VANIER | |
| Liberal | 57.6 |
| NDP-New Democratic Party | 19.2 |
| Conservative | 19.1 |
| Green Party | 3.1 |
| Libertarian | 0.8 |
| Marxist-Leninist | 0.2 |
| OXFORD | |
| Conservative | 45.7 |
| Liberal | 32.2 |
| NDP-New Democratic Party | 16.5 |
| Green Party | 3.5 |
| Christian Heritage Party | 2.1 |
| PARKDALE—HIGH PARK | |
| Liberal | 42.0 |
| NDP-New Democratic Party | 40.2 |
| Conservative | 13.1 |
| Green Party | 3.0 |
| Libertarian | 1.0 |
| Radical Marijuana | 0.3 |
| Marxist-Leninist | 0.2 |
| Independent | 0.2 |

| District and Party | Vote % |
|---|---|
| PARRY SOUND—MUSKOKA | |
| Conservative | 43.3 |
| Liberal | 38.9 |
| NDP-New Democratic Party | 10.1 |
| Green Party | 7.2 |
| Pirate | 0.2 |
| CAP | 0.2 |
| Marxist-Leninist | 0.1 |
| PERTH—WELLINGTON | |
| Conservative | 42.9 |
| Liberal | 37.6 |
| NDP-New Democratic Party | 15.0 |
| Green Party | 2.6 |
| Christian Heritage Party | 1.5 |
| No Affiliation | 0.4 |
| PETERBOROUGH—KAWARTHA | |
| Liberal | 43.8 |
| Conservative | 35.1 |
| NDP-New Democratic Party | 18.7 |
| Green Party | 2.2 |
| Forces et Démocratie — Allier les forces de nos régions | 0.2 |
| PICKERING—UXBRIDGE | |
| Liberal | 50.3 |
| Conservative | 38.2 |
| NDP-New Democratic Party | 9.2 |
| Green Party | 2.3 |
| RENFREW—NIPISSING—PEMBROKE | |
| Conservative | 45.8 |
| Liberal | 32.7 |
| Independent | 11.0 |
| NDP-New Democratic Party | 8.6 |
| Green Party | 1.9 |
| RICHMOND HILL | |
| Liberal | 46.9 |
| Conservative | 43.3 |
| NDP-New Democratic Party | 8.0 |
| Green Party | 1.7 |

| District and Party | Vote % |
|---|---|
| SARNIA—LAMBTON | |
| Conservative | 38.8 |
| NDP-New Democratic Party | 31.1 |
| Liberal | 27.3 |
| Green Party | 2.8 |
| SAULT STE. MARIE | |
| Liberal | 44.8 |
| Conservative | 31.1 |
| NDP-New Democratic Party | 21.8 |
| Green Party | 2.1 |
| Marxist-Leninist | 0.2 |
| SCARBOROUGH CENTRE | |
| Liberal | 50.5 |
| Conservative | 32.7 |
| NDP-New Democratic Party | 11.6 |
| Libertarian | 3.1 |
| Green Party | 2.1 |
| SCARBOROUGH NORTH | |
| Liberal | 48.2 |
| Conservative | 27.4 |
| NDP-New Democratic Party | 22.1 |
| Green Party | 1.5 |
| Independent | 0.4 |
| Independent | 0.4 |
| SCARBOROUGH SOUTHWEST | |
| Liberal | 52.5 |
| NDP-New Democratic Party | 23.7 |
| Conservative | 21.2 |
| Green Party | 2.6 |
| SCARBOROUGH—AGINCOURT | |
| Liberal | 51.9 |
| Conservative | 38.0 |
| NDP-New Democratic Party | 7.9 |
| Green Party | 1.4 |
| Christian Heritage Party | 0.8 |

| District and Party | Vote % |
|---|---|
| SCARBOROUGH—GUILDWOOD | |
| Liberal | 60.0 |
| Conservative | 26.5 |
| NDP-New Democratic Party | 11.3 |
| Green Party | 1.4 |
| Independent | 0.4 |
| Radical Marijuana | 0.3 |
| SCARBOROUGH—ROUGE PARK | |
| Liberal | 60.2 |
| Conservative | 27.4 |
| NDP-New Democratic Party | 10.4 |
| Green Party | 2.0 |
| SIMCOE NORTH | |
| Conservative | 43.5 |
| Liberal | 39.8 |
| NDP-New Democratic Party | 10.6 |
| Green Party | 4.5 |
| No Affiliation | 1.1 |
| Christian Heritage Party | 0.6 |
| SIMCOE—GREY | |
| Conservative | 46.6 |
| Liberal | 38.6 |
| NDP-New Democratic Party | 9.6 |
| Green Party | 4.4 |
| Christian Heritage Party | 0.8 |
| SPADINA—FORT YORK | |
| Liberal | 54.7 |
| NDP-New Democratic Party | 27.3 |
| Conservative | 15.7 |
| Green Party | 2.1 |
| PACT | 0.2 |
| Marxist-Leninist | 0.1 |
| ST. CATHARINES | |
| Liberal | 43.2 |
| Conservative | 37.6 |
| NDP-New Democratic Party | 16.5 |
| Green Party | 2.6 |
| Communist | 0.2 |

| District and Party | Vote % |
|---|---|
| STORMONT—DUNDAS—SOUTH GLENGARRY | |
| Conservative | 51.1 |
| Liberal | 38.5 |
| NDP-New Democratic Party | 8.2 |
| Green Party | 2.2 |
| SUDBURY | |
| Liberal | 47.4 |
| NDP-New Democratic Party | 27.8 |
| Conservative | 21.1 |
| Green Party | 3.0 |
| Independent | 0.3 |
| Communist | 0.2 |
| Independent | 0.2 |
| THORNHILL | |
| Conservative | 58.6 |
| Liberal | 33.8 |
| NDP-New Democratic Party | 5.2 |
| Green Party | 1.2 |
| Libertarian | 1.1 |
| Seniors Party | 0.3 |
| THUNDER BAY—RAINY RIVER | |
| Liberal | 44.0 |
| NDP-New Democratic Party | 29.7 |
| Conservative | 21.1 |
| Green Party | 5.2 |
| THUNDER BAY—SUPERIOR NORTH | |
| Liberal | 45.0 |
| NDP-New Democratic Party | 23.2 |
| Conservative | 17.4 |
| Green Party | 13.8 |
| Independent | 0.6 |
| TIMMINS—JAMES BAY | |
| NDP-New Democratic Party | 42.9 |
| Liberal | 34.7 |
| Conservative | 20.4 |
| Green Party | 2.0 |

| District and Party | Vote % |
|---|---|
| TORONTO CENTRE | |
| Liberal | 57.9 |
| NDP-New Democratic Party | 26.6 |
| Conservative | 12.2 |
| Green Party | 2.6 |
| Independent | 0.3 |
| Communist | 0.3 |
| Marxist-Leninist | 0.2 |
| TORONTO—DANFORTH | |
| Liberal | 42.3 |
| NDP-New Democratic Party | 40.2 |
| Conservative | 9.9 |
| Green Party | 4.7 |
| PC Party | 2.3 |
| Animal Alliance/Environment Voters | 0.6 |
| TORONTO—ST. PAUL'S | |
| Liberal | 55.3 |
| Conservative | 27.0 |
| NDP-New Democratic Party | 14.7 |
| Green Party | 3.0 |
| UNIVERSITY—ROSEDALE | |
| Liberal | 49.8 |
| NDP-New Democratic Party | 28.6 |
| Conservative | 17.5 |
| Green Party | 2.9 |
| Libertarian | 0.4 |
| Animal Alliance/Environment Voters | 0.2 |
| The Bridge | 0.2 |
| Communist | 0.2 |
| Marxist-Leninist | 0.1 |
| VAUGHAN—WOODBRIDGE | |
| Liberal | 48.7 |
| Conservative | 43.9 |
| NDP-New Democratic Party | 4.6 |
| Libertarian | 1.5 |
| Green Party | 1.3 |

| District and Party | Vote % |
|---|---|
| WATERLOO | |
| Liberal | 49.7 |
| Conservative | 32.3 |
| NDP-New Democratic Party | 14.9 |
| Green Party | 2.9 |
| Animal Alliance/Environment Voters | 0.2 |
| WELLINGTON—HALTON HILLS | |
| Conservative | 50.9 |
| Liberal | 36.5 |
| NDP-New Democratic Party | 8.3 |
| Green Party | 4.0 |
| CAP | 0.3 |
| WHITBY | |
| Liberal | 45.0 |
| Conservative | 42.1 |
| NDP-New Democratic Party | 10.3 |
| Green Party | 2.2 |
| Independent | 0.4 |
| WILLOWDALE | |
| Liberal | 53.4 |
| Conservative | 37.0 |
| NDP-New Democratic Party | 7.0 |
| Green Party | 2.2 |
| Independent | 0.5 |
| WINDSOR WEST | |
| NDP-New Democratic Party | 51.3 |
| Liberal | 25.2 |
| Conservative | 20.8 |
| Green Party | 2.3 |
| Marxist-Leninist | 0.3 |
| WINDSOR—TECUMSEH | |
| NDP-New Democratic Party | 43.5 |
| Conservative | 27.5 |
| Liberal | 26.6 |
| Green Party | 2.0 |
| Marxist-Leninist | 0.5 |

| District and Party | Vote % |
|---|---|
| YORK CENTRE | |
| Liberal | 46.9 |
| Conservative | 44.0 |
| NDP-New Democratic Party | 7.3 |
| Green Party | 1.8 |
| YORK SOUTH—WESTON | |
| Liberal | 46.0 |
| NDP-New Democratic Party | 30.4 |
| Conservative | 19.2 |
| Libertarian | 2.4 |
| Green Party | 2.0 |
| YORK—SIMCOE | |
| Conservative | 50.2 |
| Liberal | 37.8 |
| NDP-New Democratic Party | 8.9 |
| Green Party | 3.1 |
| **MANITOBA** | |
| BRANDON—SOURIS | |
| Conservative | 50.3 |
| Liberal | 37.3 |
| NDP-New Democratic Party | 6.3 |
| Green Party | 6.1 |
| CHARLESWOOD—ST. JAMES—ASSINIBOIA—HEADINGLEY | |
| Liberal | 52.0 |
| Conservative | 39.0 |
| NDP-New Democratic Party | 6.0 |
| Green Party | 2.9 |
| CHURCHILL—KEEWATINOOK ASKI | |
| NDP-New Democratic Party | 45.0 |
| Liberal | 42.0 |
| Conservative | 10.3 |
| Green Party | 1.8 |
| Libertarian | 0.9 |

| District and Party | Vote % |
|---|---|
| DAUPHIN—SWAN RIVER—NEEPAWA | |
| Conservative | 46.3 |
| Liberal | 29.5 |
| NDP-New Democratic Party | 12.3 |
| Independent | 8.1 |
| Green Party | 3.8 |
| ELMWOOD—TRANSCONA | |
| NDP-New Democratic Party | 34.1 |
| Conservative | 34.0 |
| Liberal | 29.5 |
| Green Party | 2.4 |
| KILDONAN—ST. PAUL | |
| Liberal | 42.7 |
| Conservative | 39.8 |
| NDP-New Democratic Party | 14.3 |
| Green Party | 1.8 |
| Christian Heritage Party | 1.1 |
| Independent | 0.3 |
| PORTAGE—LISGAR | |
| Conservative | 60.8 |
| Liberal | 25.8 |
| NDP-New Democratic Party | 6.2 |
| Green Party | 4.0 |
| Christian Heritage Party | 3.2 |
| PROVENCHER | |
| Conservative | 56.1 |
| Liberal | 34.7 |
| NDP-New Democratic Party | 5.3 |
| Green Party | 4.0 |
| SAINT BONIFACE—SAINT VITAL | |
| Liberal | 58.4 |
| Conservative | 28.7 |
| NDP-New Democratic Party | 10.6 |
| Green Party | 2.3 |

| District and Party | Vote % |
|---|---|
| SELKIRK—INTERLAKE—EASTMAN | |
| Conservative | 51.9 |
| Liberal | 31.4 |
| NDP-New Democratic Party | 11.4 |
| Green Party | 3.5 |
| Libertarian | 1.8 |
| WINNIPEG CENTRE | |
| Liberal | 54.5 |
| NDP-New Democratic Party | 28.0 |
| Conservative | 12.4 |
| Green Party | 4.1 |
| Christian Heritage Party | 0.7 |
| Communist | 0.4 |
| WINNIPEG NORTH | |
| Liberal | 68.9 |
| Conservative | 15.3 |
| NDP-New Democratic Party | 13.4 |
| Green Party | 2.4 |
| WINNIPEG SOUTH | |
| Liberal | 58.3 |
| Conservative | 34.7 |
| NDP-New Democratic Party | 5.0 |
| Green Party | 2.1 |
| WINNIPEG SOUTH CENTRE | |
| Liberal | 59.7 |
| Conservative | 28.2 |
| NDP-New Democratic Party | 9.0 |
| Green Party | 3.1 |

**SASKATCHEWAN**

| District and Party | Vote % |
|---|---|
| BATTLEFORDS—LLOYDMINSTER | |
| Conservative | 61.0 |
| NDP-New Democratic Party | 17.6 |
| Liberal | 16.5 |
| Independent | 3.2 |
| Green Party | 1.7 |

| District and Party | Vote % |
|---|---|
| CARLTON TRAIL—EAGLE CREEK | |
| Conservative | 64.7 |
| NDP-New Democratic Party | 18.7 |
| Liberal | 14.4 |
| Green Party | 2.2 |
| CYPRESS HILLS—GRASSLANDS | |
| Conservative | 69.2 |
| Liberal | 14.9 |
| NDP-New Democratic Party | 13.2 |
| Green Party | 2.7 |
| DESNETHÉ—MISSINIPPI—CHURCHILL RIVER | |
| NDP-New Democratic Party | 34.2 |
| Liberal | 33.9 |
| Conservative | 30.1 |
| Green Party | 1.8 |
| MOOSE JAW—LAKE CENTRE—LANIGAN | |
| Conservative | 55.5 |
| NDP-New Democratic Party | 23.8 |
| Liberal | 18.0 |
| Green Party | 2.3 |
| Rhinoceros | 0.5 |
| PRINCE ALBERT | |
| Conservative | 49.8 |
| NDP-New Democratic Party | 28.5 |
| Liberal | 19.8 |
| Green Party | 1.9 |
| REGINA—LEWVAN | |
| NDP-New Democratic Party | 35.2 |
| Conservative | 34.9 |
| Liberal | 27.5 |
| Green Party | 1.8 |
| Libertarian | 0.6 |

| District and Party | Vote % |
|---|---|
| REGINA—QU'APPELLE | |
| Conservative | 44.7 |
| NDP-New Democratic Party | 30.2 |
| Liberal | 22.8 |
| Green Party | 2.3 |
| REGINA—WASCANA | |
| Liberal | 55.1 |
| Conservative | 30.3 |
| NDP-New Democratic Party | 12.6 |
| Green Party | 2.1 |
| SASKATOON WEST | |
| NDP-New Democratic Party | 39.6 |
| Conservative | 32.9 |
| Liberal | 24.5 |
| Green Party | 1.7 |
| Canada Party | 0.7 |
| Libertarian | 0.6 |
| SASKATOON—GRASSWOOD | |
| Conservative | 41.6 |
| NDP-New Democratic Party | 30.2 |
| Liberal | 26.4 |
| Green Party | 1.8 |
| SASKATOON—UNIVERSITY | |
| Conservative | 41.5 |
| NDP-New Democratic Party | 31.5 |
| Liberal | 25.2 |
| Green Party | 1.5 |
| Rhinoceros | 0.2 |
| SOURIS—MOOSE MOUNTAIN | |
| Conservative | 70.1 |
| NDP-New Democratic Party | 13.7 |
| Liberal | 13.5 |
| Green Party | 2.6 |

| District and Party | Vote % |
|---|---|
| YORKTON—MELVILLE | |
| Conservative | 59.2 |
| NDP-New Democratic Party | 20.2 |
| Liberal | 17.8 |
| Green Party | 2.8 |
| **ALBERTA** | |
| BANFF—AIRDRIE | |
| Conservative | 63.4 |
| Liberal | 26.1 |
| NDP-New Democratic Party | 6.8 |
| Green Party | 3.8 |
| BATTLE RIVER—CROWFOOT | |
| Conservative | 80.9 |
| Liberal | 9.4 |
| NDP-New Democratic Party | 6.5 |
| Green Party | 3.2 |
| BOW RIVER | |
| Conservative | 77.4 |
| Liberal | 13.7 |
| NDP-New Democratic Party | 5.2 |
| Green Party | 1.8 |
| Independent | 1.1 |
| Christian Heritage Party | 0.6 |
| Democratic Advancement | 0.2 |
| CALGARY CENTRE | |
| Liberal | 46.5 |
| Conservative | 45.3 |
| NDP-New Democratic Party | 5.6 |
| Green Party | 2.2 |
| Independent | 0.4 |
| CALGARY CONFEDERATION | |
| Conservative | 45.9 |
| Liberal | 43.5 |
| NDP-New Democratic Party | 7.1 |
| Green Party | 3.2 |
| Marxist-Leninist | 0.2 |

| District and Party | Vote % |
|---|---|
| CALGARY FOREST LAWN | |
| Conservative | 48.0 |
| Liberal | 36.0 |
| NDP-New Democratic Party | 9.8 |
| Green Party | 3.0 |
| Libertarian | 2.0 |
| Communist | 1.0 |
| Democratic Advancement | 0.3 |
| CALGARY HERITAGE | |
| Conservative | 63.8 |
| Liberal | 26.0 |
| NDP-New Democratic Party | 7.3 |
| Green Party | 2.1 |
| Libertarian | 0.4 |
| Independent | 0.2 |
| Independent | 0.1 |
| Independent | 0.1 |
| CALGARY MIDNAPORE | |
| Conservative | 66.7 |
| Liberal | 22.6 |
| NDP-New Democratic Party | 7.7 |
| Green Party | 2.7 |
| Marxist-Leninist | 0.2 |
| CALGARY NOSE HILL | |
| Conservative | 60.0 |
| Liberal | 26.9 |
| NDP-New Democratic Party | 8.9 |
| Green Party | 2.5 |
| Libertarian | 1.3 |
| Democratic Advancement | 0.3 |
| CALGARY ROCKY RIDGE | |
| Conservative | 60.4 |
| Liberal | 31.7 |
| NDP-New Democratic Party | 5.8 |
| Green Party | 2.1 |

| District and Party | Vote % |
|---|---|
| CALGARY SHEPARD | |
| Conservative | 65.9 |
| Liberal | 24.7 |
| NDP-New Democratic Party | 6.8 |
| Green Party | 2.6 |
| CALGARY SIGNAL HILL | |
| Conservative | 60.6 |
| Liberal | 30.6 |
| NDP-New Democratic Party | 5.0 |
| Green Party | 2.5 |
| Libertarian | 1.1 |
| Christian Heritage Party | 0.3 |
| CALGARY SKYVIEW | |
| Liberal | 45.9 |
| Conservative | 39.8 |
| NDP-New Democratic Party | 8.0 |
| PC Party | 2.1 |
| Green Party | 1.9 |
| Democratic Advancement | 1.7 |
| Independent | 0.4 |
| Marxist-Leninist | 0.2 |
| EDMONTON CENTRE | |
| Liberal | 37.2 |
| Conservative | 35.0 |
| NDP-New Democratic Party | 24.5 |
| Green Party | 2.6 |
| Rhinoceros | 0.5 |
| Independent | 0.3 |
| EDMONTON GRIESBACH | |
| Conservative | 40.0 |
| NDP-New Democratic Party | 34.0 |
| Liberal | 21.7 |
| Green Party | 2.4 |
| Libertarian | 0.9 |
| Radical Marijuana | 0.6 |
| Rhinoceros | 0.3 |
| Marxist-Leninist | 0.2 |

| District and Party | Vote % |
|---|---|
| EDMONTON MANNING | |
| Conservative | 45.2 |
| Liberal | 27.6 |
| NDP-New Democratic Party | 23.6 |
| Green Party | 2.2 |
| Independent | 1.1 |
| Marxist-Leninist | 0.3 |
| EDMONTON MILL WOODS | |
| Liberal | 41.2 |
| Conservative | 41.1 |
| NDP-New Democratic Party | 12.8 |
| Green Party | 2.2 |
| Independent | 1.1 |
| Libertarian | 0.8 |
| Christian Heritage Party | 0.6 |
| Communist | 0.2 |
| EDMONTON RIVERBEND | |
| Conservative | 49.9 |
| Liberal | 30.2 |
| NDP-New Democratic Party | 17.1 |
| Green Party | 2.2 |
| Libertarian | 0.7 |
| EDMONTON STRATHCONA | |
| NDP-New Democratic Party | 44.0 |
| Conservative | 31.3 |
| Liberal | 20.7 |
| Green Party | 2.3 |
| Libertarian | 0.6 |
| Pirate | 0.4 |
| Rhinoceros | 0.2 |
| Independent | 0.2 |
| Independent | 0.2 |
| Marxist-Leninist | 0.2 |

| District and Party | Vote % |
|---|---|
| EDMONTON WEST | |
| Conservative | 49.3 |
| Liberal | 34.9 |
| NDP-New Democratic Party | 13.0 |
| Green Party | 1.9 |
| Libertarian | 0.6 |
| Marxist-Leninist | 0.2 |
| EDMONTON—WETASKIWIN | |
| Conservative | 65.8 |
| Liberal | 21.5 |
| NDP-New Democratic Party | 9.7 |
| Green Party | 2.3 |
| Libertarian | 0.7 |
| FOOTHILLS | |
| Conservative | 75.7 |
| Liberal | 13.4 |
| NDP-New Democratic Party | 6.4 |
| Green Party | 3.3 |
| Libertarian | 0.7 |
| Christian Heritage Party | 0.6 |
| FORT MCMURRAY—COLD LAKE | |
| Conservative | 60.6 |
| Liberal | 28.4 |
| NDP-New Democratic Party | 7.7 |
| Green Party | 1.6 |
| Libertarian | 1.2 |
| Christian Heritage Party | 0.6 |
| GRANDE PRAIRIE—MACKENZIE | |
| Conservative | 72.9 |
| Liberal | 14.7 |
| NDP-New Democratic Party | 8.1 |
| Green Party | 3.1 |
| Libertarian | 1.1 |

| District and Party | Vote % |
|---|---|
| LAKELAND | |
| Conservative | 72.8 |
| Liberal | 13.7 |
| NDP-New Democratic Party | 10.1 |
| Green Party | 2.3 |
| Libertarian | 1.1 |
| LETHBRIDGE | |
| Conservative | 56.8 |
| NDP-New Democratic Party | 20.5 |
| Liberal | 18.5 |
| Green Party | 2.6 |
| Christian Heritage Party | 1.3 |
| Rhinoceros | 0.4 |
| MEDICINE HAT—CARDSTON—WARNER | |
| Conservative | 68.8 |
| Liberal | 17.9 |
| NDP-New Democratic Party | 9.7 |
| Green Party | 2.6 |
| Independent | 1.0 |
| PEACE RIVER—WESTLOCK | |
| Conservative | 69.4 |
| NDP-New Democratic Party | 14.4 |
| Liberal | 12.8 |
| Green Party | 2.5 |
| Libertarian | 0.9 |
| RED DEER—LACOMBE | |
| Conservative | 70.7 |
| Liberal | 15.0 |
| NDP-New Democratic Party | 11.4 |
| Green Party | 2.9 |
| RED DEER—MOUNTAIN VIEW | |
| Conservative | 74.3 |
| Liberal | 13.4 |
| NDP-New Democratic Party | 8.4 |
| Green Party | 2.6 |
| Libertarian | 0.7 |
| Pirate | 0.5 |

| District and Party | Vote % |
|---|---|
| SHERWOOD PARK—FORT SASKATCHEWAN | |
| Conservative | 63.9 |
| Liberal | 20.4 |
| NDP-New Democratic Party | 9.8 |
| Green Party | 2.5 |
| Independent | 2.3 |
| Libertarian | 1.0 |
| ST. ALBERT—EDMONTON | |
| Conservative | 45.2 |
| Liberal | 22.5 |
| Independent | 19.7 |
| NDP-New Democratic Party | 11.2 |
| Green Party | 1.4 |
| STURGEON RIVER—PARKLAND | |
| Conservative | 70.2 |
| Liberal | 15.6 |
| NDP-New Democratic Party | 10.0 |
| Green Party | 3.0 |
| Christian Heritage Party | 1.1 |
| YELLOWHEAD | |
| Conservative | 72.3 |
| Liberal | 14.2 |
| NDP-New Democratic Party | 9.0 |
| Green Party | 2.9 |
| Libertarian | 1.6 |
| **BRITISH COLUMBIA** | |
| ABBOTSFORD | |
| Conservative | 48.3 |
| Liberal | 32.8 |
| NDP-New Democratic Party | 13.7 |
| Green Party | 5.0 |
| Marxist-Leninist | 0.2 |

| District and Party | Vote % |
|---|---|
| BURNABY NORTH—SEYMOUR | |
| Liberal | 36.1 |
| NDP-New Democratic Party | 29.6 |
| Conservative | 27.8 |
| Green Party | 5.3 |
| Libertarian | 0.5 |
| Independent | 0.4 |
| Communist | 0.2 |
| Marxist-Leninist | 0.1 |
| BURNABY SOUTH | |
| NDP-New Democratic Party | 35.1 |
| Liberal | 33.9 |
| Conservative | 27.1 |
| Green Party | 2.8 |
| Libertarian | 1.1 |
| CARIBOO—PRINCE GEORGE | |
| Conservative | 36.6 |
| Liberal | 31.5 |
| NDP-New Democratic Party | 25.8 |
| Green Party | 3.5 |
| Independent | 1.2 |
| No Affiliation | 0.7 |
| Christian Heritage Party | 0.6 |
| CENTRAL OKANAGAN—SIMILKAMEEN—NICOLA | |
| Conservative | 39.6 |
| Liberal | 37.2 |
| NDP-New Democratic Party | 19.3 |
| Green Party | 3.9 |
| CHILLIWACK—HOPE | |
| Conservative | 42.3 |
| Liberal | 33.8 |
| NDP-New Democratic Party | 18.2 |
| Green Party | 4.7 |
| Libertarian | 0.8 |
| Marxist-Leninist | 0.2 |

| District and Party | Vote % |
|---|---|
| CLOVERDALE—LANGLEY CITY | |
| Liberal | 45.5 |
| Conservative | 34.8 |
| NDP-New Democratic Party | 15.7 |
| Green Party | 4.1 |
| COQUITLAM—PORT COQUITLAM | |
| Liberal | 35.3 |
| Conservative | 32.0 |
| NDP-New Democratic Party | 27.3 |
| Green Party | 3.7 |
| Libertarian | 1.8 |
| COURTENAY—ALBERNI | |
| NDP-New Democratic Party | 38.1 |
| Conservative | 28.2 |
| Liberal | 21.8 |
| Green Party | 11.7 |
| Marxist-Leninist | 0.2 |
| COWICHAN—MALAHAT—LANGFORD | |
| NDP-New Democratic Party | 35.9 |
| Liberal | 23.8 |
| Conservative | 22.8 |
| Green Party | 16.9 |
| Marxist-Leninist | 0.6 |
| DELTA | |
| Liberal | 49.1 |
| Conservative | 32.8 |
| NDP-New Democratic Party | 14.9 |
| Green Party | 3.2 |
| ESQUIMALT—SAANICH—SOOKE | |
| NDP-New Democratic Party | 35.0 |
| Liberal | 27.4 |
| Green Party | 19.9 |
| Conservative | 17.5 |
| Communist | 0.2 |

| District and Party | Vote % |
|---|---|
| FLEETWOOD—PORT KELLS | |
| Liberal | 46.9 |
| Conservative | 29.3 |
| NDP-New Democratic Party | 21.5 |
| Green Party | 2.4 |
| KAMLOOPS—THOMPSON—CARIBOO | |
| Conservative | 35.3 |
| NDP-New Democratic Party | 30.8 |
| Liberal | 30.4 |
| Green Party | 3.6 |
| KELOWNA—LAKE COUNTRY | |
| Liberal | 46.2 |
| Conservative | 39.8 |
| NDP-New Democratic Party | 14.1 |
| KOOTENAY—COLUMBIA | |
| NDP-New Democratic Party | 37.2 |
| Conservative | 36.8 |
| Liberal | 19.5 |
| Green Party | 6.5 |
| LANGLEY—ALDERGROVE | |
| Conservative | 45.6 |
| Liberal | 36.6 |
| NDP-New Democratic Party | 12.5 |
| Green Party | 4.4 |
| Libertarian | 0.9 |
| MISSION—MATSQUI—FRASER CANYON | |
| Liberal | 37.2 |
| Conservative | 34.9 |
| NDP-New Democratic Party | 20.5 |
| Green Party | 5.1 |
| Independent | 2.0 |
| Marxist-Leninist | 0.1 |

| District and Party | Vote % |
|---|---|
| NANAIMO—LADYSMITH | |
| NDP-New Democratic Party | 33.2 |
| Liberal | 23.5 |
| Conservative | 23.4 |
| Green Party | 19.8 |
| Marxist-Leninist | 0.2 |
| NEW WESTMINSTER—BURNABY | |
| NDP-New Democratic Party | 43.5 |
| Liberal | 29.0 |
| Conservative | 20.0 |
| Green Party | 4.7 |
| Libertarian | 2.6 |
| Marxist-Leninist | 0.3 |
| NORTH ISLAND—POWELL RIVER | |
| NDP-New Democratic Party | 40.2 |
| Conservative | 26.2 |
| Liberal | 25.5 |
| Green Party | 8.2 |
| NORTH OKANAGAN—SHUSWAP | |
| Conservative | 39.3 |
| Liberal | 29.9 |
| NDP-New Democratic Party | 25.6 |
| Green Party | 5.2 |
| NORTH VANCOUVER | |
| Liberal | 56.7 |
| Conservative | 26.9 |
| Green Party | 8.3 |
| NDP-New Democratic Party | 7.8 |
| Libertarian | 0.2 |
| Independent | 0.1 |
| PITT MEADOWS—MAPLE RIDGE | |
| Liberal | 33.9 |
| Conservative | 31.4 |
| NDP-New Democratic Party | 29.6 |
| Green Party | 4.2 |
| Independent | 0.9 |

| District and Party | Vote % |
|---|---|
| PORT MOODY—COQUITLAM | |
| NDP-New Democratic Party | 36.0 |
| Liberal | 30.9 |
| Conservative | 29.5 |
| Green Party | 3.4 |
| Marxist-Leninist | 0.2 |
| PRINCE GEORGE—PEACE RIVER—NORTHERN ROCKIES | |
| Conservative | 52.5 |
| Liberal | 24.9 |
| NDP-New Democratic Party | 15.5 |
| Green Party | 5.2 |
| Libertarian | 1.1 |
| PC Party | 0.9 |
| RICHMOND CENTRE | |
| Conservative | 44.2 |
| Liberal | 41.4 |
| NDP-New Democratic Party | 11.5 |
| Green Party | 2.9 |
| SAANICH—GULF ISLANDS | |
| Green Party | 54.4 |
| Conservative | 19.5 |
| Liberal | 16.7 |
| NDP-New Democratic Party | 9.1 |
| Libertarian | 0.4 |
| SKEENA—BULKLEY VALLEY | |
| NDP-New Democratic Party | 51.1 |
| Conservative | 24.8 |
| Liberal | 18.7 |
| Green Party | 3.6 |
| Christian Heritage Party | 1.8 |
| SOUTH OKANAGAN—WEST KOOTENAY | |
| NDP-New Democratic Party | 37.3 |
| Conservative | 29.8 |
| Liberal | 28.1 |
| Green Party | 4.2 |
| Independent | 0.6 |

| District and Party | Vote % |
|---|---|
| SOUTH SURREY—WHITE ROCK | |
| Conservative | 44.0 |
| Liberal | 41.5 |
| NDP-New Democratic Party | 10.4 |
| Green Party | 3.4 |
| Libertarian | 0.5 |
| PC Party | 0.2 |
| STEVESTON—RICHMOND EAST | |
| Liberal | 45.1 |
| Conservative | 38.5 |
| NDP-New Democratic Party | 12.1 |
| Green Party | 3.7 |
| Libertarian | 0.6 |
| SURREY CENTRE | |
| Liberal | 45.1 |
| NDP-New Democratic Party | 30.1 |
| Conservative | 19.8 |
| Green Party | 3.5 |
| Christian Heritage Party | 1.3 |
| Communist | 0.3 |
| SURREY—NEWTON | |
| Liberal | 56.0 |
| NDP-New Democratic Party | 26.1 |
| Conservative | 15.7 |
| Green Party | 2.2 |
| VANCOUVER CENTRE | |
| Liberal | 56.1 |
| NDP-New Democratic Party | 20.0 |
| Conservative | 16.9 |
| Green Party | 5.8 |
| Libertarian | 1.1 |
| Marxist-Leninist | 0.1 |

| District and Party | Vote % |
|---|---|
| VANCOUVER EAST | |
| NDP-New Democratic Party | 49.9 |
| Liberal | 28.2 |
| Conservative | 10.8 |
| Green Party | 9.2 |
| Communist | 0.9 |
| Independent | 0.4 |
| Marxist-Leninist | 0.4 |
| Pirate | 0.3 |
| VANCOUVER GRANVILLE | |
| Liberal | 43.9 |
| NDP-New Democratic Party | 26.9 |
| Conservative | 26.1 |
| Green Party | 3.1 |
| VANCOUVER KINGSWAY | |
| NDP-New Democratic Party | 45.7 |
| Liberal | 27.8 |
| Conservative | 21.0 |
| Green Party | 3.3 |
| Libertarian | 1.0 |
| Communist | 1.0 |
| Marxist-Leninist | 0.2 |
| VANCOUVER QUADRA | |
| Liberal | 58.7 |
| Conservative | 25.8 |
| NDP-New Democratic Party | 10.9 |
| Green Party | 4.2 |
| Pirate | 0.2 |
| Radical Marijuana | 0.1 |
| Independent | 0.1 |
| VANCOUVER SOUTH | |
| Liberal | 48.8 |
| Conservative | 33.9 |
| NDP-New Democratic Party | 14.0 |
| Green Party | 2.6 |
| Marxist-Leninist | 0.4 |
| PC Party | 0.4 |

| District and Party | Vote % |
|---|---|
| VICTORIA | |
| NDP-New Democratic Party | 42.3 |
| Green Party | 32.9 |
| Liberal | 11.8 |
| Conservative | 11.8 |
| Libertarian | 0.7 |
| Animal Alliance/Environment Voters | 0.3 |
| Independent | 0.2 |
| WEST VANCOUVER—SUNSHINE COAST—SEA TO SKY COUNTRY | |
| Liberal | 54.6 |
| Conservative | 26.2 |
| NDP-New Democratic Party | 9.9 |
| Green Party | 8.9 |
| Radical Marijuana | 0.3 |
| Marxist-Leninist | 0.2 |
| **YUKON** | |
| YUKON | |
| Liberal | 53.7 |
| Conservative | 24.3 |
| NDP-New Democratic Party | 19.4 |
| Green Party | 2.6 |
| **NORTHWEST TERRITORIES** | |
| NORTHWEST TERRITORIES | |
| Liberal | 48.3 |
| NDP-New Democratic Party | 30.5 |
| Conservative | 18.3 |
| Green Party | 2.8 |
| **NUNAVUT** | |
| NUNAVUT | |
| Liberal | 47.1 |
| NDP-New Democratic Party | 26.6 |
| Conservative | 24.8 |
| Green Party | 1.5 |

## NOTES ON CONTRIBUTORS

**Éric Bélanger** is Professor in the Department of Political Science at McGill University and a member of the Centre for the Study of Democratic Citizenship. His research interests include political parties, public opinion, and voting behaviour, as well as Quebec and Canadian politics. His work has been published in a number of scholarly journals, including *Comparative Political Studies*, *Political Research Quarterly*, *Electoral Studies*, *Publius: The Journal of Federalism*, the *European Journal of Political Research*, and the *Canadian Journal of Political Science*. He is also the co-author of *French Presidential Elections* and *Le comportement électoral des Québécois* (2010 Donald Smiley Prize).

**Harold D. Clarke** is Ashbel Smith Professor, University of Texas at Dallas, and Adjunct Professor, Department of Government, University of Essex. He is a former principal investigator for the British and Canadian Election Studies. Recent publications include *Making Political Choices: Canada and the United States*, with Allan Kornberg and Thomas Scotto (University of Toronto Press) and *Affluence, Austerity and Electoral Change in Britain*, with David Sanders, Marianne Stewart, and Paul Whiteley (Cambridge University Press).

**David Coletto** is Adjunct Professor at the Arthur Kreoger College of Public Affairs at Carleton University. He is also a founding partner and the CEO of national public opinion research firm Abacus Data. He has published in the *Canadian Journal of Political Science* and the *Canadian Political Science Review*. His research interests include public opinion, research methodologies, voting behaviour, and election financing.

**Christopher Dornan** is Associate Professor in the School of Journalism and Communication at Carleton University. He has worked as a journalist for the *Ottawa Citizen*, the *Edmonton Journal*, the *Globe and Mail*, and CBC Radio. His work has appeared in venues as disparate as the *Literary Review of Canada*, *Critical Studies in Communication*, the research reports of the *Royal Commission on Electoral Reform and Party Financing*, the *Media Studies Journal*, and the *Canadian Medical Association Journal*. He is the co-editor of, and contributor to, this and five previous volumes in the Canadian Federal Election series.

**Faron Ellis** is Research Chair in the Citizen Society Research Lab at Lethbridge College. His research in Canadian politics focuses on parties and elections and includes *The Limits of Participation: Members and Leaders in Canada's Reform Party* and *Parameters of Power: Canadian Political Institutions, Brief Edition*. In 2010 he was elected as alderman to the Lethbridge City Council. This is his eighth contribution to the Canadian Federal Election book series.

**Mary Francoli** is an Associate Professor in the School of Journalism and Communication at Carleton University. Her research focuses largely on the impact of new media on governance, the state, and society. She received her Ph.D. in political science from the University of Western Ontario and was the Leverhulme Visiting Fellow in New Media and Internet Politics at Royal Holloway, University of London.

**Josh Greenberg** is Director of the School of Journalism and Communication at Carleton University and Associate Professor in Communication Studies. His areas of teaching and research interest include media analysis, qualitative research, public relations, crisis and risk communication, social media, and political communication. He has explored these topics as they pertain to several areas of public policy: immigration, labour relations, energy, climate change, and crime and surveillance. He is the co-editor of *Communication in Question* (Nelson, 2009, 2014), *The Surveillance Studies Reader* (The Open University Press, 2007), and *Surveillance: Power, Problems and Politics* (UBC Press, 2010).

**Susan Harada** is an Associate Professor, Associate Director of the School of Journalism, and Communication and Journalism Program head at Carleton University. A former national news and documentary journalist with the CBC, her posting prior to joining Carleton was that of National Parliamentary Correspondent for CBC News *The National*. She has contributed several chapters to the Pammett and Dornan Canadian Election series since 2004, focusing mainly on the Green Party of Canada.

**Brooke Jeffrey** is Professor of Political Science at Concordia University and Director of the Masters Program in Public Policy and Public Administration. A former public servant and Director of the Liberal Caucus Research Bureau, she is the author of several books on Canadian federalism, political parties, and public policy, including a history of the Liberal Party, *Divided Loyalties: The Liberal Party of Canada 1984–2008*. Her most recent book is *Dismantling Canada: Stephen Harper's New Conservative Agenda*.

**Lawrence LeDuc** is Professor Emeritus of Political Science at the University of Toronto. His publications on Canadian elections include *Political Choice in Canada*, *Absent Mandate*, and *Dynasties and Interludes: Past and Present in Canadian Electoral Politics*. In the comparative field, his publications include *Comparing Democracies 4* (with Richard G. Niemi and Pippa Norris) and *The Politics of Direct Democracy: Referendums in Global Perspective*.

**Louis Massicotte** is a Professor in the Department of Political Science at Université Laval in Quebec, where he also holds the Research Chair in Democracy and Parliamentary Institutions. He also taught at the Université de Montréal from 1992 to 2006. A graduate of Laval and Carleton Universities, he was a research officer in the Library of Parliament from 1980 to 1990. As Chief, Policy and Strategic Planning at Elections Canada (1990–92), he has been involved in the democratic development of thirteen countries. He also acted as an adviser to Quebec's Secrétariat à la Réforme des institutions démocratiques on the reform of the electoral system in 2003–05. In 2007 he prepared a report for the Commissioner of Official Languages on the impact of an elected Senate on language minorities.

He is the author of *Establishing the Rules of the Game: Election Laws in Democracies* (2003) and *Le Parlement du Québec depuis 1867* (2009). His most recent work is a comparative study of durational residence requirements for electors, commissioned by Quebec's Department of Justice.

**David McGrane** is an Associate Professor in Political Studies at St. Thomas More College and the University of Saskatchewan. He is the Principal Investigator of the Canadian Social Democracy Study (www.canadiansocialdemocracy.ca), which is a SSHRC-funded research initiative tracing the activity of the federal NDP from 2000 to 2015. He most recent book is *Remaining Loyal: Social Democracy in Quebec and Saskatchewan*, published by McGill-Queen's University Press. He is currently the President of the Prairie Political Science Association.

**Richard Nadeau** is Professor of Political Science at the University of Montreal and a member of the Centre for the Study of Democratic Citizenship. His interests are voting behaviour, public opinion, political communication, and quantitative methodology. A Fulbright Scholar, Professor Nadeau has authored or co-authored more than 160 articles (published in the most prestigious political science journals), chapters, and books, including *Unsteady State*, *Anatomy of a Liberal Victory*, *French Presidential Elections*, *Le comportement électoral des Québécois,* and *Health Care Policy and Public Opinion in the United States and Canada*.

**Brenda O'Neill** is Head and Associate Professor of Political Science at the University of Calgary. Her current research examines gender and party leadership, women's political behaviour, and women's feminist and religious beliefs and their role in shaping political behaviour. Her research has appeared in *Ethnic and Racial Studies*, *The Canadian Journal of Political Science*, *Party Politics*, *The Journal of Women, Politics and Policy*, and *The International Political Science Review*. She is the co-editor with Elisabeth Gidengil of *Gender and Social Capital* (2006).

**Jon H. Pammett** is Professor Emeritus of Political Science and Distinguished Research Professor at Carleton University in Ottawa. He is also co-director of the Carleton University Survey Centre and Canadian delegate to the International Social Survey Programme. He is co-author of *Political Choice in Canada* and *Absent Mandate*, books about voting behaviour in Canadian elections. He is co-editor of, and contributing author to, the previous volumes in the Canadian Federal Election series. His most recent book is *Dynasties and Interludes: Past and Present in Canadian Electoral Politics* (with Lawrence LeDuc, Judith I. McKenzie, and André Turcotte), soon to appear in a second edition.

**Jason Reifler** is a Senior Lecturer at the University of Exeter. He studies political behaviour, focusing on public attitudes about foreign policy and voting behaviour. He is co-author of *Paying the Human Costs of War* (Princeton University Press) and has published scholarly articles in the *British Journal of Politics and International Relations*, *International Studies Quarterly*, *International Security*, *Political Behaviour*, and other academic journals. He received his B.A. from Colby College and his Ph.D. from Duke University.

**Thomas J. Scotto** is Senior Lecturer in the Department of Government at the University of Essex in the United Kingdom. He is the co-author of *Making Political Choices: Canada and the United States* (University of Toronto Press, 2009). His interests lie in the areas of public opinion, polling, and voting behaviour, and his articles on the topics have appeared in *Public Opinion Quarterly*, *International Studies Quarterly*, the *Journal of Politics*, and *Electoral Studies*.

**Marianne C. Stewart** is a Professor in the School of Economic, Political and Policy Sciences at the University of Dallas. Her research areas include the logic, methodology, and scope of political science; political attitudes, electoral choice, and political participation; and social science data collection and analysis. She has been co-principal investigator of the British Election Studies (2001, 2005, 2009–10) and other projects supported by the Economic and Social Research Council (U.K.), the National Science Foundation (U.S.), and other organizations. Her recent publications include *Affluence, Austerity, and Electoral Change in Britain*, with Harold Clarke, David Sanders, and Paul Whiteley, and published by Cambridge University Press.

**Melanee Thomas** is an Assistant Professor in the Department of Political Science at the University of Calgary. Her current projects include an edited collection entitled *Mothers and Others: Understanding the Impact of Family Life on Politics*, an exploration of the effect of gender, stereotype threat, and psychological orientations on politics, and an examination of the selection of women to the premier's office in Canada.

**Allan Thompson** was the Liberal Party of Canada candidate in the riding of Huron-Bruce for the 2015 election. Thompson was born and raised in the riding, studied journalism at Carleton University and international relations at the University of Kent at Canterbury before beginning a seventeen-year career with the *Toronto Star*. Since 2003 he has been a journalism professor at Carleton University. He is the editor of *The Media and the Rwanda Genocide* and co-author of the journalism textbook *The Canadian Reporter*.

**André Turcotte** is an Associate Professor at Carleton University's School of Journalism and Communication. Between 1992 and 1993, he was the co-editor of The Gallup Poll. He was part of the polling team for the Chrétien Liberals in the 1993 federal election. Between 1994 and 2000, he was the official pollster of the Reform Party of Canada and its leader, Preston Manning. André has also provided advice to several political leaders. He is the co-author of the recent book *Dynasties and Interludes: Past and Present in Canadian Electoral Politics*.

**Christopher Waddell** is an Associate Professor at Carleton's School of Journalism and Communication. Prior to joining Carleton in 2001, he was parliamentary bureau chief for CBC Television news from 1993 to 2001, senior producer of *The National* from 1991 to 1993, and a reporter, Ottawa bureau chief, associate editor, and national editor for the *Globe and Mail* from 1985 to 1991. He has authored or co-authored the media chapter in the four previous election books in this series. His research interests include political communication, the media and national politics, elections, public policy as it affects business and the economy, and the business of the media.

Visit us at

*Dundurn.com*
*@dundurnpress*
*Facebook.com/dundurnpress*
*Pinterest.com/dundurnpress*